THE SAINT'S LIFE AND THE SENSES OF SCRIPTURE

THE SAINT'S LIFE and
THE SENSES OF SCRIPTURE

Hagiography as Exegesis

ANN W. ASTELL

University of Notre Dame Press
Notre Dame, Indiana

Copyright © 2024 by University of Notre Dame
Notre Dame, Indiana 46556
undpress.nd.edu
All Rights Reserved

Published in the United States of America

Library of Congress Control Number: 2024937290

ISBN: 978-0-268-20811-0 (Hardback)
ISBN: 978-0-268-20810-3 (WebPDF)
ISBN: 978-0-268-20814-1 (Epub3)

For Catherine (†2020) and Michael Griffin,
and their children,
Benedict, Basil, and Miriam

For the promise is for you and for your children and for all who are far off, everyone whom the Lord our God calls to himself.

— Acts 2:39

*At length when almighty God determined . . .
to have Benedict's life for an example known to the world,
that such a candle, set on a candlestick,
might shine and give life to the Church of God,
our Lord vouchsafed to appear to a certain priest.*

— Gregory the Great, *Life of Saint Benedict*

Out, out, brief candle!

— *Macbeth*, 5.5.23

CONTENTS

List of Illustrations ix
List of Tables xi
Acknowledgments xiii
Abbreviations xvii

INTRODUCTION
Brief Candle: The Saint's Life as Biblical Illumination 1

PART 1
The Saint's *Life* in the Age of Monasticism

CHAPTER 1
Psalm Use, Prayer, and Prophecy in the *Lives* of Saint Guthlac 17

CHAPTER 2
Hexaemeral Miracles in Saint Aelred of Rievaulx's *Life of Ninian* 38

CHAPTER 3
The Song of Songs and Saint Bernard of Clairvaux's
Life of Saint Malachy 61

CHAPTER 4
Eadmer's Parabolic *Life* and *History* of Saint Anselm of Canterbury:
A Twice-Told Tale 83

viii   Contents

PART 2
The Saint's *Life* in the Scholastic Age

CHAPTER 5
Saint Francis of Assisi as "New Evangelist" in Thomas of Celano's
Vita prima and Bonaventure's *Legenda maior*   119

CHAPTER 6
Heroic Virtue in Blessed Raymond of Capua's
Life of Catherine of Siena   149

CHAPTER 7
Mary Magdalene and the Eucharist:
Reading Jacobus de Voragine's *Legenda aurea* with Catherine of Siena,
Raymond of Capua, and Osbern Bokenham   172

PART 3
The Saint's *Life* in Modernity

CHAPTER 8
The Ends of Hagiography:
Erasmus's *Jerome*, Harpsfield's *Life of More*, and More's Epitaph   209

CHAPTER 9
Modern Literary Experiments in Biblical Hagiography   236

CHAPTER 10
Historical Truth, Biblical Criticism, and Hagiography   252

Notes   265
Bibliography   340
Index   372

ILLUSTRATIONS

Plate 1.1 Harley Y 6, "Guthlac Roll," British Library, Roundel 6, late twelfth century. https://www.bl.uk/collection-items /guthlac-roll. 24

Plate 2.1 Hildegard von Bingen, *The Redeemer of Creation*, ca. 1151, from *Scivias* II.I. T.10, in CCCM 43, © Brepols Publishers, Turnhout, Belgium. 48

Plate 2.2 Mary J. Zore, *The Seven Days of Creation Mandala*, 2021. Courtesy of the artist. 49

Plate 7.1 Sebastian Conca, *The Death of the Magdalene*, 1700–1764, oil on copper. Raclin Murphy Museum of Art, University of Notre Dame. Mr. and Mrs. Al Nathe Fund, 1990.003. 185

Plate 7.2 Giovanni di Paolo, *The Miraculous Communion of St. Catherine of Siena*, 1447–1465. The Metropolitan Museum of Art, New York. https://www.metmuseum.org /art/collection/search/436511. 193

Plate 7.3 *Horae ad usum romanum*, ca. 1430. Bibliothèque nationale de France, Paris. BN Ms. lat. 1156B, fol. 174r. 204

Plate 9.1 Luigi Gregori, *Lourdes Mural*, 1887, Basilica of the Sacred Heart, University of Notre Dame. Photograph courtesy of Nancy Cavadini. 251

TABLES

Table 2.1 Six Miracles, Six Days 50

Table 5.1 Merited Rewards for the Blessed in Bonaventure's *Commentary on Luke* 138

Table 5.2 The Beatitudes Viewed under Three Aspects in *Breviloquium* 5.5 141

Table 5.3 Chapters, Beatitudes, Gifts in Bonaventure's *Legenda maior* 145

ACKNOWLEDGMENTS

The stories of the saints were with me from childhood, but hagiography as a topic of research was first proposed to me by my teachers in English at the University of Wisconsin-Madison: Sherry Reames, A. N. Doane, Donald Rowe, and Jerome Taylor, and also by Judson Boyce Allen, who had taught me at Marquette University. When I migrated in 2007 from my beloved homeland in medieval literary studies in English at Purdue University into my new, welcoming home in the Department of Theology at the University of Notre Dame, I faced the midcareer challenge of developing new courses to teach and taking up new research compatible with my personal interests, academic training, and prior experience.

As is often the case, teaching spurred my own learning, inspired investigation, fostered a sense of community with colleagues and students, and enabled intellectual continuities. This book is, in many ways, a fruit of my classroom experience in teaching various iterations of graduate seminars at Notre Dame on "Hagiography and Narrative Theology," on the *Legenda aurea*, on "Eadmer and Anselm," and on the *Lives* of Saint Francis. These classes have attracted a mix of students from English, medieval studies, and theology (historical Christianity, liturgical studies, systematics). It is a special joy to be able to cite the recently published work of some of my students in the footnotes of this book.

The book is also a fruit of greatly appreciated times of sabbatical. I wrote chapter 1 while holding the Teilhard de Chardin Visiting Chair in Catholic Studies at Loyola University Chicago (Fall 2015). Parts of chapter 1 and of chapter 9 date from my time as a fellow at the Center of Theological Inquiry in Princeton (2010–11), when I also immersed myself in patristic exegesis of the Psalms. Over the years, I have given versions of parts of this book's chapters as papers at conferences and colloquies at Boston

College (2023, 2014), Providence College (2022), Purdue University (2021, 2008), Columbia University (2019), Villanova University (2016), St. Augustine's University in Johannesburg, South Africa (2015), Loyola University Chicago (2015), the International Congress on Medieval Studies in Kalamazoo, Michigan (2014, 2016), and the University of Notre Dame (2010).

I owe great thanks to my friends and colleagues in theology at Notre Dame for the atmosphere of encouragement generated by their own work on the saints and saints' lives. I think, for example, of the "Saturdays with the Saints" lecture series begun in 2010 by John C. Cavadini and hosted by the McGrath Institute for Church Life, to which many ND colleagues have contributed: Peter Casarella, Catherine Cavadini, Kathleen Sprows Cummings, Lawrence Cunningham, Brian Daley, S.J., Leonard DeLorenzo, Keith Egan, Terrence Ehrman, C.S.C., Virgil Elizondo, Margot Fassler, Anthony Giambrone, S.J., Daniel Groody, C.S.C., Kevin Grove, C.S.C., Mary Catherine Hilkert, O.P., Jessica Keating Floyd, Robert A. Krieg, Ulrich Lehrner, Ernest Morrell, Francesca Murphy, Nathan O'Halloran, S.J., Timothy O'Malley, Timothy Matovina, Anthony Pagliarini, Margaret Pfeil, Dianne Phillips, J. Daniel Philpott, Cyril O'Regan, Gabriel Radle, Gabriel Reynolds, and Joseph Wawrykow. I think, too, of the "Saintliness across Religious Traditions" conference organized by Paul Kollman, C.S.C., and Gabriel Reynolds, to which other colleagues contributed: Robert Gimello, Michael (Tzvi) Novick, Paulinus Odozor, C.S.Sp., Trent Pomplin, and Mun'im Sirry.

An earlier version of chapter 2 appeared under the title "To Build the Church: Saint Ælred of Rievaulx's Hexaemeral Miracles in the *Life of Ninian*," *Cistercian Studies Quarterly* 49, no. 4 (2014): 455–81. Chapter 6 expands upon my article "Heroic Virtue in Blessed Raymond of Capua's *Life of Catherine of Siena*," *Journal of Medieval and Early Modern Studies* 42, no. 1 (2012): 35–57. I thank the editors of these journals for permission to include these copyrighted articles in the present monograph.

Many thanks are owed for the artwork. Nancy Cavadini kindly shared her photograph of the Lourdes mural at the Basilica of the Sacred Heart on Notre Dame's campus. Mary J. Zore painted *The Seven Days of Creation Mandala* specifically for this book. Dianne Philips assisted me in obtaining the image from the Book of Hours at the Bibliothèque nationale de France. Vitoria Perdomo and Bart Janssens facilitated the needed permissions to reproduce artworks from the Raclin Murphy Museum of Art and from

Brepols Publishing, respectively. The images from holdings at the British Library and at the Metropolitan Museum of Art in New York are generously in the public domain. Greatly appreciated subventions from the Institute for Scholarship in the Liberal Arts and from the McGrath Institute for Church Life, both at the University of Notre Dame, supported the reproduction of the artworks in color.

Eli Bortz, then editor in chief at the University of Notre Dame Press, first welcomed the submission of this book. Stephen Wrinn, director of UNDP, presented it for acceptance to the board after receiving two positive and very helpful external reports from Barbara Newman and Ian Christopher Levy, respectively. Rachel Kindler shepherded it into production. Scott Barker patiently and attentively copyedited the text, catching and correcting many of my mistakes and inconsistencies and asking helpful questions. Matthew Dowd exercised editorial oversight, Wendy McMillen carried the book forward into design and production, and Laura Moran Walton and Stephanie Marchman cared for its marketing. Please know, all of you, of my sincere gratitude.

This book is dedicated to the memory of Catherine Griffin and her family. During the last two years of her holy, young life, I could accompany Catherine spiritually, together with her devoted husband, Mike, their children, and a large, supportive community of family members and friends. It was truly an experience of the communion of the saints. I thank you, Catherine, for helping me from heaven to finish this book.

Finally, my gratitude goes to my brothers and sisters in the Astell family, to the Schoenstatt Sisters of Mary, and to the members of the Schoenstatt family in Indiana. For almost fifty years now we have shared with each other the little, real-life stories of personal and communal striving for holiness. We have told and retold anecdotes from the life of Schoenstatt's founder, Father Joseph Kentenich (†1968), whom we believe to be one of God's saints. We have prayed together in Schoenstatt's shrine. Without you this book would not be. *Deo gratias.*

Ann W. Astell
Feast of the Visitation, 2023

ABBREVIATIONS

AASS   Acta sanctorum. 67 vols. Edited by Johannes Bolland, Godefridus Henschenius, and Daniel van Papenbroeck; first published, Antwerpt: Joannem Mevrsium, 1643; rev. ed., Jean Baptist Carnandet. Paris: V. Palmé, 1863; suppl. *Analecta Bollandiana*, 1885–1983.

CCCM   Corpus Christianorum Continuatio Medievalis

CCSL   Corpus Christianorum, Series Latina

CF   Cistercian Fathers

CWE   *Collected Works of Erasmus*

EETS   Early English Text Society

FA:ED   *Francis of Assisi: Early Documents*. 3 vols. Edited by Regis Armstrong, J. A. Wayne Hellmann, and William Short. New York: New City Press, 1999–2001.

HN   Eadmer. *Historia Novorum in Anglia*. Edited by Martin Rule. Rolls Series. Wiesbaden: Kraus Reprint, 1965; *Eadmer's "History of Recent Events in England" (Historia Novorum in Anglia)*. Translated by Geoffrey Bosanquet. Philadelphia: Dufour, 1965.

LA   Iacopo da Varazze. *Legenda aurea*. 2 vols. Edited by Giovanni Paolo Maggioni. Florence: SISMEL/Edizioni del Galluzzo, 1998.

PL   *Patrologiae Cursus Completus, Series Latina.* 221 vols. Edited by J. P. Migne. Paris, 1844–1864.

ST   St. Thomas Aquinas. *Summa Theologica.* 5 vols. Translated by the Fathers of the English Dominican Province. New York: Benziger, 1948. Reprint, Allen, TX: Christian Classics, 1981.

VA   Eadmer. *The Life of St. Anselm, Archbishop of Canterbury, by Eadmer.* Edited and translated by R. W. Southern. Oxford Medieval Texts. Oxford: Clarendon, 1972.

INTRODUCTION

BRIEF CANDLE

The Saint's Life as Biblical Illumination

In a thirteenth-century manuscript of uncertain provenance, a historiated initial for Psalm 26 shows a crowned King David within the letter "D."[1] He lifts a lighted candle up before the altar, and God's outstretched hand blesses it from on high. The letter "D," David's own initial, combines with other letters to spell *Dominus illuminatio mea* ("The Lord [is] my light"). The image narrates God's enlightenment of the psalmist, and David's upheld candle also serves, literally and figuratively, to illumine the holy words on the page for the reader.

A candle's light is flickering and short-lived. During the time of its shining, however, even a brief candle no bigger than a wick can enable the king's discovery of a lost gold coin or a misplaced pearl in a dark house, as the rabbis have reminded those who would despise the minor genres of parable, narrative example, and saintly tale. Ancient Jewish commentary therefore intersperses such homiletic material into its grammatical, moral, and mystical elucidations of the biblical text and of the Talmud. Easily understood, plainly told, "the *Aggadot* . . . give delight to [the study of] Scripture," and "by [their] light, a man may fathom words of Torah."[2]

Like the Jewish Aggadot, Christian hagiography functioned in the time of its flourishing (from the fourth through the fifteenth centuries) in the overlapping forms of *exempla* and *vita*, chiefly as an illumination of the Gospels, as a narrative form of commentary upon the Bible. The book of Armagh (Codex Ardmachanus, ninth century), venerated as a relic by Irish Christians during the Middle Ages, contains the Latin texts of the Gospels and Epistles, alongside Sulpicius Severus's *Life of Saint Martin of Tours* and

2 THE SAINT'S LIFE AND THE SENSES OF SCRIPTURE

memoranda for a *Life of Saint Patrick*.[3] Such *Lives* highlighted scripture's allegorical (Christological and ecclesial) and tropological (moral and ethical) senses for the faithful, rendering them literal in the kinetic stories of saints who responded with their lives to Christ's imperative, "Come follow me" (Matt. 4:19).[4] Indeed, classic stories within the hagiographic tradition begin with the saint's response to a biblical word as a personal address. The young Antony of Egypt hears Matthew 19:21 read aloud in church and finds in it an answer to his question about living evangelical poverty.[5] Augustine, recalling this very episode in Athanasius's *Life of Antony*, reads the passage from Paul (Rom. 13:13–14) that precipitates his own conversion: "Take and read."[6] Francis of Assisi understands, commits to memory, and joyfully acts upon the Lord's command to the twelve apostles in Matthew 10:9–10, a passage Francis has heard proclaimed in the Gospel at Mass.[7]

As a literally realized tropology, the saint's life was, at the same time, a figurative allegory of Christ, who calls the saint and whose words and actions can be glimpsed, *mutatis mutandis*, through the veil of the saint's. The end of the saint's *Life*, moreover, whether witnessed in martyrdom or described as ecstasy, conveyed to its readers an anagogical anticipation of the afterlife. Composed by monks, clerics, and ascetic laypersons who practiced *lectio divina*,[8] the early and most influential saints' *Lives* echo the biblical texts from which they draw their inspiration. And like the scriptures, they were meant to be read at multiple levels of signification; indeed, the "literal sense" itself of saints' *Lives* accommodated sometimes abrupt shifts in those levels, *historia* yielding to literalized (or reliteralized) *allegoria*. In this way, the hagiographies could be seamlessly incorporated into the prayer life of the Church, with episodes from the *Lives* used as readings in the Divine Office,[9] retold as exempla in sermons,[10] and visualized in art.[11] The same readers who heard the God of Israel and the devil compared (*in bono* and *in malo*, respectively) to a devouring lion (cf. Hosea 13:8; 1 Pet. 5:8) and who read about Jonah in the whale's belly (Jon. 1:17–2:10) could easily imagine and understand in allegorical and moral terms (e.g., as reliteralized tropology) the dramatic tale of the dragon swallowing (the ultimately victorious) Saint Margaret in the darkness of her prison cell.[12]

In his *Homilies on Ezekiel*, Gregory the Great confidently asserts, "In the life of the holy Fathers we recognize what we ought to understand in the book of Sacred Scripture."[13] Hugh of Saint Victor (1096–1141) admonishes any student of the Bible who has become obsessed with interpreting difficult and occult passages to remember the plain sense, biblical teaching of virtue and to "make it a habit of going . . . to the lives of the holy fathers and the triumphs of the martyrs and other such writings dictated in a simple style."[14] Linking the biblical saints with more recent ones, Hugh explicitly directs students of the Bible to read the hagiographies composed by Gregory the Great: "Among the deeds and sayings of the saints, those marvelously written down by the blessed Gregory should, I think, be taken to heart."[15] Parallel to the Hagiography (Wisdom literature) of the Old Testament in its tripartite division (Law, Prophets, Hagiography), Hugh places the writings of the Fathers, including the saints' *Lives* by Athanasius, Jerome, and Gregory, as a hagiographic, third part of the New Testament, alongside the four canonical Gospels and the "Apostles" (Acts, Epistles, Revelation), which correspond in Hugh's schema to the Law and the Prophets, respectively.[16]

This assertion of a close association of hagiography with the Bible is at once unsurprising and startling. It is unsurprising if one begins by considering the formation of the New Testament canon during the centuries leading up to the Council of Nicaea (325). The Gospel according to St. Luke tells the story of Jesus, the "Saint of saints" (*Sanctus sanctorum*)[17] in a manner consistent with Old Testament narratives of the tabernacle, the holy of holies, filled with God's glory. The Gospel according to Saint Matthew employs typological allusion to depict Jesus as a prophet like Moses, but greater—the one whom Moses himself prophesied would come after him (Deut. 18:15–19). The other Evangelists employ a comparable pattern of citation of the Hebrew scriptures, to point to Christ as the one prophesied and prefigured in such divinely elected men as Abel, Isaac, Joseph, Moses, David, Elijah, and Jonah. The Acts of the Apostles portrays the martyr Stephen (Acts 6:5–7:60), in turn, as acting and speaking in imitation of Christ, who reveals himself to Paul as living in the persecuted members of his mystical body, the Church (Acts 9:1–6). Other ancient Christian writings ultimately excluded from the biblical canon—notably the Proto-Evangelium of James (ca. 145)—similarly use scriptural language to tell new saintly stories (e.g., that of the pious parents of the Virgin Mary, Joachim and Anne) reminiscent of Old Testament prototypes.

A claim for the biblical origin and inspiration of hagiography is plainly startling, however, if one considers the hagiographic crisis that erupted in

4 THE SAINT'S LIFE AND THE SENSES OF SCRIPTURE

the sixteenth century, when the cult of the saints was challenged by Protestant Christians as idolatrous, their images in churches defaced by iconoclasts, and their legends rejected as papist fables.[18] A fierce polemic cast the legends of the saints as antithetical to biblical truth and inappropriate for use in preaching and pious reading. One scribal critic complained about the popular legend of Saint Brendan: "A brother would be better occupied transcribing the psalms of David or singing them for his own sins and those of the brethren, than deceiving idiots with such unholy scriptures [*quam scripturis tam impuriis*]."[19] Through a dramatic semantic shift, the word "legenda," which named the readings prescribed for use in the Divine Office, became synonymous with an untrue narrative, such as those found, according to its critics, in Jacobus de Voragine's popular hagiographic anthology, the *Legenda aurea* (ca. 1260).[20] In the face of such a challenge, the very idea of a biblical hagiography seems nonsensical, a contradiction in terms.

Roman Catholics upheld, of course, the cult of the saints, but in that camp too the close relationship between hagiography and scripture was gradually altered, weakened, and interpolated by changes in reading practices, in the juridical process of canonization, and in the understanding of history itself. By the late sixteenth century, the saint's life could no longer be written as a *Life* in the hagiographic sense of that word, for which conformity to scripture, in its literal and spiritual senses, suffices as witness. Rather, the life story must be related in a way that answers to juridical questions regarding set proofs of holiness. Already in the thirteenth century, Henricus de Segusio (1200–1271), otherwise known as "Hostiensis," signaled a shift when he defended the papal reservation of the right to canonize saints by drawing a telling parallel between the correct interpretation of the Bible and of a saint's *Life*: "It is part of the pope's commission to decide doubtful places of Scripture; how much more, therefore, should it be his office to determine the doubtful cases of sanctity in which greater dangers may be involved."[21]

In the contests of the sixteenth and seventeenth centuries, scripture was set against hagiography by Protestant Christians, and Roman Catholics were ready to defend the cult of the saints through critical revision in the writing and reading of saints' stories. How is this historical shift, which marks a trajectory from a close relationship between the Bible and hagiography in the earliest period to a distancing of the two in modernity, to be explained? This obvious question has largely gone unasked. Despite the generally recognized, close relationship between the Bible and the saint's *Life* in late antiquity, biblical scholars seldom, if ever, cite hagiographies as offering evidence for biblical reception and interpretation. The same holds true for the major studies of biblical interpretation during the Middle Ages. Hagiographies go unmentioned by Beryl Smalley, *The Study of the Bible in the Middle Ages* (1952), by Henri de Lubac, *Exégèse médiévale: Les quatre sens de l'écriture* (1959), and by Ian Christopher Levy, *Introducing Medieval Biblical Interpretation: The Senses of Scripture in Premodern Exegesis* (2018). As a result, variation and change in biblical interpretation have not been correlated with changes in hagiographical styles. Studies of individual saints' *Lives* often identify biblical allusions and quotations and sometimes comment upon them, but no overarching account of historical transformations of the saint's *Life* as a genre has given serious attention to related changes in biblical study as it moved from monastic enclosure to university classroom.

One reason for this scholarly neglect is the putative impurity of hagiography at its very origin—an unstable mix of things that, some opine, is enough in itself to account for both the early assimilation of the saint's *Life* with scripture and the early modern divergence of the two. The book generally regarded as foundational for the modern study of hagiography, Hippolyte Delehaye, *The Legends of the Saints: An Introduction to Hagiography* (*Les Légendes hagiographiques*) (1905),[22] supports a premise of mixed origins for the genre, which Delehaye characterizes as an impure, syncretistic invention. Addressed *ad intra* to the Christian community, the *Life* oriented itself chiefly to biblical models in its telling of a saint's life. Addressed *ad extra* to participants in pagan cult, the *Life* oriented itself toward antique biography, myth, and romance in order to win a popular audience for the new Christian heroes and heroines who would surpass and displace the old, literally occupying the sites of their former worship. A centaur and a satyr appear, for example, in Jerome's fourth-century *Life of Paul the Hermit*.[23]

Delehaye's book gives a very tendentious account, however. It explicitly excludes from its scope and consideration the accounts of martyrdoms by early Christian eyewitnesses (those furnishing "the most pure sources of hagiography"); the *Lives* of saints written by men of letters "possessing both literary power and the necessary information . . . to discharge the functions of a historian"; and those composed by "conscientious biographers who, at various periods of the Middle Ages, succeeded in closely following these [late antique] models."[24] Setting aside, in short, the best works in the hagiographic genre, Delehaye, whose procedure evinces a markedly "two-tier" (clerical/lay) understanding of the premodern Church,[25] devoted his "full attention" instead to "those conventional and factitious productions composed at a distance from the events recorded and without any tangible relation to the facts"—in short, the legendary material that belonged to ancient and medieval popular religion.[26]

Highlighting and classifying the "conventional" aspects of mythic legends of the saints, Delehaye's influential "introduction to hagiography" opened the door for anthropological and archeological studies of saintly cult by scholars in religious studies, for local historical studies, and for literary studies of a neglected medieval genre with representative works copiously extant in manuscripts. Through its exclusion, however, of hagiographies by learned writers—Athanasius, Jerome, Augustine, Sulpicius Severus, Hilary of Poitiers, Gregory of Tours, Gregory the Great, Bernard of Clairvaux, Aelred of Rievaulx, Philip of Harvengt, Bonaventure, and others—Delehaye's *Legends of the Saints* reinforced the already wide gap between hagiography and modern biblical and theological scholarship.[27] Its focus on identifying hagiographic "conventions" did nothing, moreover, to advance a dynamic understanding of changes within the longer history of hagiographical writing and reading.

Those changes presage and contribute to changes in the historical study of the Bible. This book argues that significant changes within the hagiographic tradition itself, reflective of broader streams of change in theological practice and method (monastic, Scholastic, liturgical), resulted in a gradual disassociation of the different "senses" of hagiography—literal, historical, moral, allegorical, anagogical—that its great exemplars originally derived from their hermeneutical function, namely, to offer a form of narrative commentary upon scripture and to bear witness as its handmaid to an apostolic tradition of biblical reception in holy lives from age to age. The changes in hagiography over time are tied in particular to corresponding, interrelated changes in the canonization process, on the one hand, and in biblical study, on the other. The literal meaning of scripture, which enabled the dynamic interplay of the various spiritual senses, became increasingly detached from them, even as the hagiographical letter came finally to be replaced by a biographical history.

This pattern of disassociation becomes apparent only when the early masterworks of the genre, ignored by Delehaye, are reinserted into its historiography at its base. Strongly figurative, these early *Lives* foreground the miraculous signs of the saint—signs that point to Christ; evince biblical typology, numerology, quotation, and wordplay; and provide a strong incentive for imitation not through human strength, but through the hope of divine grace and virtuous empowerment. Significantly, in *Confessions*, Lady Continence holds out to Augustine "numerous good examples . . . to follow," and she points out to him the reason for his hesitation in following Christ: "Are you incapable of doing what these men and women have done? Do you think them capable of achieving this by their own resources and not by the Lord their God? . . . Why are you relying on yourself, only to find yourself unreliable? Cast yourself on him."[28] In the face of such an argument, whether discursive or narrative, the supposed antinomy between the saints as miracle-working friends of God, on the one hand, and imitable moral examples, on the other, crumbles.[29] In each case, God's is the power, the grace.

God's authorial fashioning of saints and God's authorship of the scriptures stand parallel to, and mutually enforce, each other, thus allowing for the Bible's intertextual relationship to hagiography. God is the primary "author" of the life of a saint (with the human being's free will cooperation being given in response to, and through, God's grace), and the "book" of each holy life is to be read, accordingly, together with all the other "books" in the communion of saints; similarly, God as the "author" of the divinely inspired scriptures authorized them to be read intertextually and at multiple levels, according to different senses, scripture interpreting scripture.[30]

The long Middle Ages upheld this understanding of the Bible as a source of divine revelation, but beginning in the twelfth century—exactly when Eadmer of Canterbury distinguished his *Life of Anselm* from his *Historia* of the same saint—biblical scholars began to pay more attention to the letter of scripture also as an expression of a human composer. Hugh of Saint Victor began to use the word "history" to name the "plain" or "literal" sense of scripture, which is foundational to the other senses. The "literal" sense subsequently became the object of new academic understandings, as various theologians addressed its relation not only to history but also to metaphor, parable, and fable (e.g., Judg. 9:7–15), to figural relationships between and among historical events and persons, to rhetorical context, to literary conventions, and to authorial intention. The application of the Aristotelian causes to the exegesis of scripture acknowledged the human biblical writer as a secondary efficient cause, in the service of God as the primary cause, even as it differentiated between human and divine intentionality.[31] This had the unintended effect of introducing a greater distance between the literal and spiritual senses of the scriptures.

Parallel to the new interest in the human writers of the biblical books, the *Lives* of saints written with a view to their canonization shifted attention from miracles worked during their earthly lives to the character of the saints, their motivations, and heroic virtue. The *Lives* composed as dossiers are less figural, less biblical in their formal orientation, more focused on the saints themselves as objects of judicial testing. The goal of demonstrating specific virtues, one by one, competed with the older narrative tendency in hagiography to present the life of the saint in conformity to the overarching pattern of Christ's life, in which the compendium and perfection of all virtue are to be found.[32] Hagiographic tropology thus became relatively detached from its typology.

This relative detachment of historical "letter" and virtuous "spirit" found its structural and thematic expression in "dualist" saints' *Lives*, such as Bonaventure's *Legenda maior* of Francis of Assisi, where the chronologically arranged chapters narrating the "Outer Life" of the saint (chapters 1 through 4 and 13 through 15) literally frame chapters devoted to the "Inner Life" of his individual virtues (chapters 5 through 12). Unlike Suetonian biographies with a similar structure, these saints' *Lives* thematize the debated relationship between the physical and spiritual senses of the saint—a relationship mirroring that between the carnal "letter" and the "spirit" of scriptures. For Bonaventure, Francis's stigmata seal their unity in a marvelous and unprecedented way, but he writes his *Life* of the saint of Assisi in answer to antimendicant critics disputing that very thesis. The hagiographic questions prove to be profoundly exegetical, focused on the very meaning of the evangelical imperatives obeyed by Francis. Similarly, in Raymund of Capua's *Life of Catherine of Siena*, a final chapter on the question of her heroic virtue invites a rereading of all the preceding chapters, even as questions concerning her inner mystical experience are raised recurrently throughout the *Life* in tension with those concerning her outwardly observable, controversial behavior.

At roughly the same time, moreover, the same Scholastic impulse that fostered compilation, contest, and *quaestio* gave rise to hagiographic encyclopedias, such as Jean de Mailly's *Abbreviatio in gestis et miraculis sanctorum* (*Summary of the Deeds and Miracles of the Saints*), Bartholomew of Trent's *Epilogus in gestis sanctorum* (*Afterword on the Deeds of the Saints*), Vincent of Beauvais's *Speculum historiale*, and Jacobus de Voragine's *Legenda aurea* (*Golden Legend*). Combining abbreviated saints' legends with Scholastic commentaries on the feasts of the Church year, arranged by season, Jacobus's famous, liturgically inspired work exhibits dualist features of its own that juxtapose time and eternity. A prodigious compiler and a paratactic narrator, Jacobus includes conflicting and improbable accounts in the *Legenda aurea*, and not infrequently interjects his own opinion that this or that bizarre story is apocryphal and unworthy of credence.[33] This sort of inclusivity in a collection radically oriented toward the eschaton, patiently awaiting that day when weed and wheat will finally be separated (cf. Matt. 13:29–30), proved scandalous to Reformation and Counter-Reformation readers, who desired trustworthy sources and imitable models for sober, virtuous living in this world. Ironically, the *Legenda aurea*—the great achievement of an anagogical hagiography, widely read by Christians for three centuries—also presaged the end of time for the genre per se. The abbreviated *Life* both mirrored and announced the outing of the brief candle.

The concern about the legendary's claim to historical truth gave rise in the sixteenth and subsequent centuries, in Protestant and Catholic circles alike, to hagiography's successor, biography.[34] Renaissance humanists made many and important contributions to the transition, typically blending classical and biblical allusion and linguistic precision, on the one hand, with a judiciously selective translation and pruning of medieval sources, on the other.[35] Erasmus of Rotterdam's *Life of Saint Jerome* (1516), which famously includes sharp criticism of legends such as those found in the *Legenda aurea*, is often called "the West's first modern biography."[36] The *Lives* of men and women from the early modern period subsequently canonized as saints—Thomas More, John Fisher, Ignatius de Loyola, Teresa of Avila—were first composed as biography and even (in the case of the latter two Spanish reformers) autobiography. No longer woven together from the scriptures—its words and its spiritual senses—the *Life* of a saint was assembled instead from historical documents, including especially the saint's own letters and writings.

The Protestant protest against saints' legends that cast them as fables detracting from biblical truth—a protest also sounded, albeit with differing accent, among Catholic reformers of the fifteenth and sixteenth centuries—is thus a complex indictment. Protestant theology sought to free the Bible from encumbering traditions and to defend it as the sole or primary source of divine revelation (*sola scriptura*); it rejected the legends of the saints as false likenesses of the biblical stories and the saints themselves, so constructed, as idols whose cult detracted from Christ's worship.[37] But hagiography as a genre—once closely tied to scripture as its handmaid, providing it both with a kind of narrative commentary upon itself and with a hermeneutic for the faithful's appropriation—had, in fact, already been distanced (however unintentionally) from the Bible through the disassociation of its literal and spiritual senses. This disassociation left hagiography (in the guise of the *legenda*) vulnerable to criticism, even as it left scripture itself increasingly alone (*sola*) and exposed, in its turn, to attack in the rapidly emerging new era of secular modernity.[38] Hagiography's fate in the sixteenth century proved, in short, a bellwether for the Bible's in the seventeenth, eighteenth, and nineteenth.

In the nineteenth century, the criticisms once leveled against hagiographies were leveled against the Gospels themselves, which David F. Strauss (1808–74) characterized in *Das Leben Jesu kritisch bearteitet* (1835–36) as "mythic,"[39] especially in their miracle stories. The equally controversial *Vie de Jésus* (1863) of Ernst Renan (1823–92) followed Strauss's lead. Renan's "Author's Introduction" to the book explicitly compares the Gospels to the legends of the saints. Treating the Gospels simply as human writings and attributing a very limited "historical value" to them, Renan declares: "They are neither biographies after the manner of Suetonius, nor fictitious legends in the style of Philostratus; they are legendary biographies. I would willingly compare them to the Legends of the Saints . . . in which historical truth and the desire to present models of virtue are combined in various degrees."[40]

PREVIEW OF THE CHAPTERS

Taking a cue from Hans Frei's account in *The Eclipse of Biblical Narrative*,[41] this book treats the "brief candle" of premodern hagiography as a bellwether for the modern reception of the Bible. Its tripartite division of chapters traces biblically inflected changes in hagiographical writing across three periods: (1) monasticism in its rise, (2) Scholasticism, and (3) the early Reformation. Chapters 1 through 3 illustrate a maximal integration of hagiography with scripture through the direct quotation of, allusion to, and intertextual evocation of multiple biblical passages. Composed between the eighth and the early twelfth centuries by monastic writers (Felix of Croyland, Aelred of Rievaulx, Bernard of Clairvaux), these hagiographies not only extend scripture tropologically and Christologically into the lives of the saints whose stories they narrate, but they also perform an often startling exegesis of scripture. The first function has long been recognized; the second, exegetical function has been largely invisible to modern readers.

The fruit of monastic *lectio divina*, the hagiographies discussed in the first three chapters offer a narrative commentary upon scripture. Felix of Croyland's Latin *Life of Saint Guthlac* (ca. 730), explored in chapter 1, aligns the Christological prophecy of the Psalms with the prophecy of Christ's saints. Aelred of Rievaulx's twelfth-century *Life of Saint Ninian*, discussed in chapter 2, narrates a series of six miracles that recall the six days of creation as interpreted by scripture itself (especially John 1) and by Augustine of Hippo in his *Confessions*. Bernard of Clairvaux's *Life of Saint Malachy* (ca. 1148), the topic of chapter 3, provides a narrative exegesis of the Song of Songs, discovering both the Bridegroom and the Bride in the saint.

What M. D. Chenu has called "a new awareness of history" in the twelfth century affected biblical exegesis and hagiography alike.[42] Reporting on the tumultuous, recent events in England, Eadmer's paired *Life* and *History* of Anselm of Canterbury, studied in chapter 4, marks and mirrors a disturbance in the relationship between the literal/historical sense of the Bible and hagiography, on the one hand, and the spiritual senses, on the other. In order to unite the *Life* with the *History*, Eadmer consciously interprets the tumultuous events in the *History* through Jesus's parable of the great feast in Luke 14:16–24, and in the *Life* he provides an allegorical interpretation of that same parable. Chapter 4 is a pivotal chapter that detects in hagiography the first signs of the disassociation of the literal/historical sense of scripture from the spiritual senses—a disassociation that Eadmer's younger contemporary Hugh of Saint Victor strove to prevent.

12 THE SAINT'S LIFE AND THE SENSES OF SCRIPTURE

Chapters 5, 6, and 7 continue the exploration of dualistic hagiography in the saints' *Lives* composed by three different Scholastic writers: Bonaventure's *Legenda maior* of Francis of Assisi (chapter 5), Raymond of Capua's *Legenda maior* of Catherine of Siena (chapter 6), and Jacobus de Voragine's "Legend of Mary Magdalene" in the *Legenda aurea* (chapter 7). The formal expression of dualism differs in each case, but all three show a tension in the effort to join the spiritual senses with the literal/historical.

The explicit discourse of heroic virtues in Bonaventure's *Legenda maior* and in Raymond's *Life of Catherine of Siena* reflects changes in the canonization process, but also what Kevin Hughes calls the "disintegration of mystagogy"[43] in biblical reading itself, as the tropological sense of the saint's life becomes, in effect, separated from the historical storyline. Against antimendicant critics, Bonaventure must defend the virtue of the (already canonized) saint, and Raymond, that of Catherine, for whose canonization he hopes. Jacobus's thirteenth-century legend of Mary Magdalene similarly turns the anagogical sense of the biblical saint's life into a separate, legendary narrative of ecstasies that were, first, reliteralized in the historical fasting and trances of Catherine, as Raymond of Capua (1303–39) narrates her imitation of the earlier saint, and then remoralized for pious laywomen in the Middle English poetry of Osbern Bokenham (1393–1447).

Chapter 8 links radical changes in the writing of saints' *Lives* to those reforms inaugurated in biblical studies at the literal level by Erasmus of Rotterdam and his contemporaries. Inspired by Erasmus's editorial principles, applied both to scripture and to the writing of saint's *Lives*, Nicholas Harpsfield's documentary biography of Thomas More (ca. 1556)—the first such biography in the English language—marks both the end of the writing of a saint's *Life* in the form of biblical hagiography and the start of what Frei calls the "eclipse" of biblical narrative.

Chapter 9 surveys some brilliant, novelistic attempts to revive hagiography as a "brief candle" for the Bible. Dostoevsky's *Crime and Punishment* (1866) and *The Brothers Karamazov* (1879–80) stage the luminous reading aloud of significant pericopes from the Gospels by characters who perceive the passages as relevant to their lives. Willa Cather's *Death Comes for the Archbishop* (1927) conveys Bishop Latour's transformative perceptions of New Mexico—its people and places—in language saturated with biblical echoes, joining evocation with eschatological vocation. Franz Werfel's

Song of Bernadette (1941) narrates the story of a young, visionary saint as an apocalyptic allegory, prophetic of times to come. More so than the modern biographers of saints, these novelists all take the inspired scriptures to be hagiography's primary source and exegetical end.

Chapter 10 draws parallels between the divergent strands of modern-day biblical study, as analyzed by Hans Frei, and those found in contemporary hagiographic study. Mirroring each other along lines that recall the biblical senses of traditional exegesis, these strands make a case for a lost connection between the Bible itself and premodern hagiography. A brief look at Gregory the Great's *Life of Saint Benedict* confirms this important, intertextual relationship at the origin of the genre. A backward glance at the preceding chapters recalls the book's unfolded argument and awakens the hope that a renewed biblical scholarship, combining historical-critical methods with an exegetical theology conscious of a long, living history of biblical reception, will find its partner in a renewed hagiography.

PART I

The Saint's *Life* in the Age of Monasticism

CHAPTER ONE

PSALM USE, PRAYER, AND PROPHECY IN THE *LIVES* OF SAINT GUTHLAC

Composed within a classical, biblically inspired, hagiographic tradition stemming from Saint Athanasius's fourth-century *Life of Anthony* of Egypt (251–356), Felix of Croyland's Latin *Life of Saint Guthlac* (ca. 730) records the hermit-saint's ardent practice of psalmody and his use of specific psalms both in his combat with demons and in his prediction of future events. Felix's *Life* and its prose translation into Old English emphasize that Guthlac speaks prophetically ("velut prophetico ore," "mid witegiende muðe," "witedomlice muþe") when he voices psalms both in prayer and in prediction.[1] The only study of prophecy in the extant Guthlac materials—a fine 1983 *Viator* article by Sally Musseter—focuses on *Guthlac B*, where the Psalms are not quoted, and, for that reason, it ignores the Latin hagiographer's insistent association of psalm use with prophecy.[2] This use, I argue, extends to the *Life* of the saint the understanding of the Psalms as prophetic of events in the earthly life of Jesus—a use well attested in the New Testament, the Fathers of the Church, and Christian liturgy. By this extension, the Psalms are also seen to prophesy the life of every Christian, in accord with Augustine's doctrine of the *Totus Christus*.[3] Jean Danielou wrote fifty years ago, "What is said of Christ is also true of the Christian."[4]

Against the anti-Judaism of the Marcionites and the Manichees and as a remedy for pride, Augustine of Hippo (354–430) preached on each of the 150 psalms over the course of three decades in order to lay claim to the Psalter as the Church's book of prayer.[5] Building upon the clear teaching in the New Testament that the Psalms prophesied Christ—the prophet David having been inspired to announce his divine Lord and his great descendant *secundum carnem*—Augustine understood and taught that the preexistent Christ, the Eternal Word, also prophesied in the Psalms, signified in them his union in prayer with his Bride, the Church, and effected that same union liturgically through psalm use. Previous commentators had distinguished different voices in the Psalms. Augustine does too, but he insists that when the Church speaks, Christ speaks too, *in persona ecclesiae*. Leading the Church as a whole and each of her members in praying to God, Christ speaks in the Psalms with and as the sinner, prescribing inspired prayers for purgation and conversion. He joins with the suffering in their outcry, making it his own. He meditates with the righteous on the law. He prompts the praises of the saints. Christ thus prophesies the Christian, whom he joins to himself through the Psalms, conforming their lives through prayer to the pattern of his own life.

The concept is a theo-dramatic one. Does Christ also speak, pray, and prophesy in Felix's Guthlac, when the hermit sings the Psalms? If so, how? To what effect? Like Musseter, but on a different basis, I see in Guthlac a "conflation of type and prophet."[6] In Felix's composition, Guthlac's psalm use in prayer enables and guarantees the prophetic power of his utterance, and presages the specific typological character of his death on April 11, 714, a Wednesday during Easter Week.

My argument here proceeds in four sections. First, I suggest the high stakes involved in a prophetic reading of Guthlac's psalm use, given the claim it makes for the Psalter's own dual character as prayer book and prophecy—an interactive duality, so recognized (I hope to show) by Guthlac himself, by his hagiographer Felix, and by Felix's near contemporary, Alcuin of York (735–804). Second, I analyze the specific psalm references in the *Vita Sancti Guthlaci* and its complete Old English prose translation. Third, I argue for intertextual connections between the hagiographer's psalm citations, on the one hand, and the Liturgy of the Hours, on the other. Fourth, I highlight Vercelli "Homily 23," a short, selective translation of Felix's *Life of Saint Guthlac*. That homily helps to explain the special association of Guthlac with the Rogation Days celebrated in Anglo-Saxon England with psalmic processions in preparation for Ascension Thursday.

ON PRAYER AND PROPHECY IN THE PSALMS AND PSALM USE

In various ways, the dual identity of the book of Psalms as prayer and prophecy has influenced the whole long history of their reception. Liturgical theologians frequently present the history of psalm use as a movement away from an early period, wherein the Psalter's Christological prophecies were emphasized, to a time when the personal use of the psalms in prayer (a practice encouraged by Alcuin of York) predominates. In a chapter entitled "The Changing Role of Psalmody," Paul Bradshaw, first of all, observes, "The Book of Psalms is cited more frequently in the New Testament than any other Old Testament Scripture, and it is there chiefly viewed as a book of prophecy—or one might say as *the* prophetic work *par excellence* of the Old Testament," written by "King David under the inspiration of the Holy Spirit."[7] Bradshaw explains that, beginning in the third century, "under the influence of the exegetical method adopted by Origen, . . . Christological interpretation was gradually extended from certain select psalms to encompass virtually all the psalms."[8] The use of psalms, thus interpreted, "as hymns" in Christian worship probably "has its roots in the use of psalms as prophecy," according to Bradshaw.[9] Contrasting these early "content-related" uses with those later emphasizing the "action and intention of the pray-er," Bradshaw lists the personal uses of the Psalms in praise, penance, and intercession (a short list that curiously omits mention of psalm use in exorcism, for healing, and at times of temptation).[10]

Bradshaw's historiography of psalm use arguably gives insufficient attention to the early uses of psalms in personal prayer, abundantly attested, for example, in Athanasius's "Letter to Marcellinus," alongside the recognition of the Psalms as prophetic of Christ's earthly life and second coming.[11] Bradshaw's contrast of Christo-prophetic and prayerful psalm use is meaningful, both descriptively and in the light of modern trends, which frequently separate the two. Responding to critics of the traditional Christological interpretation of the Psalms, Danielou articulates the persistent question: "Would there not be an advantage in disengaging the Psalms from Messianism and only retaining their lasting value as inspired prayers?"[12] Danielou himself responds in the negative, reminding his real and imagined interlocutors that "the whole of ancient tradition concerning the liturgical use of the Psalms rests on their Messianic significance."[13]

The form-critical analysis of the Psalms by Old Testament scholars also militates against a sharp separation of psalmic prayer and prophecy and helps indirectly, via a process of historical reconstruction, to explain the eager early Christian discovery of Christological prophecy in the Psalter, which was understood to include oracles. Sigmund Mowinckel's now classic study *The Psalms in Israel's Worship* associates the book of Psalms with an ancient Temple cult, within the context of which seer-priests, temple-prophets, and anointed kings spoke oracles, preserved (Mowinckel argues) in the very text of the Psalms, which are often characterized by abrupt shifts from verse to verse in voice (first person, second person, third person). In the royal psalms (Pss. 2, 110, 89), Mowinckel finds "enthronement oracles," spoken at the anointing of Israel's kings.[14] Similarly, concerning penitential petition, Mowinckel asserts, "The psalms handed down to us show that it was part of the very ritual of the penitential festivals that (the priest or) the temple prophet would promise the suppliant salvation and the granting of his prayer by means of an *oracle* or a *promise* to that effect."[15] The note of thanksgiving and confidence with which psalms of lamentation typically end is not, Mowinckel instructs, only an expression of the "assurance of faith" (cf. Heb. 11:1), nor is it simply a psychological outcome of having prayed.[16] Rather, it is also something "objectively based" on a "promise of salvation uttered by the priest or temple prophet."[17]

Mowinckel's influential theory is based chiefly on a form-critical analysis of the Psalms themselves, but it also draws upon key passages in the historical books of the Old Testament, where prophecy and psalmody are combined. After his anointing with oil by Samuel, for example, Saul goes out toward the city of Gibeah (as the prophet has instructed him), where he encounters (as Samuel has predicted) "a band of prophets coming down from the high place with harp, tambourine, flute and lyre before them, prophesying," whereupon Saul, moved by "the spirit of God," prophesies among them.[18] To cite another example used by Mowinckel: when the king of Israel in his distress poses a crucial military question to Elisha, the prophet first requests that a minstrel be brought; he speaks his inspired oracle only after the minstrel plays (2 Kings 3:9–19).[19]

All of this may seem far removed from Felix of Croyland's *Life of Saint Guthlac* (a prophet who, perhaps not coincidentally, also offers psalmic predictions to the future king of Mercia, Aethelbald). Alcuin of York's *De laude psalmorum* (sometimes called the preface to *De psalmorum usu*) suggests otherwise, however. Composed in the second half of the late eighth century, *De laude* emphatically and instructively treats the matters of prayer and prophecy as inseparable from each other. Its most recent editor, Jonathan Black, reports "at least 200 extant manuscripts from the ninth to fifteenth centuries containing the text, which has come down to us in versions of different length, with various titles and incipits."[20] Although *De psalmorum usu* can no longer credibly be attributed to Alcuin,[21] that ninth-century compilation was regularly joined in manuscripts to Alcuin's *De laude* and confirms other evidence that "in the decades after his death Alcuin was associated with the psalm uses."[22]

In the earliest extant version, based on a corrupt archetype, *De laude* begins abruptly with five sentences taken from Gregory the Great's homilies on Ezechiel,[23] which comment on the prophetic episode in 2 Kings mentioned above: "Also since the spirit of prophecy is not always in their minds, to the extent that they do not have it, they recognize that when they have it, they have it as a gift. Thus, when the prophet Elisha was asked about the future and knew the spirit of prophecy was not with him, he called for the psaltery to be played so that the spirit of prophecy would descend upon him."[24]

Alcuin, following Gregory (who goes unnamed), draws the following conclusion from the Old Testament story:

> For when the psalmodic voice is directed by the heart's intent, through this a way to the heart [*ad cor iter*] is prepared for the almighty God, so that it pours the mysteries of prophecy and grace of compunction into the intent mind. As it is written, "The sacrifice of praise has glorified me," etc. Thus, in sacrifice through divine praise, a way of showing [*iter ostensionis*] is made (that leads) to Jesus, since while compunction is poured out through psalmody, a path by which we may reach Jesus is made in the heart.[25]

A rich and complex passage, reflective of a profound Gregorian doctrine of sacrifice and compunction,[26] it correlates the opening of the lips in psalmody to that of the rightly intended heart. Rendered receptive to grace through psalm-singing and psalm-prayer,[27] the heart then receives from God a prophetic insight in and through the illumined words of the psalm, which reveals them to be referring to Jesus. "And so, no mortal can explain the power of the psalms," in which, Alcuin (echoing Gregory) insists, "you will find . . . the incarnation of the Word and the Lord's passion and resurrection and ascension."[28]

Alcuin then proceeds to list eight uses of the Psalms, all of which, given the proper intent of the heart, can open it to a share in "the mysteries of prophecy" (*prophetiae mysteria*) veiled in the psalm texts. One can use the Psalms (Black summarizes) "when one wishes (1) to do penance, (2) to pray, or (3) to praise God; in times of (4) temptation, (5) world-weariness, (6) tribulation, or (7) regained prosperity; and (8) when one wishes to contemplate divine laws."[29] Supplying his own numbering in the Regensburg edition of 1777, an earlier editor, Johann Froben, counted a ninth use (preserved as such in Migne's edition),[30] but Black is certainly correct to regard the closing section instead as Alcuin's overall conclusion. What troubles Black is that this conclusion "seems to be as much a redundancy as a recapitulation,"[31] so closely does it paraphrase the opening promise of prophetic understanding: "You will also find in the psalms the incarnation and passion and resurrection and ascension of the Lord and all the power of divine words if you study them with your innermost mind and attain through the grace of God the marrow of innermost understanding."[32]

The textual problems surely remain, but what is certain is that Alcuin's *De laude psalmorum* stands squarely within a Gregorian tradition that closely integrates both psalmody and heartfelt, personally intended psalm prayer with the prophetic, Christological understanding of the biblical text—the sort of understanding that gives a person an actual share in the prophetic experience, its vision and enunciation. Rather than moving from Christological prophecy to personal prayer use, Alcuin's *De laude* actually reverses that putative trajectory by presenting psalmody and psalm-prayer as a biblically attested means to render one open to the Holy Spirit of prophecy. Gregory's language, appropriated by Alcuin, aligns the pray-er who uses the Psalms to prepare "a way to the heart [*ad cor iter*] . . . for the almighty God," on the one hand, with the great precursor of the Lord, on the other, John the Baptist who, fulfilling Isaiah's prophecy, preached in the desert, "Prepare the way of the Lord" (*parate viam Domini*) (Matt. 3:3).[33]

FELIX'S GUTHLAC AS PSALMIC PROPHET

Even as Athanasius's "Letter to Marcellinus"—the greatest early Christian exposition of psalmic spirituality—sheds light on psalm use in Athanasius's monumental *Life of Antony* (355–62), Alcuin's *De laude psalmorum* elucidates, *mutatis mutandis*, Felix's *Life of Saint Guthlac*. Athanasius's *Vita Antonii* (in Evagrius's translation), Sulpicius Severus's *Life of Martin of Tours*, Jerome's *Vita Pauli*, Gregory the Great's *Life of Saint Benedict* (in the *Dialogues*, book 2), and Bede's prose *Life of Saint Cuthbert*, are, in fact, important sources for Felix's *Life of Guthlac*, alongside Virgil's *Aeneid* and the Bible.[34] Bertram Colgrave, the editor of Felix's text, cites "thirty-five direct quotations from Scripture" in the *Life of Saint Guthlac* and calls particular attention to Felix's use of the Psalms.[35]

Describing twelfth-century roundels,[36] which repeatedly depict Guthlac with a Psalter,[37] and a later, confused legend that Guthlac had himself translated the Psalter into Old English,[38] Colgrave remarks, "It is clear . . . that the psalter played an important part in the Crowland tradition,"[39] which stemmed in many ways from Felix's influential hagiography. At least five of the eighteen roundels depicting scenes from the *Life of Guthlac* in Harley Y 6, the twelfth-century "Guthlac Roll" housed in the British Library, display the Psalter, usually on the lap of the seated saint (roundels 4, 6, 12), but also upon the altar in his hermitage (roundel 9) and in the hand of Guthlac's helper, Saint Bartholomew (roundel 7). In roundel 6 (see plate 1.1), a seated Guthlac, the Psalter upon his lap, welcomes a winged angel and Bartholomew, his special patron.

Felix's *Life* records that Guthlac, after his sudden and deep conversion at age twenty-four, abruptly leaves the Mercian army and goes to the monastery at Repton, where he receives the tonsure under the abbess Aelfthryth and takes a penitential vow of total, lifelong abstinence from alcoholic beverages. At the monastery he learns the "chanting of the psalms" (*psalmorum canticum*),[40] whereupon the intent desire of his sober mind is answered by an irrigation of grace: "the divine grace sprinkled this same man's fertile heart copiously with the moist showers of heavenly dew" (*tunc frugifera supra memorati viri praecordia roscidis roris caelestis imbribus divina gratia ubertim indigabat*).[41] During a two-year novitiate, he learns virtue from his fellow monks and is initiated "in canticles, psalms, hymns, prayers, and church routine" (*canticis, psalmis, hymnis, orationibus moribusque ecclesiasticis*).[42]

Plate 1.1. Harley Y 6, "Guthlac Roll," British Library, Roundel 6, late twelfth century. https://www.bl.uk/collection-items/guthlac-roll.

Then, striking out on his own, Guthlac betakes himself into wild fens near Cambridge and, from there, to the more remote island called Crowland, where he begins his solitary life and his battles with demons. He does so armed "with the arrows of holy psalmody" (*sagittas psalmodiae*).[43]

In his hagiography of Guthlac, the monk Felix uses psalm quotations and the language of prophecy in discernible patterns. During the four demonic attacks recorded in chapters 29 through 34, Guthlac *prays* prophetically in the words of the Psalms. Then, his own spiritual trials at an end, Guthlac begins to manifest charismatic endowments, including foreknowledge. In this virtuous state, he *prophesies* prayerfully, using phrases drawn from the Psalms to speak to others. In a stunning episode near the end of the *Life*, Guthlac's protégé, Aethelbald, prays to Saint Guthlac, echoing the Psalms in his prayer, and the saint replies, also in psalmic phrases, prophecy answering prayer, and prayer proving prophetic.

Guthlac's first temptation upon his arrival at Crowland, a seemingly God-forsaken place infested with demons, is to despair over the rigors of the eremitical life he has commenced. On the evening of the third day of this bout of dark depression, Guthlac—weak and alone, but still resistant— "began to sing as though through the spirit of prophecy" (*velut prophetico spiritu psallere coepit*) the words of Psalm 17:7: "'In my distress I called upon the Lord,' and the rest." (*In tribulatione invocavi Dominum, et reliqua*).[44] At the sudden appearance of his patron, Saint Bartholomew, on whose feast day he had arrived at Crowland, Guthlac takes heart and sings triumphantly in the words of Psalm 117:7, "'The Lord is my helper and I shall see my enemies,' and the rest" (*Dominus mihi adiutor est, et ego videbo inimico meos, et reliqua*).[45]

The two quoted verses in the chapter contain verbs in three tenses: "I called" (present perfect, *invocavi*), "is" (present, *est*), and "shall see" (future, *videbo*). Taken together, they represent and help to effect Guthlac's movement from despair to faith and confident hope. By casting his despair into the past, Guthlac joins his personal narrative prophetically to that of David, who first sang Psalm 17 on the day of his rescue from the hands of all his enemies. When Bartholomew appears, in answer to the hermit's prophetic prayer, the arrival of Guthlac's helper matches that of David's divine helper in the psalm. The "et reliqua" in Felix's narrative art keys in the entirety of the cited psalms, whose subliminal poetry almost surfaces in Felix's prose—the "thick clouds dark with water" ("tenebrosa aqua in *nubibus aëris*") of Psalm 17:12, for example, standing parallel to Guthlac's beclouded, despairing thoughts ("nefandarum cogitationum *nebulis*"), both of which are suddenly illuminated (Ps. 17:13: "prae *fulgore* in conspectu eius"; *Life*: "*inluminato . . . gremio*").[46]

In a second trial, narrated in chapter 30, two devils come to Guthlac in human form, playing the false part of friends who tempt Guthlac not to despair (as in chapter 29) but to presumption (a vice that, like despair, violates hope, but through overreliance on one's own powers) and disobedience. Misusing biblical examples of fasting (Moses, Elijah, Jesus), the devils urge Guthlac to violate the strict but moderate, eremetical rule he has chosen for himself as an "unalterable rule of life" (*vitae . . . illius haec inmota ortonomia*).[47] That rule prescribes one meager meal of barley bread and water taken daily at sunset. The demons encourage him to fast instead for six days at a stretch, eating only on the seventh day, in order to accomplish in himself God's new creation.[48] Guthlac recognizes the idolatrous nature of the temptation, which weirdly mirrors through inversion Satan's temptation of Eve to eat forbidden fruit in order to become "like God" (Gen. 3:5). Rising up (*exsurgens*), Guthlac begins to sing Psalm 55, starting at verse 10: "Let mine enemies be turned back" (*Convertantur inimici mei retrorsum*),[49] and the devils immediately vanish like smoke before his face, *velut fumus a facie eius* (Ps. 67:2).[50]

The hagiographer's statement that Guthlac sang the whole of Psalm 55 (*et reliqua*) provides a hint concerning the hermit's insight into the sinfulness of the superficially God-pleasing asceticism promoted by his adversaries. The psalmist complains that his enemies have banded together against him. He repeats again and again that he trusts in God, not men; in God, not the flesh. The phrase *in Deo* is repeated four times in the short psalm, with *in Domino* counting as a fifth, variant iteration. Most importantly, perhaps, the twelfth verse of the psalm, "My vows to thee I must perform, O God; I will render thank offerings to thee" (*in me sunt Deus vota tua / reddam gratiarum actiones tibi*) serves to renew Guthlac's vow to keep the hermit's rule he has chosen. Guthlac's daily barley bread, obediently eaten and thankfully received, corresponds to the daily bread petitioned in the Lord's Prayer. A thank offering, it also has Eucharistic overtones that prefigure Guthlac's viaticum, the sacrament he, an ordained priest, gives to himself on Easter Sunday, April 8, 714, three days before his death, and on the very night of his dying.

The single verse from Psalm 55 quoted in the episode, "Let mine enemies be turned back" (*Convertantur inimici mei retrorsum*) (v. 10), reminds Augustine of Hippo, in his commentary on the psalm, of Jesus's words to Peter, "Get behind me, Satan! You are a stumbling block for me" (*Vade post me Satana scandalum es mihi*) (Matt. 16:23).[51] Like Guthlac's false friends, the two demons in human form, Peter had spoken against the path of obedience leading to the cross: "God forbid, Lord! This shall never happen to you!" (Matt. 16:22). Impatient and presumptuous, Guthlac's tempters would also hinder the hermit in his way of obedience, recommending to him instead a quick (and suicidal) way to eternal rest: a short series of six-day (or seven-day) fasts.

Victorious in these two temptations, Guthlac endures a third great trial, recounted by Felix in chapters 31–33. Physically dragged through the fen and tortured by fiends who command him to leave Crowland, Guthlac (like Antony of Egypt in his temptation by shape-changing demons) remains steadfast in mind (*stabilita mente*) and sings "as though with prophetic words" (*prophetico velut ore*) the eighth verse of Psalm 15: "The Lord is at my right hand, lest I should be moved" (*Dominus ad dextra est mihi, ne commovear*).[52] Taken in context, the refusal to move answers literally to the demonic demand that he depart from a physical place, Crowland, even as it reveals that same place to be the symbol of a spiritual location, the "place" of his closeness to the eternal, unchanging God. The art of the hagiography quotes a single verse from Psalm 15 in order to point to its other verses, which name the Lord himself as the psalmist's only "good" (v. 2), his "chosen portion" and "lot" (v. 5), his "heritage" (v. 6).

The prophetic framing of Guthlac's psalm quotation (*prophetico velut ore*) suggests more, however. Preaching to the crowds in Jerusalem on Pentecost, Peter quotes Psalm 15:25–28 as a prophetic foretelling of Jesus's resurrection from the dead: "I saw the Lord always before me, / for he is at my right hand that I may not be shaken; / therefore my heart was glad, and my tongue rejoiced; / moreover, my flesh shall dwell in hope. / For you will not abandon my soul to Hades, / nor let thy Holy One see corruption. / Thou hast made known to me the ways of life; / thou wilt make me full of gladness with thy presence" (Acts 2:25–28). Guthlac speaks the first of these words just before he is carried off, body and soul, to the very gates of hell, where he rebukes the demons, taking the strong, combative stance of Job, another "man of God" (*vir Dei*).[53]

Rebuffed by Bartholomew, Guthlac's helper from heaven, the demons immediately obey his command to return Guthlac, safe and sound, to his hermitage, while celestial voices are heard singing Psalm 83:8, "They [the saints] shall go from strength to strength" (*Ibunt sancti de virtute in virtutem*).[54] In fulfillment of Psalm 15, then, Guthlac is preserved from the pit, the prophecy of Christ's resurrection proving to have been prophetic also of Guthlac's own return from the underworld. Guthlac's victorious homecoming to his home in Crowland, moreover, offers the foretaste of the eschatological fulfillment of the prophecy of Psalm 83. The battles with demons have strengthened Guthlac in virtue, to be sure, but the horrifying sight of hell has also effectively increased Guthlac's longing for heaven's beauty. Therefore Guthlac can sing also the still unvoiced words of Psalm 83, which is a hymn of homesickness for the house of God: "How lovely is thy dwelling place, O Lord of hosts! / My soul longs, yea, faints for the courts of the Lord" (*Quam dilecta tabernacula tua Domine virtutum / concupiscit et defecit anima mea in atria Domini*) (vv. 1–2). Meanwhile, the fiends vanish again "like smoke" (*velut fumus a facie*), Felix repeating for a second time this echo of Psalm 67:2.[55]

Guthlac's fourth and last struggle with temptation, described in chapter 34 of the *Life*, takes the form of a troubled dream-vision of a Briton attack on his retreat in East Anglia—a realistic vision that plays upon the hermit's memories of his own military past and also his waking anxieties about warfare in nearby Mercia. Recognizing the nightmare as nightmare and not reality, Guthlac perceives the devils' trick and puts the whole phantasmagorical army to flight by singing "as if prophetically" (*velut prophetico ore*) the first verse of Psalm 67: "Let God arise, and the rest" (*Exsurgat Deus, et reliqua*).[56] For a third and final time, Felix echoes Psalm 67:2, relating that the imaginary Britons "vanished like smoke" (*fumus a facie eius*) before his eyes.[57]

The thrice-repeated citation of the second verse; the specific mention of Psalm 67 in the title of chapter 34; the invocation of that entire psalm, starting at the first verse; and the third narrative use of the formula "as if prophetically" (*velut prophetico ore*)—all suggest the special importance Felix ascribes to this particular psalm as a key to the reader's understanding of Guthlac's holy life. Arguably, Felix even employs *exsurgens* as an epithet (*exsurgens Guthlac*) in chapter 30, in order to link the saint to the God he invokes and follows: "Exsurgat Deus" (Ps. 67:1). The participle "exsurgens" modifies Guthlac again in chapter 50, in the Easter week of his death. In section three of this chapter a study of Psalm 67 in its liturgical use reveals it to be a prophecy of the Lord's "rising" in his resurrection and ascension, and thus also a prophecy of Guthlac's own dying and rising in Eastertide.

For now, it suffices to say that Psalm 67 appropriately responds to Guthlac's famous, warring dream-vision. Its opening verse, "Let God arise," recalls the prayer of Moses at the marching out of the tribes of Israel, carrying the ark: "Arise, O Lord, and let thy enemies be scattered; and let them that hate thee flee before thee" (Num. 10:35). Psalm 67 celebrates the mighty deeds of the Lord of Hosts, who sets to flight the armies of Israel's enemies: "The kings of the armies, they flee! They flee!" (Ps. 67:12). Dispersing the Britons in his dream, Guthlac dispels the demons of his violent past in Mercia, but he also prophesies Mercian victory over the Britons and safety for East Anglia. The hagiographer Felix thus brings good hope also to King Aelfwald, the king of East Anglia, at whose request he has composed the *Vita Sancti Guthlaci*.

After chapter 34, Guthlac no longer battles personally with demons, except for one nocturnal skirmish with fiends in the shapes of wild beasts (*Life*, chap. 36).[58] Instead, he encounters them in others, whom he frees through performing exorcisms (chaps. 41–42). He tames the animals of the fens—jackdaws, fish, swallows (chaps. 37, 38, 39, 40)—creatures very unlike the wild beasts of his fiendish nightmare.[59] Possessing the "spirit of prophecy" (*prophetico spiritu*), Guthlac reads the thoughts of his disciple Beccel, exposes his intent to kill his master, and converts him.[60] By the "spirit of prophecy" (*prophetiae spiritu*), Guthlac has knowledge from a distance of the faults and sins of others, whom he admonishes.[61] Through the spirit of foresight (*providentiae spiritu*), he knows what doubts and questions to expect from his visitors.[62] By that same charism of foresight (*spiritu providentiae*), he describes his still unbaptized successor,[63] and he predicts that his own death will occur "on the eighth day" of his illness.[64]

Felix echoes the Psalms in the later chapters of the *Life*, but only in Guthlac's conversations, in life and after death, with Aethelbald, who has been exiled from Mercia, where he will later reign (716–57). "As if interpreting a divine oracle" (*velut divini oraculi interpres*), Guthlac reveals Aethelbald's future to him in some detail, after explaining that he already knows of the Mercian's calamitous exile and has prayed for him: "I have asked the Lord to help you . . . and He has heard me" (*rogavi Dominum . . ., et exaudivit me*).[65] Guthlac's prayer is, it seems, the precondition for his prophecy. The oracle he delivers is the Psalter he has read, and upon which he has meditated. A pastiche of psalm citations (Colgrave counts six in nine lines), Guthlac's prophecy to and for Aethelbald does foretell the exile's victorious return to Mercia, but it also exhorts him to patient waiting and trust in the Lord, who is his helper (*Dominus adiutor*) (Ps. 27:7).[66]

After Guthlac's death, a tearful Aethelbald prays at the saint's tomb. His words echo the Psalms, in part because they also echo Guthlac's prayers for him and psalmic exhortation. The disciple imitates his father, Guthlac. Adapting Psalm 80:8, the exile tells Guthlac, "Through you, I called upon the Lord, and He freed me" (*per te invocabam Dominum, et liberavit me*).[67]

Echoing Psalm 30:15, Aethelbald declares that he has trusted in the Lord, but also in Guthlac, the Lord's servant: "In you I have hoped, and the hope has not failed me" (*in te sperabam, nec me spes fefellit*).[68] Answering to the exile's petition for continued assistance, Guthlac appears to him in a vision of light to banish his fears. Like the psalmist (Pss. 117:7; 27:7; 77:35), Guthlac names the Lord as Aethelbald's "helper" (*adiutor*). He goes on to prophesy the exile's kingship and to confirm the prophecy by a sign, a provision of needed food that comes, in fact, to Aethelbald the following day, exactly as predicted. After that, Felix relates, the Mercian "placed unshakeable confidence in the prophecies of the man of God" (*in vaticiniis viri Dei defixit*).[69]

In this last display of psalm use in prayer and prophecy in the *Life*, Felix effectively recalls Guthlac's own first, despairing temptation in chapter 29. The prayer of Aethelbald as a tearful invocation of the Lord (*invocabam Dominum*) through Guthlac imitates Guthlac's prophetic singing of Psalm 17:7, *In tribulatione invocavi Dominum*.[70] Guthlac's sudden sight of his helper, Saint Bartholomew, prefigures Aethelbald's vision of his friend and father, Guthlac. On that occasion in his youth, Guthlac declared his trust in the Lord as his helper (*Dominus mihi adiutor est*), using the words of Psalm 117:7, even as he experienced that divine aid through the consoling presence of Bartholomew. Similarly, at the end of the *Vita Sancti Guthlaci*, Aethelbald experiences the Lord as *adiutor* ("helper") through Guthlac's shining presence and spoken words. The prophecy Guthlac has heard and prayed in the Psalms has become the prophecy he speaks and gives in his own life to Aethelbald and, through Aethelbald, to the reader of Felix's hagiography.

GUTHLAC'S PSALMODY AND THE LITURGY

Of the fifteen psalms explicitly cited in Felix's *Life* (Pss. 17, 117, 55, 67, 15, 83, 27, 26, 20, 89, 143, 72, 80, 30, and 77, with Ps. 67 being echoed four times), four (Pss. 26, 67, 89, and 117) also appear in Athanasius's *Life of St. Antony*, which was certainly known to Felix.[71] Like Antony, Guthlac wields Psalms 67:1 and 117:7 as weapons in battles with demons.[72] These and other psalms have a long history of use in rites of exorcism,[73] but Felix's Guthlac (unlike Athanasius's Antony) also (and emphatically) uses them in prophecy. Felix employs the phrase *velut prophetico ore* three times to introduce Guthlac's psalm-singing. Felix's Guthlac also differs from Athanasius's Antony in having prophetic glimpses of hell and heaven while still in the flesh—visions Jane Roberts describes as possessing "more in common with the Fursey–Drichthelm tradition than with the Antonian."[74]

To mark his victory over his tempters at hell's mouth, Guthlac, like Saint Fursey (d. 650), hears the angels singing Psalm 83:7, *Ibunt sancti de virtute in virtutem*. Known to Bede (673–735), the *Life of Fursey* (composed 656–57), inclusive of the *Visio Sancti Fursei*, must have been known also to Bede's contemporary, Felix.[75] Remembering Paul's own visionary account in 2 Corinthians 12:2, Bede describes the otherworldly journey of the Irish monk-missionary to East Anglia in his *Ecclesiastical History of the English People* 3.19: "He was snatched from the body . . . and during that time he was privileged to gaze upon the angelic hosts and to listen to their blessed songs of praise. He used to say that he heard them sing among other songs, 'The saints shall go from strength to strength' [Ps. 83:7a] and again, 'The God of gods shall be seen in Sion' [Ps. 83:7b]."[76]

Oriented toward the prophesied second coming of Christ and each one's expected encounter with the Lord at the time-ending hour of death, early Christians practiced psalmody (in its fullest form, the daily or weekly recitation of the 150 psalms) as a way of heeding the exhortation in 1 Thessalonians 5:17, "Pray without ceasing."[77] Just as the Psalter prophesied events in Christ's earthly life, so too did psalm use ready souls for Christ's return and prophesy the eschaton, training vigilant pray-ers to anticipate Christ's judgment, to ward off hellish punishment by renouncing sin, to merit Christ's reward through virtuous living, and to commence already here on earth a share in heaven's unending praise. In this prophetic understanding of the Psalms (to echo Walter Brueggemann), "the future . . . impinges on the present."[78]

Guthlac, unlike Antony of Egypt, lived in a monastic community prior to his embarking upon an eremitical life, and he was schooled there (his hagiographer reports) "in canticles, psalms, hymns, prayers, and church routine" (*canticis, psalmis, hymnis, orationibus moribusque ecclesiasticis*).[79] Guthlac's psalm use at Crowland must be understood, therefore, also in the context of monastic *cursus*, the ordered schedule of weekly psalm recitation. His prophetic use of Psalm 67, in particular—a repeated use, thematic in Felix's *Life*—demands a liturgical interpretation.

32 THE SAINT'S *LIFE* IN THE AGE OF MONASTICISM

Historians of the Divine Office distinguish two chief forms of the Office, the Benedictine and the Roman (the latter sometimes called "secular"). Jesse D. Billett has established that "the form of the Office introduced by the Augustinian mission [from Rome to England] cannot have been 'Benedictine' in the later medieval sense," nor was "the Benedictine form of the Office . . . used in England before the monastic reform of the tenth century."[80] In Billett's account, the liturgical decrees of the Council of Clofesho (747) — a council supported by the Mercian king Aethelbald (Guthlac's protégé) and Aelfwald, king of East Anglia (Guthlac's devotee) — show "consolidation and strengthening of a form of the Office liturgy first introduced by Roman missionaries,"[81] rather than a new imposition of the Roman *cursus*, over and against the Benedictine. Piecing together corroborating evidence, Billett argues, in particular, that the Roman Office was used in East Anglia under Aelfwald, for whom Felix composed his *Vita Sancti Guthlaci*.[82]

According to Billett's schema for the Roman *cursus* (based, in part, on the ninth-century descriptions of it by Amalarius of Metz),[83] the psalms Felix places either on the lips of Saint Guthlac (or of his protégé Aethelbald or of unseen angels heard by Guthlac) would have been sung in the Office as follows:

Sunday and festal nocturns: Pss. **17*** and **15*** (2nd nocturn);
   Ps. 20 (3rd nocturn)
Sunday at lauds (from Septuagesima to Palm Sunday) or at prime
   (except from Septuagesima to Palm Sunday): **Ps. 117**
Monday nocturn: Pss. 26, 27, 30
Wednesday nocturn: Pss. **55, 67***
Thursday nocturn: Pss. 72, 77
Thursday lauds: Ps. 89
Friday nocturn: Pss. 80, **83**
Saturday vespers: Ps. 143

In this tabulation, I highlight in bold those psalm citations to which Felix calls special attention through the direct quotation of an entire verse, and I star those psalms Felix introduces with some variant of the solemn phrase "with prophetic voice." This sketch allows the immediate recogni-

Psalm Use, Prayer, and Prophecy in the *Lives* of Saint Guthlac 33

tion that Felix's hagiography associates the life of the saint especially with the night offices for Sunday, Wednesday, Thursday (lauds being joined with the night vigil to form a single "hour" in the sevenfold Roman *cursus*), and Friday.[84] The *Life* is anchored in these days and hours, which recall weekly the mysteries (1) of Christ's rising from the dead (Sunday), (2) his betrayal by Judas (Wednesday), (3) the institution of the Eucharist and the Ascension (conjoined mysteries, both occurring on Thursday), and (4) Christ's passion and death (Friday).

The connection to the night office(s) on Sunday, the first day of the week, is literally obvious and theologically important. Felix quotes from both Psalm 17 and Psalm 117 in retelling the first of Guthlac's temptations, and he returns to them (somewhat more allusively) in Guthlac's final, posthumous appearance to Aethelbald. Billett notes that Psalm 17, "the longest psalm recited in the Sunday night office," is decorated in both the Vespasian and the Salaberga Psalter (and possibly also in the Blickling), a feature that suggests Psalm 17 began the second nocturn at an early stage in the development of the Roman Office.[85] Psalm 15, also chanted during the Sunday nocturns, figures in Guthlac's great victory during the third temptation at the very gates of hell; it prophecies the resurrection of Christ (cf. Acts 2:25–28), recalled weekly on Sunday, the day of Christ's rising.

Wednesday designates a climax or turning point in the drama of salvation that is mirrored in the Divine Office, and in Guthlac's *Life*. Psalm 55, recited during the Wednesday nocturn, proves key to Guthlac's second victory in temptation—that over his false friends, the two fiends, who would, like Judas, betray Guthlac "with a kiss" (cf. Luke 22:48). The liturgy for Holy Week recalls on Wednesday the decision of Judas to seek an opportunity to hand Jesus over to his enemies (Luke 22:1–6; Mark 14:10–11; Matt. 26:14–16).

Felix relates that Guthlac fell mortally ill on Wednesday during Holy Week, feeling sudden pangs while he was at prayer at night. A week later, "again on a Wednesday, being the fourth day of the Easter festival, his illness came to an end, and he went to be with the Lord."[86] Felix's Latin text, more ornate than Colgrave's English translation would suggest, here echoes Bede's prose *Life of Saint Cuthbert*, who, like Guthlac, died on a Wednesday, the monks at Lindisfarne hearing of his death as they were at the night office, singing Psalm 59.[87]

In Guthlac's case, Psalm 67 is the prophetic text that, more than any other, foretells his life, death, and saintly destiny. Sung during the Wednesday nocturn in both the Roman and the Benedictine *cursus*, Psalm 67 is the only psalm to be quoted thrice in the *Life* (chaps. 30, 31, 34) and mentioned in a chapter title. This psalm receives special prominence in Guthlac's fourth trial, the vision of the assailing Briton hordes (chap. 34). Guthlac dies at dawn on Easter Wednesday, but (Felix relates) "from midnight until dawn" the hermitage is filled with an extraordinary light that begins to shine suddenly,[88] when Guthlac's companion, Beccel, "was engaged upon his nightly vigils," praying the Wednesday nocturn (*nocturnis vigilis*).[89] In this way, Psalm 67, albeit unquoted directly here, announces the saint's death.

Psalm 67 is sung in the Divine Office not only on Wednesday nights, but also in the festal liturgy for Ascension Thursday.[90] Danielou names Psalm 67 "the third psalm of the Ascension," alongside Psalms 23 and 109.[91] Like the latter, Psalm 67 is "an essential source for the theology of the Ascension," and Saint Paul interprets it as such in Ephesians 4:7–11: "But to each of us grace was given according to the measure of Christ's bestowal. Thus it says, 'Ascending on high, he led away captives; he gave gifts to men' [cf. Ps. 67:18]. Now this 'he ascended' what does it mean but that he also first descended into the lower parts of the earth? He who ascended, he it is who ascended also above all the heavens, that he might fill all things. And he himself gave some men as apostles, and some as prophets."[92]

Before his ascension, Jesus instructs the apostles to return to Jerusalem to await there the coming of the promised Holy Spirit with his gifts (Acts 1:4). After the Ascension, angels appear to prophesy Christ's return: "This Jesus, who was taken up from you into heaven, will come in the same way as you saw him go into heaven" (Acts 1:11). Numbered among the twelve apostles, Guthlac's helper, Bartholomew, also known as Nathaniel, is suggestively foretold in his role as psychopomp by Jesus himself, who tells Nathaniel, "Truly, truly, I say to you, you will see heaven opened, and the angels of God ascending and descending upon the Son of Man" (John 1:51).

In chapter 34 of the *Life*, Felix has Guthlac sing Psalm 67:1, "Let God arise," as a battle cry, begging for the Lord's intervention against spiritual foes. Felix quotes Psalm 67:2 repeatedly to say that Guthlac's enemies "vanish like smoke."[93] In the liturgical context of the Ascension, the disappearance of the fiends from Guthlac's sight corresponds paradoxically to the vanishing of Christ's body, lifted up into the clouds (Acts 1:9) to mark the victorious fulfillment of his earthly mission and to complete the trajectory of his resurrection from the dead. Christ literally rises up, as God and man, reversing the pattern of his humble descent in the Incarnation, Crucifixion, and harrowing of hell. Raised on high, he distributes the victor's booty in the form of charisms granted to the members of his mystical body—a body mysteriously formed on earth through the ascension of his human body and its hidden, real presence in the Eucharist.

Holy Thursday, the day of the Last Supper, and Ascension Thursday, are thus mysteriously intertwined and recalled together on a weekly basis in the memory of the Church. In a Johannine passage highlighted by Douglas Farrow, the "twin mysteries of the ascension and the eucharist" are explicitly linked.[94] Responding to those who are scandalized by his "hard saying" concerning the eating of his flesh and the drinking of his blood, Jesus retorts, "Do you take offense at this? Then what if you were to see the Son of Man ascending where he was before?'" (John 6:60, 62).

Through the long chapter narrating Guthlac's illness and dying—a weeklong process that spans Holy Week and Easter, Passion and Resurrection— Felix lets his readers confront the scandal of death through Guthlac's weeping disciple, Beccel, whom Guthlac comforts. "So great was his faith," writes Felix, "that death, which seems something to be feared and dreaded by all mortals, he considered to be, as it were, a rest and reward for his labour."[95]

At Beccel's abjuration, the dying Guthlac reveals for the first time that, from the second year of his eremitical life, he has had daily converse with an angel. This mention of the comforting angel recalls the verse from the night office on Fridays—Psalm 83:8: "The saints shall go from strength to strength"—which Guthlac is said to have heard sung by angelic voices at the end of the terrible trial that had brought him to the threshold of hell. Reminiscent of the angelic strengthening given to Jesus during his agony in the garden (Luke 22:43), the verse now figures in Guthlac's immediate preparation for death. The angel's narrated descent at God's command enables Guthlac's final participation in the Lord's own rising, in his resurrection and ascension.[96] "Rising up" (*exsurgens*), Guthlac celebrates Mass at Easter and gives himself the sacrament. On the morning of his death, he again takes "Christ's Body and Blood," and with eyes uplifted to heaven (*elevatis oculis ad caelum*) and hands upraised (*extensisque in altum manibus*), he sends forth his spirit.

GUTHLAC'S "ASCENSION" AND ROGATIONTIDE

The same psalms voiced by Guthlac in Felix's *Life* of the saint were chanted in the liturgy, which occasioned in turn the saint's remembrance in readings, homilies, and poetry.[97] Because of its use in the Office for the Feast of the Ascension and because of its processional imagery, which, like that of Psalm 77, recalls Israel's journey through the wilderness, Psalm 67 found a natural place in the ritual for the minor Rogation Days (*laetanias minores*) — described by Stephan Borgehammar as "three days of penitential processions — Monday to Wednesday before Ascension Thursday,"[98] when the Easter candle was typically extinguished.[99] Another psalm important to Felix's *Life of Guthlac* — Psalm 55 — is also the proper to the procession for Rogation.[100]

The name of Guthlac — a saint whose life took Psalm 67 as its prophecy — appears in twenty of the Old English litanies of the saints edited by Michael Lapidge — litanies virtually identified with the Rogation Days (*letaniae/laetaniae*) and their "litanic processions or 'litanies.'"[101] In the invocation before the litany of the saints, they are asked to rise up: "Surgite, sancti."[102] The saints in heaven are called, as it were, to help to lead an earthly procession of wayfaring Christians who seek paradise itself as their final goal. "In a physical analogy," writes Stephen Harris, "the processors will be heading back to their church, whose entrance is called the *Paradisum*."[103] At least ten churches (in the dioceses of Ely, Peterborough, Lincoln, and Norfolk) were dedicated to Guthlac.[104]

Appropriate for use at Rogationtide, Vercelli "Homily 23," the final piece (fols. 133r–135v), in the Vercelli Book (ca. 1000), is a close translation of selected parts of Felix's *Vita Sancti Guthlaci*, fused together to form a clear pattern of *descensus/ascensus*. It presents Guthlac as a model of penitence, humble fasting, and prayerful trust in God. It concludes with the image of Guthlac's soul in its ascent to God, after narrating the saint's descent to hell's doors. It forms, as Samantha Zacher has demonstrated, "an entirely fitting conclusion to the Vercelli book as a whole."[105]

Following chapters 28–32 of Felix's *Life*, Homily 23 begins abruptly with Guthlac's establishment of his hermitage at Crowland and proceeds to retell the first three of Guthlac's temptations: to despair over his past sins and present weakness, to excessive fasting, and to terror before the gates of hell. It includes his singing "with prophetic mouth" (*witedomlice muðe*) of Psalm 17:7 (lines 23–24), Psalm 55:10 (lines 59–60), and Psalm 15:8 (lines 87–88), and it retains also at least an echo of Psalm 67:2 in the image of the demon vanishing like smoke before Guthlac's face (*se awyrgeda feond efne swa rec beforan his onsyne aidlode*) (lines 60–61).[106] At the sudden appearance of Saint Bartholomew at the end of his third trial, however, Guthlac simply flies, happily and speedily, with the apostle into heaven: "And then, after that, the holy Guthlac flew with the apostle Saint Bartholomew to the glory of heaven's kingdom, and the Savior received him there, and he lives there and reigns in the glory of the kingdom of heavens always without end in eternity. Amen fiat!" (*Þa æfter þam fleah se haliga Guðlac mid þam apostole sancta Bartholomei to heofonarices wuldre 7 hine se Hælend þær onfeng 7 he þær leofað 7 rixaþ in heofonarices wuldre a butan ende on ecnesse. Amen fiat!*) (lines 117–19).[107]

Possessed with three sermons (19–21) for the minor Rogation Days, but lacking a concluding Ascension Day sermon,[108] the Vercelli compiler seems to have provided in substitution two homilies about the soul's end, either in hell (22) or in heaven (23), with *Elene*'s poetic narrative about the finding of the true cross meditating between them.[109] The Feast of the Invention of the Holy Cross was celebrated in Anglo-Saxon England on May 3, a date sometimes coinciding with the Rogation Days or Ascension. Abridging Felix's *Vita Sancti Guthlaci* as he does, the Vercelli homilist offers an almost startling interpretation of the *Life* as an Ascension narrative, wherein the Christian saint, after a discipleship of humbling descent and battle with demons, follows Christ's lead in a procession of saints moving heavenward as they sing the Psalms.

Guthlac—a penitent, hermit, and exemplary saint—certainly found the Psalms to be (in Alcuin's words) a way to Christ: "For when the psalmodic voice is directed by the heart's intent, through this a way to the heart [*ad cor iter*] is prepared for the almighty God, so that . . . a path by which we may reach Jesus is made in the heart."[110] The Psalter's prophecy of Christ and Christian is self-fulfilling, as it were, through the reader's practiced prayer, especially the singing of the Psalms and meditation upon them. The pray-er of the psalms, like John the Baptist, the greatest and the least of the prophets, thus prepares the way of the Lord (cf. Luke 3:4) and joins the procession led by Christ and Christ's saints, Guthlac notable among them.

CHAPTER TWO

HEXAEMERAL MIRACLES IN SAINT AELRED OF RIEVAULX'S *LIFE OF NINIAN*

The remarkable combination in the *Life of Ninian* (*Vita Niniani*) by Aelred of Rievaulx (1110–67) of a hagiographic plain style, biblical quotation, and sophisticated Augustinian intertext makes it a masterpiece of medieval hexaemeral literature. But it has not been recognized as such, in large part because scholars have underestimated the transformative power of Aelred's translation of his source materials, which include (I hope to show) Augustine's commentary on Genesis 1 in *Confessions*, book 13. Marsha L. Dutton has pointed to some obvious parallels between the lives of Ninian and Aelred.[1] Aelred's implicit closeness to Ninian, the apostle to the southern Picts, invites further reflection upon Aelred's explicit, close, self-identification elsewhere with Augustine of Hippo. A triangulated relationship emerges, wherein the saint's story, as Aelred tells it, works effectively to mediate between Aelred and Augustine not only as historical persons but also as commentators on the creation account in Genesis 1.

I argue that Aelred uses the *Life of Ninian* to narrate his own story in a hidden way and, in that same process, to transform Augustine's theological memoir in *Confessions* effectively into the *Life* of a late fourth-century British saint, who was, if Aelred's sources be trusted, Augustine's close contemporary and fellow bishop. (The year of the death of Saint Martin of Tours, 397, is held to mark the start of Ninian's missionary activity.) An astute reader of Augustine, Aelred imitates in the hagiographic terms of the *Life* the yoking together in *Confessions* of a life story with a commentary on the days of creation in Genesis. As narrated by Aelred, Ninian's six miracles comment upon the Creator's miraculous work at the making of heaven and earth and thus also at Scotland's first evangelization.

Although Augustine's influence upon Aelred's other writings has long been acknowledged, it has escaped the attention of readers of the *Vita Niniani*. Indeed, among the works of Aelred, the *Life of Ninian* has received little critical attention, apart from the important source studies of John MacQueen and Winifred W. MacQueen.[2] Comparing Aelred's *Vita Niniani* both to Bede's brief account of the life of the same British saint in the *Historia Ecclesiastica* 3.4 (ca. 731) and to the *Miracula Nynie Episcopi*, a "religious epyllion composed in Latin heroic (hexameter) verse," dating from the time of Alcuin of York (ca. 735–804), John MacQueen has argued that all three of these documentary sources stem from a common Latin prose source, no longer extant, to which Aelred had indirect access through a (now lost) Old English translation.[3]

Such studies highlight and help to explain important commonalities between Aelred's *Vita Niniani* and the *Miracula Nynie Episcopi*, but they shed little light upon the notable differences between them — in particular, Aelred's apparent addition of two miracle stories, attributed to the saint during his lifetime, to the four contained in the *Miracula*; his reordering of the account of Ninian's missionary activity (to place its narrative after, not before, that of the building of the stone church at Whithorn in Galloway); and everything (especially his use of biblical quotations, allusions, and Augustinian intertext) that belongs to the consummate art of Aelred's hagiography as a work of narrative theology. Aelred's *Vita Niniani* "follows the *Miracula* fairly closely in the main outlines of the story," Winifred MacQueen observes, "but there is virtually no verbal resemblance, and a constant shift of emphasis."[4] Some of the differences between Aelred's *Vita* and the *Miracula* are reasonably explained by Aelred's immediate source (notably, the reference in Aelred's *Vita* to the Old English place-name *Farres Last*),[5] but Aelred's own disparaging remarks in the prologue about the literary and linguistic qualities of his "barbarous" source[6] render plausible — indeed, highly probable — the hypothesis that Aelred has not merely accomplished a stylistically pleasing, literal translation into Latin prose, but also effectively transformed the *Life of Ninian* through a retelling of his miracles that reveals their deep theological significance.

Aelred explains in the prologue that he has endeavored to "draw the life of this illustrious man out of rustic speech, as if bringing it from a kind of darkness into the light of Latin eloquence," thus enhancing its power to delight and to edify its readers.[7] The process from darkness into light suggests not merely an outward adornment, but a creative illumination of the rough and formless materials (cf. Gen. 1:1–3) through Aelred's meditation upon them in the light of scripture. For such a transformative retelling of a saint's life and miracles in biblical terms, Aelred could have drawn inspiration (as he often did) from the writings of Augustine, especially his commentaries on Genesis.

Aelred's debt in *Speculum caritatis* (*The Mirror of Charity*) to Augustine's treatment of Sabbath rest in *De Genesi ad litteram* (*On the Literal Interpretation of Genesis*) has long been recognized.[8] A close correspondence between Aelred's moral interpretation of the six days of creation in the *Mirror*,[9] on the one hand, and the six miracles in his *Life of Ninian*, on the other, enables a further reconstruction of Aelred's reading of Augustine's commentary on Genesis in book 13 of *Confessions*, where the works of the days are interpreted allegorically and tropologically. In this chapter, I first discuss the Augustinian basis for Aelred's original correlation of a saintly life and miracles to the days of creation. I then sketch the biblical sources inspiring the variety of artistic renderings of the creation story, including Aelred's own. Finally, I turn to a close reading of the six miracles in book 1 of Aelred's *Life of Ninian* and of the narrative interludes that divide them into three thematic pairs.

AELRED'S AUGUSTINIAN CONCEPT: CONFESSING MIRACLES OF A NEW CREATION

As Marco Carlos Emerson Hernández has emphasized, Augustine's understanding of creation as miraculous is inseparable from his thought concerning its re-creation in Christ.[10] The first Christian theologian to offer a definition of *miraculum*,[11] Augustine uses the notion of the miraculous in various ways in his many writings,[12] but he ascribes at least three different purposes to miracles understood as extraordinary signs and wonders wrought by God. First of all, miracles are useful in converting unbelievers through the awakening of wonderment. In *Confessions*, Augustine sees this purpose as explaining the relative frequency of miracles in the age of the apostles, when the preaching of the gospel was regularly accompanied by miraculous healings: "Their preaching and proclamation used miracles and sacred rites and mystical prayers to attract the attention of ignorance, the mother of wonder, inducing the awe aroused by secret symbols."[13] In *The City of God*, Augustine reiterates this point: "Miracles were necessary before the world believed, in order that it might believe."[14] Remembering Ninian's historic missionary work (late fourth century) among the southern Picts, Aelred no doubt saw this first purpose of miracles in ample evidence.

Second, Augustine teaches that God uses extraordinary signs to make the faithful more deeply and gratefully aware of the standing miracles of creation and re-creation, of the sheer existence of things created out of nothing (*ex nihilo*), of the completely gratuitous gift of grace granted to undeserving sinners, of the marvel of moral conversion, and of the beautiful pattern of providence in human history, individual and collective: "Although . . . the standing miracle of this visible world is little thought of, because always before us, yet when we rouse ourselves to contemplate it . . . it is a greater miracle than the rarest and most unheard of miracles. For man himself is a greater miracle than any miracle done through his instrumentality."[15] Linking the miracle of miracles of the Eternal Word's incarnation to that of humanity's paradisiacal creation as a being of body and soul, Augustine marvels "that a miraculous person was born miraculously."[16] Affirming the wondrous signs recorded in scripture, Augustine does not separate them from, but rather joins them to, the works of creation: "For it is God Himself who has wrought all these miracles, great and small, . . . and who has enclosed [them] in this world, itself the greatest miracle of all."[17]

Finally, miracles bear witness to the Church as the Bride of Christ and to the communion of saints. For Augustine, the story of Eve's creation from Adam's rib (Gen. 21–22) was a miracle pointing to the Church herself, born from Christ's side during his sleep in death on the cross, and to humanity's need of grace for the perfection of its nature: "All things that have been made not in the natural development of things, but in a miraculous way to signify this grace, have had their causes also hidden in God."[18] Augustine bears witness in *City of God* that "even now miracles are wrought in the name of Christ, whether by His sacraments or by the prayers or relics of His saints,"[19] and in *Confessions* he celebrates cures wrought in Milan through the relics of the martyrs Protasius and Gervasius.[20]

According to Augustine, moral miracles too, when properly observed, have an arresting, marvelous quality that points to God as their originator. Hence the miraculous fruitfulness of holy men and women, who are "an example to the faithful by the life they live before them" and who "arous[e] them to imitation" (1 Thess. 1:7).[21] All persons, because created in the "image and likeness" of God (cf. Gen. 1:26), are called to imitate the divine and are capable of conversion through Christ's grace. Indeed, all things, because created *ex nihilo*, possess a deep, natural capacity for obedience to God, so that no miracle, properly speaking, is contrary to nature, but rather, revelatory of nature's secret power to obey.[22] "For how is it contrary to nature," Augustine asks, "which happens by the will of God, since the will of so mighty a Creator is certainly the nature of each created thing?"[23] He concludes that "a portent ... happens not contrary to nature, but contrary to what we know as nature."[24]

In the *Confessions*, Augustine famously identifies the miraculous pattern of his own life's conversion with that of the creation story. There the traditional *divisio* of the six ages of man, which subtly inflects his chapter-by-chapter account of his own life, from infancy to adulthood, is matched, *mutatis mutandis*, with his allegorical interpretation of the six days of creation, followed by Sabbath rest, in the concluding book 13. Aelred imitates this Augustinian pattern in the *Life of Ninian*, which recounts exactly six miracles worked by God through the British saint during his lifetime, hexaemeral miracles bearing witness to the saint as the evangelizer of the southern Picts, a moral exemplar for his flock, and the cosmological agent of a "new creation" in Christ (2 Cor. 5:17).

From his youth, Augustine's *Confessions* was dear to Aelred. Walter Daniel, Aelred's scribe, friend, and biographer, records that the abbot of Rievaulx had a particular attachment to the *Confessions*, "for it was these which had been his guide when he was converted from the world."[25] In the oratory where Aelred read and prayed during his final illness, he kept near him "his glossed psalter and the *Confessions* of Augustine and the text of John's Gospel and the relics of certain saints and a little cross which had belonged to Henry, archbishop of York."[26] These treasures, in which (he declared) he had "delighted," were bequeathed by him on his deathbed to his fellow monks: "whatever I have and I myself are yours."[27]

Marsha Dutton remarks, however, that "the best evidence of Ælred's familiarity with the *Confessions* is his own writing, full of Augustinian words and phrases, even when apparently characterized by highly personal reminiscences."[28] In *Mirror of Charity* (*Speculum caritatis*), Aelred echoes Augustine's *Confessions* in acknowledging his own existential crisis at the court of King David and in recalling his unspeakable grief at a young friend's death.[29] Aelred's close identification with Augustine is evident in these autobiographical passages, but the abbot of Rievaulx wrote no extended first-person account of his life similar to that of the famous fourth-century convert.

Aelred's *Life of Ninian*, however, "tells of a man whose life in many ways anticipated Ælred's."[30] Both men, after all, spent their youth at a royal court,[31] delighted in learning, and suffered a spiritual restlessness.[32] Both traveled to Rome, where they were each received warmly by a pope.[33] Both were personally acquainted with an older saint—Ninian with Martin of Tours and Aelred with Bernard of Clairvaux.[34] Both were involved in evangelical missions in Galloway, a land that Aelred's hagiographer, Walter Daniel, describes as "a wild country, . . . altogether barbarous."[35]

In Aelred's *Life of Ninian*, book 1, which is the life proper, effectively divides into two parts. The first of these chronicles Ninian's life from his youth at a royal court until the time when the bishop-saint, newly returned to the British Isles after his studies and episcopal ordination in Rome, builds a stone church at Whithorn—the first of its kind in Scotland (chaps. 1–3).[36] The second part describes Ninian's miraculous episcopal ministry from the building of the church until his burial there (chaps. 4–11). Just as Augustine in book 13 of *Confessions* finds the Church mystically present in the story of creation in Genesis 1, Aelred uses the historic building of the stone church, the "White House" (*Candida Casa*), to lead the reader into an allegorical interpretation of the six miracle stories that follow.

Neatly paired in three groups of two, with short intervening passages, these six miracle stories evoke the six days of creation. They do so in a recognizable but complex way—the storyline of each miracle-account also alludes to related stories in the New Testament and mediates between them typologically. The result is an astonishing narrative theology that translates Augustine's biblical exegesis of Genesis back into a saint's history that concludes with an entrance into Sabbath rest, Ninian's time-ending burial in the church he had built, and his soul's flight into Christ's embrace. References to the church in chapters 3 and 11 thus frame the miracle stories, enclosing them, as it were, within its walls. Whereas Augustine in *Confessions* 13 finds the life of the Church hidden within the letter of Genesis 1, Aelred discovers the Christian life exemplified in Ninian's to be a hexaemeral "new creation" in Christ (2 Cor. 5:17) made possible in and through the Church, Christ's mystical body, symbolized in, and safeguarded by, the church building.[37]

John MacQueen points out, "In MNE [*Miracula Nynie Episcopi*] the conversion of the Picts follows immediately upon Ninian's return from

Rome, and precedes the foundation of *Candida Casa*, whereas in VN [*Vita Niniani*] the foundation of *Candida Casa*, together with the miracles involving Tudwal and the priest . . . have first place."[38] Aelred's arrangement gives prominence to the building of the church as an inaugural event. A student both of Augustine and of Bede, from whose *Ecclesiastical History* he quotes in his preface to the *Life of Ninian*, Aelred may also have been inspired by Bede's prose *Life of Saint Cuthbert* to use an architectonic symbolism in his *Life of Ninian*. As Walter Berschin and John Eby have noted, Bede, the author of *De Templo*, narrates the story of Cuthbert in precisely forty-six chapters—a number matching the number of years required for the reconstruction of the Temple in Jerusalem (John 2:20).[39]

The biblical texture of Aelred's prose hagiography of Ninian, which works into its artistic fabric numerous quotations from scripture, instructs its readers, moreover, to expect a numerological symbolism inviting allegoresis. Augustine, after all, exhorts his readers: "We must not despise the science of numbers, which, in many passages of holy Scripture, is found to be of eminent service to the careful interpreter."[40] MacQueen emphasizes in his discussion of *Miracula Nynie Episcopi* that "numerological structure is one feature of the [hagiographic] tradition."[41] Indeed, MacQueen's studies of other saints' *Vitae*—notably the *Navigatio Sancti Brendani Abbatis* and Heiric of Auxerre's *Life of Germanus*—have underscored the biblical, Platonic, and Augustinian numerology at work in them. Heiric's composition, MacQueen argues, is "based on the number six"—the number "of the perfection of [God's] works" to which Augustine devotes a chapter in book 11 of *City of God*.[42]

In *Mirror of Charity*, Aelred similarly devotes a chapter to explaining "why six is the number commended in God's work, seven in his rest" (*cur senarius numerus in Dei opera, septenarius in eius requie commendetur*).[43] More important than this chapter, however, is a subsequent chapter ("Quomodo opera sex dierum caeteris aptentur virtutibus . . ."), to which we shall return, in which he systematically assigns different virtues (faith, hope, temperance, prudence, fortitude, and justice) to the respective works of the six days of creation, reserving the virtue of charity, "the consummation of all virtues," to the seventh day.[44] Given this numerological framework, one can reconstruct the Augustinian reading that underlies Aelred's writing of the *Vita Niniani* as the life of a virtuous saint, a resplendent "new creation" in Christ (2 Cor. 5:17).

AELRED'S HAGIOGRAPHIC AESTHETICS: FASHIONED "IN MEASURE, NUMBER, AND WEIGHT" (WISDOM 11:21)

Aelred's rendering of the six miracles recalls the six days in Genesis 1, but also arranges the miracles in thematic pairs. His ordering of the first four miracles (and possibly that of the fifth and sixth) matches that found in his putative, hagiographic source, with the result that the order of the miracles does not correspond exactly to that of the days in Genesis 1.[45] Aelred draws authority for this sort of imaginative adaptation of the theme of the days of creation from the scriptures. Indeed, Aelred's use of scripture to interpret scripture supports the visionary transparency in which he views events of salvation history together.

Most obviously, perhaps, the account of the creation of man and woman in Genesis 2 complements the rather different account given in Genesis 1:26–29—a circumstance that led the bishop Augustine to wonder whether the creation of humankind might be understood to have occurred both on the sixth day and on the seventh and, if so, how.[46] "The two versions offer different interpretations [of humanity's creation], and each offers information not contained in the other," observes Dorothy Glass,[47] who points to examples of medieval art where the scene of Eve's creation from Adam's rib (Gen. 2:21–25) or that of God's formation of Adam from clay (Gen. 2:7) substitutes for, or combines with, the scene described in Genesis 1:26–30.

Psalm 104 (to cite another notable example of hexaemeral variation) is a seven-part psalm that praises God as the creator and as the sustainer of creation. Each part roughly corresponds to the respective day mentioned in Genesis 1, but the psalmist's purpose authorizes also departures from that scheme. Psalm 104 alludes, for example, to the great flood of the time of Noah in its second section (vv. 5–9), which stands parallel to the "second day" of Genesis 1, when the waters below the dome are separated from those above (Gen. 1:6–8). References to human existence and work, to bread, oil, and wine, appear in the third section of Psalm 104 (vv. 10–18), correspondent to the day on which God created vegetation. Psalm 104 similarly mentions ships at sea in its fifth section (vv. 24–26), which corresponds to the fifth day, when God created "the great sea monsters" (Gen. 1:21). Throughout Psalm 104, systematic allusions to Genesis 1 allow the psalmist as a theologian to link the divine works of creation with those of providential sustenance, to point to human participation in them, to place the days of creation within the context of human history, and to praise the Lord as mighty, gracious, wise, and good.

The most important biblical warrant for the Christian reimagination of the creation story in Genesis is, of course, the opening verse of the Gospel according to Saint John, "In the beginning was the Word," which clearly echoes the first words of Genesis 1 ("In the beginning God created . . ."), thus opening the way for a rich exegetical tradition of Trinitarian, Christological, and ecclesial interpretations of the days of creation. This commentary tradition, for which Augustine's works are foundational, experienced a revival in the twelfth century in *On the Sacraments of the Christian Faith* (*De sacramentis christianae fidei*) by Aelred's older contemporary, Hugh of Saint Victor (1096–1141), who devotes the entire first book to the topics of creation and restoration: "True faith rests in two: Creator and Redeemer. And the Creator and Redeemer are one."[48]

Commenting on the figure of the Christ-Logos in medieval art, Emile Mâle explains that "God the Father created *in principio*, which is to say *in verbo*, that is, by His Son. Jesus Christ is at once Creator and Redeemer."[49] As a result of this Christology, Christian artists of the Middle Ages rarely depict the six days of creation in a "precisely literal" way, according to Glass;[50] rather, they incorporate into their artwork a variety of elements deriving from the theological commentary tradition. "Even at the very beginning of Christian art, . . . illustrations of the creation do not follow a linear pattern. Instead," writes Glass, "the diversity and the reasons for it, become increasingly complex."[51] David L. Simon agrees, observing that "the vital relationship between Creation and Salvation is a virtual leitmotif of the study of Genesis illustrations, from the Cotton Genesis recensions where the Creator is depicted as Christ-Logos to the illustrations in the Paris *Antiquitates Judaicae* [of Flavius Josephus], where the Virgin and Eve are juxtaposed to each other."[52]

Such typological juxtapositions, which place the days of creation in the context of salvation history, argue for a comprehensive, providential design in keeping with the Augustinian theme of a single "day" of creation repeated six times—a simultaneous creation of everything encompassed in "heavens and earth" (Gen. 1:1),[53] as Sirach 18:1 was understood to attest: "Qui vivit in aeternum creavit omnia simul" (He who lived in eternity created all things at once).[54] The timeless quality of creation scenes represented in murals, manuscript illuminations, relief-carvings, tapestries, and domes is suited to apprehending a paradoxical simultaneity of chronologically sequential events, all of which are present to the viewer's eye at once. This quality remains in force,[55] even as the viewer reads the assembled individual scenes in a given order, whether clockwise or counterclockwise, left to right, top to bottom, or back and forth (as, for example, in the early twelfth-century Girona tapestry, studied by Glass, where the image of a dove hovering over the waters at the top, directly over that of the Christ-Logos at the center, is mirrored by the image of birds flying over the fishes of the deep at the tapestry's bottom).[56]

In the first illumination of the second book of Hildegard of Bingen's *Scivias* (composed ca. 1141–51),[57] the six days of creation are represented in six small medallions within a dark circle (see plate 2.1).[58] A shaft of light descending from a radiant, larger circle at the top (symbolizing "the Omnipotent and Living God")[59] divides the six medallions visually into two sets of three (vertically arranged), even as it joins three pairs of scenes (when viewed horizontally). The horizontal pattern joins (1) the first day's creation of light and of the angels, on the viewer's left, to the dome's separation on the second day of the waters above from those below, on the right; (2) the third day's separation of water from the land and its vegetation, on the left, to the fourth day's creation of sun and moon, night and day, on the right; (3) the fifth day's creation of birds and fish, on the left, to the sixth day's creation of humans and land animals, on the right. The vertical pattern, by contrast, joins the three medallions on the viewer's left (representing the first, third, and fifth biblical days of creation), even as it links the three on the right (representing the second, fourth, and sixth biblical days).[60]

Mandala-like, the illumination allows for both horizontal and vertical readings, holding them in an equipoise that is disrupted by the mystery of sin and salvation—a mystery granted to the beholder's understanding only through "a miracle of faith."[61] In Hildegard's vision, depicted in the illumination, the circumference of the sixth medallion (that representing mankind's creation) opens fluidly onto two other scenes in the same illumination that show humanity's fall and its re-creation in Christ. As the Voice instructs the visionary to understand, "The Living God, then, who created all things through His Word, by the Word's Incarnation brought back the miserable human who had sunk himself in darkness."[62]

Quod homo secreta di ñ debet   in sua ueritatis de morte ad uitā
plus scrutari. quā ipse uult manife   ostensa ē.   Ideo eos apparuit.
  Quod filius di nat' in   stare.   Qd' filii di a morte resurgent. dis
mundo morte sua diabolū supauit   cipulis suis frequent' ad corroboran
τ electos suos ad hereditatē suā re   Qd' filio di ascendente ad pa
  Verba osee de eadē re. Sdixit   tre. sponsa ei diuersis ornamtis sun
  Qd' corp' filii di in sepulchro   sdata ē.
p tiduu iacens resurrexit. τ homi

Plate 2.1. Hildegard von Bingen, *The Redeemer of Creation*, ca. 1151, from *Scivias* II.I. T.10, in CCCM 43, © Brepols Publishers, Turnhout, Belgium.

Plate 2.2. Mary J. Zore, *The Seven Days of Creation Mandala*, 2021. Courtesy of the artist.

Inspired by the Girona tapestry and by the illustration of Hildegard's vision, Mary J. Zore's colorful *The Seven Days of Creation Mandala* (see plate 2.2) shows Christ, the Eternal Word, the Alpha and Omega, at the center of a circular painting, his right hand raised up in a Trinitarian gesture.[63] Below Christ a bleeding pelican signifies Christ's saving work of re-creation, its outstretched wings mirroring those (at its side) of the Creator-Spirit in the form of a dove, hovering over the churning chaos. A burst of light emanating from Christ haloes the head of the dove to represent the light of the first day. A white, cloudlike firmament appears next, separating the waters above from those below to mark the second day. A wavy, blue sea next to a brown bank symbolizes the separation of water and land on the third day. A sun surrounded by stars symbolizes the fourth; a bird and

Table 2.1 Six Miracles, Six Days

Cure of Tudvallus's blindness	Creation of light (Gen. 1:1, 14); Coming of true light (John 1:9; Luke 1:76–79)	Days 1 and 4
Testimony of the speaking infant	Human creation and procreation (Gen. 1:28); Divine incarnation (John 1:1, 14; Luke 1:26–45)	Day 6
Miracle of the leeks	Creation of vegetation (Gen. 1:11–12, 29)	Day 3
Miracle of the cattle thieves	Creation of the land animals (Gen. 1:24–26)	Day 6
Miracle of the Psalter and the rainfall	Creation of the firmament and the separation of waters above and below (Gen. 1:6–8)	Day 2
Miracle of the runaway oblate in the leaking boat	Separation of land and sea, of the birds and fishes (Gen. 1:9–10, 20–21); Ps. 1:3	Days 3 and 5

a fish, the fifth. Green vegetation in the background joins the third, fourth, and fifth days. A man and woman, framed by flowers, represent the creation of humankind on the sixth day, their faces not unlike Christ's own human face, in whose incarnate image they have been created. Christ's incarnation defines the seventh day, which combines time and eternity, the human and the divine, in the ongoing work and rest of re-creation. Communion with Christ, made possible by the Eucharistic sacrifice symbolized in the blood of the pelican, secures the communicants' resting in God, their partaking in God's peace.[64]

Aelred's *Vita Niniani* realizes the hagiographic implications of this doctrine of creation and re-creation. Since the saints are, above all, sharers in the singular life of Christ (cf. John 14:6), who was divinely present and active "in the beginning" (Gen. 1:1, John 1:1) and who lives forever,[65] the *Life* of the apostle Ninian appropriately calls to mind and renews on earth the works of the six days (see table 2.1). The same God who is the author of the books of scripture and of creation is the author of the lives of the saints, God's "new creation" (2 Cor. 5:17) in Christ.

IN THE BEGINNING: MIRACLES OF LIGHT AND INCARNATION

The first miracle in the *Vita Niniani* thematizes darkness and light, as Ninian spreads the light of the gospel into the benighted land of the southern Picts through the cure of the blindness of Tudvallus, a proud king, who initially opposes Ninian. Tudvallus has succumbed to the three lusts that guide Augustine's analysis in *Confessions* of his own concupiscence: the "pride" of life, the "lust of the flesh, and the lust of the eyes" (1 John 2:16).[66] Indeed, Tudvallus's condition and that of his kingdom recalls Augustine's tropological interpretation of the dark abyss in Genesis 1:2: "For we also, we are a spiritual creation in our souls, and have turned away from you our light. In that life we were 'at one time darkness' (Eph. 5:8)."[67]

As in Genesis on the first day, when God created light (Gen. 1:3), in Aelred's account of Ninian's first miracle, the saint appears explicitly as "the lamp set upon a stand" (Matt. 5:15; Mark 4:21), whose mission it is "to illumine those in the house of God with heavenly signs and the radiant flames of the virtues, to enlighten darkened minds with the lucid and fiery word of the Lord and to enkindle the indifferent."[68] Aelred quotes directly from Genesis 3:18 in his narration of this first miracle, which brings God's light and blessing upon a darkened land "near to being cursed," a land that "'brought forth thorns and thistles' instead of useful grass."[69]

Portraying Ninian as a light shining into the darkness, Aelred allusively associates the creation of light on the first day with the creations of the heavenly lights (sun, moon, and stars) on the fourth day. In this, Aelred follows Augustine, who, in *Confessions* 13, allegorizes the saints as lights created by God: "Then it is not only you [Lord] in the secret place of your judgment who divide between light and darkness, as you did before the making of the firmament; it is also your spiritual people established in the same solid firmament and distinguished by your grace manifested throughout the world. May they 'give light over the earth and divide day and night and be signs of the times' (Gen. 1:14)."[70] In *Mirror of Charity*, Aelred similarly connects the virtue of prudence manifested "like the light of the fourth day" in spiritual leaders and saints, such as Ninian.[71] The miracles of Tudvallus's cure from blindness and of his conversion to Christianity aptly reflect, moreover, Aelred's association in *Mirror of Charity* of the virtue of faith with the first day of creation: "Let faith be for us, then, like the first day on which we believers are separated from unbelievers, as light from darkness."[72]

Ninian's first miracle is paired with a second, complexly allegorical miracle, which recalls the creation of humanity on the sixth day, the fall of mankind through a tempter's seduction of a virgin, and the incarnation of the Word-made-flesh as the "new Adam" (cf. 1 Cor. 15:45–47). This strange and challenging miracle story, in which a speaking infant defends the innocence of an accused priest, reflects Aelred's hagiographic meditation upon Genesis 1–3 in the light of John 1:1: "In the beginning was the Word," and the immediately following verses of that Gospel. In books 12–13 of *Confessions*, and in his other commentaries upon Genesis, Augustine interprets the opening verse of Genesis, "In the beginning God created the heavens and the earth," precisely in relation to the eternal Word, "the beginning" of all created things.[73] Through the miracle of the speaking infant, Aelred tells of God's visitation of his people, echoing the prophecy of Zachariah, whose speech had been miraculously restored at the birth of John the Baptist: "God has visited his people" (Luke 1:68).[74]

Ninian commands the newborn babe to speak, and Aelred praises the saint's faith, even as Elizabeth praised the faith of Mary, who had accepted the angel's word to her: "Truly all things are possible to a believer" (cf. Luke 1:37; 1:45).[75] The mother of that baby, initially portrayed as an Eve, seduced by a tempter, doubles as a New Eve, the Virgin Mary, when Aelred applies to her the words of the Lucan nativity story: "The time came for the woman to be delivered, and she bore a son" (Luke 2:6–7).

These typological characterizations of the woman are Aelred's invention. "The author of the *Miracula* (chapter 6) treats the story from the point of view of the priest only. The woman is not mentioned except as mother of the child," Winifred MacQueen points out.[76] Aelred, by contrast, centers attention on the woman and her experience, interpreting her human plight within the context of salvation history. Her desperate "pact with death" recalls the mortal curse of Adam and Eve, the biblical "mother of the living" (Gen. 2:15, 19–20).[77]

The woman's dual identity as Eve and Mary places her baby between her and two different fathers: the biological father of the infant and the accused, but innocent priest, an ironic stand-in for Joseph, Mary's celibate husband and Jesus's adoptive father, perhaps, but also for Christ himself, one with the Father (cf. John 10:30), the sinless bearer of humanity's guilt, accused before the high priest (John 18). When Aelred quotes Psalm 8:2–3, "out of the mouth of a babe and a nursling," to characterize the witness of the infant to the priest's innocence, he recalls Jesus's own quotation of that same verse in Matthew 21:17, in answer to the demand of the chief priests and the scribes that he silence the praises of the "children crying out in the temple, 'Hosanna to the Son of David'" (Matt. 21:15).

When the miraculously speaking infant tells the bishop, "Your priest . . . is innocent of this wicked deed. We have nothing in common except our nature,"[78] the explicit affirmation of the babe's humanity inevitably recalls the Incarnate Word's assumption of human nature. The oxymoron of the speaking infant (*infans* = "one incapable of speech")[79] in the context of biblical allusions to the Lukan nativity recalls a repeated theme in *City of God* and in the Christmas sermons of Augustine. In Sermon 84, Augustine declares: "He who sustains the world lay in a manger, a wordless Child, yet the Word of God."[80] Sermon 187 praises the incarnate Christ-Logos as the "maker of heaven and earth brought forth on this earth overshadowed by the heavens; unspeakably wise, wisely speechless."[81] Similarly, in Sermon 188, Augustine hails Christ "in the manger in mute infancy, He the Word without whom all human eloquence is mute."[82] Exciting the wonderment of his listeners at the miracle of Christ's incarnation and birth, Augustine asks, "Who is this Infant whom we so call because he is not able to speak? He is both a speechless child and He is the Word."[83]

The very righteousness of God, sent to "proclaim justice to the Gentiles" (Matt. 12:18) and to justify sinners (cf. Gal. 2:17), this Word is appropriately figured in a babe whose speech exonerates a falsely accused priest. "Let justice declare for us the sixth day," writes Aelred in the *Mirror of Charity*. "On it, let us, clothed again with divine likeness, . . . render to each his due."[84]

Interpreting theologically the wondrous story he relates, which tells not only of a speaking infant, but also of the Incarnation and the restoration of human nature, Aelred echoes Augustine's doctrine of miracles as events not truly contrary to nature (*contra naturam*), but only contrary to our customary understanding of the natural order: "O marvel worthy of all wonder! . . . Should not nature yield to the Lord of nature?"[85]

IN THE MIDDLE EARTH: MIRACLES OF GARDEN AND PASTURE

The first two miracles of Ninian allegorically join the creations of the first, the fourth, and the sixth days—the creations of light and of lights (the sun, moon, and stars) and of humanity—through a Christological intertext (Christ being our Light, the Incarnate Word of our salvation, True Man). The third and fourth miracles similarly recall the works of the third and sixth days in Genesis, namely, the vegetation and the grass-eating animals of the earth. Placing these paired miracles in the middle position accords with the Old English cosmological idea of the *middangeard* (later, middle earth)[86]— a notion symbolized by the yard of the garden in the third miracle and by Ninian's encirclement in the fourth miracle of the grazing cattle all around with a protective furrow to ward off dangers from every direction.

The narrative of the third miracle, wherein an obedient brother, acting at Ninian's command, looks and finds an unexpected abundance of leeks and other herbs in a previously infertile garden, explicitly recalls Genesis 1:11: "Let the earth put forth vegetation, plants yielding seed." Aelred tells us: "He saw leeks and other kinds of herbs not only growing, but even producing seed," a sight that moves the amazed brother, "as if caught up in ecstasy he thought he was seeing a vision."[87]

Caring miraculously for the needs of the brothers, who have hungered, leekless, at the monastery's table, Ninian performs one of the virtuous works of mercy (Matt. 25:35–36) that Augustine in *Confessions* 13 associates explicitly with the growth and fertility of seed-bearing plants: "As the earth produces her fruit, so at your command, the command of its Lord God, our soul yields works of mercy 'according to its kind' (Gen. 1:12), loving our neighbor in the relief of physical necessities, 'having in itself seed according to its likeness.' Aware of our own infirmity, we are moved to compassion to help the indigent."[88] Fittingly, too, this miracle of the third day concerns an episode of mortification by monks, who sit hungry, but humbly and without complaint, at a table where neither vegetables nor herbs have been served. "Let temperance dawn on us like the third day on which . . . we mortify our bodies," Aelred writes in *Mirror of Charity*.[89]

Even as the third miracle is reminiscent of the seasonal renewal that brings a flourish of new life in the springtime after winter, the fourth miracle includes the violent death and resurrection of a would-be cattle thief who dares to cross the line demarcating the cattle yard, only to be gored to death by a bull; it goes on to relate that same thief's complete restoration to life and health through Ninian's prayers and the conversion of his fellow robbers.

Augustine's allegorical interpretation of the land animals in *Confessions* 13 helps to explain this miracle, which focuses on the shepherd's proper control of cattle—a word that the English language associates with (Anglo-Norman) "chattel" and (Middle English) "catel," meaning "property," "bovine" and human, and also "human beings" grouped together "en masse" in a herd.[90] Latin similarly connects the words for cattle (*pecus*) and money (*pecunia*), and applies the former term contemptuously to humans acting in a servile herd.[91] Connecting the creation of vegetation on the fifth day to the creation of cattle and humans on the sixth, Augustine asks, "If the earth is fruitful, whence come so many thorns?"[92] "Go," he answers, "destroy the thorny jungle of avarice" that opposes the works of mercy.[93]

Commenting on the cattle as herd animals in *Confessions* 13, Augustine compares them to human beings who imitate each other, covet their neighbors' goods, grow alike through rivalry with one another, and thus fail to conform themselves to the divine "image and likeness" (Gen. 1:26) in which they have been created. Quoting the words of Saint Paul, "Be not conformed to this world" (Rom. 12:2), Augustine adds, "For you [Lord] did not say 'Let man be made according to his kind,' but 'let us make man according to our image and likeness' (Gen. 1:26)."[94] The person who is properly human shepherds his possessions and restrains his desires, taming them, even as Ninian established spiritual boundaries for the cattle. The trespassing thief, by contrast, is destroyed by the very goods he sought to steal, his own unrestrained desires finding a counterpart in the ravaging bull.

When Ninian raises the dead man to life and then converts his comrades, the second action of the saint explains the spiritual significance of the first. Augustine puts it thus: "When our affections were restrained from loving the world by which we were dying through living an evil life, then there began to come into being a 'living soul.'"[95] He adds: "So in the 'living soul' there will be beasts that have become good by the gentleness of their behavior.... There will be good 'cattle,' experiencing neither excess if they eat nor want if they do not eat.... For these animals serve reason when they are restrained from their deathly ways."[96] In *Mirror of Charity*, Aelred follows Augustine in interpreting the creation of humans and land animals together on the sixth day as a sign that humans properly "govern with noble authority the savage beasts of our vices, the reptiles of our earthly desires, and the beasts of burden of our bodily impulses."[97] Aelred's hagiography of Ninian thus reliteralizes Augustine's exegesis of the created cattle in order to prompt a similar allegorical interpretation of Ninian's miracle.

AT THE END: MIRACLES OF SEPARATION

The same may be said of the final pair of miracles in the *Life of Ninian*, both of which allude to a work of creation involving separation. These two miracle stories have no counterpart in the *Miracula Nynie Episcopi* and provide a hermeneutical key for the hexaemeral framing of the *Life* as a whole. The fifth miracle clearly corresponds to the work of the second day in Genesis 1, the separation of the waters above and below the firmament. The sixth miracle recalls both the work of the third day (the separation of the sea from the dry land) and the teeming of the waters with fish and of the air with birds on the fifth day. Taken together, they prepare—in accord with Aelred's narrative theology—for the death of the saint, the separation of his soul from his body, and the entrance into Sabbath rest. In each case, the discovery of the miracle's meaning depends upon a prior knowledge of Augustine's exposition of the creation story.

In Aelred's account of the fifth miracle, we learn that, while on a journey, Ninian and his companion, a holy brother named Plebia, "opened their psalters to refresh their spirits with holy reading."[98] When a rainstorm suddenly broke, they and their Psalters were miraculously protected from the downpour: "The thin air curved like a vault over the servants of God as if it were a kind of wall that remained impenetrable."[99] This miracle, we are told, was often repeated in Ninian's life; raindrops touched him and his book only on those fleeting occasions when, yielding to a distractive thought, he failed to concentrate upon his prayers and thus on the reign, the kingdom, of God. In such moments, the raindrops and the reproof of his companion had a merciful, monitory effect upon Ninian, who, like the prodigal son, "returned to himself" (*in se autem reversus*) (cf. Luke 15:17).[100]

Readers familiar with Augustine's *Confessions* cannot fail to be reminded of his interpretation there of the firmament of Genesis 1:6–8, which he identifies with the sacred scriptures, "a solid firmament of authority over us."[101] Reading and submitting to God's authoritative teaching in the Bible, the faithful are to find their way to the heavenly *patria*, where angels read the eternal book that is God himself and discern "the immutability of [his] design" in "a codex . . . never closed," a book never "folded shut."[102] The miracle of the rain thus bears witness to Ninian's submission to God's reign through obedience to the biblical word, which, in Aelred's hagiography, literally effects a protective dome or umbrella over the saint, who would otherwise have been soaked to the skin.

Significantly, Augustine compares the firmament of the sky to a stretched skin, a vellum that is not only a writing surface but also a sign of the mortality of the biblical authors through whom God has revealed his eternal truth.[103] In *Mirror of Charity*, Aelred similarly connects the creation of the firmament with the virtue of hope in eternal life: "Let hope be the second day: through it, dwelling in the heavens and . . . hoping only for things above the heavens with God, we are distinguished from those who, . . . importuning God for only earthly things, flood and ebb like waters under the firmament of heaven."[104]

According to John MacQueen, "The emphasis on the book as part of the story suggests that the narrative was originally linked to a supposed relic of the saint—a psalter which showed traces of exposure to the elements."[105] This proposal is plausible, but it misses the significance of what is certain: Aelred's allusion to Genesis 1:6–8 and Augustine's interpretation of that passage.[106]

If the separation of earth and sky in miracle five is vertical, enforcing the difference between God and men, that between sea and land in miracle six is horizontal, expressive of differences between humans. Miracle six relates the tale of a boy oblate, a young, runaway disciple of Ninian, who, rejecting discipline, runs away from the saint, absconding with Ninian's staff. Choosing an unsealed coracle as his means of escape, the boy soon finds himself in danger of drowning far from shore. This threat associates the miracle story not only with the separation of water and land on the third day, but also and especially with the teeming of the waters on the fifth day with "the great sea monsters and every living creature that moves, with which the waters swarm" (Gen. 1:21).

Aelred links the virtue of fortitude to the fifth day of creation: "On it let us endure the storms of the great, vast sea of the world."[107] He exhorts his readers, "At God's working become spiritual fish, let us save our lives amid tempests and billows, and by raising heavenwards like winged birds both the desires and attachments of our mind and setting our mind on things above, with God's blessing, let us bear many fruits of good works."[108]

Like the repentant Ninian who "returned to himself" in miracle five, the boy "comes back to himself" in the face of the "waves avenging the wrong [he has] done to the father" through his flight.[109] The idea of repentance and conversion as a return to one's proper home, position, or resting place is biblical (cf. Luke 15:17), but also thoroughly Augustinian and Aelredian.[110] Meditating upon the gravitational pull exerted upon the restless soul by the Holy Spirit, which, like a bird hovering over the watery abyss (Gen. 1:2), "is immutably borne above all that is mutable," Augustine considers the impropriety of human sinfulness, which leaves humankind lower than itself.[111] "In a good will is our peace," Augustine writes. "A body by its weight tends to move toward its proper place. The weight's movement is not necessarily downwards, but to its appropriate position: fire tends to move upwards, a stone downwards. They are acted upon by their respective weights. . . . Once they are in their ordered position, they are at rest. My weight is my love."[112]

Praying to Ninian through the relic of his staff, the repentant boy receives the saint's aid. Indeed, the saint's staff proves to be multipurpose as his instrument: sealing the leaks in the boat, catching the wind like a sail, guiding the boat like a rudder, holding it steady like an anchor. Significantly, the saint himself does not appear in this miracle story, which John MacQueen likens to "sensational romantic fiction," unlike "anything in the other miracle stories."[113] The disappearance of the saint into the staff serves the theological purpose, however, of signaling the saint's complete spiritual "death" into Christ, in accord with the saying of Saint Paul: "I live, no longer I, but Christ lives in me" (Gal. 2:20). Aelred exclaims, "Yours are these deeds, O Christ! . . . You impressed your sacred footsteps on the waves of the sea; Ninian's power suppressed the natural power of the sea."[114]

Returned safely to shore, the boy plants the staff in thanksgiving, and at his prayer it turns into a rooted tree, next to which a "crystal-clear spring" bursts forth, a source of healing drink.[115] This final image recalls, of course, Psalm 1, which compares the just man to "a tree planted near running waters" (Ps. 1:3). A rich exegetical tradition associates this tree with the tree of life in Genesis 2:9, with Christ himself (the *beatus vir* of Psalm 1:1), with the tree of his cross, and with the tree of life in the New Jerusalem (Rev. 22:2). Indeed, the invocation of Psalm 1 in the final miracle recorded before Ninian's death confirms the hexaemeral pattern of the miracles as a set. Augustine notes in his exposition of Psalm 150, "The first psalm is generally agreed to have prophesied about Christ," the latest Adam (1 Cor. 15:45), even as the first chapter of Genesis refers "to the Father's creation of the world through his Son."[116] Both Psalm 1 and Genesis 1 stand "at the foremost place in the book" (Ps. 40:7) and give witness to Son's perfect obedience to the Father.

Interpreted *in bono* by Ambrose and Augustine, the water flowing by the tree in the Psalm 1 refers to the Holy Spirit and his gifts, poured out upon Jesus and given through him to others in baptism; interpreted *in malo*, however, the running waters symbolize the temptations and persecutions that threaten to overwhelm the just one who stands in close proximity to forces that seek to undermine his or her stability, as Jesus did in his passion.[117] In either case, whether interpreted *in bono* or *in malo*, the image of the tree rooted next to a river or flowing spring evokes the story of the primeval separation of water from land in Genesis 1 on the third day—a separation upon which Augustine comments in *Confessions* 13.

In flight from Ninian and in danger of death by drowning at sea, the boy finds himself (to quote Augustine's *Confessions*) in "the midst of the waters of the world's temptations."[118] Indeed, he himself is "like a sea in a stormy swell, restlessly unstable."[119] A means of his conversion, the same waters also produce in him a renewal of his baptism, expressed in the prayer of his faith, and they support the boat that carries him back to the shore. Augustine phrases it thus: "For now the earth is believing and baptized, separated out from the sea-water bitter with faithlessness."[120] Like the staff of Moses, which parted the waters (Exod. 14), the staff of Ninian commands the elements, bringing the boy to a veritable promised land.

This homeward journey of the boy in the boat immediately precedes that start of Ninian's own. The saint, we are told, "came by a happy course to the day of his summoning."[121] He awaited the hour of his death, we are told, joyfully, for "to be separated any longer from Christ seemed intolerable" to him.[122] Ninian's entrance into eternal rest is symbolized by the burial of his body "in the church of blessed Martin, which he himself had raised from its foundation."[123] Ninian's rest, however, is active, a participation in the Sabbath of the Lord, who, Augustine affirms, is "always working and always at rest," since he is his "own rest."[124]

Ninian's activity in book 2 takes the form of posthumous miracles: "At his most sacred tomb the infirm are cured, lepers are cleansed, the wicked are cast into fear, and the blind are enlightened."[125] "By all of these," Aelred adds, "the faith of believers is strengthened to the praise and glory of our Lord Jesus Christ."[126] Ninian also continues his apostolic work through his hagiographer, who publicizes the biblically illumined miracle stories of the holy bishop and thus participates in and continue the saint's missionary activity, his preaching of the gospel.

Aelred, who has divided the six miracles of the saint in book 1 into three pairs, intersperses between the first and second sets of *miracula* a summary narrative of Ninian's evangelization of the southern Picts. The holy bishop's spoken message to the southern Picts, we are told, was accompanied and confirmed by miraculous signs, like those recorded in Christ's ministry (Mark 16:20), with the result that untold numbers were "joined to the crowd of believers by faith, by voice, and by the sacraments."[127] Similarly, between the second and third sets of miracle stories, Aelred again takes up a verbal theme, albeit this time focusing on Ninian's edifying conversation, prayer, and self-control in speech. Whether in preaching, counseling, or prayer, Ninian's words are seen to have a transformative effect that assists in re-creating the world that God first created out of nothing through his Eternal Word: "And God said, 'Let there be . . .'"

By translating Ninian's *Life*, Aelred has, in effect, given the saint a renewed opportunity to speak to later generations, as he did to the people of his own time. As Aelred puts it, he has, like hagiographers before him, tried "to save from oblivion and perpetuate in memory the example of a more perfect life for the edification of posterity,"[128] relying (in this case) upon Ninian's own intercession for him as he writes. Aelred also relied, it seems, upon the aid of Augustine, whose commentaries upon Genesis certainly inspired him, and of Moses, who recorded what happened "in the beginning when God created heaven and earth" (Gen. 1:1). Recapitulating the hexaemeral tradition in an Augustinian mode, Aelred appropriates the dynamic power of new creation in the life of the saint and employs it to fortify the Church of his own time and ours as a temple of "living stones" (1 Pet. 2:5).

CHAPTER THREE

THE SONG OF SONGS AND SAINT BERNARD OF CLAIRVAUX'S *LIFE OF SAINT MALACHY*

At the close of his *Life of Ninian*, Aelred of Rievaulx (1110–67) narrates the saint's death using a flourish of quotations from the Song of Songs. Wavering between the desire to continue to live on earth for the sake of his endangered flock and the desire to be with Christ in heaven, Ninian hears Christ's call: "Arise, hasten, my beloved, my dove, and come. Arise, my beloved!"—an invitation that echoes and combines two verses from the biblical love song (Sg 2:10, 5:2).[1] Repeating that call a little later, Aelred adds to it another verse: "for the winter is past, the rain is over and gone" (Sg 2:11), interpreting the end of the rain as the saint's victorious escape at his life's end from "the rain of temptation and the hail of persecution."[2] Addressing the saint, Aelred celebrates the virtuous fruit of Ninian's long, apostolic labors as the appearance of "flowers . . . in our land" (Sg 2:12), the roses of martyrdom and the lilies of purity. The saint's soul, as Christ's bride, is finally to "ascend from Lebanon to be crowned" (Sg 4:8), Aelred explains, "for the time of pruning has come" (Sg 2:12).[3]

Such a rich intertextual use of the Song of Songs by a Cistercian hagiographer is not surprising, given what might be called the hagiographic character of Bernard of Clairvaux's exegesis of the Song. Most famous as a biblical interpreter for his eighty-six sermons on the Song, Bernard (1090–53) regularly identifies such biblical saints as Paul, Peter, and the Virgin Mary with the bride of the Song; he invites his listening monks and his wider audience of devout readers to discover in the Song the story of

61

their own life and to read it in moral and ethical terms as the "book of our experience";[4] he seamlessly incorporates into his explication of the Song's verses a eulogy for his departed brother Gerard, whom he praises as a saint, the "black but beautiful" bride of Christ, whose darkness and comeliness resemble "the tents of Kedar, . . . the curtains of Solomon" (Sg 1:4).[5]

According to Bernard, the Song's love story, lyrically expressed, is simply the story of every saint's life, joined to Christ's. Aelred of Rievaulx, however, only quotes from the Song at the *beginning* and *end* of his retelling of Ninian's life, when the dying bishop suddenly reappears as Christ's bride. Ninian's ardent desire in his youth to go to Rome, seeking "him [Christ] whom [his] soul loves," initially identifies him with the Bride of Song of Songs 3:1–2.[6] At Ninian's passage from this life, the Bridegroom calls to him in the words of Song 2:10–12. During the narrated time of his episcopate, however, Ninian is never identified with the Bride, but rather with the Bridegroom, whose power manifests itself in him: "Yours are these deeds, O Christ!"[7]

Bernard's own *Life* of a bishop-saint—the *Life of Saint Malachy*—is similarly restrained in its direct allusion to verses of the Song of Songs. Modern editors of the *Life of Saint Malachy* have identified more than 800 scriptural citations from 52 different books of the Bible in Bernard's hagiography, which is 76 paragraphs long. Among these they cite only seven echoes of the Song. How is this somewhat surprising dearth of citation to be explained? Surely it cannot be without significance, given Bernard's endless fascination with the Song of Songs, which he understands to "celebrate the praises of Christ and his Church, the gift of holy love, the sacrament of endless union with God,"[8] the very life of the saints.

In this chapter, I argue that the direct citations of the Song, though relatively few in number, are highly significant and support a dominant pattern of marital imagery in the *Life of Malachy* that presents the bishop-saint of Ireland as the bridegroom of his diocese and thus aligns him less (or at least less obviously) with the Bride of the Song than with her spouse. Recognizing this pattern makes Bernard's hagiography of Malachy—Bernard's sole composition in that genre—a worthy companion piece to his *Sermons on the Song of Songs*, in which the abbot of Clairvaux emphasizes the bride's mystical experience of love and languishing in this land of unlikeness (*regio dissimilitudinis*). Joining the *Life of Malachy* to the *Sermons on the Song* through tracing this spousal symbolism provides, moreover, a biblically mediated insight into a question of considerable interest to historians who marvel at the Cistercian combination of monastic withdrawal and spiritual reform, on the one hand, and of social and ecclesiastical influence, on the other. "The fundamental contrast," writes Shawn M. Krahmer, "is finally that between the masculine/active bishops and the feminine/contemplative monks."[9] This gendered contrast undoubtedly holds, but it points also to a fruitful union of these vocations and to their complementary functions, both in the Church as a whole and in the life of the individual monk-bishop.

Bernard's *Life of Malachy* is among the least studied of his works.[10] Much suggests, however, that Bernard himself attached great importance to it and to the memory of the man whom he called "my Malachy" and (speaking for and to his Cistercian brothers) "our Malachy."[11] According to Geoffrey of Auxerre, Bernard's hagiographer in the *Vita prima*, Bernard donned the tunic of Malachy of Armagh after his death at Clairvaux during the night between the feasts of All Saints and All Souls in 1148; the abbot then clad the body of the departed saint in his own clothes for burial. Bernard presided and preached at the funeral Mass, using the common for a bishop-saint already on that occasion, far in advance of Malachy's official canonization in 1160. Bernard composed Malachy's epitaph and possibly also a hymn in his honor. Especially through writing Malachy's *Life*, Bernard promoted the cult of the Irish saint, whose body was buried at Clairvaux right next to the place where Bernard himself would later be buried. Chrysogonus Waddell has argued that the early Office of Saint Malachy was composed at Clairvaux, and that parts of it were subsequently used for the Office for Saint Bernard, thus forcing the composition of a new Office for the bishop.[12]

The symbolic, posthumous twinning of Bernard and Malachy, who had wished to become a Cistercian and to die at Clairvaux,[13] suggests that Bernard saw a providential sign in the bishop's attraction to Clairvaux and in his fruitful apostolate as an episcopal reformer—a sign that the Cistercian movement would positively affect every rank of the Church, active and contemplative. Martha Newman reports: "Some twenty-nine Cistercian monks were elected as bishops during Bernard's lifetime, seven more became cardinals, and one became pope."[14] In the life of Malachy of Armagh, Bernard saw realized the virtues and the practices that he had once enjoined, twenty years before (ca. 1127), upon an apparently less receptive bishop, Henry, archbishop of Sens, and which he would recommend also, with appropriate variation, to the Cistercian pontiff, Pope Eugenius III (1145–53) in *De consideratione*, a lengthy treatise he was writing at the time of Malachy's death. The example of a holy monk and bishop such as Malachy confirmed Bernard's sense that the "virtues taught by a contemplative life were also necessary for those who were to become society's leaders," and that the monasteries effectively "provided a training ground for a reformed clergy."[15]

At the same time, however, Bernard insisted on the distinction between the episcopal and monastic ways of life and warned monks against desiring ambitiously to become bishops. "What sort of presumption is this, monks?" he asks. "It is the [religious] profession which makes the monk; only necessity makes a prelate, and to prevent necessity from prejudicing profession, prelacy must be added to and not replace the monastic state."[16] In exegetical terms, that same distinction manifests itself in Bernard's writings in different uses of the Song of Songs. When Bernard evokes it in writings to and about bishops, he is careful to exhort them to a bridegroom's responsibility for the bride that is the diocese and to a guardian's care for Christ's Bride, the Church.

In *De consideratione*, for example, Bernard refers allusively to the Song of Songs only twice, and that within adjacent chapters in book 3 (3.5.19 and 3.5.20). In the first, he exhorts the pope to be vigilant to see "whether the vineyard [of the Church] blossoms with honorable and holy priests" and "whether these flowers bear fruit" (cf. Sg 7:12). In the second, after decrying clerics who dress and live luxuriously, Bernard laments, "O how the bride must be pitied who is entrusted to such attendants, who do not fear to keep for themselves what was assigned for her adornment!"[17]

When Bernard echoes the Song in a single passage in *On the Conduct and Office of Bishop*, he presupposes that the bride of Christ that is the bishop's own soul is completely lost in Christ, enabling the bishop to represent the Bridegroom to his Bride. As Bernard explains, echoing Saint Paul, the pastoral concern for the Church requires the "wounding" of the individual bridal soul by charity (Cf. Sg 2:5), so that the bride "is dead" to herself, but "not dead to Christ,"[18] who lives and acts in her as the Bridegroom he is: "You have died and your life is hidden with Christ in God."

But when Christ your life is revealed, you too shall be revealed with him in glory" (Col. 3:3–4).[19] "Love indeed is as strong as death," Bernard writes to the archbishop of Sens, echoing Song of Songs 8:6, "and it is death, not life, that it kills in us."[20]

This pattern of carefully limited and directed citation of the Song in Bernard's writings to bishops—a pattern clearly evident in his *Life of Malachy*—shows that the abbot of Clairvaux, famous for his mystical and moral exegesis of Solomon's Canticle, also contributed in a unique fashion to another recognized stream of Songs exegesis, namely, that initiated by reformers during the Investiture Controversy of the late eleventh and early twelfth centuries. John of Mantua, Bruno of Segni (d. 1123), Robert of Tumbalena (fl. 1094), and others had commented upon the Song of Songs in order to move their contemporaries to support the Gregorian program of clerical reform,[21] which ultimately entailed (as codified by canon law) celibacy for priests (who represented Christ in his marriage to the Church; cf. Eph. 5:29–32), the inalienability of Church property (as the Bride's dowry), and noninterference by kings in the investiture of bishops.[22] Megan McLaughlin points out that "the reformers of the eleventh and early twelfth centuries found in marriage a compelling symbol of the clergy's special relationship with the church and in marital imagery a flexible tool for advancing many aspects of the reform program."[23]

Judging by Bernard's *Life of Malachy*, prior to the activity of that holy bishop and of Archbishop Cellach, who ordained him, the Church in Ireland was badly in need of reform. Consecrated bishop of Connor at age thirty, the young monk-bishop Malachy "realized he had been sent not to men but to beasts," to a "people so wanton in their way of life, so cruel in superstition, so heedless of faith" that they were "Christians in name, yet pagans at heart"—indeed, a pack of "wolves and no [flock of] sheep."[24] Bernard describes "a total breakdown of ecclesiastical discipline, a relaxation of censure, a weakening of the whole religious structure," partly because of hereditary succession of eight married archbishops at Armagh, none of whom had been sacramentally ordained.[25]

Through Malachy's tireless service, exhortation, and prayer in the diocese of Connor, churches were rebuilt, the sacraments properly performed, the ranks of ordained priests replenished, and the marriages of the laity celebrated and honored.[26] Bernard relates that Archbishop Cellach had hoped that Malachy would succeed him as archbishop, but Malachy long hesitated to accept the post after Cellach's death, knowing that his election would be fiercely opposed and its legitimacy challenged, even at the cost of bloodshed, by members of that powerful clan who regarded the see of Armagh as their inheritance by blood-right. A certain Maurice, a man of this clan, had in fact immediately claimed his right to the title and office of archbishop when Cellach died.

To this reason for refusing appointment to the see of Armagh, Malachy added another that gives positive expression to a marital understanding of his relationship to his own diocese of Connor, saying that "he was already joined to another spouse whom he could not lawfully put away."[27] Urged by Gilbert, the legate of the Apostolic See, and others, Malachy, anticipating martyrdom at the hands of Maurice, finally accepts election as archbishop, but only under the condition that he might be allowed to "return to [his] former spouse" after accomplishing the work of reform at Armagh.[28] Malachy thus submits to a situation of temporary infidelity to his bride, the diocese of Connor, in order to remedy another, worse state of disorder, namely, that which Bernard names "the adultery of the Church and the dishonor paid to Christ in the course of three years of Maurice's presumption and Malachy's indecisiveness."[29]

Bernard reports that Malachy was troubled in conscience throughout this period of indecision and resistance by his vivid memory of a prophetic dream that had announced to him Cellach's impending death and the dying archbishop's wish for him to espouse the Church at Armagh in his stead: "While Cellach lay ill, there had appeared to Malachy a woman of great stature and reverend appearance.... When he asked her who in the world she was, she replied that she was Cellach's wife. Then she handed to him the pastoral staff which she held in her hand and disappeared. Several days later the dying Cellach sent his staff to Malachy, to the man who was to succeed him, and it was then that he realized the meaning of what he had seen."[30]

The symbol of the staff, given to Malachy both by the woman in the dream and by Cellach, points, of course, to the bishop's role as shepherd of his flock, in imitation of Christ, the Good Shepherd, who gives his life for his sheep (John 10:11). When a relative of Maurice named Niall followed Maurice in claiming to be archbishop of Armagh, he tried to fortify his claim by absconding from the city with "certain insignia of that see, namely the text of the Gospels which had been Saint Patrick's and the staff embellished with gold and precious stones which the people called the 'staff of Jesus.'"[31] In Bernard's *Life of Malachy*, the true archbishop triumphs over his opponent only after he humbles himself to go to meet a prince, a powerful member of the same clan to which Niall belongs, to discuss terms of peace. Suspecting treachery, Malachy goes at the risk of his life, explaining to his brother priests, "It may be that by humility I shall turn the tyrant, but if not I shall still conquer by showing myself a shepherd to the sheep. . . . It does not behoove a bishop to lord it over his clergy, but to be an example to his flock."[32] Malachy's brave appearance among his enemies leads, miraculously, to their conversion, wolves turning, as it were, into sheep.

A second symbol, given to the bishop-elect during the rite of consecration — the bishop's ring — signifies and seals a relationship of marital fidelity between the bishop and his diocese. McLaughlin discusses the "mystical significance" of the ring, which came to represent not just the bishop's juridical authority over his diocese, but also a "token of faith," "a kind of engagement or wedding ring."[33] When Malachy must decide, later in the *Life*, between three candidates for the office of bishop, he chooses a man named Edan: "You, Edan, . . . take the burden."[34] Responding to Edan's fears, Malachy speaks the comforting words: "Don't be afraid. You have been pointed out to me by the Lord, for I have just foreseen on your finger the gold ring by which you will be espoused."[35]

Citing Saint Paul's advice to Titus and Timothy that a bishop should be the "husband of one wife" (Titus 1:6; 1 Tim. 3:2), the reformers of the eleventh and twelfth centuries interpreted the verse to enjoin a bishop's fidelity to a single diocese and thus to ward off the dangers of clerical careerism and of simony in its various forms. Those same verses, when joined to Song of Songs 6:9, "My dove, my perfect one, is only one" (*una est columba mea perfecta mea*), inspired a ritual development that set the bishop's consecration increasingly parallel to the rite of Christian marriage, itself the "great sign" (*sacramentum magnum*) (Eph. 5:32) of Christ's love for his Bride, the Church.

Given this strong pattern of marital imagery in the *Life of Malachy* — a pattern rooted in the scriptures, in the rite for episcopal consecration, in the developing theology of the sacraments of holy orders and of matrimony, and in the recently mandated discipline of priestly celibacy[36] — Bernard's textual and intertextual allusions to the Song of Songs in his tale of a holy bishop assume a qualitative significance that far exceeds their quantitative measure. The *Life of Malachy* effectively gives Bernard a new opportunity to comment upon the Song, bringing it to bear upon the specific issue of the episcopal calling as an active way of holiness dependent upon a contemplative foundation. If Bernard's Bride is "virile" in her virtuous perfection, veiling a "masculine" potential (as Krahmer argues), the opposite is also true: the bishop as bridegroom veils the bride, nourishing her inner life through his spiritual surrender to Christ and his outward service to Christ's Bride, the Church.

In the pages that follow, I comment upon each of Bernard's citations of the Song of Songs in the *Life of Malachy*, showing how narrative context enables him to interpret the Song differently, discovering new meanings in the biblical text that are often unstated in, but complementary to, those spelled out in his *Sermons on the Song of Songs*. Rereading those collected sermons through the lens of the *Life of Malachy* brings to the fore, moreover, an ecclesial and ecclesiastical content that is frequently overlooked by scholars who emphasize too exclusively Bernard's personal and monastic mysticism.

"MY SISTER, MY BRIDE" (SONG OF SONGS 4:9, 10, 12)

In the *Life of Malachy*, Bernard does not literally quote this lyrical expression, nor does he paraphrase it. Neither the editor of the critical edition of the Latin text nor that of the English translation notes its hidden presence. Bernard's intertextual citation of the book of Tobit, however, enables its discovery in the midst of a cautionary tale about the dangers of a merely literal reading of scripture. The opening pages of the *Life of Malachy* instruct us, in short, to read the *Life* itself not only historically, but also allegorically, according to the biblical model of a multilayered significance.

Bernard thus proves himself ever the master of a rhetorical art that aims at enlisting the reader actively in the work of reading. Mary Carruthers tells us that medieval authors understood that the starting point of a meditative exercise, such as the reading of scripture or of a saint's *Life*, should awaken the reader's energy through "energizing devices" designed to put the reader's memory "in gear and to keep it interested and on track."[37] Among the possible "energizing devices," Carruthers mentions *allegoria*, "an ornament that [by its very nature as a figure of difficulty] initiates meditative thinking," and *enargeia*, a "bringing-before-the-eyes," a vivid word-painting, which sometimes takes the form of *ekphrasis* (the verbal description of a work of visual art) or of an occult dream-vision.[38] Bernard's *Life of Malachy* employs both, leading to the intertextual remembrance of the Song of Songs and its ecclesial allegory.

In paragraphs 6 and 11 of the *Life*, Bernard mentions Malachy's sister, who appears suddenly, unnamed and unannounced, first to reprove Malachy's virtuous, youthful practice of burying the dead and then, posthumously, to haunt Malachy's dreams with her need of his prayers. The first episode immediately precedes Malachy's ordination as a priest. The second comes just before Malachy's rebuilding of the ancient monastery at Bangor (paras. 12–15) and his election as bishop of Connor (para. 16). The two (and only two) appearances of the sister are puzzling, and Bernard carefully links them, reminding his readers that "we spoke of her earlier."[39]

What are we to make of Malachy's sister and her mysterious presence in the *Life* of a holy monk-bishop? "Although not all male saints were associated with a sister (and some holy men continued to avoid female relatives), the persistence with which sisters appear in recorded *Lives* of holy men nevertheless raises several important questions," observes Fiona Griffiths.[40] Griffiths herself focuses on this hagiographic feature as a clue pointing to the historical fact of "deep, affectionate, and ongoing familial ties" between biological brothers and sisters in religious life during the Middle Ages,[41] but she also admits the likelihood that some hagiographic sisters—notably Saint Benedict's sister, Scholastica—also served an allegorical function.[42]

Malachy's sister certainly belongs to this latter category. Although she is his sister, Bernard characterizes her relationship to Malachy by likening her to two troublesome wives: Eve, the seductress of Adam, and Anna, the wife of Tobit. Even as Anna rebuked her blind husband for misjudging her, Malachy's sister scolds Malachy, who has been burying the dead—the same charitable work that Tobit had undertaken at the risk of his own life. To Malachy, whom Bernard calls "our new Tobias," she says, "What are you doing, you idiot? Let the dead bury the dead."[43]

The episode is strange in many ways. Although Malachy acts like Tobit, he is identified with Tobit's son, Tobias, who is not known to have buried the dead, but to have been God's instrument (through the accompanying agency of the archangel Raphael in human disguise) in the healing of Tobit's blindness and in the expelling of the demon Asmodeus, who had killed the seven former bridegrooms of his kinswoman Sarah (his own future bride) on their wedding night. Is the hagiographer Bernard, so well versed in the scriptures, guilty of confusing Tobit and Tobias, or is he allusively conflating father and son in order to link Malachy's corporal works of mercy to his later spiritual work as a bishop-bridegroom in setting free his much beleaguered bride, the diocese of Connor and, by extension, the archdiocese of Armagh? The problem of the text leads to the reader's discovery of the answer.

The sister's scolding of Malachy, which places her within a misogynistic tradition of bad women, only superficially resembles Eve's temptation of Adam and ironically recasts Anna's rebuke of her husband, Tobit, whom she does not scold for burying the dead but for his moral blindness in wrongly judging her a thief. Irony abounds, too, in the sister's misappropriation of the words of Jesus, "Let the dead bury the dead" (Luke 9:16). Malachy's reply to his sister, "Wretched woman, you keep to the pure word, but you are unaware of its meaning,"[44] doubles as an instruction to the reader of Bernard's hagiography, who is taught to seek a deeper significance not only in the Gospel verse but in the saint's *Life*.

Who or what, then, does Malachy's sister symbolize? Bernard furthers the development of this inquiry when she makes her second appearance in the text. Malachy's sister has died. "Repelled by her carnal life," Malachy had previously broken off contact with her, but, upon her death, he begins "to see in spirit her whom he would not see in the flesh."[45] The juxtaposition of carnal and spiritual sight in Bernard's narrative, reminiscent of that between the letter and the spirit in 2 Corinthians 3:6, signals a new understanding of the sister both in Malachy's understanding and in the reader's. Bernard devotes an entire section to describing a series of three dream-visions in which Malachy sees his departed sister. In the first, a voice reveals that she stands "just outside in the yard," starving for the food of which he has deprived her through his cessation of masses offered for her soul.[46] Reminded of her need of his prayers, he begins anew his Eucharistic intercession for her and sees a vision of her coming "to the threshold of the church, not yet able to come in and wearing a dark garment."[47] Persevering in prayer, he sees her a second time, dressed in a lighter garment and "admitted inside the church, but still not allowed close to the altar."[48] In his final sight of her, she stands "in the midst of the white-clothed choir, arrayed in bright clothing."[49]

The story of Malachy's dream-visions of his sister and of her successive transformations serves several purposes. Literally and obviously, it exemplifies the power of the practice of prayer for the dead. It focuses attention on the Eucharist as a sacramental means of healing, sanctification, and unity among the members of the Church. It suggests, more subtly, Malachy's own spiritual growth through his perseverance in praying for his sister, whose soul he loves (Cf. Sg 3:3), but not her sin.[50] Bernard concludes this section of the *Life* with his own prayer to Jesus: "Oh, good Jesus, you give this power, you have suffered; strong and merciful to save, you show mercy and strength in your arm."[51]

At yet another, more hidden level of significance, however, the sister's third and final transformation, her joining of the "white-robed choir, arrayed in bright clothing," assimilates her to Christ's Bride, the Church: "For the marriage of the Lamb has come, and his Bride has made herself ready; it was granted to her to be clothed with fine linen, bright and pure" (Rev. 19:7–8). In becoming Christ's bride, Malachy's sister—through her various stages of purification and transformation—prefigures the reform of the Church in Ireland as it will be accomplished through the holy bishop's pastoral care and apostolic ministry. Allegorically considered, Malachy's sister is the bishop's bride, to the extent that Christ lives and acts in Malachy: "My sister, my bride" (Sg 4:9, 10, 12).

The spiritual healing of Malachy's sister is mirrored in later miracles involving Malachy's healing of women. Although Malachy's miracles are greatly varied in kind and benefit both men and women, Bernard relates a high proportion of stories that involve women and girls—a choice justified symbolically, in part, by the controlling allegory of the bishop as a bridegroom who participates in Christ's spousal desire "to present the church to himself in splendor, without spot or wrinkle or any such thing . . . , holy and without blemish" (Eph. 5:27; cf. Sg 4:7). Bernard records Malachy's cures of a mute girl (three different cases), a mad woman (two cases), a paralyzed woman, a woman possessed by demons (two cases), a self-mutilating woman, and a pregnant woman unable to give birth (two cases), and others.[52]

Among the many miracles stories, Bernard groups together three involving women in a sequence (paras. 52–54) that mirrors that found in Malachy's three visions of his sister. In the first, a woman who is dear to Malachy suffers from a hemorrhage and is near death from the loss of blood. When she sends word of her condition to Malachy, requesting his prayers for her soul, he replies from afar by sending a young runner who carries to her three apples blessed by the saint. Weak as she is, from loss of blood and hunger, she asks to be propped up. She tastes of the blessed apples and falls into a deep sleep, during which the hemorrhage ceases. She awakens, healed.

This first miracle evokes Malachy's first encounter with his dead sister, whose starving soul Malachy begins to nourish from a distance through his celebration of the Eucharist, a spiritual food that an Augustinian tradition associates with the fruit of the Tree of Life and identifies as an antidote for the eating of the forbidden fruit.[53] The Bride in the Song of Songs describes the Beloved as "an apply tree [*sicut malum*] among the trees of the wood," whose fruit is "sweet to [her] taste" (Sg 2:3). "Sick with love" during the Bridegroom's absence, the Bride begs, "Refresh me with apples" (*stipate me malis*) (Sg 2:5).

In the second miracle account, Malachy attends a dying noblewoman. Taking counsel with others present, he decides to delay anointing her until the morning. During the night, however, she dies suddenly, without having received the sacrament—a circumstance for which Malachy blames himself. Anointing her body with his tears and praying fervently, Malachy awakens the woman from death and anoints her with the holy oil, which leads to her complete recovery in body and soul.

The passage is replete with scriptural echoes from various sources, but it strongly evokes the raising of Lazarus, for whom the Lord wept (John 11:33); the anointing of Jesus's own body with tears and ointment (Luke 7:46; John 12:3); and verses from the Song of Songs that speak of oils (Sg 1:3; 5:5). Malachy's delay in this case recalls his earlier negligence in failing to care for his sister's spiritual need. Crossing the boundary between death and life, the woman in this second tale, who recovers life and health in stages, resembles Malachy's sister as she appears to him posthumously—at first outside, then at the threshold of the church, then safely inside it, but at a distance from the altar, and finally in the midst of the choir.

The spiritual significance of the second miracle becomes explicit in the third. According to Bernard, the third miracle in this ascending series "is to be put ahead of the miracle of raising up the dead woman," because it involves a moral miracle that "brought back to life" a person's inner life.[54] Bernard describes a woman who was "foolhardy, outrageous, and quick-tempered, formidable in both tongue and hand, impossible to live with and despised."[55] Brought to Malachy by her desperate children, she obeys his command to confess her sins, accepts his order "never to lose her temper again," and receives through his prayer "the spirit of meekness," with the result that "a miraculous change" in her occurs.[56]

This last and greatest story in the sequence relates a moral transformation in this life that parallels the purification of the soul of Malachy's sister after death. Just as the children interceded with the saint for their mother, Malachy interceded with Christ both for his sister and for the woman, whose angry tongue and constant harping recalls the rebukes of Malachy's sibling. Even as Malachy could not bear to be near his sister, the relatives of the abusive woman had separated themselves from her. Her healing restores the whole community, even as that of Malachy's sister portended the restored peace of the bishop's bride, the diocese of Connor.

"THE FOUNTAIN OF THE GARDENS, THE WELL OF LIVING WATERS" (SONG OF SONGS 4:15)

Immediately following the moral miracle tale of the once angry woman's conversion, Bernard relates three wondrous stories, each involving water, to conclude a section, of fifteen paragraphs (paras. 42–56), about the "heavenly miracles" that took place to ratify Malachy's program of reform.[57] This section begins with Bernard's portrayal of Malachy himself as "the greatest miracle" — someone whose humble bearing, voluntary poverty, powerful prayer, and evangelical zeal mark him as an apostolic man, a "true heir of the Apostles."[58] Fittingly, then, the last two miracles in the section are miracles (obviously reminiscent of the miraculous hauls of fish in Luke 5:1–12 and John 21: 4–8) involving the sudden multiplication and catch of fish in waters where fish, formerly in abundance, had died out.[59]

What precedes the two miracles of fish, however, is an account of an unusual petition for the gift of tears and its granting through Malachy's prayer. Troubled by the dryness of his soul, a God-fearing layman begs Malachy to pray that he might be granted to weep tears as an expression of his spiritual yearning. Malachy responds with a smile and a gesture of singular intimacy: "He laid his cheek on the other's cheek, as if joining him in a caress, and said: 'May it happen for you as you have asked.'"[60] From then on, we are told, the man wept "rivers of waters" in cascading, nearly continual tears of contrition and devotion and thus became an embodiment of "that saying of Scripture: the fountain of the gardens, the well of living waters" (Sg 4:15).[61]

Associated with spiritual life, the overflowing fountain and the deep well from which spring water may be drawn seem to represent the two streams of compunction that Gregory the Great saw symbolized in the dowry of Caleb's daughter, to whom her father bequeathed "the upper springs and the lower springs" of water (Josh. 15:19) as a wedding gift.[62] In the *Dialogues* and in *Moralia in Job*, Gregory distinguishes two different streams of compunction, "because the soul thirsting for God is first pierced [*compungitur*] by fear and then by love."[63] These, in turn, correspond to a twofold gift of tears: tears of shame and remorse, on the one hand, and tears of longing and joy, on the other.[64] Gregory associates the second piercing with the wound of love suffered by the Bride in Solomon's Canticle (Sg 4:9).[65]

Malachy's cheek-to-cheek gesture and Bernard's quotation of Song 4:15 suggest a complex biblical and exegetical intertextuality in the miracle story. The man who wants to weep for God's sake, though a layman and not a monk, is likened to the Bride of the Song, whose "cheeks are beautiful as the turtledove's [*sicut turturis*]" (Sg 1:9). Commenting on that verse, Bernard explains to his fellow monks: "And therefore, to seek God for his own sake alone, this is to possess two cheeks made beautiful by the two elements of intention [i.e., matter and purpose, what you intend and why]. This is the bride's own special gift."[66] Praying for the petitioner, Malachy joins the Bridegroom, Christ, in granting the bride's request. Touching cheek to cheek and awakening tears, Malachy in this moment symbolizes the spiritual marriage between Christ and Christ's Church, the bishop and his diocese, the monk and the layman — charity overflowing all boundaries, combining ranks.[67]

DOVELIKE CHEEKS, EYES, AND VOICE
(SONG OF SONGS 1:9, 1:14, 5:12, 2:12)

The Bride in the Song of Songs praises the Bridegroom's eyes, which are "like doves above the streams of waters" (*sicut columbae super rivulos aquarum*) (Sg 5:12), even as the Bridegroom celebrates the beautiful Bride's eyes as dovelike (*ecce tu pulchra oculi tui columbarum*) (Sg 1:14b). Similarly, Bernard praises Bishop Malachy in the *Life*: "Oh pure heart! Oh dovelike eyes!"[68] In his letter to Henry, archbishop of Sens, Bernard paints the portrait of an ideal bishop, using the same image: "Faithful is the pontiff who looks *with dove-like eyes* at everything good which passes through his hands, whether it be God's favors showered on humankind or their prayers to God, and holds on to nothing for himself."[69] This sentence appears in a passage discussing the virtue of charity, which issues "from a pure heart, a clear conscience, and a sincere faith."[70] The pure-hearted bishop, according to Bernard, is "a bridge [*pons*] between God and neighbor," a "good mediator," who "offers to God the prayers and vows and longings of the people, bringing back to them from God blessing and grace."[71] In this same passage, Bernard explicates the bishop's "death to self" in this exchange by referring explicitly to the wound of the Bride in Song of Songs 2:5.[72]

Dovelike in his eyes and cheeks (Sg 1:9)—that is, as glossed above, "in what he intends and why"[73]—the holy bishop speaks also with "the voice of the turtledove" (Sg 2:12). Bernard prefaces his *Life of Malachy* with a complex citation of this poetic image, identifying the dove's voice simultaneously with Malachy's, Christ's, and his own as hagiographer. "If I should awaken my sleeping friend [the recently deceased saint, Malachy]," writes Bernard, "'the voice of the turtledove shall be heard in our land' [Sg 2:12], saying: 'Lo, I am with you all days, even unto the end of the world' [Matt. 28:20]."[74] Writing to Pope Eugenius, Bernard similarly identifies the "voice of the turtledove" with that of an inspired messenger of Christ, Eugenius himself, whose letter to the abbot of Clairvaux has been read in chapter: "'The voice of the turtledove has been heard' in our chapter, and it has filled us with joy. Certainly a clear voice, and a voice burning with zeal, weighty with knowledge. The spirit of life breathed through your words, a mighty spirit, a spirit crying aloud, chiding and arousing us to 'a jealousy that is the jealousy of God himself.'"[75]

The combination of the nouns "voice" and "dove" in Song of Songs 2:12 seems to have triggered in Bernard the remembrance of the Word of God, through whom "in the beginning . . . all things were made" (John 1:1–3); of the Spirit of God, who "in the beginning . . . was moving [dovelike] over the face of the waters" (Gen. 1:1–2); of John the Baptist's preaching of repentance; and of Jesus's own baptism at the Jordan River—an event marked by the Spirit's descent "in bodily form, as a dove" and by the sound of "a voice from heaven," bearing witness to Christ's divinity (Luke 3:22). The sound of "the voice of the turtledove" (Sg 2:12) thus announces good news and effects a vernal renewal of creation through repentance.

Bernard himself glosses "the voice of the turtledove" in Sermon 59 on the Song of Songs, where he instructs his monks both to hear and to speak with that same voice: "With her voice more akin to mourning than to singing, she reminds us that we are pilgrims. I listen willingly to the voice of the teacher who does not stir up applause for himself but compunction in me. You really resemble the turtledove if you preach repentance. . . . Practice what you preach."[76] Bernard goes on to connect the mourning of dovelike souls with the "groaning" of creation itself (Rom. 8:22) and with the inward sighing of the Holy Spirit (Rom. 8:26), whose "voice sounds through the lips of all," interceding for "the needs of each."[77]

In paired visions described near the end of the *Life*, immediately before Malachy departs from Ireland to begin his final journey to Clairvaux, Bernard directly associates Malachy again with iconic signs of the Holy Spirit's presence and activity. In the first vision, a deacon who attends Malachy during the saint's celebration of Mass sees a dove fly into the church through a window. The dove, "a rare bird in that land," brought with its sudden appearance a great light that shone upon Malachy "in great brilliance" and dispelled the darkness, moving the deacon to fall prostrate before the altar in fear and trembling.[78] In the second, an auxiliary bishop, walking with Malachy one early morning among the tombs of saints in the cemetery of Saint Patrick, first witnesses a mysterious, fiery blaze at the tomb of one such saint (presumably that of Saint Patrick himself) and then sees Malachy plunge himself "into the midst of the flames, embracing the altar with outstretched arms," only to emerge from "that fire more ablaze than usual with a heavenly fire."[79]

The Song of Songs and Saint Bernard of Clairvaux's *Life of Saint Malachy* 77

"IN THE STREETS AND IN THE SQUARES I WILL SEEK HIM"
(SONG OF SONGS 2:3)

A missionary bishop with the zeal of a second Saint Patrick, Malachy is depicted throughout the *Life* as a Christlike good shepherd who goes out in search of his lost sheep (John 10:14; Luke 15:3–7). Malachy, who realizes "that he must be a shepherd and not a mere hireling," chooses again and again "to stand his ground rather than to flee, being prepared to give up his life for his sheep if need be."[80] Similarly, the Song of Songs, replete with pastoral imagery, describes the Bridegroom as both a king (King Solomon is named in Sg 3:9, 11) and a shepherd—a combination reminiscent of the shepherd-king David, Solomon's father and the royal ancestor of Jesus "according to the flesh" (*secundum carnem*) (cf. Rom. 1:3). The Bride in the Song wonders, for example, where her beloved pastures his flock (Sg 1:7); she finds that he "feeds [them] among the lilies" and "in the gardens" (Sg 2:16; 6:2–3).

Bernard describes Malachy as intent upon nourishing his flock properly, "ingenious in every ruse by which to make wolves into sheep," using public speeches, private arguments, compassionate assistance to individuals, "whichever way he saw would be best for each one."[81] Traveling on foot, "he also went out to the country and to the small towns," patiently enduring injury, insult, hunger, cold, and nakedness.[82] Bernard's list of Malachy's sufferings for his flock evokes those of Saint Paul (see 2 Cor. 11:27), who felt a "divine jealousy" for the church at Corinth, which he had "betrothed . . . to Christ" as "a pure bride to her one husband" (2 Cor. 11:2).

Identifying the bishop as bridegroom of his diocese with the Bridegroom of the Song, Bernard takes the Bride's painful, repeated searches for her beloved, described in the Song (Sg 3:1–3; 5:6–8), and assimilates them to those of the bridegroom-bishop. "How many nights he gave over entirely to vigils, stretching out his hands [in a cruciform posture] in prayer!" Bernard exclaims. "And when they would not come willingly to church, he went about in the city in the highways and the byways, seeking earnestly anyone he might gain for Christ."[83] In this passage, the night vigils of Malachy evoke the wakeful sleep of the Song's Bride (Sg 3:1, 5:2), even as they transform them, inventing a mysticism of pastoral care. Malachy's missionary trips into the city similarly transform the Bride's lonely nocturnal quest "about the city, in the streets and in the squares" (Sg 3:2) in search of her beloved. Finally, Malachy's Christlike sufferings redeem those suffered by the Bride at the hands of the mysterious watchmen, who beat her, wound her, and strip her of her mantle (Sg 5:7).

In a series of sermons (76–86), Saint Bernard comments extensively on the episode of the Bride's nocturnal search. In these sermons, Bernard discovers in the Bride's intense yearning the certain proof of a hidden reality, namely, that she has first been loved by God and received from him his prevenient grace: "We love because he first loved us" (1 John 4:19). Bernard brings this Johannine verse (amidst a panoply of others) to bear upon the Bride's quest for the one who has first stirred her heart through his gifts and favors: "Since I love, I cannot doubt that I am loved, any more than I can doubt that I love."[84] "From this [awareness of being loved] comes the zeal and ardor to seek him whom your heart loves," Bernard explains, "because you cannot seek unless you are sought, and when you are sought you cannot but seek."[85]

Looking for the Bridegroom, the Bride encounters instead the night watchmen, who are said to have "found" her (Sg 3:3); she questions them about the one whom she seeks. In Song of Songs 3:3–4, the Bride simply passes the watchmen after questioning them (their answer is not recorded) and immediately finds "him whom [her] soul loves." This sequence contrasts with that in Song of Songs 5:6–8, where the questing lover is found by watchmen who beat her—sentries to whom she poses no question and from whom she receives no guidance, spurring her to ask instead the "daughters of Jerusalem" about her beloved's whereabouts.

Bernard interprets the contrastive figures of the watchmen within the larger context of his argument about prevenient grace. In the positive scenario in chapter 3, the watchmen on duty have actually come looking for the Bride in order to direct her toward the Bridegroom, whom she immediately finds: "Scarcely had I passed them [the watchmen], when I found him" (Sg 3:4). Bernard identifies the watchmen with "they who are to instruct the new bride in the things she needs to know, to prepare her for her marriage to the heavenly Bridegroom, and to teach her the faith and counsel her in the ways of holiness and true religion."[86] Vigilant in prayer by night, "they . . . care with all their heart for the Lord's flocks committed to their charge."[87] "Friends of the Bridegroom" (John 3:29), these watchmen bear the responsibility to protect the Church—whether she is figured as a city, a flock, or a Bride—against earthly tyrants, heretics, and the temptations of evil spirits.[88] Alluding to the negative scenario in chapter 5 of the Song, Bernard explains that these same foes sometimes appear as untrue friends, false watchmen, when vicious men pursue episcopal office for the sake of their own gain, "not to adorn the Bride but to despoil her; not to guard her but to destroy her" (cf. Sg. 5:7).[89] The true watchmen, by contrast, include not only the genuine successors of the apostles on earth, but also the angels and saints in heaven—all who have prepared the way for, and contributed to, the Bride's homeward journey to her Lord. [90]

Depicted in the *Life* as vigilant by night in prayer, by day in searching for the members of his flock, Malachy clearly resembles these virtuous watchmen who participate, in turn, in the Good Shepherd's own task. Significantly, Malachy's nightlong prayer with arms outstretched is said to precede his apostolic endeavors.[91] Robert T. Meyer, the English-language translator of the *Vita Sancti Malachiae episcopi*, describes the *cross-figil*, "praying with arms extended in the form of a cross," as a "customary monastic practice," mentioned in the Old Irish penitentials.[92] The holy bishop's cruciform prayer points to the prevenient grace given through Christ's death, by which Jesus paid a bride-price for his elect, the Church (1 Cor. 6:20).

In the Song of Songs, the Bridegroom's outstretched hands (and, by implication, arms) are mentioned twice, each time with allegorical reference (in Bernard's understanding) to Christ's passion, death, and resurrection. In the first, the Bride exclaims, "O that his left hand were under my head, and that his right hand embraced me!" (Sg 2:6). In *On Loving God*, Bernard interprets the left hand as conveying "all the signs of love she had received during her lover's first visit," namely, the earthly life of Jesus, and the right hand as proffering the eternal joys of heaven, when "she will experience what she had heard: 'The flesh is of no use; it is the spirit that gives life' [John 6:64]."[93] "His left hand," writes Bernard, "is symbolic of his unsurpassable charity which made him lay down his life for his friends [John 15:13], while his right hand portrays the beatific vision which he promised them and the joy of his majestic presence."[94]

In the second, the Bridegroom appears by night at the Bride's locked door, calls to her, and "put[s] his hand to the latch," whereupon the Bride opens the door, her "hands dripp[ing] with myrrh" (Sg 5:4–5), only to find him gone. Bernard comments only briefly on this verse, alluding to it in his comment on the ointments mentioned in Song of Songs 1:2–3. Fusing the two images, Bernard first recalls the anointing of Jesus's feet with oil that "trickled from the hands of a courtesan" (namely, the sinful woman of Luke 7: 37–38, but also Mary of Bethany in John 12:3, who anointed Jesus's head and feet in anticipation of his burial) and exhorts the penitents in his audience: "Safely may your hands drip with the bitterness of myrrh in the course of this salutary anointing, because God does not scorn this crushed and broken spirit [Ps. 50:19]."[95]

Curiously, after discussing the ointments of contrition and devotion, Bernard again references Song of Songs 5:5, using it this time to describe "another ointment, far excelling these two, to which I give the name loving-kindness."[96] In a rousing speech obviously intended to reach an audience beyond his listeners at Clairvaux, Bernard calls out: "Whoever you may be, if your soul is thus disposed, if you are saturated with the dew of mercy, ... so dead to yourself that you live only for others—if this be you, then you obviously and happily possess the third and best of all ointments and your hands have dripped liquid myrrh that is utterly enchanting."[97] Bernard then presents a series of exempla, all of whom are said to have possessed hands so dripping with the myrrh of selfless service: Paul, Job, Joseph, Samuel, Moses, and David. The Bride's hands are wet with myrrh as they open the door to her beloved, but his hands precede hers in their movement, trying the latch. When Bernard speaks of a soul "saturated with the dew of mercy," he thus alludes to the prevenient presence of the Bridegroom, who calls to the Bride, "Open to me, ... for my head is wet with dew, and my locks with the drops of the night" (Sg 5:2). In compassion, the Bridegroom and the Bride are one, their hands joined.

In the *Life of Saint Malachy*, the gestures of uplifted and outstretched hands are so often repeated as to suggest that Bernard, Malachy's hagiographer, was proposing them as iconographic for the saint. Echoing a biblical instance of paronomasia (Ws 3:1: "qui re*man*ent in *man*u Dei"), Bernard states, "Malachy remained in God's hands."[98] Already in the first paragraph of the *Life* we read that Malachy, when still a boy, secretly "lifted up holy hands everywhere [1 Tim. 2:8], stretching them out to heaven."[99] By a "pious fraud" he made this gesture frequently behind the back of his unsuspecting teacher, for whom "he used to send up a prayer, quickly as though it were a dart."[100] Later, after he has been consecrated bishop, God himself intervenes to rescue Malachy, when at the "lifting up [of Malachy's] hands,"[101] a sudden, violent storm brings death to the bishop's enemies, who were lying in wait to kill him. At the monastery at Bangor, Malachy cures a lame beggar after looking up to heaven, "raising his hands at the same time."[102] Bernard records that Malachy used the same gesture of upraised hands when he prayed for the life of the woman who had died before receiving the sacraments.[103] Malachy is said to have worked the moral miracle of the angry woman's transformation "by the [power of] the right hand of the Most High [Ps. 77:10]."[104] On the night of his death at Clairvaux, Malachy lays his hands in blessing upon all those assembled at his bedside.[105] Shortly after the holy bishop dies, Bernard himself touches the withered hand of a cripple to Malachy's hand, and the first of the saint's posthumous miracles occurs.[106]

Bernard's sermon at the funeral Mass for Malachy includes a veritable blazon of the saint's body, which has served so well the virtues of his soul. The abbot praises Malachy's "faithful eyes," his "undefiled hands," his "beautiful footsteps" and travel-worn feet, his "holy lips," mouth, and tongue.[107] Among these, the praise of the hands is the most elaborate. Bernard remembers gratefully "those undefiled hands which had always loved to be exercised in laborious and humble deeds; which had so often offered up for sinners the saving host of the Lord's body and were lifted up to heaven in prayer without anger or contention; which were known to have conferred many blessings on the sick and to have shone with various signs."[108]

"I HELD HIM AND WOULD NOT LET HIM GO"
(SONG OF SONGS 3:4)

As he himself had wished and prophesied, Malachy died on All Souls' Day and was buried at Clairvaux: "If I happened to be on a journey and God so permits it, I have chosen Clairvaux."[109] Using a daring image, Bernard appropriates the paraphrased words of the Bride in Song of Songs 3:4 to recall his own ardent welcome of Malachy to the monastery: "With what eager face and mind, my Father, I brought you into my mother's house and into the chamber of her who bore me."[110] The unquoted part of that same verse, "I held him and would not let him go" (Sg 3:4), silently attests to the Cistercian abbey's honor as Malachy's last resting place.

The end of Bernard's *Life of Malachy* thus returns us to its beginning. In his preface to the *Life*, Bernard explains why he has undertaken to write it.

He has always regarded the recording of "the illustrious lives of the saints" to be a praiseworthy work, because the saints can "serve as a mirror and example" for the faithful.[111] Calling the saints to mind through writing and reading brings them back from the dead, making them "still alive among us," even as they, by their prayer and example, "call back many of those who are dead while they live."[112] Like John the Baptist, Malachy was and is a "burning and shining light" (John 5:35) for Christians.[113] Bernard therefore feels justified in recalling him as a witness to Christ's enduring presence: "If I should awaken my sleeping friend, the voice of the turtledove shall be heard in our land [Sg 2:12], saying, 'Lo, I am with you all days, even unto the end of the world' [Matt. 28:20]."[114]

The subtle allusion to John the Baptist, together with the melding of Song 2:12 with Matthew 28:20, adds poignancy to the image of Malachy as a "sleeping friend." Like the martyred John the Baptist, Malachy sleeps in death. Like John, too, Malachy is Christ's friend, and Bernard's. In a passage Bernard does not quote, John the Baptist names himself "the friend of the bridegroom": "He that hath the bride, is the bridegroom: but the friend of the bridegroom, who standeth and heareth him, rejoiceth with joy because of the bridegroom's voice. This my joy therefore is fulfilled" (John 3:29). Acknowledging Jesus as the Church's Bridegroom, John rejoices at hearing his voice, which Bernard identifies with "the voice of the turtle" (Sg 2:12). About to tell Malachy's story in a way that associates him with the Bridegroom of the Song of Songs, Bernard gratefully recalls, "The saint held me among his special friends."[115] The bridelike monastery at Clairvaux, therefore, holds him: "He was buried here."[116]

As bishop, Malachy made Christ the Bridegroom present to Christ's Bride, the Church, in the dioceses of Connor and of Armagh, strengthening the bond between them through his episcopal ministry in word and sacrament. In the end, that same service united Malachy himself mystically to Christ as Christ's bridal spouse and, in Christ, to Christ's company at Clairvaux. In Bernard's *Life of Malachy*, the Song of Songs tells the story, and the story interprets the Song. Just as in his sermons on the Song Bernard declares the "book of our own experience" to be necessary for the monks' understanding of the biblical love song,[117] here the abbot of Clairvaux maintains the book of the saint's *Life* also to be necessary and, indeed, to be part of their experience.

CHAPTER FOUR

EADMER'S PARABOLIC *LIFE* AND *HISTORY* OF SAINT ANSELM OF CANTERBURY

A Twice-Told Tale

Writing in the early twelfth century (ca. 1109–15) after the death of Anselm of Canterbury (1034–1109), the monk Eadmer put the finishing touches on two complementary works that he had begun writing in the 1090s, after the start of Anselm's archiepiscopate in 1093. The first four books of the *Historia novorum in Anglia* (*History of Recent Events in England*) end with Anselm's death at age seventy-six, marking the close of the *History* as originally intended by its author.[1] The two books of the *Vita Anselmi* (*Life of Anselm*) conclude with Anselm's death and burial, a couple of added, posthumous miracle accounts, and Eadmer's guilty confession (to which we will return).[2] The contents of the *History* and of the *Life* partly overlap, especially in their narratives of Anselm's troubles in England and his exiles, but the emphasis in each work differs. In the preface to the *Life*, Eadmer refers to the *History* as the earlier of the two writings, the record of controversies open to the public, which he wishes to supplement with an account of Anselm's private conversations, personal manner of life, and miracles.[3]

As Anselm's secretary, friend, and companion in exile, Eadmer tells the saint's story in both its public and its private settings with an unprecedented attention to detail and liveliness of expression, echoing the natural, spoken language of Anselm and his interlocutors. "Eadmer's chief claim to fame as a biographer," writes R. W. Southern, "lies in his rediscovery and mastery of the difficult art of recording the spoken word in a vivid and natural way."[4]

The *Historia novorum* is indeed "widely regarded as a landmark in the development of English historical writing,"[5] "a remarkable, innovative leap into the twelfth-century world of experience."[6] The *History*'s companion piece, the *Vita Anselmi*, deserves equal recognition as a landmark text in hagiography, in part because of its specifically parabolic relationship to the *Historia novorum*—a text increasingly recognized as existing (as Charles Rozier puts it) in a space "between history and hagiography."[7] With the aid of a cited, biblical parable, the *History* leans toward the hagiographic, and the *Life* comments on the *History*, functioning to some extent as its allegory.

In the *History*, Eadmer explicitly interprets Anselm's archiepiscopate as an ironically dramatic, historical realization of the Lukan parable of invited dinner guests (Luke 14:16–18); the *Life* elaborates upon that exegesis. In the interpretive process, which entails a narrative retelling of Anselm's story in the *Life*, Eadmer seeks to smooth the rough stones foundational to Anselm's difficult history, to direct its interpretation, and to defend Anselm's sanctity before its doubters. Pairing the *History* with the *Life*, however, Eadmer also separates elements of action and character that earlier hagiographies had seamlessly joined. Eadmer's innovation thus calls attention inadvertently to a widening gap between historical and hagiographic accounts—a gap with broader implications both for biblical reading in the twelfth century, an age imbued with what M. D. Chenu has called "a new awareness of history,"[8] and for the canonization process.

EADMER'S "BIOGRAPHICAL DUALISM"

The relationship between the *History* and the *Life* has inspired much scholarly interest, but not from the angle of biblical intertextual interpretation. Using a Pauline metaphor (1 Cor. 3:2) important to Anselm's own educational thought and practice, Sally Vaughn does call the *History* a "meaty" work, in comparison to the "milk" of the *Life*, and usefully suggests that Eadmer had different intended audiences for his two writings,[9] but she does not draw out the full implications of that metaphor, especially in application to those members of Eadmer's ideal audience who were exhorted to read both works. In his preface to the *Life*, Eadmer "give[s] warning . . . that readers of the former work [*Historia novorum*] cannot fully understand Anselm's actions without the help of this work [*Vita Anselmi*], nor can readers of this work do so without the help of other."[10] The pertinent questions of order in writing and reading thus remain. When, how, and (most importantly) why did Eadmer write both a *History* and a *Life* of Anselm? What generic distinctions does Eadmer see between the two? What different purposes did he hope to achieve through them separately? What intent directs their combination as complementary texts?

The answers to the "when" and "how" questions are and must remain tentative. Since, as Southern acknowledges, "we have no copy of the work in its original state," and Eadmer "has left very little trace of his methods of composition,"[11] we can only speculate about the authorial process that led to Anselm's sacred biography being a tale twice-told. Southern casts doubt on Eadmer's apparent claim that he had completed the *History* before beginning the *Life*. According to Southern's reconstruction of things, both were works-in-progress before 1100, when "the *Vita Anselmi* . . . was probably well advanced."[12] It must have been around 1100, Southern proposes, when Anselm discovered Eadmer secretly at work on the *Life*, offered some corrections to it, and then, after further reflection, commanded Eadmer to destroy the work, protesting his unworthiness of such a memorial. Eadmer did so, but not (he confesses belatedly in the *Life*'s final chapter) without first copying the *Life* to preserve it, against the express will of his abbot and archbishop. Uneasy in conscience, Eadmer then temporarily abandoned his work on the *Life* and the *History* alike, completing them only after Anselm's death in 1109. In this way, Southern accounts for the brevity of later chapters of the *Life* (starting at 2.50), which lack the remembrance of Anselm's spoken words, and for the heavily reliance in books 3 and 4 of the *History* on documents—in particular, letters quoted verbatim—as substitutes for recorded speeches.[13]

Following Southern, Rozier describes the *Life* and the *History* as written "in tandem."[14] Vaughn, by contrast, imagines that Eadmer was engaged in the process of collecting materials ("taking notes") for a unified biography of Anselm when the archbishop discovered his secretary's secret enterprise, and only then—in an effort to save Anselm as an example for future generations—did Eadmer decide, post 1100, to divide the collected material for use in two different compositions.[15] She takes Eadmer's words about the *History*'s priority in time as referring to the date of its final completion sometime after Anselm's death, when the preface to the *Life* was also presumably composed.

Whether Eadmer decided early or late to make Anselm's story a tale twice-told, the choice itself is remarkable and has prompted a search for possible literary models. Vaughn argues persuasively concerning the *Historia novorum* (*HN*) that "one model seems to be the words and deeds of Canterbury's founders as portrayed in Bede's History of the English Church."[16] Vaughn shows that the first pages of Eadmer's *History* evoke patterns and precedents found in Bede's *Ecclesiastical History*.[17] At the start of book 1, Eadmer briefly provides a prehistory for the time of Anselm, starting with the positive relationship between King Edgar (943–75) and Saint Dunstan (909–88), archbishop of Canterbury (*HN* 3). Following this peaceful, iconic portrait of cooperation, Eadmer presents the negative example of King Ethelred (ca. 966–1016), whom Dunstan denounced for the murder of his own brother, King Edward (d. 978). Dunstan's prophecy of foreign invasions, oppression, and devastation to come is then shown to have been fulfilled during the reigns of Ethelred and subsequent kings (*HN* 3–5), leading eventually to the invasion of William of Normandy in 1066 (*HN* 6–9). Eadmer associates Saint Dunstan and his prophecy with Saint Elphege (ca. 953–1012), archbishop of Canterbury, who was taken captive by the Danes and martyred during Ethelred's reign (*HN* 4–5); by extension, Eadmer links both saints with the sorely tried archbishop, Anselm of Canterbury.

Focusing his research similarly on the *Historia novorum*, Rozier reports: "Eadmer made no references to any of the histories housed in the Canterbury collection, either as sources or as models for his writing."[18] More important for Eadmer the historian, according to Rozier, were the sacred histories of Bede — the *Ecclesiastical History of the English People* and the *Life of Saint Cuthbert* — and Eadmer's own hagiographies of Anglo-Saxon saints: *Life of Saint Dunstan*, *Life of Saint Breguwine* (archbishop of Canterbury from 761 to 764), *Life of Saint Oda*, a *Life of Saint Oswald* (of Worcester), *Life of Saint Wilfrid* (of York). Eadmer's "historical account of Anselm could not exist independently of the hagiographical," Rozier insists.[19] In this, he underscores Antonia Gransden's thesis: "Hagiography provided Eadmer with his historical training."[20]

Surveying the already established models for biographical writing — (1) the "heroic pattern" of Anglo-Saxon saints, such as Bede celebrated; (2) the "commemorative pattern" used to honor the abbots of Cluny; (3) the "secular model" found in Suetonius's *Lives of the Twelve Caesars* and Einhard's ninth-century *Life of Charlemagne*; and (4) the *Lives* and *Sayings* of the Desert Fathers—Southern finds narrative elements, especially those exhibited in the "heroic pattern," that appear in Eadmer's combined *History* and *Life*, but no single literary exemplar for Eadmer's particular public/private division of material. "Taking the work as a whole," Southern observes, "the parallels are slight, and the deposit of the past does not lie heavily on Eadmer's work."[21] Grandsen finds "the division between public and private life in a rudimentary form"[22] in earlier writings—for example, Coleman's *Life of Saint Wulfstan* and Suetonius's *Life of Caesar Augustus*. Like Southern, however, Grandsen concludes that Eadmer's work is highly original in its structure and expression: "Eadmer wrote less to emulate past biographers than to express his personal loyalty to and affection for Anselm."[23]

The private/public distinction between the *Life* and the *History*—a distinction important to Southern's influential characterization of the *Life* as "intimate biography"[24]—is somewhat misleading, however. The *Life* itself arguably divides chronologically into "private" and "public" parts: book 1 concerns Anselm's early life and years as monk, prior, and abbot at Bec, and book 2 deals with Anselm's tumultuous career as archbishop, but happenings in book 1 are also presented in sophisticated ways as prophetic of those in book 2. Book 2 of the *Life*, like book 1, emphasizes Anselm's private conversation and personal manners in circles friendly to him, but it also paints that picture against the insistent background of public events occurring at the same time and described in greater detail in the *Historia novorum*. Michael Staunton rightly points out, "[Historians] neglect the extent to which Anselm's public life is dealt with in the *Vita*."[25]

The *Life* and *History* do not combine in a simple chronological or topical sequence, one after the other, to produce a unified "bipartite biography" (to use Grandsen's preferred term); rather, they stand in a constant, dynamic interchange with one another, enabled by the history and the protagonists they share and the cross-referencing Eadmer provides. The dialectic effect achieved is that of a "biographical dualism" (to use Thomas Heffernan's preferred term) that highlights a significant biblical and hagiographic difference from the classical convention that simply orders an account of deeds (*praxeis*) logically before an account of character (*ethos*).[26] In the exegetical terms appropriate to biblical and hagiographic reading, deeds (human and divine) belong to *historia*; doctrine, to *allegoria*; morals and ethics, to *tropologia*.

A VICTORINE EXEGETICAL FRAMEWORK FOR EADMER'S *LIFE* AND *HISTORY*

Hugh of Saint Victor composed his influential *Didascalicon* in Paris in the late 1120s, shortly after Eadmer's death in 1124. Hugh's guide to the arts both "recapitulates an entire antecedent tradition" and (in the words of Jerome Taylor) "interprets that tradition . . . at the very dawn of the twelfth-century renaissance,"[27] endeavoring to further its renovation and thus safeguard its continuance within a rapidly changing educational environment. Anselm of Bec and of Canterbury, the "father of scholasticism,"[28] contributed directly (through his writings and pedagogical methods) and indirectly (through his students, notably Anselm of Laon and Honorius Augustodunensis) to the changes that were afoot.[29] Although Eadmer's work predates Hugh's, the Victorine's treatise sheds light upon the traditions Eadmer sought to preserve, on the one hand, and the novelty he embraced as a means of renewal, on the other.

Hugh's *Didascalicon*, like Cassiodorus's *Institutiones divinarum et saecularium lectionum* (*On Divine and Human Readings*), is a bipartite treatise that examines the arts and sciences (in books 1–3) in their relationship to biblical study (treated in books 4–6). Though it is tempting to try to draw structural comparisons between Hugh's two-part *Didascalicon* and Eadmer's "bipartite biography" of Anselm, I restrict my discussion here to Hugh's remarks about history in general and about scripture's historical, allegorical, and tropological senses in particular. For Hugh, history is foundational, allegory is fitted to history through the rule of faith as "a sort of second foundation,"[30] and tropology arises from the combination of the first two. This layered construction and orderly approach yield a twofold fruit: "Twofold is the fruit of sacred reading, because it either instructs the mind with knowledge or it equips it with morals. Of these, the first, namely knowledge, has more to do with history and allegory; the other, namely instruction in morals, has more to do with tropology."[31]

Both Eadmer and Hugh see a close relationship between the understanding of the Bible's tropology and the reading and writings of saints' lives. Hugh worries about the cosmological and philosophical trends then current in theology at Chartres and seeks to secure the centrality of the Bible in education and spiritual formation. Responding to the new academic study of the Bible associated with the assembling of glosses,[32] Hugh insists that biblical study should never become an end in itself, a feast for the curious, but should increase one's love for God and neighbor, as the lives of the saints, who have been schooled in the gospel, bear witness. The puzzles presented by obscure passages should not feed the pride of exegetes, but lead them in humility to the plain sense meaning of passages that clearly teach what is to be believed and practiced. Warning against "an empty desire for knowledge" and an addictive zeal for "untangling the enigmas of the Prophets and the mystical meanings of sacred symbols," Hugh admonishes anyone so addicted and "scorning the simpler Scriptures" to abandon curious pursuits, and "make it a habit of going instead to the lives of the holy fathers and the triumphs of the martyrs and other such writings dictated in a simple style."[33]

The lives of the saints, Hugh teaches, exemplify the goal to which scripture directs its readers and help to ensure the proper interpretation of the Bible. Following Augustine, who in *De doctrina Christiana* (*On Christian Doctrine*) famously reduced the meaning of the scriptures to the twofold law of charity,[34] Hugh places emphasis on the Bible's teaching of virtue by word and example: "This knowledge is got in two ways, namely, by example and by instruction: by example, when we read the deeds of the saints; by instruction, when we learn what they have said that pertains to our disciplining."[35]

Important to note, Hugh makes no distinction here between the virtuous examples set by biblical saints—the patriarchs, for example, and the apostles—and those set by the saints and martyrs of later ages. In fact, he explicitly directs students of biblical tropology to read the hagiographies composed by Gregory the Great: "Among the deeds and sayings of the saints, those marvelously written down by the blessed Gregory should, I think, be taken to heart."[36]

This lack of distinction between "biblical" and "nonbiblical" saints' lives suggests that, for Hugh, there simply can be no such distinction, every saint being—by definition—biblically normed. His specific pointing to Gregory as a hagiographer, moreover, has canonical force. In Hugh's vocabulary, the "hagiography" of the Old Testament includes all the Wisdom literature: "The Old Testament contains the Law, the Prophets, and the Hagiographers."[37] In his thought, the New Testament, broadly understood, is tripartite in a parallel way: the "Gospels" correspond to Law, the "Apostles" to the Prophets, and "the Fathers" to the Hagiographers.[38] Hugh includes "in the third group, first, . . . the Decretals, which we call canons or rules," and, second, "the writings of the Holy Fathers of the Church—Jerome, Augustine, Gregory, Ambrose, Isidore, Origen, Bede, and many other orthodox writers."[39]

Not surprisingly, Eadmer's *Vita Anselmi* (*VA*) describes Anselm as a lover of the scriptures who seeks to understand them,[40] takes them as a practical guide for his daily living, and whose words can therefore be applied to him. For example, Eadmer relates that Anselm sought the advice of Bishop Maurilius about his vocation, "lest he should seem in anything to disobey the commands of Holy Scripture," where it is written, "Do all things with counsel" (Sir. 32:24).[41] As a young monk, newly appointed prior of the monastery at Bec, Anselm, in love with Truth, devotes himself to biblical study: "He applied his whole mind to this end, that according to his faith he might be found worthy to see with the eye of reason those things in the Holy Scriptures which, he felt, lay hidden in a deep obscurity" (*VA* 12). Endeavoring to "overcome evil with good" (Rom. 12:21), Anselm wins the good will and affection of those who initially envied his preferment as prior (*VA* 15–16). Conformed to the pattern of scripture, Anselm also makes its teaching his own, for example, when he, echoing 1 Corinthians 3:2 and explaining his own practice, counsels an abbot to distinguish wisely between the "solid food" that is fitting for "strong souls" and the "milk" to be given to boys who are still infants in the spiritual life (*VA* 39). The young prior's good counsel of others is such, Eadmer opines, that Sulpicius Severus's praise of Saint Martin of Tours can be applied to Anselm of Bec: "The name of Christ, or of justice, or whatever else belongs to the true way of life was always on his lips" (*VA* 14).

For the most part, book 1 of the *Vita Anselmi* joins biblical precepts seamlessly with those of the Rule of Saint Benedict and sees them realized in the virtuous example set by Anselm, who strives to live virtuously in accord with what has been commanded. Anselm's deeds (*historia*) and moral teaching (*tropologia*) by word and example in book 1 are so much in harmony as to be virtually identical. The actions and events narrated in book 2 of the *Life* (corresponding to those in the four books of the *History*), however, are not so easily decipherable, as we shall see, in moral and ethical terms. Anselm's critics in the *History* and (albeit to a lesser extent) in the *Life* include not only kings, barons, and bishops, but also monks of Canterbury, who suffer long and hard during Anselm's prolonged absence from Christ Church Priory at the cathedral through two periods of exile. Anselm himself fears for his own salvation, and the pope in the *History* chastises him as a self-seeking, unfaithful shepherd when he seeks to resign his burdensome duties as archbishop.[42] Southern observes: "It was difficult to know what to think about Anselm."[43] Eadmer's appended book of *Miracles* includes visionary assurances of Anselm's blessedness in heaven, among them the story of a young monk at Christ Church who, perplexed by the devotions of some at Anselm's tomb, "did not know whether to pray for Anselm or to solicit his prayers for himself."[44]

To the *History* and its often scandalous twists and turns, Eadmer ascribes a priority in composition and effectively rests upon its rough foundation, in ways I hope to show, the second, hagiographic account of Anselm's life, *Vita Anselmi*. A famous image in Hugh of Saint Victor's *Didascalicon* similarly places the literal/historical sense of scripture at the foundation of the exegetical edifice, comparing the biblical *historia* to the first layer of rough and uneven stones laid by masons:

> The foundation is in the earth, and it does not always have smoothly fitted stones. The superstructure rises above the earth, and it demands a smoothly proportioned construction. Even so the Divine Page, in its literal sense, contains many things which seem both to be opposed to each other and, sometimes, to impart something which smacks of the absurd or the impossible. But the spiritual meaning admits no opposition; in it, many things can be different from one another, but none can be opposed.[45]

Hugh's preferred name for the foundation is not "letter" but "history": "First you learn history and diligently commit to memory the truth of the deeds that have been performed, reviewing from the beginning to end what has been done, when it was done, where it was done, and by whom it was done."[46] Even as a mason uses a taut cord to guide him in laying a second foundation upon the first, thereby leveling the surface as a base for the next layers, so too the rule of faith guides the interpreter of biblical *historia*: "The taut cord shows the path of true faith."[47] The layers of stone that are fit together upon the foundation, Hugh likens to *allegoria*: "The foundation which is under the earth we have said stands for history, and the superstructure which is built upon it we have said suggests allegory."[48]

Beryl Smalley and others have seized upon this passage as proof (alongside other proofs) that the twelfth century saw a new interest in the historical sense and, insisting upon its fundamental importance and dignity, sought to restrain fanciful allegorization.[49] Henri de Lubac, however, argues that "far from revolutionizing the principles of exegesis by attacking the old allegorizing routine, Hugh of St. Victor is merely trying to consolidate the imperiled tradition."[50] Endangered from opposite directions, this tradition faced, on one side, a rising, philosophical Scholasticism that, in the words of Chenu, "detached itself from sacred history;"[51] on the other side, an apocalypticism that too quickly identified current events with signs of the end-time, labeled public figures with the biblical names of "Antichrist" and "Whore," and divided human history into Trinitarian stages.[52] Summarizing this situation, Kevin Hughes writes: "What M. D. Chenu described as the 'new awareness of history' is reflected in the tendency to immanentize the eschatological and to historicize the mystical."[53]

Hugh of Saint Victor's memorable, architectural image reduces the traditional three or four senses of scripture to a twofold division—foundation (history) and superstructure (allegory and tropology)—as a means of teaching and preserving what Chenu calls the two essential "pieces" of biblical theology, its "letter" and "spirit," "plain" meaning and "hidden" mystery, "the *lectio historiae* and the construction of *allegoria*."[54] The interrelation between the two is such that (as de Lubac puts it) "allegory is in truth the truth of history; the latter, just by itself, would be incapable of bringing itself intelligibly to fulfillment; allegory fulfills history by giving it its sense."[55]

Appearing within a guide to the arts, Hugh's pedagogical innovation in layering allegory atop history had a conservative intent, but his schematic response to the crisis at hand may also have mirrored it and thus contributed to what Kevin Hughes calls the "disintegration of mystagogy."[56] The Victorine's image is artisanal, featuring inert building materials subject to rearrangement, whereas traditional exegetical images capture organic processes. Hugh borrows the famous image from Gregory the Great, but the Victorine also transforms it.[57] Instead of the biblical letter opening to spiritual discovery and nourishment—like bread broken, shared, chewed, and savored, or like a planted seed sprouting through its husk—Hugh's stones laid in the earth may remain there, separable from the superstructure ideally fitted to it. In his schema, which first separates parts and then seeks to join them, Hugh presents history and allegory as "distinct 'orders,' studied under two different but consecutive *disciplinae*, one 'historical' and one 'theological.'"[58] Over the course of time this curriculum had serious consequences, according to Hughes: "*Allegoria*, as a distinct order, came to have a method and structure separate from *historia*, and so, in practice, from exegesis itself."[59]

Pairing his *Historia novorum* with the *Vita Anselmi* as he does, Eadmer constructs his own edifice with a historical foundation and a hagiographic superstructure. The history recounted in the *Vita* is closely fitted to that of the *Historia*, and the two works are necessary to each other for a reader's full understanding, but yet, Eadmer insists, each is self-sufficient enough to be read alone. For Eadmer, the happenings he witnessed during the archiepiscopate of Anselm of Canterbury—politically complicated, scandalous, sublime, miraculous—were all participatory in an unfolding sacred history in which God was acting in and through his saint to accomplish his mysterious purpose in a sinful world. "One of the principal activities of sacred biography is to chronicle the appearance of the inbreaking of the divine in the world," Heffernan remarks.[60] Eadmer found himself too close to the complicated events he recorded to achieve both a detailed, blow-by-blow account of what he heard and saw, on the one hand, and an idealized synthesis of the sacred and the secular in a single, unified history, similar to that effected from a distance by Bede in his *Ecclesiastical History*, on the other. His solution? To set the *History* opposite the *Life*, while using a biblical intertext—itself a narrative, a history—in a sophisticated way to unite them across the gap.

EADMER'S PARABOLIC *HISTORY*

In the preface to the *Historia novorum*, Eadmer declares its purpose: "The main purpose of this work is first to describe how Anselm, Abbot of the Monastery of Bec, was made Archbishop of Canterbury, and then to shew how it came about that, a disagreement having arisen between him and the King of England, he was so often and for so long absent in exile from his country and what has been the outcome of the question in dispute between them" (*HN* 2). Eadmer also briefly identifies the chief point of that disagreement, referring explicitly to the novelty in England of the investiture of bishops and abbots as practiced by the Norman rulers—William I (the Conqueror), William II (Rufus), and Henry I—and of the related demand for clerical homage to be paid to the king. That homage, as the *History* relates, entangled clergymen in feudal obligations that set Church property at risk, that compromised them in the fulfillment of their ecclesiastical obligations to the faithful and to the archbishop of Canterbury as primate, and that hampered the archbishop himself in carrying out his manifold responsibilities. Anselm, therefore, "wished to put an end to this practice of investiture by the King, as being contrary to God and to the canons of the Church, and thereby to prune away the mischiefs resulting from it" (*HN* 2).

The language of pruning is arguably biblical, a subtle allusion to Christ's comparison of the Church to a vine in need of pruning (John 15:2). More obvious biblical allusions of various sorts occur throughout the *History*. Anselm and his critics, for example, quote scripture rhetorically in making their arguments. Anselm's impassioned second speech at the Council of Rockingham uses Christ's words in Matthew 16:18 ("Thou art Peter and on this rock will I build my Church") and Matthew 22:21 ("Render to Caesar the things that are Caesar's and to God the things that are God's) to challenge the English bishops to support his position against that of the king (*HN* 57–58). When William Rufus threatens to take back Anselm's archbishopric should he go to Rome, Anselm answers with the words of the apostles, "It is right to obey God rather than men" (Acts 5:29; *HN* 81). Pope Urban II refuses to accept Anselm's resignation as archbishop, alluding to the parable of the Good Shepherd (John 10:11–18) and Hebrews 12:4: "Bishop! Shepherd! You have not yet suffered bloodshed, no, nor wounds, and are you already seeking to steal away from the care of the Lord's sheep-fold?" (*HN* 103). When Anselm too passively (it seems) prolongs his second exile, a letter of protest likens him to a cowardly shepherd who has abandoned his sheep, leaving them behind to be torn by the wolves (*HN* 161; cf. John 10:12). Pope Pascal writes to King Henry, opposing his investiture of bishops on biblical grounds: the Lord himself, not any earthly king, is "the door" to the sheepfold (John 10:9), and every Christian king is obliged (as is everyone) to "render to God the things that are God's" (Matt. 22:21; *HN* 128–29).

Biblical echoes are also used to describe situations and persons and to express emotions. When the bishops seek to put Anselm on trial (a dramatic scene that inevitably recalls Christ's own trial and that of Stephen in Acts 6–7), one soldier breaks from the crowd, kneels before Anselm, and encourages him to take heart, remembering "the blessed Job how he overcame the devil" (*HN* 61). Anselm's innocence of personal wrongdoing is acknowledged even by the king, and the bishops condemning him are individually dubbed "by some such nickname as Judas the traitor, Pilate, or Herod, or the like" (*HN* 65). A short-lived, superficial reconciliation between the king and Anselm inspires Walter, bishop of Albano, recently arrived from Rome, to exclaim ironically, "Behold, how good and joyful a thing it is for brethren to dwell together in unity!" (Ps. 132:1; *HN* 71). Confronted with the king's demand for reparations, Anselm laments spontaneously in the words of the prophet Jeremiah: "We looked for peace and no good is come, for a time of healing and behold confusion" (Jer. 8:15; *HN* 78).

Eadmer records a vivid, public exchange that suggests that the authority of the Bible itself is being put on trial along with Anselm. Sealed letters from Pope Pascal to King Henry and to Anselm affirm the Church's strict position vis-à-vis the investiture of bishops and abbots and threaten the punishment of excommunication for noncompliance. The three bishops, emissaries for the king, who have returned to England with these letters claim, however, that the pope told them something quite different in a private audience, promising leniency to the king and tolerating his continued practice of investiture. Solemnly they stake their word and that (supposedly) of the pope himself against the pope's own written documents. Anselm's emissary to Rome, the monk Baldwin, decries the duplicity they ascribe to the pope and contests their report. Denigrating the witness of monks like Baldwin and of "sheepskins," Anselm's opponents arouse the protest of monks in the assembly: "Alas then! Are not the gospels themselves written upon sheepskins?" (*HN* 139).

Among the biblical quotations in the *History*, Eadmer attaches special weight to passages read in the context of the liturgy. On the first day of Anselm's entering into his see, for instance, the Gospel reading was

Matthew 6:24: "No man can serve two masters" (*HN* 44). The archbishop himself recalls this verse and discovers its significance as a "forewarning" (*HN* 44) when, early in his archiepiscopate, a quarrel over money arises between him and the king, who regularly sets a price upon his friendship.

Eadmer quotes a single biblical verse three times and singles it out for commentary, thus highlighting its thematic importance. According to the prescribed ritual, at Anselm's consecration as archbishop, the presiding bishops opened a copy of the Gospels and held it, thus opened, over his head. When they examined the book afterward, the following verses were found at the top of the page: "He called many. And at the time of the supper he sent his servant to say to them that were bidden that they should come, for all the things were now ready. And they all with one consent began to make excuses" (Luke 14:16–18; *HN* 43–44).

After supporting the Bible in its two testaments as a yoke upon his shoulders, the bishop-elect is presented with that same Bible at his ordination as a symbol of his teaching authority and duty as a successor of the apostles.[61] The liturgical practice described here by Eadmer is a variant form, attested in some dioceses during the Middle Ages.[62] The opening of the book of the Gospels at random on the solemn occasion of his ordination provides a means for the new bishop to receive a meaningful, personally prophetic word at the start of his ministry. The randomness of the selection likens the liturgical practice superficially to the drawing of lots (attested positively and negatively in scripture as a means of decision-making)[63] and to forms of *sortes bibliae* or *sortes sanctorum* condemned by the Church as divination,[64] but the spirit of the rite, taken in context, is quite different. Here the opening of the Gospel book above the head of the one being ordained recalls the Christ's appropriation in the Letter to the Hebrews of the psalmist's words: "Behold I come: in the head of the book it is written of me: that I should do thy will, O God" (Heb. 10:7; Ps. 39:8).[65] The verse given at ordination bespeaks the minister's vocation and destiny.

The verses read aloud at Anselm's ordination begin a two-part parable. The first part (Luke 14:16–20) details the excuses given by dinner guests who have accepted the host's invitation, but who then refuse the servant's summons to the feast: "Come; for everything is ready now" (Luke 14:17). In this way, they commit "a grievous insult to the host,"[66] who has made his costly preparations based on their initial acceptance. In the second part (vv. 21–24), the master, angry at the initially invited guests, sends his servant out twice into the streets and lanes to fill the empty places at table with "the poor, the crippled, the blind, and the lame" (Luke 14:21). Read in its Lukan context, the guests who make excuses are (as Ernst Wendland explains) "the Pharisees and other religious leaders of the day who were refusing to accept both the message concerning the 'kingdom of God' as well as the divinely chosen messenger."[67]

At Anselm's reception of the pallium, the very same Lukan passage is read, astonishing some of those present, "as it was clear that this had occurred without any fore-thought or pre-arrangement on the part of anyone" (*HN* 73). Eadmer omits "what some said, what some foretold," but he clearly regards the verse as prophetic and alerts his readers to its value in guiding their interpretation of the *History*: "From the subsequent occurrences which, to present a true picture of events, we shall with God's help speak of in their turn, it will be quite evident that it was not by mere chance that on the first occasion of his consecration those particular words of the Lord were found above his head, nor without significance that the second time at the confirmation of his consecration the same words were read in the hearing of the people" (*HN* 73).

At this point, Eadmer leaves interpretation of the parable open to his readers, but his narration of the historical events clearly suggests his own exegesis. By the time Anselm receives the pallium from the altar at Christ Church,[68] the king and the bishops who initially forced the archbishopric upon Anselm (thus accepting, as it were, the divine invitation to be spiritually ruled and nourished at Anselm's hand) have already made their opposition to the archbishop clear (thus refusing the summons). Eadmer records that "a quarrel between [Anselm] and the king" arises even before Anselm's consecration, when the archbishop-elect, "unwilling to despoil the Church" (*nolens ecclesiam . . . expoliare*) (*HN* 40), refuses to renounce claim to lands that had been confiscated by the Crown. Later, when Anselm offers King William five hundred pounds in support of his military campaign in Normandy, the king rejects that amount, demanding a thousand from him—an amount Anselm refuses to give, lest it appear to be "the price of the archbishopric," and his preferment a matter of simony (*HN* 44–45). Soon the king declares his "hatred" of Anselm and refuses him permission to go to Rome to receive the pallium from Urban II, a pope Anselm (unlike the king) has already recognized against the rival claimant, Clement III (*HN* 52). The bishops of England, called to assembly at Rockingham, tell

Anselm that his first loyalty and theirs must be to the king, not the pope—a position Anselm firmly rejects (*HN* 58–59). The bishops then adjudge him "guilty of death" (*HN* 57), and the king deprives Anselm of royal protection, rejecting him as spiritual father (HN 63). At this impasse, a truce is called through the mediation of the barons (*HN* 66–67); William manages to have the pallium brought secretly to England from Rome, with the intention to remove Anselm from his see and to invest another with the archbishop's staff, ring, and pallium (*HN* 68). That proving impossible, and Anselm refusing to receive the pallium from the king's hands, the archbishop receives it from the altar (*HN* 73).

The preceding description of events at the start of Anselm's episcopate indicates the pattern that repeats itself throughout the *History*, as William Rufus and his successor Henry I, together with the bishops, continue to harass the primate, limit him in the exercise of his powers, seize the Church's property, demand clerical homage, and defend their right to invest bishops. These actions and the justifications given for them constitute (in the language of the Lukan parable) the refusals and excuses of those summoned to the supper. When the penalty of excommunication becomes attached to the king's stubborn investiture of bishops and to their acceptance of such an investiture, the parable's imagery of empty seats at the table assumes a special fittingness.

But Eadmer's historical narrative of necessity also shows Anselm declining invitations from, and refusing the summons of, the king and the bishops, who pressure him to take their side, "trying to make him under pretext of doing right do what is not right" (*sub obtentu justitiae contra justitiam*) (*HN* 104). Eadmer defends Anselm against the suspicion of clerical ambition and simony by relating, in dramatic detail, the excuses Anselm gives at the time of his own investiture as archbishop, when he passionately resists the election (*HN* 32–37).[69] "I am already old and unfit for any worldly work," he declares, adding the plea, "Leave me in peace and entangle me not in business which I have never loved, or no good can come of it" (*HN* 33). In Anselm's own understanding, he is no match for the king—a "feeble sheep" yoked with "an untamed bull" (*HN* 36). When the bishops urge him to submit himself to the king, to support what has become customary in the kingdom, and to do his duty to his see (as they perceive it), Anselm refuses, resting "all his reasoning . . . upon the words of God" (as William of Durham admits to the king) (*HN* 62).

As the long contest between the archbishop and the English kings—first William, then Henry—plays out, however, some of the reasons Anselm gives for his actions appear to his contemporaries not as humble or heroic, but rather as selfish excuses to avoid the burden of his office, to flee across the Channel and to remain on the Continent, thus avoiding suffering in solidarity with his flock. Eadmer records the reproof of Pope Urban: "Has Anselm, Anselm the Saint [*ille sanctus*], a man so good and so great, no compunction in leaving Christ's sheep, and that before any fighting, to be torn by the ravening wolves, caring only for his own peace of mind?" (*HN* 103). Anselm's second exile arouses a similar outcry, expressed in one of the letters from England that Eadmer includes in the *History*: "Of your own accord, without being in fact compelled by anyone, you have let yourself be snatched away from our dangers, perhaps in order that you might not feel what we are forced to suffer" (HN 160).

Eadmer's words in defense of Anselm's conduct in the delicate case of King Henry's chosen wife and queen, Matilda of Scotland (1080–1118), might be applied to many other cases where the monk historian both carefully details the sequence of public events and official procedures and also claims personal insight into Anselm's character: "We at any rate who have known his *inmost heart* [*cor ejus*] in this and many other difficulties bear him witness that, as he himself used to say, he had not at that time either the knowledge or the ability to enable him to act more rightly or more justly than he in fact did" (*HN* 126; emphasis added).

Eadmer's insight into, and revelation of, the "inmost heart" (*HN* 126) motivating Anselm's outward conduct—his reading, in short, of the saint's life in its duality—is strikingly parallel to the monk historian's reading of scripture in its intertextual relation, literal and allegorical, to the *History*. After his account of Anselm's death and burial, Eadmer returns again to the passage from Luke 14 and offers his own retrospective interpretation of the significance of the parable of the great feast for understanding Anselm's life. The reading of this parable at Anselm's episcopal consecration and at his reception of the pallium "foreshadowed" all the subsequent events, "seeing that to almost everything which Anselm in his preaching taught or in his teaching forbade, some excuse was made [*excusatio objecta est*] and never were his words effectually obeyed" (*HN* 213).

After recalling in gloomy detail the failure of Anselm's reforms and the backsliding of those who temporarily accepted them, Eadmer laments: "Few are found (I am speaking of men in this world) who, taking the way which the illustrious Father Anselm in his teaching set before them, strive to hasten to the Lord's supper [*ad cœnam Domini*] with pure and single hearts" (*HN* 214). Even as the lord's servant in the parable goes out twice to summon people to fill the banquet hall, taking the places left empty by the originally invited guests, so too, Eadmer explains, Anselm went out twice from England to the Continent. There, in sharp contrast to his reception in England, Anselm finds willing feasters: "That, in these goings-out he, by preaching, by warning, by correcting, brought a vast number of men of other nations to the Lord's supper, we know without any shadow of doubt, we who were his companions in his journeyings and in his labours" (*HN* 214).

Eadmer's interpretation obviously takes more of the Lukan parable into account than just the initial verses that were "at the top of the page" (*in summitate paginae*) (*HN* 43) and previously quoted. His closing remarks about the two goings-out also provide a smooth segue for readers who turn from the *History* to the *Life*, the first book of which (almost half of the whole) presents Anselm at home in his native Aosta and then at Bec. The *History*'s gravitational center is England during the time of Anselm's archiepiscopate, the realm of the initially invited, then refusing, supper guests; the *Life*'s spiritual center is Anselm himself, the monk of Bec who becomes an exile from England and who finds hospitality on the Continent. There he experiences and provides to others (to continue the metaphor of the supper) a foretaste of heaven. Whereas the *History* literally quotes and self-consciously foregrounds the parable, which it sees historically realized during Anselm's term as archbishop, the *Life* provides another interpretation of the parable that focuses not so much on earthly refusals and excuses (though these are recorded), but on divine acceptance. In the process, it also renarrates episodes in the *History*, making Anselm's sanctity—manifest to his closest companions—his best defense.[70]

EADMER'S ALLEGORICAL *LIFE*

The parable in Luke 14:16–24 does not describe the host's supper per se, but, interpreted in its biblical context, the meaning of the supper to which the guests are summoned is clearly eschatological.[71] God is the host. In fact,

Jesus tells the parable at table in the house of a Pharisee, responding to the exclamation of another dinner guest: "Blessed is he that shall eat bread [*panem*] in the kingdom of God!" (Luke 14:15). Eadmer places the image of eating heavenly bread at the beginning of the *Vita Anselmi*. There he tells of a dream-vision that Anselm had as a little boy and liked to recall as an adult. Living in a mountainous region, Anselm imagined God to live high up above the mountains. In his dream one night, the boy is called to climb the mountain and to come to the court of the great king, God. There he finds God alone with his steward. Summoned forward, the boy sits at the king's feet and answers his questions. After this conversation, he is given "the whitest of bread" (*panis nitidissimus*) to eat, and he refreshes himself with it "in God's presence" (*VA* 5). Awakening, the boy believed what he had dreamt to have actually occurred, so real was the experience, and he told others "that he had been fed with the bread of God [*ex pane Dei*]" (*VA* 5).

Two chapters later, Eadmer again refers to "bread of exceptional whiteness" (*panem nitidissimum*) that Anselm's servant discovers, against his expectation and at a time of great hunger, in their backpack, as they trek through the Alps (*VA* 7).[72] The incident occurs literally in the mountains and points to the Divine Providence directing and sustaining the difficult course of Anselm's life from his youth.

Eadmer refers a third time to the dream-vision of Anselm's boyhood when he describes Anselm as the young prior of the Abbey at Bec. A teacher of moral virtue and a wise discerner of the roots of vice, Anselm has become a wise counselor for his fellow monks. To Anselm, Eadmer applies Sulpicius Severus's praise of Saint Martin that "the name of Christ, or of justice or whatever else belongs to the way of true life was always on his lips" (*VA* 14). Following the allegorical linkage of bread with teaching in Gospel accounts (e.g., Matt. 16:5–12; Mark 8:13–21),[73] Eadmer observes: "The reader can easily see that there was something prophetic in that early vision of his in which he was fed with pure bread [*nitido pane*] from the Lord's table" (*VA* 14).

Eadmer's bold decision to echo Anselm's spoken language in the *Life* is not only meant to reveal his character but also to allow the saint to continue to feed and to instruct his listeners by extending that fortunate company to include Eadmer's readers. Significantly, Anselm's teaching regularly occurs during meals as table-talk, sometimes substituting (somewhat controversially) for the reading regularly prescribed by the Benedictine Rule.[74] "We shall describe how Anselm talked at meal-times," Eadmer announces (*VA* 73), going on to give as an example a well-chosen story about a monk who, after having left the world, is now commanded by his abbot to busy himself with the temporal concerns of the monastery. This monk, seated with Anselm at table, raises his concern about this spiritual endangerment, to which Anselm replies with an extended similitude comparing the "whole life of man" to a "a mill built over a swift-flowing river," where three types of men grind their flour (*VA* 74). The man of the third type, practicing obedience and other virtues, keeps his flour "pure and without loss so that it may feed him in eternity" (*VA* 76).

Staunton has observed that the selection of this particular similitude, out of Anselm's many similitudes, sheds light on Anselm's own situation and self-understanding, since he—like his conversation partner—is also a monk who, first as prior, then as abbot, and now as archbishop of Canterbury, is heavily engaged in worldly affairs, in submission (he believes) to God's direct will and not merely with God's permission.[75] In this way it answers to some of Anselm's contemporary critics, who imagine him to have actively sought the archbishopric. At the same time, we may add, the specific choice of a similitude involving flour and the bread of eternal life fits well with Eadmer's extended exegesis in the *Life* of the Lukan parable of the great supper, highlighted in the *History*. Concerning the man of the third type, Anselm relates, "He asks, he begs to be excused [*excusat se*]" from his duty at the grindstone, but he answers the summons in obedience (*VA* 76).

The biblical imagery of the great, eschatological feast adds significance to Anselm's miracles involving food. When food supplies run short at the monastery, Anselm exhorts the cellarers: "Trust in God, and I am confident that he will supply what is needful for you" (*VA* 47)—a confidence that is wondrously rewarded. His hospitality to guests at Bec is generous and famous (*VA* 46–47). When an inhospitable baron fails to offer Anselm lodging and supper, he leaves, hungry and without shelter for the night, meeting on the way another monk who offers a place for his lodging, but who has only "bread and cheese" to offer the abbot—a menu Anselm supplements through his order that a net be cast quickly into the nearby river (*VA* 26–27). The miraculous haul of an "unusually large trout" (*tructam insolitae magnitudinis*) (*VA* 27) recalls, of course, miracles of Jesus,[76] but

Eadmer's selection and narration of this particular episode contrasts the inhospitableness of the baron with the feasting of Anselm and his monks, who trust in God to supply their needs.[77] Anselm's need was a summons to kindness that the baron in the story, like the originally invited guests in the Lukan parable (and, by extension, like the English bishops, barons, and kings), declined to heed, but which first the poor monk and then Anselm himself accepted.

Just as the miracles of multiplied loaves and fishes in the Gospels are understood to foreshadow the institution of the Eucharist, Anselm's miracles of bread and fish are coupled in Eadmer's *Life* with Eucharistic signs and symbols. Instructed by a vision, a leper drinks from the water with which Anselm has washed his hands during Mass, and he is healed (*VA* 57–59). Like the Canaanite woman who begs for her daughter's healing as puppies beg for the "crumbs that fall from the table of their masters" (Matt. 15:27), two knights beg for scraps of food from Anselm's table in order to be healed (*VA* 117–18). A baron, present at Anselm's Mass, is healed there (*VA* 119). William of Warelwast, by contrast, eats "daily at the Father's table" (*VA* 97–98), when Anselm's journey from England is delayed at Dover by an adverse wind, only to act later as King William's Judas-like agent in searching the archbishop's baggage, humiliating him publicly at the shore before his departure into exile (*VA* 98).

The *Life* emphasizes Anselm's warm reception on the Continent, where he is met "by crowds of people . . . with joy and enthusiasm" (*VA* 102). Even in places where he is unknown, people point him out "as a man of God [*virum vitae*]" (*VA* 104). The Roman Curia rejoices at his arrival, and the pope speaks before the assembly, praising Anselm as a "man of high religion and virtue . . . to be venerated [as primate of England] almost as our equal" (*VA* 105). The Muslim soldiers of Roger of Apulia are drawn to him by his manifest humility and gentleness (*VA* 111–12). English pilgrims to Rome prostrate themselves before him (*VA* 114). The people of Rome—even the enemies of Urban II—honor Anselm as a saint (*sanctus homo*) (*VA* 115). At Lyons, where Anselm takes up a longer residency, the local archbishop treats Anselm as his friend and superior (*VA* 116).

Anselm's acceptance on the Continent during two exiles—a welcome that answers a divine summons—bears out the historian's interpretation at the close of the *Historia novorum* of the servant's successful goings out in

Luke 14: "In these goings out [Anselm] . . . brought a vast number of men of other nations to the Lord's supper" (*HN* 214). Eadmer seals this line of interpretation in the *Life*—with the words of the Gospel read to Anselm at the very hour of his death on Wednesday during Holy Week: "Ye are they which have continued with me in my temptations; and I appoint you a kingdom, as my Father hath appointed unto me, that ye may eat and drink at my table in my kingdom" (Luke 22:28–30; *VA* 142–43). This passage closes an envelope pattern that begins, as it were, with the words of the dinner guest that prompt the beginning of the parable of the great feast: "Blessed is he that shall eat bread [*panem*] in the kingdom of God!" (Luke 14:15).

READING THE *LIFE* AS ALLEGORICALLY FITTED TO EADMER'S *HISTORY*

The *Vita Anselmi* is carefully constructed. As in the later *Life of Aelred of Rievaulx* (ca. 1167) by Walter Daniel, Eadmer narrates Anselm's inception of monastic life precisely in chapter 7 of book 1, signaling the young man's sharing in the Lord's rest on the seventh day (Gen. 2:2–3). The description of Anselm as an educator of young monks (*VA* 16–21) is balanced and explicated later by Anselm's corrective instruction of an abbot regarding the proper treatment of boys (*VA* 37–39). The prophetic command of Maurilius, archbishop of Rouen, that Anselm neither resign his post as prior nor refuse a higher office (*VA* 21–22) prepares both for Anselm's election as abbot (*VA* 44–45) and for his investiture and consecration as archbishop (*VA* 64–65, 66). Staunton notes that Eadmer puts on the lips of the devil accusations of Anselm, prior to his election as abbot at Bec, that were also on the human lips of Anselm's detractors, then and later (*VA* 43).[78] In an important conversation with Archbishop Lanfranc (1005–89) about the saints of England, Anselm interprets the martyrdom of Saint Elphege as a choice to die rather than to commit injustice by despoiling his own men of their money: *nisi homines suos eorum pecunia spoliaret* (*VA* 51); later Eadmer uses this same language to explain Anselm's consequential decision not to pay the sum demanded by the king at the cost of despoiling his own men (*spoliatis hominibus suis*) (*VA* 67). Eadmer places Anselm's bipartite dream-vision of the worldly way (symbolized by people carried off in a swift and muddy torrent) and of the monastic way (envisioned as a grassy paradise) precisely at the center of the chapters in book 1 that narrate his years at Bec (*VA* 35–36). Anselm awakes suddenly from it after declaring his heartfelt desire to see what true patience (*patientia vera*) is (*VA* 36).

Anselm's unfulfilled desire in the dream is what the reader is allowed to see in Eadmer's portrait of the long-suffering saint, who has decided firmly to take heaven as his goal in life. Precisely here at the end of this visionary chapter, Eadmer explains why he has scattered Anselm's own words throughout the *Life*: "For it seems to me impossible to obtain a full understanding of the tenor of his life if only his actions are described" (*VA* 36). Anselm's talk, especially with those closest to him, provides a needed gloss.

Similarly, Eadmer judges it impossible to understand Anselm fully if one reads either the *History* or the *Life* alone. In the preceding analysis, we have taken seriously Eadmer's claim that the *History* has some sort of priority in the orders both of composition and of reading, so that the Lukan parable literally proclaimed and meditated upon in the *History* is extended allegorically in the *Life*. The likelihood that the two works were also somehow written in tandem, however, allows for the priority of history to be taken also in an episodic sense that enables and requires a back-and-forth reading of individual scenes that appear from different perspectives in the *History* and the *Life*. This layered approach is analogous to the way scripture interprets scripture, a second foundation smoothing the uneven first foundation of Hugh of Saint Victor's biblical edifice.

Southern has commented on one illustrative example, comparing the accounts given in the *History* and in the *Life* of Anselm's dedication of the church at Harrow. In the much longer account in the *History*, the bishop of London disputes Anselm's right to dedicate the church, situated on land belonging to Canterbury, because it stands within the boundaries of his diocese (*HN* 45–47). Maintaining the practice and tradition of his predecessors, Anselm dedicates the church. In the *Life*, by contrast, there is no mention of the dispute over jurisdiction. Instead Eadmer relates that a clerk from London arrives on the scene and manages to steal the chrismatory to be used in the rite, causing a delay as people search for it. Miraculously the clerk carrying the stolen chrismatory loses his sense of direction and keeps returning to the scene of the crime instead of going away from it. His odd behavior is observed by the crowd, and he is seized, the chrismatory recovered, and the rite of dedication performed by the archbishop (*VA* 67–68). Southern remarks that the *History* and the *Life* present here "two sides of the story"— one "public," the other "private."[79] The odd story in the *Life* is comprehensible, he adds, if one knows the historical backstory: "The theft of the chrismatory was no doubt an attempt to prevent the consecration going forward."[80] Exactly this historical interconnection, however, undermines Southern's public/private distinction, since the theft was publicly known. Using exegetical language instead, Staunton more fittingly calls the account in the *Life* "an allegory of the challenge to Anselm's archiepiscopal rights."[81]

Observing that "patristic works of exegesis display aspects of thought and attitude easily identifiable in Eadmer's work,"[82] Staunton underscores the hagiographer's careful attention to the exact placement of stories (both miracles and parabolic similitudes) in the *Life*, such that they do not stand alone; rather, they both gain significance from, and impart significance to, the historical events that contextualize them. Harassed by the king and the king's men, Anselm weeps at the sight of a hare, chased by hounds, that flees for safety under the legs of Anselm's horse, which the barking dogs then surround (*VA* 89–90). The reader immediately senses Anselm's affective identification with the little animal at the literal/historical level of interpretation. Anselm himself provides an eschatological interpretation, likening the frightened hare to a soul bereft of help and surrounded by mocking, menacing demons at the hour of death (*VA* 89–90). Anselm's eschatological exegesis enables the story to be extracted from the *Life* and put to sermonic uses, but in its own context it reinforces the view suggested in the *Historia novorum*, namely, that Anselm's frustrations in the exercise of his archbishopric put him in fear for his own soul's salvation: "He began to fear that all this might spell his own condemnation in the sight of God" (*HN* 79; see also 92–93).

The story in the *Life* that immediately follows that of the cornered hare tells of a bird whose foot is tied to a string (*VA* 90–91). After repeated attempts to fly away, the bird breaks the string and escapes his captor. Anselm sees in the bird's attempts an allegorical representation of an individual's efforts to break the chains of vicious habits. In its narrative context, however, it also symbolizes Anselm's thrice repeated attempts to gain the king's permission to fly away (so to speak) from England and, then, his final decision to go to Rome, regardless of the king's threats (*VA* 91–93). Eadmer includes in this chapter one of his many explicit cross-references to the *Historia novorum*: "Many more things than these took place over this affair, but since we have written of them elsewhere, we shall here shortly dispose of them" (*VA* 92).[83] This historical context allows one to draw a comparison between the boy tormenting the bird and the king inhibiting Anselm. It also implies that Anselm's decision to leave is a virtuous one, made firmly and in inner freedom from enslaving fear.

Anselm's similitudes imitate Jesus's own parabolic teaching in the Gospels; Eadmer's hagiography makes use of them not simply to illustrate Anselm's talk, but also to interpret events in Anselm's life, endowing them with a biblical significance that is not always immediately apparent. In the *History*, for example, Anselm speaks to the assembled bishops at the Council at Rockingham. Reminding them of their earlier promises to support him in the exercise of the archbishopric as primate of England, Anselm also recalls his great reluctance to accept that office and insists that his humble protests at the time of his election were genuine: "But lest anyone not knowing my conscience in this matter should be offended in me, I protest (I speak the truth) that, were it not for submission to the Will of God, I should that day, if offered the choice, have chosen *to be thrown upon a blazing pyre and to be burned alive* [*in ardentem rogum comburendus praecipitari*] rather than be raised to the dignity of the archbishopric" (*HN* 55; emphasis added).

The rhetoric is high, and the image is graphic. Anselm had foreseen that things would go badly between him and the king; perhaps he also foresaw that he would not be able to rely on his fellow bishops, who now stand with the king against him. Anselm insists that he would rather have been burned alive, thrown bodily on a pyre, than be raised to the primacy. Why does Anselm use this particular image? Is it simply to express in the strongest possible terms his earlier terror at the thought of becoming archbishop of Canterbury? Is it an indirect way of describing his present, tortuous situation as comparable to be being burned alive? Eadmer describes how the bishops physically lifted Anselm up and carried him (*portaverunt*) to the church upon his election against his will—an action that indeed resembles being picked up and thrown "upon a blazing pyre" (*HN* 35, 55). Does the archbishop see himself even now as a burnt offering, a sacrifice, a scapegoat? Has the will of God left him without a choice? Has he not freely accepted God's will? Or does he believe his election not to have been God-willed, but only God-permitted?[84]

In the *History*, matters remain somewhat opaque. The fiery image is not interpreted by Eadmer. The reader senses Anselm's self-defensiveness. Some of his listeners have taken offense at him, been scandalized by him. The truth of Anselm's conscience, his inmost thoughts, and intentions are finally hidden from others, despite his public declarations.

In the *Life*, however, Eadmer makes a significant use of fire imagery in three different passages and links it specifically to Anselm's assumption of his duties as archbishop of Canterbury. Staunton calls attention to the telling placement of the first of two miracle stories that are virtually doublets.[85] The first miracle took place at Winchester on Easter Sunday, April 17, 1093, occurring precisely in the interval between Anselm's forced investiture on March 6 and his episcopal consecration as archbishop on December 4. A fire breaks out in the city and threatens to consume the house where Anselm lodges. Anselm and his companions are forced to flee. Bishop Gundulf and Baldwin, Anselm's fellow monk and faithful assistant, urge Anselm to make the sign of the cross in the face of the flames. Anselm at first resists, declaring himself unworthy of a miracle: "'On my account?' he answered, 'these are idle words [*nichil est*]'" (*VA* 66). When Anselm finally does raise his hand to make the sign, however, the flames immediately die down.

Related in the chapter between those describing Anselm's election (*VA* 64–65) and his consecration (*VA* 66–67), this miraculous episode involving a fiery conflagration gives figurative expression to the life-threatening danger Anselm faces in the form of the archbishopric, which will put him gravely to the test.[86] It symbolizes God's will and his submission to it in the sign of the cross Anselm finally makes. In the quoted words "nichil est," Eadmer not only gives voice to a characteristic idiom of Anselm's, but also echoes Anselm's very words of resistance to his election, as recorded in the *History*. There, as in the *Life*, Eadmer describes Anselm being forcibly seized and physically carried into the church while the bishops sing the *Te Deum*; the *History* adds, however, that Anselm, protesting his lack of consent, cries out, "It is a nullity, a nullity, [*nihil est . . . nihil est*] all this that you are doing" (*HN* 35).

The second miracle involving fire virtually repeats the first, but with important variations that clearly signify God's powerful providence and Anselm's greater submission to God's will. Like the first, Eadmer places it, both chronologically and rhetorically, at an important turning point, sandwiching it between three chapters that record mysterious foretellings of the death of King William Rufus (*VA* 122–24), on the one hand, and the chapter that actually announces that news, bringing with it a summons from the new king, Henry I, to return to England (*VA* 125–26), on the other. Eadmer specifies that the fire broke out at a monastery called La Chaise-Dieu, located in Auvergne, about seventy miles from Lyons, three days after (*post triduum*) the latest of the previously mentioned revelations had been received (*VA* 125). The temporal allusion has, of course, a liturgical resonance, hinting at Anselm's share in Christ's resurrection.

Unlike the fire at Winchester, for which no cause is given, the fire at La Chaise-Dieu literally falls from heaven: a bolt of lightning during a storm at night strikes a building, setting stored hay ablaze. Alone together, Eadmer observes Anselm's complete calm, his unhurried rising from his bed, and his free decision, without urging from anyone, to go to meet the fire. Anselm immediately (*mox*) raises his hand. Whereas the flames in the first of the two miracles simply die down at the sign of the cross, the flames at La Chaise-Dieu "sink down as if they were stooping to receive his blessing" (*VA* 125). The damage caused by the fire in Winchester is also much greater than that of the second, where a special protection is noticeable: "While some of the surrounding houses were destroyed, no damage was done to the hay of the monks whose guest Anselm was" (*VA* 125–26).

At King Henry's summons to England, Anselm crosses the Channel. Precisely at this point in the *Vita Anselmi*, Southern notes, Eadmer's reporting becomes short, concise, almost entirely lacking in the detail characteristic of the earlier chapters.[87] Anselm's actual crossing of the Channel in September 1100 goes without note; Eadmer simply reports that Anselm met with the king in Salisbury, with the result that the old battle over clerical homage and investiture was renewed and eventually led to Anselm's return to Rome.

Anselm's return to England after his first exile, however, inevitably recalls the archbishop's earlier flight from that land. Eadmer's artistic hagiography places there, between the two fiery miracles, a third, explicitly biblical, allusion to fire. Out of England and safely arrived at Wissant, we are told, Anselm "rejoiced exceedingly and gave thanks repeatedly to God because he saw that he had escaped *as from the great furnace of Babylon*, and had attained a sort of peak of calmness and rest" (*VA* 100; emphasis added).

This sentence in the *Life* is followed immediately by a passage quoted almost from the *History* that narrates King William II's rapid and ruthless seizure of the properties belonging to the see of Canterbury and the nullification of any agreements concluded during Anselm's term of office, which the king now regards as ended. The narrative effect is that of a split screen that shows Anselm rejoicing on one side of the Channel and William Rufus raging on the other side. The quotation of the *History* within the *Life* here and elsewhere also demonstrates how the two works are made to fit together to form a double foundation, historical and allegorical, at the base of a rising edifice of anticipated future narratives looking back to Anselm's actions as setting a precedent for imitation.[88]

The allusion to the "great furnace of Babylon" (*VA* 100) directs readers to chapter 3 of the book of Daniel, which narrates the story of Shadrach, Meshach, and Abednego—three Judean exiles who are bound and "thrown into the furnace of blazing fire" (Dan. 3:21) for their refusal to worship the golden statue made by King Nebuchadnezzar in violation of God's commandment against idolatry. The brief allusion brilliantly picks up on Anselm's cryptic comment, recorded in the *History*, about being "thrown upon a blazing pyre . . . to be burned alive" (*HN* 55). In so doing, it interprets Anselm's resistance to election as archbishop as including an anxious recognition that that election will entail temptations to idolatry, to worshipping the king instead of God, out of weakness and mortal fear. Biblically interpreted, Anselm's stated preference for the pyre now signals his refusal of idolatry and his willingness to suffer a sort of martyrdom in submission to God's will, not in the end by escaping the archiepiscopate but by accepting its duties. Shadrach, Meshach, and Abednego are singled out for accusation, after all, by Chaldeans who envy their preferment for leadership positions in the province of Babylon (Dan. 3:8–12), a scenario strangely parallel to that of the abbot of Bec made archbishop of Canterbury and then accused of treason by the English bishops.

Anselm's prayers of rejoicing and thanksgiving at his escape from the furnace do not remove from him the responsibilities of the archiepiscopate; to the king's chagrin and confusion, Anselm leaves England still carrying the staff of the archbishop of Canterbury. His rejoicing is thus an escape *from* the furnace that occurs, ironically, while still *in* the furnace. Similarly, the three Judean exiles in Babylon sing their famous songs of praise from within the furnace, where they are protected from the blaze by an angel and by a mysterious, moist wind.[89] This detail also strengthens the pattern of correspondence. In the *Life*, the wind at first pushes the ship on which Anselm has embarked back to England, but it suddenly changes direction at Anselm's tearful word of unconditional submission to God's will, enabling him to cross the channel. "I am ready to obey [God's] will," Anselm confesses, "for I am not mine, but his" (*VA* 99).

"Were it not for submission to the Will of God," Anselm tells the bishops assembled at Rockingham, he would have preferred the pyre to the archbishopric (*HN* 55). Given that hellfire is reserved for those who reject God's will, Anselm's graphic image inevitably calls up yet another pattern of biblical imagery. In Matthew 13, for example, the parables of the wheat and the tares describes the weeds at harvest time being bound up in bundles and then burnt in the fire (Matt. 13:30); Jesus himself then explains that the weeds represent the "children of the wicked one," who will be "cast . . . into the furnace of fire" (Matt. 13: 38, 44) at the time of judgment.

Anselm certainly worries about his own salvation, writing to Pope Urban from Lyons: "And now that I have been four years in that episcopate, I have borne no fruit, but in vexations of my soul innumerable and horrible have lived uselessly, so that day after day I desired rather to die out of England than to live there. Were I to end there this present life as I was, I foresaw the damnation rather than the salvation of my soul" [*plus videbam animae meae damnationem quam salutem*] (*HN* 92). He confesses: "I kept seeing in that country many evils which it were wrong for me to tolerate but which I had not a bishop's freedom to correct" (*HN* 92), his hands being tied by the king and his fellow bishops. Lest his soul be "plunged into suffering eternal," he begs to be released from "the chain of . . . slavery" (*HN* 93). Anselm cannot claim success as archbishop of Canterbury; his unfulfilled duties and curtailed activities, compounded by his flight from England at the cost of banishment by the king, stand, in his own mind and that of others, in judgment against him. In the *Life*, Eadmer uses the "great furnace of Babylon" rather than the "furnace of fire" of Matthew 13 to make Anselm's sanctity under persecution his best defense. Eadmer's marvelous *in bono* commentary in the *Life* on the fiery image in Anselm's first speech at Rockingham resists any possible *in malo* interpretation of it, but a tension remains between *History* and *Life*, between outward action and moral character—a tension that Eadmer's allegory, laid on the stony, uneven foundation of history, only imperfectly remedies.

THE TEST OF CANONIZATION

During the twelfth century, when Eadmer was finishing his twofold, sacred biography of Anselm and Hugh of Saint Victor was about to write his *Didascalicon*, a trend was developing in the Church that would eventually reserve the canonization of saints to the authority of the pope. The first papal canonization was that of Saint Gerard of Toul by Pope Leo IX in 1050. Eric Waldram Kemp describes the development: "The first papal canonizations coincide with the early stages of the recovery of the see of Rome from its tenth-century degradation, and with the beginning of the religious revival of the eleventh century which was to contribute so much to the increase of papal power."[90] The Gregorian reforms (ca. 1050–1110) that mandated clerical celibacy, fought lay investiture, and punished simony also endeavored to safeguard against abuses in the recognition of saints. Pope Urban II, to whom Anselm appealed during his first exile, canonized two saints, Saint Nicholas Peregrinus and the Empress Adelaide; Pope Paschasius II canonized Saint Peter of Anagni in 1109.[91]

As the canonization process gradually developed and centralized, the bishop of the local diocese came to bear responsibility for presenting the candidate for consideration to the higher ecclesiastical authority (i.e., the archbishop or primate), who then brought the matter before the pope through both a written *Life*, attesting to that person's virtues and orthodox belief, and also eyewitness accounts of miracles. In this scenario, miracles alone do not suffice to prove sanctity, nor does local acclaim. The pope by the grace of his office must finally enter the saint's name into the *catalogus sanctorum*, "the canon of saints."[92]

Jay Rubenstein suggests that Lanfranc, Anselm's former teacher at Bec and his predecessor as archbishop of Canterbury, was inspired by this development in his effort to scrutinize the existing cults of Anglo-Saxon saints: "It is perhaps natural that he [as primate of England] would take upon himself the papal duty of determining if reputed saints were in fact saints."[93] The *Vita Anselmi* records a telling conversation between Lanfranc and Anselm in which Lanfranc openly expresses his "doubts about the quality of their sanctity" and about the veneration of Elphege, in particular, as a martyr (*VA* 51). Citing the example of John the Baptist, universally recognized as a martyr, Anselm replies with a theological argument that broadens the idea of dying for Christ to include a Christlike dying for justice (an argument that guides his own conduct). Eadmer, too, replies, recalling the wider context of Christian witness within which Elphege was first taken captive by his enemies.

Rubenstein has persuasively argued that Eadmer ardently supported the continued cult of Anglo-Saxon saints and the veneration of their relics; he also associated the decline in devotion to these same saints with England's troubled recent history. The *Historia novorum* pointedly links Dunstan and Elphege with Anselm. It also includes a lengthy digression on the cope of the bishop of Benevento, which recalls to Eadmer's remembrance the time of King Cnut and Queen Emma (ca. 984–1052), to whom an earlier bishop of Benevento had presented the arm of Saint Bartholomew as a precious relic, vouching for its authenticity with a solemn oath at Christ Church in Canterbury (*HN* 107–10). Eadmer relates, too, a self-deprecating story about his coming to possess only a small relic of Saint Prisca (*HN* 162–63; *VA* 133–34). Remembering England's past devotion, Eadmer implies criticism of his own, less pious time: "For in those days people in England usually considered the relics of saints [*patrocinia sanctorum*] more valuable than anything else in the world" (*HN* 109). In sharp contrast to Eadmer's devotion to the saints, King William Rufus habitually swears by the "Holy Face of Lucca" (*per Vultum de Luca*) (*HN* 101); the king is reported, too, to have publicly denied God's knowledge and justice and to have refused to invoke the saints, denying their power of intercession (*HN* 101–2).

Writing at this critical time, when saints were put to the test not only by their own trials and tribulations but also by the Church, Eadmer knew and understood that the credibility of the saint depended also on the credibility of the hagiographer, whose duty it was both to be historically accurate and thus believable, on the one hand, and as a believer to confess the faith that transfigures earthly experience, on the other hand. Eadmer answered to this challenge by writing both a *History* and a *Life*, cross-referencing the two writings in various ways in order to join them. The *Life* often refers its readers explicitly to the *History*, and the *History* points implicitly to the *Life* through its parabolic ambiguities and its own closing exegesis.

Eadmer is careful in the *Life* to name his sources for some of the recounted miracles and to claim his own status as an eyewitness to others. He calls down a curse upon any hagiographer who perjures himself through spreading falsehoods: "I affirm that it is a shocking thing for anyone knowingly to write what is false in sacred histories [*in sacris historiis*]. For the soul of the writer is slain every time they are read or listened to, since in the things which he has falsely written he tells abominable lies to all his readers" (*VA* 149). The phrase "in sacred histories" recalls an earlier age in hagiographic writing—the age, perhaps, of Bede and of Sulpicius Severus—when there was no need for dualistic biography, for both a *History* and a *Life*, because no temporal event occurred outside the experience of faith; at the same time, however, the phrase, applied particularly to the *Life*, clearly sets it as "sacred history," akin to biblical history, apart from the "secular" history of the *Historia novorum*.

Eadmer's hope that his readers would read both works seems not to have been generally realized, judging by the extant manuscripts. The *Historia novorum* survives in only two early manuscripts, both of English provenance, whereas nineteen copies of the *Vita Anselmi* dating from the twelfth through the fourteenth century are extant, most of which were copied not in England but on the Continent.[94] Eadmer's *Vita Anselmi* "seems never to have enjoyed in England even the modest popularity which it obtained abroad," Southern remarks. Indeed, everything suggests that in England Anselm only slowly gained the reputation belonging to a saint and supportive of his canonization.

The great advocate of Anselm's cause was Thomas Becket (1118–70), who used Anselm's prayers and who took Anselm as a model for his own archiepiscopate, its legal contests, and its time of exile. Consecrated archbishop of Canterbury in 1162, Becket requested Anselm's canonization at the Council of Tours in May 1163, and presented Pope Alexander III with an account of Anselm's *Life* and *Miracles*, probably composed by John of Salisbury (1110s–80).[95] According to Southern, John of Salisbury based his *Life of Anselm* on Eadmer's, which Salisbury abridges, providing no new information; the miracles Salisbury reports are also (with one exception) those found in Eadmer's book of *Miracles*.[96] On June 9, 1163, Pope Alexander wrote in reply to Archbishop Becket, instructing Becket, as primate, "'to determine whether Anselm ought to be canonized or not' in consultation with 'an assembly of his suffragans, abbots, and other prominent ecclesiastics of the province,' reserving to himself [as pope] only the right of confirmation."[97] Since Becket's own fight in defense of the Church's independence from royal control began soon thereafter, leading to his exile in October 1164, and his murder in Canterbury in 1170, the decision about Anselm's canonization was apparently left in suspense. Becket himself was canonized, however, in 1173, setting an important precedent for Anselm's own eventual recognition as a saint, albeit one generally remembered more today for his prayers, meditations, and extraordinary theological writings than for his sufferings in exile. Anselm, declared a doctor of the Church in 1720 by Pope Clement XI, was finally canonized, it seems, only belatedly and irregularly when his name and feast (April 21) first appeared in John Molanus's 1568 edition of the Roman Canon, which included additions to the Canon based on the calendars of Belgian churches. Tracing this complicated history, Southern credits Eadmer's *Vita Anselmi* for Anselm's canonization, since his fame had spread "in Flanders, where Eadmer's biography had gained an early popularity."[98]

Inspired by scripture's own double foundation in history and allegory, Eadmer sought in his *History* and *Life* of Anselm to render his tempestuous career as archbishop of Canterbury intelligible as a Christlike acting and suffering. Anselm's eventual canonization and that of other saints controversial in their own lifetimes had consequences, in turn, for biblical reading in the early modern period. I mentioned in the introduction to this book that the great thirteen-century commentator on the *Decretals* of Gratian, Henricus de Segusio (1200–1271), otherwise known as Hostiensis, defended the authority and the responsibility of the pope to canonize saints by drawing a telling comparison between the correct interpretations of the Bible and of a saint's life: "It is part of the pope's commission to decide doubtful places of Scripture; how much more, therefore, should it be his office to determine doubtful cases of sanctity in which greater dangers may be involved."[99] For Eadmer, the interpretive challenges of scripture and of a saintly candidate such as Anselm are similarly set side by side, neither being able to illumine the other perfectly. Anselm's own appeal to the arbitration of the pope, echoed by his hagiographer, signals the direction to which hagiographers of a new, Scholastic era would turn increasingly in the quest for what Donald Prudlo calls "certain sainthood."[100]

PART 2

The Saint's *Life* in the Scholastic Age

CHAPTER FIVE

SAINT FRANCIS OF ASSISI AS "NEW EVANGELIST" IN THOMAS OF CELANO'S *VITA PRIMA* AND BONAVENTURE'S *LEGENDA MAIOR*

His highest aim . . . was to pay heed to the holy gospel
in all things and through all things,
to follow the teaching of our Lord Jesus Christ,
and to retrace His footsteps completely.

— Thomas of Celano, Vita prima

The strong, literal affinity between sacred scripture and hagiography reached both a zenith and a crisis in the successive early *Lives* of Francis of Assisi (1181–1226). Pope Gregory IX canonized Francis in July 1228, prior to the composition (commissioned by that same pope and completed in 1229) of Thomas of Celano's first *Life* of the saint (*Vita prima*). In the papal bull announcing Francis's canonization, *Mira circa nos* (1228), Gregory places Francis squarely within a biblical tradition, likening him in his virtues to Samson, Abraham, Jacob, Paul, and Christ himself, who "although rich, became poor for our sake" (2 Cor. 8:9).[1] Dominique Poirel has argued, however, that Francis's reception of the stigmata of Christ's own wounds (an unprecedented marvel) marks a rupture in the history of sanctity and in the narration of a saint's life.[2] In the pages of his legends, "Francis has not merely *acted* like Christ, but he has, in a way, *become* Christ," observes Matthew Kozlowski.[3]

Francis's ardent, literal fulfillment of the gospel's counsels, his evangelical preaching, and the divine seal of the stigmata worked together to constitute a hagiography of the *poverello* ("little poor man") not only as an illustrative commentary upon the gospel, but also even as a sort of fifth Gospel that renewed the apostolic four—Matthew, Mark, Luke, and John—and vied with them as a source of contemporary exemplarity for the faithful. In the *Vita prima*, Thomas of Celano praises Francis as "a new Evangelist" (*novus evangelista*) whose charismatic life, teaching, and preaching "filled the whole world with the gospel of Christ, ... edifying his listeners by his example as much as by his words, as he made of his whole body a tongue"[4] for the Word of God.[5]

In the *Lives* of Francis, that maximal, saintly closeness to the gospel triggered a crisis in the genre of hagiography itself, which took on new Scholastic forms in the overlapping contexts of two forums: academic debates about evangelical perfection and an increasingly well-defined, centralized canonization process that sought to certify both a candidate's heroic virtue and the miracles wrought by God through his or her intercession. Francis lived in strict accord with his understanding of the gospel's demands,[6] making the canonization of the saint and the papal approval of the Rule of the Ordo Fratrum Minorum akin to the magisterial approval of Francis's biblical understanding. Buttressing the oral approval given in 1209/10 by Pope Innocent III, Pope Honorius III in 1223 confirmed "with Our Apostolic Authority" the Rule and Life of the Lesser Brothers, namely, "to observe the Holy Gospel of Our Lord Jesus Christ by living in obedience, without anything of one's own, and in chastity."[7] The Church's approving decrees were, moreover, linked by Francis's hagiographers to God's own inerrant sign of approbation in the stigmata marking Francis's hands, feet, and side; Bonaventure likens these imprinted marks to the writing of the commandments on stone tablets by "the finger *of the living God*" (Rev. 7:2; Deut. 9:10).[8]

In this chapter, in the first section, I describe how hagiography's traditional affinity to scripture, both in content and form, is maximized in episodes in Francis's life as they are narrated in both the *Vita prima* of Thomas of Celano and Bonaventure's *Legenda maior* (*Longer Life*, 1260–63), albeit in contrastive ways. In the second section, I sketch the Scholastic disputes about evangelical perfection that were raised by the canonization of Francis and the papal approval of the Franciscan Rule. In Bonaventure's response to these disputed questions, biblical exegesis and the lives of the saints are significantly intertwined. In the third section, I probe parallels between biblical and saintly authorship and authority. Here, moving beyond John Coakley's important argument about the process of Francis's early conversion,[9] I consider the contrastive ways that Celano and Bonaventure present the converted life of Francis as a work of grace. In the fourth, fifth, and sixth sections, I argue that Bonaventure's sustained, narrative presentation of Francis's virtues in the "Inner Life" of the *Legenda maior* (chapters 5 through 12) functions as a commentary on the beatitudes in Jesus's Sermon on the Mount, enlisting its authority to answer the disputed questions about evangelical perfection. In the brief seventh section, I consider how Bonaventure's biblical theology, broadly conceived, influences his understanding and performance of the contested hagiographer's task.

"NO DEAF HEARER OF THE GOSPEL": SAINT FRANCIS AS HAGIOGRAPHIC HERALD OF THE WORD

For Thomas of Celano, Francis's own, expressive love of the Word of God was best conveyed in a hagiography that was itself rich in biblical echoes and citations—a *Life* imitative of the saint's life that allowed Francis, as it were, to continue to be heard, seen, and touched by an extended audience of readers. Through its wealth of biblical echoes, the *Life of Saint Francis* continues the hagiographic tradition, chiefly monastic, in which Celano was well versed,[10] as evidenced by his echoing of passages found in Athanasius's *Life of Anthony*, Gregory the Great's *Life of Saint Benedict*, Sulpicius Severus's *Life of Martin of Tours*, William of Saint-Thierry's *Vita prima of Abbot Saint Bernard of Clairvaux*, and Eadmer's *Life of Anselm*.[11]

Through its strong Augustinian accents—especially evident in the portrayal of Francis in book 1 as a sinner enslaved to sin by natural inheritance, upbringing, and the "voluntary servitude" of his own carnal desires[12]— Celano's *Vita prima* also recalls Augustine's *Confessions* more broadly as a narrative about that saint's changing relationship to the Bible.[13] When Francis hears the gospel proclaimed as the Word of God in the Portiuncula (an episode discussed below), he responds to it much as Augustine does at the moment of his conversion in book 8 of his *Confessions*, when he reads Romans 13:13-14, and again in book 9, when, moved especially by the words of Psalm 4, he is filled with the desire to preach the Psalms to the world as a protest against its pride.[14]

Celano's first *Life of Saint Francis* (the *Vita prima*) celebrates the saint's canonization by the pope in Assisi, narrating that event with the detail and the emotion of an eyewitness. Present at Francis's canonization in Assisi on July 16, 1228, Thomas of Celano details the itinerary of Pope Gregory IX in the immediately preceding months; the hagiographer emphasizes that the "Lord Pope" had carefully considered the matter of the canonization in two solemn assemblies of the cardinals, during which "miracles were heard, verified, accepted, and approved" and reports concerning "the life and conduct of the holy man" were attested.[15] The unanimous judgment of the consistory supported the canonization of Francis, whose enrollment "in the catalogue of the saints" Gregory then proclaimed.[16] Writing almost thirty years later, Bonaventure similarly describes the process and the cardinals' unanimous affirmation, but calls greater attention to the pope's personal conviction of Francis's holiness and to his desire, as Christ's vicar, to glorify on earth the saint whom the Lord himself had assuredly glorified in heaven.[17]

The canonization at the start of Celano's book 3, which recounts Francis's posthumous miracles, imbues the saint's entire story not only with the divine authority of the gospel Francis so confidently preached, but also with the papal and episcopal authority that had approved the friars' evangelical way of life. Echoing the Acts of the Apostles (Acts 9:28), Celano explains that Francis "*acted confidently* in all matters because of the apostolic authority granted him."[18] Indeed, "Apostolic authority resided in him; so he refused to flatter kings and princes."[19]

Firmly rooted in this authoritative tradition celebratory of saints, Thomas of Celano subsequently responded to particular requests from within the Franciscan community to retell the story of Francis three more times — in the recently discovered *Vita brevior* (*Shorter Life*, ca. 1232-40),[20] *Remembrance of the Desire of a Soul* (ca. 1244), and *The Treatise on the Miracles* (1254)[21] — making in these diverse texts timely variations upon the themes first sounded in the *Vita prima*.[22] Writing his *Legenda maior* of Francis in 1260-63, more than thirty years after Celano's *Vita prima*, Bonaventure of Bagnoregio (1221-74) draws extensively on earlier hagiographies, especially

Celano's, but also those by Julian of Speyer (1232–35), Anonymous of Perugia (1240), and *The Legend of the Three Companions* (1241–47).

Like Thomas of Celano, Bonaventure underscores the evangelical force of the saint's life, but he does so in an altered theological context affected by heated Scholastic debates concerning evangelical perfection, papal authority, and biblical interpretation. For Bonaventure, as we shall see, the disputed questions about Francis's life, example, and work are ultimately also questions about the Bible itself, passages from which (and glosses upon) are quoted by parties on each side of the respective debates; the disputed exegetical questions therefore require a defense of hagiography. In Bonaventure's *Disputed Questions on Evangelical Perfection*, we read: "Blessed Francis was inflamed by the example of the apostles from the words of the Gospel proclaimed in the church to undertake this way of living, as shines forth more clearly *in the accounts of his life*."[23]

Responding to William of Saint-Amour (1200–1272), who denied that Christ, the apostles, and the early saints (Basil, Benedict, Augustine, Jerome, Gregory, Hilary, Paulinus) had begged, and who decried the "begging recently introduced by Dominic and Francis" as "superstitious and senseless,"[24] Bonaventure declares, "Now against this attack that arms itself with doubt, it is necessary to resist without doubt. For if we entertain doubts about what we read in the lives of St. Alexius and Blessed Francis, for that same reason anything we read in the lives of other saints becomes questionable. As a result, all the examples of virtues and deeds of the saints are then rendered doubtful."[25]

Resisting such doubt, Bonaventure seeks in his own theological work as a hagiographer to defend the truth of saints' *Lives* as rooted in the authority of sacred scripture, ecclesial tradition, orthodox belief, and the decree of the pope, who has been empowered by the God-given grace of office to canonize saints, interpret the Bible, teach, and commission preachers.[26] In many ways, Bonaventure's *Legenda maior* is thus not only a hagiography of Saint Francis, but also a Scholastic experiment in narrative theology suited both to Franciscan devotion and to resolving academic arguments about evangelical perfection and papal authority.[27] Robert Karris observes, "If one reads carefully between the lines, one realizes that this work has as one of its goals to answer the objections of William of Saint-Amour."[28] In the *Disputed Questions*, Bonaventure takes William's objections to Franciscan poverty and preaching to be a challenge to Christ's own teaching in the Sermon on the

Mount;[29] he answers William, in part, in the *Legenda maior* by presenting blessed Francis's life as a fulfillment of the beatitudes.

Focusing on the *Vita prima* of Thomas of Celano, Wayne Hellmann has highlighted four key gospel events in that *Life*: (1) the hour when Francis hears the priest read from the Gospel of Matthew at the Portiuncula; (2) the reenactment at Greccio of Christ's nativity; (3) Francis's opening of the scriptures three times on the altar at the hermitage; and (4) Francis's asking to hear the Gospel of John before his death.[30] Here I briefly recall these same moments as the hagiographer describes them, comparing Celano's account of Francis's biblical witness with Bonaventure's account to demonstrate the potent interweaving of the saint's *Life* with the sacred scriptures.

Celano relates that Francis hears the priest at the Portiuncula proclaim the words of the Gospel about "how the Lord sent out his disciples to preach,"[31] and then he stays in the church afterward to ask the priest to explain the passage. The hagiographer summarizes the synthetic explanation given, which includes quotations not only from Matthew 10, but also from related passages in Luke 9 and Mark 6. Francis immediately recognizes in the Lord's command to his disciples the desire of his own heart ("This is what I want") and hastens "to implement the words of salvation," devoutly putting "into effect what he heard."[32] Francis, in short, listens to the priest with an inner disposition that is completely receptive and prepared to do what he hears. God's prevenient grace has already worked in him. "No deaf hearer of the gospel," Francis responds actively to the Word of God, following its instructions, which he "was careful to carry out to the letter."[33]

Although this encounter with the gospel is a pivotal experience for the saint, other encounters with Christ's recorded words have apparently preceded it and prepared for it. At some indeterminate time and place, Francis must have been struck by the parables of the hidden treasure (Matt. 13:44) and of the pearl of great price (Matt. 13:45), because (as Celano relates) in the early days of his conversion Francis, after having cut short his ventured trip to Apulia, speaks in secret to an unnamed, close friend, albeit "cautiously and in riddles," about his intentions to follow Christ through a radical renunciation of worldly possessions, saying that "he had found a great and valuable treasure."[34] In the *Legenda maior*, by contrast, Bonaventure omits any reference to Francis's guarded conversations with an uncomprehending, close friend, substituting for them (as it were) a visionary dialogue between Christ and Francis on the way to Apulia.[35] The future saint's clear realization of his calling in Bonaventure's hagiography results from this audition (unmentioned in the *Vita prima*), during which Christ himself speaks to him directly and explains the meaning of his earlier dream of stockpiled weapons of war.[36] Hearing Christ on the way to Apulia, where he had intended (again) to enter military service, Francis immediately reverses course and returns in haste to Assisi because (Bonaventure relates) "he realized that he had found a *hidden treasure*, and, like a wise merchant, planned to buy *the pearl he had found by selling everything*."[37]

What first triggers Francis's change of mind about going to Apulia and then gives rise to his coded conversations with his unnamed friend remains completely mysterious in Celano's *Vita prima*. According to the hagiographer, Francis also wonders at the "sudden change in himself,"[38] whereby he has lost interest in things that formerly attracted him. We are only told that Francis suddenly decides against the proposed military adventure and seeks instead to "keep Jesus Christ in his inmost self."[39] Coakley rightly observes that "[Thomas of Celano] presents the saint's conversion in terms of the effects of God that occur only within his inner experience rather than in events of the world around him," whereas Bonaventure construes "the divine as a separate presence in the narrative to which the narrator has access, but which stands now in a sphere distinct from the saint's self-contained human integrity."[40]

When Bonaventure goes on to tell about Francis's hearing the Gospel read in the Portiuncula, he narrates the episode itself more briefly than Celano does, but he adds expressions that frame the story theologically. He first sets the scene "in the church of the Virgin Mother of God," and then draws an explicit parallel between Mary's conception of "*the Word full of grace and truth*" (John 1:14) and Francis's own conception and bringing to birth of "the spirit of the Gospel truth."[41] For Bonaventure, Francis's initial hearing of the Gospel is a grace-filled moment of incarnation of the Word in the life of the saint. Bonaventure describes Francis's immediate, joyful obedience as a response to the "divine prompting" that leads him to become "a model of evangelical perfection and to invite others to penance"; that same "divine prompting" imbues his preaching, we are told, with a prophetic power that "proclaim[s] peace" to those who have previously been "at odds with Christ and far from salvation."[42]

Among the hearers of Francis's evangelical preaching is the first of his disciples, Bernard, soon followed (in Celano's account) by ten more; for them and for himself, Francis writes "a form of life and a rule," using "primarily words of the holy gospel, longing only for its perfection."[43] Celano simply describes Bernard as embracing the evangelical counsels as he sees them being lived by Francis. Bonaventure, by contrast, intersperses a scene in which Francis and Bernard first enter the church of Saint Nicholas, pray for divine guidance, and then open "the book of the Gospels three times, asking God to confirm Bernard's plan with a threefold testimony."[44] Upon each opening of the book, their eyes fall upon a verse (Matt. 19:21, Luke 9:3, and Matt. 16:24, respectively) counseling a means for perfect discipleship through the renunciation of earthly goods. This scene in the *Legenda maior* foreshadows Francis's later triple *sortes* of the Bible concerning his own future path of suffering,[45] creating a link between the Franciscan form of life, its basis in the scriptures, and its confirmation by the stigmata. Both Celano and Bonaventure describe Francis's later, triple opening of the Bible to the account of Christ's passion as a prophecy of God's will for the saint, soon to be marked with Christ's wounds.

As in Celano's account, the growing number of disciples in the *Legenda maior* moves Francis to compose a rule with "the observance of the Holy Gospel as its unshakeable foundation"[46] and to seek its approval by the pope, Innocent III. Strengthening his defense of the mendicants against critics such as William of Saint-Amour, Bonaventure adds the quoted testimony of the bishop of Sabina, John of Saint Paul, who speaks this significant word to his fellow cardinals and the pope: "If we refuse the request of this poor man as novel or too difficult, when all he asks is to be allowed to lead the Gospel life, we must be on our guard lest we commit an offense against Christ's Gospel. For if anyone says that there is something novel or irrational or impossible to observe in this man's desire to live according to the perfection of the Gospel, he would be guilty of blasphemy against Christ, the Author of the Gospel."[47]

Both Celano and Bonaventure emphasize that Francis was illumined by the Holy Spirit in his understanding, interpretation, and explanation of the scriptures, "although he had not studied."[48] More than Celano, however, Bonaventure points to Francis's approval of members of the order, such as Anthony of Padua (and himself), who "were devoting themselves to the study of Sacred Scripture"; Bonaventure also adds the anecdote of a religious from Siena, "a Doctor of Sacred Theology," who posed "certain questions [to Francis] that were difficult to understand," to which Francis replied "with such clarity in teaching that the learned man was absolutely dumbfounded."[49] Bonaventure thus envisions Francis as capable of answering, both in word and by the example of his life, the very questions that had prompted disputations in the universities.

Celano and Bonaventure emphasize that Francis's reverence for the scriptures honored them both in their letter and spirit. Adept at symbolic recognitions, Francis is said by Celano to have loved and reverenced the scriptures in their physicality as books to be kept in places of honor and as lettered pages to be copied.[50] At the same time, his spiritual exegesis of the scriptures led him to a sacramental vision of the world and its creatures. "He used to embrace more warmly and to observe more gladly anything in which he found an allegorical likeness to the Son of God," writes Celano.[51] For example, Francis pitied and ransomed lambs on the way to slaughter, "since in Sacred Scripture the humility of our Lord Jesus Christ is fittingly and rightly compared to the lamb."[52] Biblical images similarly inspired Francis's real-life dealings with sheep, goats, worms, and flowers.[53] Narrating Francis's care for lambs, rabbits, fish, falcons, pheasants, and waterbirds, Bonaventure similarly notes Francis's particular discovery of the likeness of Christ in all those creatures named "in the symbols of Scripture."[54] Celano and Bonaventure both point to Francis's care for lepers, but Bonaventure adds that Francis kissed "their hands and their mouths" and makes explicit the biblical inspiration for Francis's actions in Isaiah's prophecy (Isa. 53:3) of Christ "despised *as a leper*."[55]

At the end of book 1 of the *Vita prima*, Celano offers a detailed account of the nativity scene Francis had asked to be erected at Greccio — a scene that the hagiographer employs rhetorically to illustrate Francis's sustained, formative meditation on "the humility of the Incarnation and the charity of the Passion"[56] (the latter topic being illustrated in book 2 by Francis's reception of the stigmata, his mortal illness, and his holy death). As Celano relates, the scene at Greccio fulfills Francis's stated wish "to enact the memory of that babe who was born in Bethlehem: to see as much as is possible with [his] own bodily eyes the discomfort of [Jesus's] infant needs, how he lay in a manger, and how, with an ox and an ass standing by, he rested on hay."[57] The manger is positioned at the foot of the altar on which the host is consecrated: "Over the manger the solemnities of the Mass are celebrated."[58] Francis himself, robed as a deacon, sings the Gospel during the Christmas Mass and preaches the sermon, referring often to Jesus as "the babe from Bethlehem" (*puerum de Bethlehem*) and pronouncing the word "Bethlehem" with a peculiar intonation of the first syllable ("Baaath") to make the word resemble the sound of a bleating sheep.[59] The Word of the Gospel is thus enfleshed in such a way that the mystery of the Lord's nativity becomes a sensory event in which all present may participate, the very hay in the manger subsequently effecting miracles of healing.

Bonaventure briefly retells the story of the manger scene at Greccio in the *Legenda maior* at the end of chapter 10, which concerns Francis's zeal for prayer. He omits the detail of Francis's mimetic, bleating pronunciation, but adds that "Francis petitioned for and obtained permission from the Supreme Pontiff" to create the manger scene[60]—an addition illustrating Francis's humble obedience and consistent with Bonaventure's stress on the papal authorization given to Francis and the order he founded.

Since Bonaventure's *Life* of Francis is structured quite differently from that of Thomas of Celano's, this particular episode lacks the structural and theological importance it has in the *Vita prima*. There book 1 ends with a focus on the biblical mystery of the Nativity, reenacted at Greccio, and prepares for the mirrored representation of Christ's passion in Francis's stigmata and death at the conclusion of book 2. "Francis has heard the scriptures in such a way that their many words have been condensed into the person of Christ, and not all the many possible interpretations of the person of Jesus, but into two episodes—his humble birth and painful death," states Dominic Monti.[61] For Bonaventure, by contrast, Francis's hearing of the gospel gains expression in his virtuous living and preaching of the Sermon on the Mount. The saint's evangelical work, detailed in eight chapters at the structural center of the *Legenda maior*, is rewarded by his reception of Christ's stigmata on Mount La Verna.

For both hagiographers, the chapters dealing with Francis's reception of the stigmata, his illness, and his death are replete with biblical significance. Like Bonaventure after him, Celano recalls how Francis, desirous of a more perfect conformity to Christ, had reverently placed a book of the Gospels upon the altar in the hermitage at La Verna, prostrated himself before it in ardent petition to know God's will for his life, and then opened the book three times. Each time his eyes fell upon a prophecy of Christ's passion, which Francis understood to mean that many trials still awaited him.[62] Bonaventure adds that the threefold opening of the book was "in honor of the Trinity," and that Francis then foresaw that he was to be conformed to Christ not only in his actions but also in his suffering before death.[63]

The vision of the crucified seraph comes to Francis soon thereafter. Powerfully moved by the seraph's beauty and frightened, at the same time, by his attachment to the cross, Francis suffers the piercing impression of the vision "upon his heart" (as Celano relates) in this double movement of love and fear.[64] Wondering at the meaning of the vision, the saint then observes upon his own hands and feet and at his side the marks of the wounds he had seen upon the seraph's body. Bonaventure's account of the stigmatization follows Celano's closely, but incorporates the mystical vocabulary of excessive love, compassion, and enkindling (*incendium mentis*) to name the affects associated with Francis's transforming ecstasy.[65] For Bonaventure, Francis is "the angelic man," who, like a new Moses, comes down from Mount La Verna "bearing with him the likeness of the Crucified, depicted not on *tablets of stone* [Deut. 4:13] or on panels of wood carved by hand, but engraved on parts of his flesh *by the finger of the living God* [Deut. 9:10]."[66]

Just as the triple opening of the Gospels prepares Francis (and the readers of his hagiographies) for the saint's reception of Christ's wounds, so too the reading of the Gospel on Francis's deathbed reveals the meaning of the saint's death as a sharing in Christ's. According to Celano, the dying Francis himself recites Psalm 142 and then asks that the Gospel according to Saint John be read, starting at John 12:1, "Six days before the Passover..."[67] Bonaventure reverses the order of these readings, so that Francis's psalm recitation "to the end" responds, as it were, to the Gospel.[68] In both cases, the selection from the Gospel consciously joins the time of Francis's dying to the Holy Week of Jesus's passion and death. In Celano's *Vita prima*, Saint Clare and her sisters at San Damiano lament over Francis's body in a manner that inevitably recalls the grief of the sorrowful mother and of Mary Magdalene at Calvary.[69] Bonaventure omits that scene, so that Francis's passage in death is followed almost immediately by testimonies and miraculous signs that provide "a glimpse of the resurrection" and of the glorious ascension of Francis's soul as it rises and enters "a home of eternity."[70]

PITTING SCRIPTURE AGAINST HAGIOGRAPHY: THE ANTIMENDICANT CRITICS

By the time Bonaventure wrote his *Legenda maior*, critics of the mendicants had already attempted to weaken the tightly knit unity of the saint's *Life* with sacred scripture by attacking one or more of its interlinked components. Some denied the authenticity of Francis's stigmata and thus the divine seal upon his person and mission, prompting an official rebuttal by Pope Alexander IV in his *Benigna operatio* (1255).[71] Other critics, such as William of Saint-Amour and Gerard of Abbeville (1225–72), raised charges of heresy against the Franciscan movement, which they associated with the apocalypticism of Joachim of Fiore (ca. 1135–1202), in part because of Friar Gerard of Borgo San-Donnino's notorious *Liber introductorius ad Evangelium aeternum* (*Introduction to the Eternal Gospel*) (1254)—a work condemned by Pope Alexander IV in 1255.[72] William and others also challenged the authority of the pope to commission the mendicants to preach—a challenge prompting Alexander IV's condemnation in July 1256 of William's *Brevis tractatus de periculis novissimorum temporum* (*Brief Treatise on the Dangers of the Last Days*).[73] The Franciscans' rejection of personal and communal ownership, their begging, and their perceived intrusion into pastoral care rankled the secular clergy, who questioned the orthodoxy of their biblical exegesis, ecclesiology, asceticism, and Christology.

Against Franciscan Joachites, such as Bonaventure (and later Petrus Johannis Olivi),[74] who saw the radical poverty embraced by Francis as a divine remedy marshaled in the final age of the world against avarice, "the root of all evils" (1 Tim. 6:10),[75] antimendicant critics such as William of Saint-Amour cited 2 Timothy 3:1–8, which warns against the distressful advent of religious imposters in the last days, and 2 Thessalonians 3:10, which instructs Christians to work for their livelihood; these critics also vehemently denied the foundational Franciscan claim that Jesus and his disciples begged, and thus that Francis and the Franciscans imitated their example.[76] "To beg," argues William, "is a sin plain and simple, unless it might sometimes be excused, for it is against the teaching of the Apostle [Paul]."[77]

William's critique of the Franciscans' poverty extends also to their refusal to accept money either as wages or as alms. Both Celano's *Vita prima* and Bonaventure's *Legenda maior* record that Francis heard Matthew 10:9–10 read in the Portiuncula and embraced it immediately as part of his rule of life: "Do not possess gold or silver or money, or carry on your journey a wallet or a sack, nor bread nor a staff, nor [are you] to have shoes nor two tunics."[78] Bonaventure takes the obedient fulfilling of this command as making it necessary for the apostles to beg—an action thus entailed in the Lord's precept.[79] Setting scripture against scripture, William objects that Christ's apostles had a money bag that was kept by Judas, according to John 12:6 and 13:29.[80] Defending Franciscan poverty, Bonaventure quotes the *Glossa* in support of the interpretation that Christ's purse was intended for charitable purposes; its existence does not, therefore, contradict the command to eschew monetary payments and donations in exchange for preaching the gospel.[81] Rather, the command of poverty given in Matthew 10:9–10 to the apostles sent on mission "pertains to evangelical perfection."[82] Bonaventure presents Christ's own example and the example of the saints, including Francis, as proof that begging belongs to Christian perfection.[83]

Focusing on the single issue of voluntary poverty as a virtue, David Clairmont asks, "If the reason for Franciscan reform was to understand in a deeper and more abiding way how to follow the Gospel counsels of poverty, to whom does the Franciscan look with regard to how to live them: Jesus Christ, who commanded them, or Francis of Assisi, who obeyed the command?"[84] Analyzing the disputes about poverty and evangelical perfection that arose in the 1270s between the Dominicans and the Franciscans and among the Franciscans themselves,[85] Kevin Madigan sees them both as continuations of earlier disputes between the secular clergy and the mendicants in the 1250s and as expressions of questions still lingering today about Christian sanctity in its relationship to the scriptures: "What is the content of the gospel? What is required of the Christian? . . . Are the commandments of Christ intended to be observed literally? Must all Christians observe the *precepta Christi* literally, or only those who would be perfect? What is the relation between the Bible and its authoritative interpretation?"[86]

AUTHORSHIP, AGENCY, AND VIRTUE IN
THE *VITA PRIMA* AND THE *LEGENDA MAIOR*

To Madigan's questions, we may add another: What is the relation between hagiography and the Bible? A comparison of Thomas of Celano's *Vita prima* (1229) with Bonaventure's *Legenda maior* of Francis (1260–63) shows a hagiographic turn from earlier, meditative, monastic forms celebrating God's wondrous work in human lives to emerging Scholastic models focused on the saints themselves as heroic respondents to God's call. This narrative turn reflects parallel theological developments in how biblical authorship is conceived, biblical commentary conducted, and evangelical perfection defined. In each case, the saint's *Life* reflects the scriptures, but the Bible itself appears differently in its hagiographic reflection.

For Celano in the *Vita prima*, Francis is a model of conversion effected mysteriously by grace alone; the accent falls upon God's authorship of the saint, which stands parallel to God's authorship of the Bible. For Bonaventure, by contrast, Francis is (in the words of Kozlowski), a model "of perfect virtue,"[87] the exemplar of a free human will in cooperation with grace, a man at the meeting point of human expression (in his longing petition for the grace of martyrdom) and divine impression (in the imposition of the stigmata).[88]

Illumined by God, in dialogue with Christ, and responsive to grace, Bonaventure's Francis thus more clearly illustrates the double mode, divine and human, that Scholastic theologians affirmed both in human sanctity and in biblical authorship, considered in its primary and secondary causality.[89] As Alastair Minnis and others have shown, the application of Aristotelian epistemology and causality to textual production, including the composition of the books of the Bible, led medieval commentators on the sacred scriptures to place more emphasis on the agency of the inspired human writers (*auctores*), while at the same time affirming God's primary authorship and thus the authority of the Bible as a source of divine revelation.[90] Gregory the Great (540–604) regarded it as "superfluous" to speculate about the authorship of the book of Job, "since . . . the Holy Spirit is confidently believed to have been the Author," who "dictated" the words of the book.[91] Bonaventure, Thomas Aquinas, and others, by contrast, find it important not only to affirm that God is the author of Holy Writ, but also to consider the biblical authors in their own right as *auctores* and prophets, divinely inspired in various ways in accord with their natural faculties.[92]

Similarly, those who upheld heroic virtue and imitability as essential criteria for sainthood gave greater recognition to human capacity for free decision in their discipleship and human participation in the process of their own sanctification by God through grace. What John Coakley has written about the difference between Thomas of Celano's *Vita prima* and

Bonaventure's *Legenda maior* can thus be applied, *mutatis mutandis*, to Scholastic discussions of biblical authorship in the thirteenth century: "Divine agency, though still the *sine qua non* of hagiographical narrative, had to share the stage increasingly with human agency—a major development in the idea of Christian biography."[93]

Bonaventure's portrayal of Francis as a free agent who responds in a meritorious way to God's call is initially accomplished in two ways. First, drawing on sources composed after the *Vita prima*, Bonaventure adds scenes in which Christ himself speaks to Francis—for example, on the way to Apulia and from the cross at San Damiano—thus distinguishing the divine and human agents and rending them both visible in their interaction to the *Life*'s readers. In this way, as Coakley has argued, "the sequence of early narratives of the 'conversion' of Francis of Assisi . . . stands as a prominent case of this increased interest in human agency on the part of the biographers."[94]

Second, the later hagiographer describes Francis even in his youth as pure, self-restrained ("he did not give himself over to the drives of the flesh"), free from greed, and kind: "Even at that time he resolved not to be 'a deaf hearer of the Gospel,' but *to give to everyone who begged.*"[95] Thomas of Celano, by contrast, describes Francis prior to his conversion as a wretched sinner living among sinners sorely in need of grace—"vain and arrogant," devoted "to things full of excess and lewdness," "flowing on the tide of every debauchery," "in the service of outrageous conduct," Christian only by name.[96] In Celano's Augustinian account of Francis's youth, God's invincible grace effects mysterious, sometimes instantaneous, changes within Francis's own soul and miraculously accounts for his conversion: "*The hand of the Lord was upon him* [Isa. 48:9], *a change of the right hand of the Most High* [Ezek. 1:3], that through him the Lord might give sinners confidence in a new life of grace."[97] Gently challenging Celano's account in the *Vita prima*, Bonaventure quotes its memorable phrase, "no deaf hearer of the Gospel," and applies it not to the moment when Francis hears the Gospel of Matthew read at the Portiuncula, but to Francis in his youth: "Even at that time he resolved not to be 'a deaf hearer of the Gospel.'"[98]

Bonaventure thus places emphasis on Francis's meritorious good resolve, his free choice of obedience. This portrayal of Francis stands in keeping with a widely accepted Scholastic principle: "A form can only be received *in materia disposita*. Sanctifying grace or justification is a form received in the will. Therefore the will must be disposed to receive it."[99] Bonaventure asserts in the *Breviloquium*, "A predisposition toward a perfecting form must itself be in the likeness of the form."[100] The Franciscan Master held that a sinner's cooperation with prevenient grace (*gratia gratis data*) paves the way for the reception *de congruo* of sanctifying grace (*gratia gratum faciens*), cooperation with which is meritorious of salvation.[101] God does not justify human beings without their consent. Despite differences in their teachings on the relationship between grace and the free will,[102] Bonaventure and Aquinas (as Michael Lawler notes) both agreed with, and sought to refine, the Scholastic maxim "that God should reward according to his power that man who does what lies in him."[103]

To these two ways (named above) of crediting Francis's virtuous agency, Bonaventure adds a third through a major restructuring of the arrangement found in the *Vita prima*. Bonaventure interrupts Celano's largely chronological narration to insert at the center of the *Legenda maior* eight thematic chapters on Francis's virtues. This alteration is remarkable, given that Celano does nothing of the sort. The *Vita prima* uses the discourse of virtues chiefly in a single digression, where Celano celebrates not Francis's personal virtues (which are self-evident in his actions) but those of the brothers, whose virtuous communal life radiates hope for the renewal of the Church as a whole: "Grounded on the solid rock of true humility," they were "to have the well-designed spiritual structure of all the virtues arise in them."[104] Celano also, somewhat awkwardly and belatedly, instructs his readers that they can follow in Francis's footsteps by imitating the virtues symbolized by the six wings of the seraph: "We too will certainly be able to reach these heights if, like the Seraphim, we *spread two wings over our heads* [Ezek. 1:22]; that is, following the blessed Francis's example, in every good work we have a pure intention and upright conduct, and directing these to God, we strive untiringly to please God alone in all things."[105]

The structural change that divides the *Legenda maior* into an "outer" life (chaps. 1–4 and 13—15) and an "inner" life (chaps. 5–12), has, not surprisingly, garnered considerable critical attention.[106] The rearrangement serves to juxtapose the approval of the Franciscan Rule by Pope Honorius (described at the end of chapter 4 as a foreshadowing of the seal of the stigmata given to Francis by Christ, "the Supreme Pontiff"),[107] on the one hand, with the impressive vision of the crucified seraph (described in chapter 13), on the other. The eight chapters on the virtues are generally recognized to show an ascending hierarchy of virtues: purgative, illuminative, perfective. The ordering of the virtues places special emphasis on poverty (chap. 7), charity (chap. 9), and preaching (chap. 12)—core charisms of the Franciscan renewal.

For Bonaventure, the moral conduct of Francis was (as Jacques-Guy Bougerol notes) "the source of moral reflection."[108] The thirteenth century saw heroic virtue being established as a standard criterion for the official recognition of a saint.[109] The twofold criteria of miracles and virtues had been challenged in Francis's case by those who doubted the stigmata and questioned whether his radical practice of poverty was indeed in accord with the Gospels. Bonaventure answers both doubts in the *Legenda maior*, using the eight beatitudes (*Beati qui sunt* . . .) of Christ's Matthean Sermon on the Mount to show the perfect conformity of blessed Francis with the gospel. The beatitudes, as Bonaventure understands them, are inseparable from *beatus Franciscus*, who lived the gospel's precepts with heroic virtue and therefore has deserved to receive the rewards Christ promises to the blessed.

THE BEATITUDES IN THE *LEGENDA MAIOR*, GLOSSED THROUGH BONAVENTURE'S *BREVILOQUIUM* AND HIS COMMENTARY ON LUKE

In the *Legenda maior*, the intertext of the beatitudes is veiled, but easily discernable through Bonaventure's numerology; the typological linkage of the three mountains of Sion, of the sermon in Galilee, and La Verna, signaled in chapter 4; occasional direct citations of Matthew 5 in individual chapters; and Bonaventure's discussions elsewhere (notably in the *Breviloquium* [1254–57] and in the *Commentary on the Gospel according to Luke* [1254–57]) of the beatitudes in relation to virtues.[110] Building upon my earlier argument about the structural importance of the eight Matthean beatitudes for the "Inner Life" of virtues,[111] I explore here more closely Bonaventure's theological understanding of the relationship between Francis's heroic virtues, perfected through the gifts of the Holy Spirit, and the beatitudes, and thus of the saint's *Life* and the Sermon on the Mount. Chapter 5 of the *Legenda maior* begins the "Inner Life" with the declaration that Francis "was encouraged to reach the palm of victory through the height of heroic virtue [*invictae . . . virtutis*]."[112] The criterion of heroic virtue for canonization gained support from Aquinas's explanation in the *Summa theologiae*, where Thomas first quotes from the Sermon on the Mount: "Be ye . . . perfect, as your heavenly Father is perfect" (Matt. 5:48).[113] Then, interpreting a Platonic dictum found in Macrobius, he explains that the cardinal virtues of the faithful—intermediate between the social or human virtues and the "exemplary virtues" in the mind of God—are of two kinds: the perfecting or purgative virtues (*virtutes purgatoriae*) and those of the perfected or cleansed mind (*virtutes purgati animi*). The latter are "attributed to the Blessed, or, in this life, to some who are at the summit of perfection."[114]

Aquinas and Bonaventure agree that the beatitudes differ from the virtues and the gifts, but they disagree about how they differ. For Aquinas, the beatitudes are not habits, but acts of virtues perfected by the gifts. Poverty, he asserts, is not a virtue.[115] For Bonaventure, by contrast, the beatitudes are habits (operative dispositions infused by the Holy Spirit), and the evangelical poverty of the blessed named in Matthew 5:3 is indeed a virtue, albeit one that has been transformed into a habit of beatitude through the Spirit's gifts. Bonaventure explains in the *Breviloquium*, "A single grace branches out into the habits of the virtues; [then] it branches out into the habits of the gifts [of the Holy Spirit]; [then] it branches out into the habits of the beatitudes."[116] The acts of the habits of the virtues (*habitus rectificantes*) belong to a beginning stage in the life of holiness, those of the gifts (*habitus expedientes*) to an intermediate stage, and those of the beatitudes (*habitus perficientes*) to the height of perfection.[117] In the *Legenda maior*, Bonaventure locates poverty "among the gifts of charisms" (*inter cetera charismatum dona*).[118] According to Bonaventure, the gifts serve to realize the beatitudes, which are "habits of perfection that are so closely related to their final end [of eternal happiness] that they are rightly called beatitudes."[119]

In his *Commentary on the Gospel according to Luke*, Bonaventure deals with the four beatitudes (Luke 6:20–23) enunciated during Jesus's sermon on the plain. Discussing the differences between the Lukan and the Matthean beatitudes (Matt. 5:1–12), Bonaventure takes the commonly accepted position that Jesus must have spoken to two different audiences, delivering the shorter sermon to a large crowd and reserving the longer and fuller discourse on the mount for the small circle of his advanced disciples.[120] "Since the perfect are made conformable to Christ through the sevenfold Spirit who rested upon him as is said in Isaiah 11:2–3," Bonaventure reasons, "there are seven beatitudes to accord with the seven gifts of the Holy Spirit."[121] Earlier in this same commentary, Bonaventure interprets the names of the twelve apostles to signify their special virtues, noting "six steps in the progress of the virtues by which one is led to *perfect love*" — steps said to parallel both the steps leading to *peace* in the beatitudes (Matt. 5:9) and the gifts of the Spirit leading to *wisdom*.[122]

The Lukan beatitudes, Bonaventure explains, complement this numerology with their fourfold promise of heavenly rewards to be merited in four different ways, "which lift us up to God and justify our free will."[123] Noting Jesus's use of the present tense, the exegete remarks: "He calls these poor *blessed*, because they are ready for beatitude,"[124] the happiness that entails a share in God's kingdom, a participation in divine power. The *hungry for justice* shall be satisfied, the *ones who mourn* now will laugh, the *ones who patiently suffer* the hatred of others will know a great and joyful reward in heaven. Bonaventure goes on to accept the *Glossa* of Bede that associates the four beatitudes with the four cardinal virtues: "Poverty corresponds to temperance; hunger for spiritual goods to justice; weeping to prudence; suffering of evils to fortitude or patience."[125] When such virtues are perfected through God's Spirit in the beatitudes, the merited rewards constitute what Bonaventure calls "the four parts of beatitude." Echoing Ephesians 3:17–18, he names the length of beatitude the *interior joy* of the soul; the depth of beatitude, the *lower joy* of the glorified body; the breadth, the *exterior joy* of companionship with the saints and the renewal of all creatures; the height, the *superior joy* of the vision of God (see table 5.1).[126]

The cruciform pattern of height, breadth, depth, and length that Bonaventure gives to the Lukan beatitudes through his invocation of Ephesians 3:18 (read within the context of Ephesians 3:14–19) is theologically significant. It implicitly links the meritorious virtues and rewards of the blessed to the grace of Christ, whose cross has won their salvation, and to the Trinity, the source of all grace. Paul's prayer in Ephesians 3:14–17 invokes all three persons of the Trinity, who are also named whenever one makes the sign of the cross, touching one's forehead, breast, and two shoulders.

This fourfold pattern provides a gloss for the *Legenda maior*'s narration of six visions of the cross that culminate in Francis's final, seventh vision of Christ as the crucified seraph in chapter 13, where the hagiographer also recaps them.[127] Three of these are particularly impressive in their silent recall of Ephesians 3:18. The priest Sylvester sees the vision of a golden cross extending from the mouth of Francis, "whose top reached the heavens [Gen. 28:12]

Table 5.1 Merited Rewards for the Blessed in Bonaventure's *Commentary on Luke*

(Luke 6:20) for yours is the kingdom of God	(Eph. 3:18) so that you may be able to comprehend with all the saints what is the height (superior joy)	Height of participation in God's power, merited by poverty (temperance)
(Luke 6:21) for you shall be satisfied	(Eph. 3:18) what is the breadth (exterior joy)	Breadth of goodness, merited by hunger for justice (justice)
(Luke 6:21) for you will laugh	(Eph. 3:18) what is the depth (lower joy)	Depth of wisdom or truth, a laughter merited by mourning (prudence)
(Luke 6:22) for surely your reward is great in heaven	(Eph. 3:18) what is the length (interior joy)	Length of eternity, merited by patient suffering (fortitude)

and whose arms stretched far and wide and seemed to extend to the ends of the world."[128] Later, Brother Pacifico sees Francis "marked with two bright swords intersecting in the shape of a cross. One of them stretched from his head to his feet, and the other across his chest from one hand to the other."[129] Hearing Anthony of Padua preach on the inscription *INRI* placed on Jesus's cross (John 19:19–20), Monaldo suddenly sees "blessed Francis lifted up in the air with his arms extended as if on a cross."[130] These visions enable the reader of the *Legenda maior* not only to anticipate the saint's reception of the stigmata, but also to see that miraculous gift as a sign of his moral virtues, which have been effected through God's grace and perfected through the Spirit's gifts. "Such grace," observes Katherine Wrisley Shelby, "is and has been on offer to all of humanity through the Crucified Christ—if they would only choose to cling to him as closely as Francis."[131]

These visions of the cross in the *Legenda maior* show Francis again and again as an exemplar of evangelical perfection, recalling Bonaventure's exegesis of the four Lukan beatitudes. In the *Breviloquium*, Bonaventure uses Ephesians 3:14–19, which he quotes in full, to structure the entire prologue to that work: "In these words the 'great doctor of the Gentiles and preacher of truth,' filled with the Holy Spirit as a chosen and sanctified instrument, discloses the source, procedure, and purpose of holy scripture, which is called theology. For he [Saint Paul] intimates that Scripture derives its origin from an inflowing of the Most Blessed Trinity; that its manner of proceeding corresponds to the demands of our human capacities; and that its purpose or fruit is an abundance of overflowing happiness."[132] In the Pauline passage, Bonaventure discovers the height, the breadth, the length, and the depth of all the sacred scriptures: the height of scripture in God; the breadth in all the books of the Old and New Testaments; its length in the history of salvation from the beginning until the end of time; and its depth in the trifold levels of mystical signification: allegorical, tropological, and anagogical.[133]

The stated, overall aim of the scriptures—to lead the saints to "the fullness of everlasting happiness"[134]—suggests, moreover, the reason for Bonaventure's special focus in the *Breviloquium* on the beatitudes as illustrative of that goal of bliss and of the means toward its fulfillment. Indeed, the Franciscan Master's intricate discussion of the virtues, gifts, and beatitudes in the *Breviloquium* sheds light on the chapters on Francis's virtues in the *Legenda maior*, but the two works are seldom studied together. The *Breviloquium*'s teaching on grace makes it clear that Francis's virtues in the *Legenda maior* are more than practiced virtues; through the Spirit's gifts, they have branched into the beatitudes of the blessed man.

In part 5, chapter 5, of the *Breviloquium*, Bonaventure first considers the role of the Spirit's seven gifts under seven headings.[135] Under the third of these, he pairs the gifts with the seven virtues they assist: fear/temperance, piety/justice, knowledge/prudence, fortitude/steadfastness or patience, counsel/hope, understanding/faith, and wisdom/charity.[136] Here he follows closely the first of two different lists of pairings given in his commentary on Peter Lombard's *Sentences*. In the second list of pairings, not given in the *Breviloquium*, Bonaventure associates the gifts with different ways of aiding the three theological virtues efficiently: understanding and knowledge both aiding faith; wisdom and piety aiding charity; fear and fortitude aiding hope.[137] To all of these, counsel is superadded as a general aid. The existence of different lists in these sources, and the flexibility with which Bonaventure treats the operation of the individual virtues and gifts here and elsewhere, offers encouragement to see his later *Legenda maior* as illustrating other suitable pairings vis-à-vis Francis's enumerated virtues and beatitudes.

In *Breviloquium* 5.5, Bonaventure discusses the seven beatitudes of Matthew 5:3–11 (counting the eighth beatitude together with the first, since they share the same promised reward) from three different points of view: "from the integrity of perfection itself, from the modalities of perfection, and from the preliminary dispositions for perfection [the gifts of the Holy Spirit]."[138] The first three beatitudes (poverty of spirit, meekness, and mourning) are seen, first, as intrinsically purgative habits, generally necessary for the soul's integrity, and its deliverance from self-inflation, rancor, and sensual lust.[139] Second, when regarded under the modality of the perfection of religious life through its three vows of poverty, obedience, and chastity, the three beatitudes of poverty, meekness, and mourning are seen to entail the renunciation of property, the recognition of the neighbor's good, and the desire for the eternal good, respectively. Third, when considered from the perspective of the seven gifts, the gift of the fear of the Lord is seen as necessary for the perfecting of poverty and humility (understood as virtues involving withdrawal from covetousness and pride) in the beatitude of poverty of spirit; the gift of piety, for the perfection of meekness; and knowledge of our fallen condition and earthly exile, for the perfection of mourning.[140]

Bonaventure similarly treats the paired beatitudes of hunger for justice and desire for mercy under three applications. Regarding the integrity of perfection, these two beatitudes are said to flourish in every soul that advances in holiness by "following the divine example."[141] God indeed is just and merciful. For those in authority in the Church *in via* who seek perfection in leadership, these beatitudes therefore are particularly vital. They are attained through the gifts of fortitude and counsel, respectively, because, as Bonaventure explains, those who hunger for justice are ready to die for justice's sake and "God counsels nothing more strongly in Scripture than to show mercy."[142]

Finally, the paired beatitudes of the peacemakers and the pure of heart are treated as appropriate to the perfect enjoyment of God in tranquil love and to the vision of God in eternity, the *visio beata* of the saints. These same beatitudes pertain to the perfection of inner holiness in cleanness of conscience and spiritual tranquility and are obtained through the gifts of understanding and wisdom, respectively, because the understanding of truth "cleanses out heart from all fantasies" and wisdom "unites us to the highest truth and good, in which all the desires of our soul find their end and their repose."[143] (See table 5.2.)

Saint Francis of Assisi as "New Evangelist" in *Vita prima* and *Legenda maior*   141

Table 5.2   The Beatitudes Viewed under Three Aspects in *Breviloquium* 5.5

Blessed are...	Integrity of Perfection	Mode of Perfection	Virtues and Gifts of the Spirit
the poor in spirit	Purged from self-inflation	Vowed to poverty	Poverty and humility, perfected through FEAR OF THE LORD
the meek	Purged from rancor	Vowed to obedience	Meekness in obedient service, perfected through PIETY
those who mourn	Purged from sensual lust	Vowed to chastity	Chaste detachment from this world, perfected through KNOWLEDGE of our fallen condition and earthly exile
those hungering for justice	Imitating God's justice	Serving the Church in pastoral office	Justice, perfected through FORTITUDE
the merciful	Imitating God's mercy	Serving the Church in pastoral office	Mercy, perfected through COUNSEL
the pure of heart	Clean in conscience	Anticipating the *Visio beata*	Virtues perfected through UNDERSTANDING
the peacemakers	Tranquil in spirit	Anticipating eternal rest	Virtues perfected through WISDOM

THE BEATITUDES IN THE EIGHT CHAPTERS OF THE "INNER LIFE"

This elaboration in the *Breviloquium* of the beatitudes in their relation to the virtues and gifts illumines the content and the arrangement of the chapters in the *Legenda maior* that present Francis in possession of heroic virtue and as an exemplar of evangelical perfection (see table 5.3). Chapters 5 through 7 form a set of three, in which the first three beatitudes of

Matthew 5:3–5 can readily be seen, but in a rearranged order that places mourning first, meekness second, and poverty of spirit third. Mourning characterizes Francis's austerity in the ascetic renunciation of sensual pleasure—an *austeritas* linked to chastity and perfected by the gift of knowledge;[144] meekness accords with his humble obedience to God and service of others, virtues perfected by piety; and poverty of spirit names his renunciation of material goods and his practice of begging as virtues perfected through the gift of the fear of the Lord.

The fear of the Lord is "the beginning of wisdom" (Prov. 9:10) and therefore usually placed first in the list of the gifts. Bonaventure has reordered the schema in order to place poverty in chapter 7 at the numerical center of the *Legenda maior*, whose chapter 15 is devoted to posthumous events: Francis's canonization and the transferal of his body. The position is rhetorically strong and symbolically significant. Bonaventure explains in the *Breviloquium*, "Poverty of spirit is the foundation of all evangelical perfection."[145] When treating poverty in chapter 7, moreover (as the editors of the early documents note), Bonaventure follows the same topical order—namely, renunciation of goods, followed by begging—as he does in the *Disputed Questions on Evangelical Perfection*.[146]

We've seen how Bonaventure associates the Gift of piety with meekness in the *Breviloquium* (5.6.5), with justice elsewhere in the *Breviloquium* (5.5.5), and with charity in the commentary on the *Sentences*. The range of the meanings of *pietas*, which Bonaventure further extends in his treatise on the gifts, *De donis*, allows it to be associated not only with Francis's meekness in chapter 6 of the *Legenda maior*, but also with his "affectionate piety" toward creatures in chapter 8 (which features the word *pietas* in its title) and with Francis's ardent life of prayer in chapter 10. Antonino Poppi notes that Bonaventure maintains in *De donis* that "the first exercise of piety is in fact honor and veneration of God," followed by the safeguarding of one's personal holiness in body and soul, and by an intimate mercy towards one's neighbor.[147] Piety honors God, the trace of God in God's creation, and the image of God in one's self and one's neighbors, thus promoting an attitude of reverence and benevolence in every direction: height, depth, length, and breadth.

Chapter 9 of the *Legenda maior* focuses explicitly on Francis's charity and his desire for martyrdom, thus pairing the saint's love with his fortitude. "Love is strong as death" (Sg 8:6). Elsewhere I have called chapter 9 a "crossover" chapter that structurally links the foreshadowing of the stigmata at the end of chapter 4 with its actual reception in chapter 13, thus bridging the "Outer Life" and "Inner Life" of the hagiography.[148] In this privileged position, charity stands at the heart of the virtues, and fittingly so, for, as Bonaventure teaches, "charity itself is the root, form, and end of the virtues, relating them all to the final end and binding them all to one another simultaneously and in an orderly fashion."[149] Francis's ardent desire to die a martyr's death leads him to risk his life in preaching to the sultan. Discussing the gift of fortitude in the *Breviloquium*, Bonaventure associates it with the beatitude of hunger for justice: "Fortitude leads to a hunger for justice, because those possessing it bind themselves to justice so avidly that they would rather be deprived of bodily life than of this justice."[150]

Francis's understanding of scripture and prophetic power, celebrated in chapter 11, are straightforwardly tied both to the Holy Spirit's gift of understanding and to the beatitude of purity of heart. "Enlightened by the splendor of eternal light, [Francis] *probed the depths* [Job 28:11] of Scripture. . . . For his genius, pure and unstained, penetrated hidden mysteries" (Col. 1:26).[151] Bonaventure writes in the *Breviloquium*, "Understanding prepares us for cleanness of heart, because the consideration of truth cleanses our heart from all fantasies."[152]

Francis's twofold activities of preaching and healing in chapter 12 can be tied with similar assuredness both to the gift of counsel and to the beatitude, "Blessed are the merciful" (Matt. 5:7). Valuing the lives both of action and of contemplation, Francis appears in Bonaventure's description as someone who, "by the prodding of the sacred Spirit," was desirous of this very gift of counsel.[153] He sought "with special eagerness in what manner and in what way he could serve God more perfectly," taking advice from others about "how he could more effectively arrive at the summit of perfection."[154] Encouraged by others, Francis devoted himself to preaching, a spiritual work of mercy, and to corporeal works of mercy, including miracles of healing. "Counsel," writes Bonaventure in the *Breviloquium*, "prepares us for mercy, . . . which [God] values more than any sacrificial offering."[155]

With chapter 12, Bonaventure concludes the "Inner Life" of the virtues; in chapter 13 he resumes the chronological account of Francis's story, picking up where he had digressed at the end of chapter 4. In the preceding analysis,

I have linked Bonaventure's account of Francis's virtues in eight chapters in the *Legenda maior* to the Matthean beatitudes and to the gifts of the Holy Spirit, as the Franciscan Master explains them elsewhere. The affiliation of three of the eight chapters with piety leave the reader, however, with a numerical conundrum: Where is wisdom, the last and greatest of the gifts? Is there no beatitude remaining with which it may fittingly be associated?

THE NINTH CHAPTER, THE SEVENTH GIFT, AND THE ANGELIC MAN

Years ago, Ewert Cousins suggested a nine-chapter sequence, beginning at chapter 5 and including chapter 13, in order to accommodate a tripart division of the virtues into purgative (chaps. 5–7), illuminative (chaps. 8–10), and unitive (chaps. 11–13).[156] Certainly Cousins is right to see an ascending sequence in the mystical unfolding. Chapter 13 explicitly refers to the hierarchical acts, whereby God "through a seraphic activity, purifies, illumines, and inflames."[157] Revising an earlier opinion, I want to suggest that Bonaventure has indeed linked the "Inner Life" with the "Outer Life" through a topical overlapping at the end, wherein the gift of wisdom takes the double form of the crucified seraph, who embodies the foolishness of the cross as the height of wisdom (cf. 1 Cor. 1: 18–24) and who imparts that wisdom to Francis with the stigmata.

What of the beatitudes? By Bonaventure's usual count, there are in fact seven, but the passage in Matthew literally includes the word "blessed" nine times. The first and the eighth are regularly treated as doublets, because they promise the same reward, and the ninth is reasonably conflated with the eighth, because both concern those persecuted for righteousness's sake. The full count of nine is useful, however, in characterizing Francis as an angelic man.[158] In the final "blessed" in Matthew 5:11, moreover, Jesus uses a second-person form ("Blessed are you") instead of the expected, third-person form ("Blessed are they") and relates the persecution his disciples endure to his own: "Blessed are you when people revile you and persecute you and utter all kinds of evil against you falsely on my account."

Bonaventure seems to have associated that sort of malicious denial of Christ's disciples with the antimendicants' denial of Francis's stigmata.

Table 5.3 Chapters, Beatitudes, Gifts in Bonaventure's *Legenda maior*

(chap. 5) On the austerity of his life and how the creatures provided him comfort	(Matt. 5:4) Blessed are those who mourn, for they shall be comforted.	Knowledge
(chap. 6) On his humility and obedience and God's condescension to his slightest wish	(Matt. 5:5) Blessed are the meek, for they shall inherit the earth.	Piety
(chap. 7) On his love of poverty and the miraculous fulfillment of his needs	(Matt. 5:3) Blessed are the poor in spirit, for theirs is the kingdom of heaven.	Fear of the Lord
(chap. 8) On his affectionate piety and how irrational creatures were affectionate toward him	(Matt. 5:9) Blessed are the peacemakers, for they shall be called sons of God.	Piety
(chap. 9) On the fervor of his charity and his desire for martyrdom	(Matt. 5:10) Blessed are those who are persecuted for righteousness's sake, for theirs is the kingdom of heaven.	Fortitude
(chap.10) On his zeal for prayer and the power of his prayer	(Matt. 5:6) Blessed are those who hunger and thirst for righteousness, for they shall be satisfied.	Piety
(chap. 11) On his understanding of scripture and his power of prophecy	(Matt. 5:8) Blessed are the pure of heart, for they shall see God.	Understanding
(chap. 12) On the efficacy of his preaching and his grace of healing	(Matt. 5:7) Blessed are the merciful, for they shall obtain mercy.	Counsel
(chap. 13) The stigmata	(Matt. 5:11) Blessed are *you* when people revile *you* and persecute *you* and utter all kinds of evil against *you* falsely on my account.	Wisdom

At the end of chapter 13, he addresses Francis in the second person and writes against the naysayers: "No truly devout person can reject this proof of Christian wisdom ploughed into the dust of your flesh. No truly believing person can attack it, no truly humble person can belittle it, since it is truly divinely expressed and *worthy of complete acceptance*" (1 Tim. 1:15, 4:9).[159] The hagiographer thus merges his own voice with that of Saint Paul, defending his *Legenda maior* of Francis as participant in the very gospel the apostle preached.

THE BIBLICAL SENSES AND THE SENSES OF THE SAINT

Bonaventure provides a comprehensive introduction to scripture in the prologue to the *Breviloquium*; he portrays Francis as an exemplary hearer, illumined reader, and blessed practitioner of the biblical Word in the *Legenda maior*. Bonaventure builds upon these earlier works in his *Collationes in Hexaemeron* (*Collations on the Six Days*) (1273). There the event of Francis, whose living of the gospel was sealed physically and spiritually with the imprinted wounds of Christ, provides the impetus for his articulation of a new understanding of the scriptures as revelation.

According to Bonaventure (Joseph Ratzinger instructs), the scriptural letter alone is not revelation; it only becomes revelation when its literal meaning is spiritually understood.[160] The senses of scripture are to be grasped conveniently by the spiritual senses of the illumined reader.[161] Thus comprehended, scripture has three levels of meaning, the first of which, the *spiritualis intelligentia*, "penetrates through the literal sense to the allegorical, tropological, or anagogical meaning."[162] "But [Bonaventure] is not satisfied with this traditional division," Ratzinger observes.[163] To it Bonaventure adds a second level, the *figurae sacramentales*, with which "Scripture speaks of Christ and of the anti-Christ in all its books,"[164] unfolding a historical pattern and a prophecy of future events. This schema recalls, of course, the first and last of Tyconius's Seven Rules for biblical interpretation,[165] but it applies them systematically across the Bible, its mysteries, and its historical ages. Finally, at a third level, Bonaventure speaks of manifold insights (*multiformes theoriae*) that scripture holds within herself in a seedlike form, but which are recognized only in the course of human history.

"The theories are almost infinite," Bonaventure writes, because the light shed by scripture illumines not only scripture itself, but also the world, which scripture reflects, and because "one man and another look differently into the mirror."[166] Like the *rationales seminales* in the present in God's creation,[167] the hidden seeds sown in the scriptures become visible and bear fruit in time. What Ratzinger terms Bonaventure's "new theory of scriptural exegesis" thus demands a high level of engagement with history, biblical and secular, "in contrast to the exegesis of the Fathers and the Scholastics which had been more clearly directed to the unchangeable and the enduring."[168]

The manifold wisdom (*sapientia multiformis*) of scripture includes all three of these levels, according to Bonaventure, but the degree to which scripture effectively imparts its infinite revelation(s) depends on its reception by the Church as a whole and by its individual members. Citing the prayer of Jesus, "I praise you, Father, Lord of heaven and earth, that thou hast hidden these things from the wise and understanding, but have revealed them to the little ones" (Matt. 11:25), Bonaventure associates biblical revelation with the saintly humility that obeys God's commands and lives by them. Francis of Assisi is (in the words of Ratzinger) "the exemplary *parvulus* [little one] in whom this word of the Lord is fulfilled in a particularly noticeable way."[169]

Indeed, Francis himself was taken by Bonaventure and many Franciscans to signal the advent of a new age, "a time of revelation,"[170] in which the multiform understandings of the letter of the scriptures would be greatly increased and shared among all the elect. For this reason, Bonaventure in the prologue to the *Legenda maior* does not hesitate to name Francis the angel of the sixth seal (Rev. 7:2), a new Elijah, and a new John the Baptist. The Franciscan Master similarly identifies Francis with the angel of the sixth seal in his *Collations on the Six Days*, where the days of creation are seen to mirror the ages of human history: "God created the world in six days and rested on the seventh, so also the mystical body of Christ has six ages and a seventh that runs concurrently with the sixth, and an eighth."[171]

Like Hugh of Saint Victor (1096–1141), who counts the writings of the Fathers as a third, hagiographic part of the New Testament that is indispensable for the correct understanding of the Bible,[172] Bonaventure too looks for biblical illumination not only in the scriptures themselves but also in extracanonical sources in the living tradition of the Church. Extending beyond

Hugh's esteem for the hagiographies of the Fathers, Bonaventure's notion of the *multiformes theoriae* allows for the Church's ever-deeper, prophetic grasp of the scriptures through the lives of canonized saints in every generation who have heard and obeyed the Word of God. In particular, Ratzinger writes, "the event of Francis effectively shattered a concept of tradition which had become too canonical."[173] Francis's life interprets scripture, enacts scripture, while Bonaventure's *Legenda maior* provides a narrative biblical commentary not only upon a host of individual passages, but also upon the very processes whereby scripture becomes revelatory for its readers. Through the awakened spiritual senses of the saint, Bonaventure teaches, others too may learn how to perceive the world and to read the Bible differently. To reject the saint's way of biblical discipleship, Bonaventure warns his disputants, is to refuse Christ's revelation itself.

CHAPTER SIX

HEROIC VIRTUE IN BLESSED RAYMOND OF CAPUA'S *LIFE OF CATHERINE OF SIENA*

*All the virtues can at times simulate perfection
when they are actually imperfect,
but they cannot deceive patience.*

—Catherine of Siena

Taking up his pen to compose his hagiography of Saint Catherine of Siena (1347–80), Raymond of Capua, O.P. (1330–99) compares himself to a host of biblical writers—David, Job, Moses, the prophets, and the Evangelists, above all John—who felt compelled to write about what they had experienced, sensing that their witness to God's marvelous deeds would bring honor and praise to God in their own and in future generations, and also benefit their readers spiritually. Raymond goes so far as to appropriate for himself the divine command given to the seer of the Apocalypse: "Write what you see in a book" (Rev. 1:11).[1] For Raymond, Catherine is prophesied and symbolically represented in the angel holding the chain with which Satan is bound (Rev. 20:1–2), but she herself is also a prophetic book to be unsealed, as it were, by him, her spiritual director, who knew her well and who can attest to her heroic virtues.

The *Life of Catherine of Siena* itself is divided into three parts. The first concerns Catherine's childhood, early visionary experiences, vow of virginity, and consecration as a Third Order Dominican; it culminates in an account of her mystical marriage to Christ (chap. 12). The second part, which also consists of twelve chapters, chronicles her public apostolate; the third part (five chapters, plus an extraordinary epilogue) focuses on her death, posthumous miracles, and heroic virtue. Raymond characterizes the first two parts under the contrastive, biblical figures of Rachel and Leah and of Mary and Martha to highlight the combination of action and contemplation in Catherine's life. He uses verses from the Song of Songs (Sg 5:2–3, 8:5) as epigraphs at the start of parts 2 and 3, respectively, to encapsulate Catherine's bridal mysticism and ecclesial significance.[2]

At the center of part 2 (chap. 6) — and thus at the center of the *Life* as a whole — Raymond provides a lengthy account of Catherine's many "ecstasies and revelations," among which her heart is riven with divine love, and she receives invisible stigmata. The near-death experiences of Catherine mark a sharp division between her body and soul, analogous to the letter/spirit distinction of the scriptural senses, but emphasizing their division rather than their organic joining. The private revelations granted to Catherine serve to affirm and renew the public revelations given to the Church through the charismatic expression she subsequently gives to them in her charitable works, hortatory letters, dictated *Dialogue*, peace-making, and preaching;[3] to the extent that the private revelations concern the still uncanonized Catherine herself, however, they also bear an uneasy relation to the Church's teaching, as Raymond's own hagiographic narrative attests. How credible a witness is Catherine to Catherine's sanctity?

"The *Legenda*, named *prolixa* or *maior*, given its remarkable length and long preparation, is an evident sign," writes Silvia Nocentini, "that Catherine's confessor, as much as her disciples and secretaries, found it arduous to explain, with the *topoi* peculiar to hagiography at the end of the fourteenth century, the holy woman's experience of God."[4] Indeed, by all accounts, Blessed Raymond of Capua's *Life of Catherine of Siena* is unusual among medieval hagiographies — "a *Legenda* with a difference," as Conleth Kearns describes it.[5] Written over a period of ten years (1384–95) by Catherine's papally appointed confessor, close friend, and Dominican co-worker, the *Life* stands at a point of significant transition in the history of hagiography as a genre. It looks back to the early legends of the Desert Fathers and Mothers — popular legends that Catherine herself read and to which Raymond frequently refers in his often difficult search for saintly precedent to validate Catherine's experience and behavior. It takes a side glance at Saint Bonaventure's *Legenda maior* (1260–63) of Saint Francis of Assisi and at Jacobus de Voragine's *Legenda aurea* (ca. 1260)—works dating, for Raymond, from the not-so-distant thirteenth century.[6] At the same time, Raymond's *Life* reflects a specifically Thomistic Scholasticism and the newly juridical process of canonization, elaborated by the Avignon popes (1309–77), with its demand for the testimony of named witnesses, for refutation of objections, and for proof of heroic virtue.[7] Biblical references frame the narrative and occasionally aid Raymond in commenting upon Catherine's words and deeds, but they remain largely marginal to the long, detailed work that, in Nocentini's words, "conditioned later bio-hagiographies."[8] Raymond's "concept of a hagiographical *vita* was to collect the greatest quantity of facts as possible in an ordered and allegorical scheme," observes Nocentini, "a manner of writing [that] reflects also the intention . . . to build in a canonical form a *legenda* that could become part of a canonization's dossier in view of papal approval of the cult."[9]

Catherine Benincasa of Siena was canonized in 1461 by Pope Pius II. The canonization of Saint Bonaventure only twenty-three years later in 1484 by Pope Sixtus IV marked the completion of the first process to look systematically for proofs of heroism in the practice of the three theological virtues (faith, hope, and charity) and the four cardinal virtues (prudence, temperance, fortitude, and justice). The criterion of heroic virtue can be said to have functioned spontaneously in the Church's popular recognition of saints from the age of the martyrs and confessors, as Augustine bears witness in book 10 of the *City of God*, where he explicitly calls the Christian martyrs "our heroes," contrasting their humble greatness with that of the pagan "men of mark."[10] The technical term "heroic virtue," however, first "entered the church's vocabulary" (according to Kenneth Woodward) in 1328, via Robert Grosseteste's translation of Aristotle's *Nicomachean Ethics*.[11] Strongly influenced by Aristotelian thought, Thomas Aquinas (1225–74) does not use the term, preferring to speak of the "*perfect virtues* . . . attributed to the Blessed, or, in this life, to some who are at the summit of perfection."[12] His study of the virtues in the *Summa theologiae*, a century earlier than Grosseteste's translation, had nevertheless already established the conceptual basis for the heuristic testing of evidence for heroic virtue in the official process of beatification and canonization.[13] A Dominican well trained in Thomistic theology, Raymond of Capua was *lector* of theology in Rome and Bologna before his election in 1380 (shortly after Catherine's death) as master general of the Order of Preachers. He was also a careful student, I hope to show, of Catherine's own, very original doctrine of the virtues.

In the late Middle Ages, attested miracles were necessary to, but not sufficient for, a saint's canonization; the personal, heroic virtue of the candidate for ecclesial recognition had to be demonstrated. The celebrated case of Catherine of Siena posed difficulties in this regard. In her own lifetime, the visionary was a controversial figure, whose virtuous practice unsettled the very understanding of traditionally accepted virtues in the minds of her friends and foes alike.[14] The *Life* itself gives ample evidence of Raymond's efforts to defend the claim of her sanctity against her detractors who found her chronic fasting a scandalous, self-willed excess; who saw in her unusual way of life a vainglorious craving to be exceptional (instead of a humble pattern-setting for others to follow); who questioned whether she had been sadly deluded by the devil; or who accused her of outright fraud in her reports of mystical experience and inedia.[15] In order to win over the skeptics in his audience, Raymond (whose vividly remembered, personal experiences of Catherine make the *Life* as much or more his life story as it is hers) casts himself as a one-time doubting Thomas (John 20:24–29), initially dubious of her virtue, who has turned into a firm believer.[16] Anticipating the response of an imagined reader, who objects that Catherine alone stands witness to her supposed mystical visions and auditions, Raymond confesses that God had once permitted him too to be very skeptical in many ways in her regard:

> I explored every avenue and tried in every possible way to find an answer to the question: are these things from God or not? Are they fact or fiction? For the thought came to me that the present age is the age of the Third Beast which the Prophet saw [Dan. 7:6]: the Beast like a leopard, with spotted skin, which signifies hypocrites. Within my experience I had come across people, especially women, who got wild notions and fell easy victims to the Enemy who beguiles us—as our mother Eve herself did in the beginning. (para. 87)

In fact, the *Life* makes Catherine's virtuous endurance of charges by scandalmongers and of doubts like Raymond's—so revealing of a general moral anxiety about the religious hypocrisy that disguises vice as virtue, and so expressive of masculine uncertainty and prejudice—a vital part of the story of her sanctity, converting them into proofs of her humility perfected in patience.

Raymond's first prologue to the *Life* previews Catherine's story as a life of interconnected virtues founded in a humility that expresses itself in charity. His epilogue—the sixth and final chapter of part 3—offers a review of Catherine's *Life* from a new and seemingly different perspective: that of her greatest virtue, patience. The initial emphasis on humility serves multiple purposes: it directly counters the charge against Catherine (that extraordinary woman, influential in public affairs) of vainglory; it sets her humble, penitential life within an apocalyptical framework comparable to that found in Bonaventure's *Legenda maior* of Francis of Assisi; and it evokes the monastic trope of the Steps of Humility (the defining route of holiness, as outlined in the Rule of Saint Benedict) to provide a familiar theological framework for the highly unusual *Life* that follows.

As Raymond constructs Catherine's *Life*, the distance between the humility of the prologue and the patience of the epilogue—a topical distance underscored by an obvious shift in hagiographical style—is bridged by the narrative theology of the *Life* proper. A long, protonovelistic work, it is filled with Raymond's own first-person reports and the colorful accounts of other named witnesses. It is punctuated, too, with frequent allusions to Jacobus de Voragine's legend of Mary Magdalene,[17] Catherine's patroness and model, whose composite history (like Catherine's own) includes times of penitence, contemplative withdrawal, miraculous abstinence and Eucharistic sustenance, ecstasy, and apostolic preaching.[18]

Outside the scope of this essay, that narrative material is systematically reviewed and cross-referenced in the epilogue of the *Life* under the aspect of patience.[19] Whereas the prologue takes a literary form that recalls an earlier hagiographic tradition, the epilogue employs the language of the new canonization process and its Scholastic moral theology. Raymond's surprising choice, in that context, of patience as the unifying and crowning virtue of Catherine's life calls attention to the originality in Catherine's own teaching on the virtues (as compared to that of Aquinas), harkens back to the Augustinian doctrine that links humility to the heroism of martyrdom, and underscores the model character of Catherine's virtuous life for the Church as a whole.[20]

RAYMOND'S ECCLESIOLOGY AND CATHERINE'S DOCTRINE OF VIRTUES

Controversial in its own time (as was the saint it celebrates), the *Life* has drawn considerable criticism from modern historians,[21] and, in recent decades, from feminist scholars, who compare and contrast Catherine's spirited, vernacular self-expression in her many letters and in *The Dialogue*,[22] with Raymond's portrayal of her.[23] The *Life* deserves to be studied in its own right, however, as a remarkable, fourteenth-century hagiographic venture, a sustained theological reflection on the meaning of Catherine's apocalyptic mission for the Church at the time of the Great Schism (1378–1415). For Raymond, Catherine's embattled life is a symbol of the Church's own life, a timely revelation to the Church of her own bridal nature, motherly calling, oneness, and holiness. Pressured on all sides, Raymond's virtuous Catherine suffers as a martyr for the truth of the Church's unity and for its peace.

For Raymond, Catherine's sanctity—her life of the virtues—is inseparable from her iconic ecclesiology, her life's witness to the Church as one, holy, catholic, and apostolic.[24] Raymond signals this inseparability in the first prologue to the *Life*, where, following an ancient hagiographic practice, he discusses the etymology of Catherine's name as an indication of her divinely appointed destiny. *Nomen est omen*. Even as "the Church is *cath*-olic," Raymond writes, "the syllable *katha* or *catha* in the name *Catharina* hints at the notion of *universality*, . . . of a 'unity' in 'diversity'" (para.10) (italicized terms underlined in the original). Glossed in a different but related way, the name "Catherine" is also a variant of the Latin word *catena*, "chain," because, as Raymond explains, "a chain is composed of a number of individual links which . . . have been combined into a single unity" (para.10). On this basis, Raymond interprets the "great chain" held by the angel, with which he binds "the ancient serpent" (Rev. 20:1–2), as a symbol referring both to the interconnected virtues in the life of the individual saint and to the bond of shared gifts and virtues holding the Church together as a communion of saints.[25] "Our Catharina was one," Raymond concludes, "in whose heart were gathered together both the universal collectivity of all the virtues . . . and the universal collectivity of all the faithful of the Church, which she loved so intensely" (para. 11).

Catherine herself uses the image of the chain of virtue in *The Dialogue* to describe the binding of Satan and of God.[26] Raymond similarly employs the symbol of the double chain, held out by the apocalyptic angel, to represent Catherine's doctrine not only of the interconnection of the virtues — such that "all the virtues are bound together, and it is impossible to have one without having them all" — but also of the interconnection of persons through the enactment of virtues or vices.[27] In *The Dialogue*, Jesus teaches Catherine again and again: "I would have you know that every virtue and every vice is put into action by means of your neighbors" (*Chè Io ti fo sapere che ogni virtú si fa col mezzo del prossimo, e ogni difetto*).[28] "Your neighbors," Jesus tells her, "are the channels through which all your virtues are tested and come to birth, just as the evil give birth to all their vices through their neighbors."[29] Whereas Saint Paul in 1 Corinthians 12 describes the Church as a body with many members, each with a different function of service, a different gift from God with which to affect and enrich the others, Catherine emphasizes the converse of moral and theological virtues that are called forth from within us in response to the need of another, effecting a vital intersubjective relationship and spiritual bond. The specific needs of our neighbors, approached in charity, give birth in us to diverse virtues.[30] For Catherine, this converse of persons and virtues results from the inseparability of the love of God and neighbor.

In Catherine's understanding, moreover, each soul possesses a "virtue which has been made primary for her," which allows for variation, growth, and community, so that "one virtue, might be, as it were the source of all the others" — one person's humility giving rise, for example, to a second person's obedience (in one instance), to gratitude (in another).[31] "I wanted to make you dependent upon one another, so that each of you would be my minister," Jesus explains to Catherine.[32]

Stressing the role of the virtues in uniting the members of the Church, one with the other, in Christ, Catherine offers a practical, biblically inspired, and mystically rich alternative to Aquinas's teaching on the four cardinal virtues: temperance, justice, fortitude, and prudence as "social virtues," appropriate to human nature as a "social animal," and perfected by the infusion of grace.[33] The respective frameworks of the two saints' thinking is so different that one hesitates even to begin to compare them. In using the image of an interconnected chain of virtues that simultaneously connects persons, one with the other, Raymond remains quietly true to Catherine, however, without contradicting Thomas; at the same time, the hagiographer uses the image to develop his own apocalyptic theme of Catherine as a prophet sent to the Church.

THE FIRST PROLOGUE: HUMILITY'S APOCALYPTIC EXALTATION

The first prologue, regularly omitted in English translations of the *Life*,[34] provides an indispensable, exegetical key for understanding Raymond's view of Catherine's person and of her mission for the world of their time. Raymond first quotes and then interprets, phrase by phrase, Revelations 20:1: "I saw coming down from heaven an angel holding in his hand the key of the abyss and a great chain" (para. 1). Recalling the Son's humble descent into the world in the Incarnation, Raymond discovers in the verse an allegorical reference to the Word-made-flesh as an "angel" embodying and announcing the gospel and holding the prophesied key of David with which to bind Satan's power over humanity.

The remembrance of Christ's self-emptying descent (see Phil. 2:5–11) inspires, in turn, Raymond's ecclesial and moral interpretation. The apostles, martyrs, and confessors of old followed the Lord's own way of redeeming humility, Raymond observes, welcoming "every kind of trial—torture, imprisonment, death itself" (para. 3). Receiving "from that Angel's hand . . . the great chain composed of all the Christian virtues linked together in an organic unity," they "overcame the Adversary" (para. 3). Faithful to himself and to his promise, the Lord continues to hold out this chain, Raymond insists, even "in our times," when the world has grown "blind and slothful" (para. 3), choosing to humble proud men by pouring out his grace "in special measure on women" (*in sexu fragiliori, videlicet femineo*) (para. 4), such as the maiden of Siena, whose very name, "Catherine," signifies her reception of the chain (*catena*) of virtues from Christ and her holding of it for and with others, to secure the unity of the Church in its present trial (para. 10). By extension, then, Catherine too merits to be called an "angel," Raymond argues, even as he, Raymond, can fittingly write as another "John," for to him, as her companion and confessor, Catherine has imparted the evangelical knowledge (*secreta revelata*) given to her by Christ (para. 6).

Raymond explains Catherine's share in Christ's unique mediation through her incorporation into his pattern of descent and ascent, her following in his footsteps. Using an ancient image that summarizes the monastic way of perfection (given classic expression in chapter 7 of the Rule of Saint Benedict), Raymond observes, "Like the angels on Jacob's ladder [Gen. 28:12–17], she kept coming down and going up again"—coming down through her humility in "her own self-knowledge and in the lowly service of works of mercy to her neighbor" and going up through prayer and contemplation, "gazing on the face of the Lord to whom that ladder leads" (para. 7). As taught by the Rule to which Raymond alludes, the steps of humility link that virtue to all the others through charity—the ladder itself being a kind of chain—so that the humility that marks the soul's conversion both grounds and preserves the soul's ascent; it is never left behind or replaced by other virtues, but perfected instead through them. Humility's exaltation, its ascent, thus opposes the false exaltation of pride, which is, in reality, the soul's Luciferian descent, its fall into a succession of vices. To highlight this relationship, crucial to Raymond's portrait of Catherine, the Rule quotes the biblical verse twice-repeated in Luke: "Everyone who exalts himself shall be humbled, and he who humbles himself shall be exalted" (Luke 14:11, 18:14).[35]

In the *Life* itself, Raymond defends Catherine against the charges of vainglory that accompanied her throughout her public career. Anticipating that need for defense, he celebrates her humility in the first prologue not by diminishing her historical influence, but rather by presenting her extraordinary achievements as humility's proof and fruit. He points to her "*Letters . . .* sent to practically every part of Christendom" and praises "the sublimity of their style and the depth of their doctrine" (para. 7). He considers "the *Book* which she composed in her own vernacular [*in idiomate proprio*], manifestly at the dictation of the Holy Spirit," again praising its style and, more importantly, its usefulness "to every soul intent on the business of eternal salvation" (para. 8). Finally, he speaks of the "burning eloquence" of her "living words," which moved people, provoked compunction, gave instruction (para. 9). These fruits, he concludes, cannot be explained by her natural endowments and education; they prove instead "the fire of the Holy Spirit present within her," endowing her with his "charisma of utterance" (para. 9). Only after emphasizing Catherine's powerful apostolic activity as writer, teacher, and preacher does Raymond turn to a direct consideration of her humility, "the foundation and support of all the other virtues" (para. 12). As Raymond indicates in the first prologue and repeatedly in the *Life* itself, Catherine characteristically chose "to be made lower than the lowest of all," because she believed herself to be "the cause of all the evils which others suffered" and thus owing "to all a debt" (para. 12). Raymond dwells upon Catherine's pronounced sense of her own guiltiness and personal responsibility for the world's evils—a sense to which Catherine herself gives clear expression in *The Dialogue*.[36]

He does so, in part, to offer an explanation of the saint's attitude and thus to protect her against the suspicion either of actual guilt (perhaps an unconfessed sin) or of a morbid scrupulosity. He confesses that he had asked her "how she could possibly say and believe" herself to be "the cause of all the wrongdoing that was committed by sinners" (para. 13). Her answer, which simply pointed to her existence and to the continued existence of sin in the world, disarmed him, leaving him "silent in the presence of such a . . . master of the life of virtue" (para. 14), whose seemingly bottomless humility gave rise, as was evident to Raymond, to "faith, hope, and the queen of . . . all [virtues], charity" (para. 14). In her, he remarks, "charity and humility were ingeniously linked together in the chain of one single good work" (para. 12).

Enumerating her works of mercy, corporal and spiritual, Raymond finds in Catherine an imitator of Christ comparable to a host of recognized saints, each in his or her outstanding virtue (para. 16). In this way, he returns to his theme (and Catherine's) of interconnected virtues, not only linked to one another in a lively manner, but also binding together the members of the Church in one single communion of saints, united to Christ and to one another. This unity, he affirms, has the power to bind Satan and his works.

Raymond's etymologies in the first prologue for the name "Catherine," together with his interpretations of it as a little chain of interconnected virtues, may have been inspired, at least in part, by a letter the English Augustinian friar William Flete (ca. 1325–ca. 1390) sent to Raymond in the summer of 1377, more than two years before Catherine's death. Flete, a hermit at Lecceto (Selva del Lago), four miles from Siena, preceded Raymond as Catherine's confessor, offering her guidance and receiving her confidences in the formative years from 1368 to 1374. In that letter to Raymond, "Brother William of England, a sinner" writes in ardent defense of Catherine against her detractors and celebrates her virtues, especially her humility, charity, and patience in bearing many trials and sufferings: "On account of her love, then, she is called a chain of virtues, but it is equally appropriate to call her a chain of sufferings, . . . since she is ever enchained in sufferings, never free."[37] William does not, however, associate Catherine's chain with that of Revelations 20:1.

The apocalyptic tone of the first prologue, controlled by its exposition of Revelation 20:1, inevitably invites a comparison to the prologue to Bonaventure's *Legenda maior* of Francis of Assisi. Echoing Acts 2:17, Bonaventure declares that the grace of the Savior has appeared "in these last days" in the poor and humble form of "his servant Francis," whom Bonaventure calls "the Angel of true peace" (Isa. 33:7), comparing him to the angel the apostle John describes in the Apocalypse "ascending from the rising of the sun, having the seal of the living God" (Rev. 7:2).[38] Like Bonaventure, Raymond compares his saint, Catherine, to an angel, naming her humble and remarkable appearance on the historical stage a prodigy, intended by God to summon humanity to repentance and reform. Raymond likens Catherine's zeal to Elijah's and her mortification to "the asceticism and poverty of John the Baptist" (para. 16), to both of whom Bonaventure similarly likens Francis of Assisi as a prophet of penitence. Bonaventure uses the apocalyptic image of "the seal of the living God" (Rev. 7:2), borne by an angel, to refer to the stigmata of Francis, whereas Raymond plays upon the language of the confessional seal, which has opened to him the secrets of Catherine's soul and of her mystical experiences (para. 6), during one of which (as Raymond relates later in the *Life*) Catherine received, like Francis before her, the imprint of Christ's wounds upon her hands, feet, and heart (paras. 194–98).

These explicit points of comparison are not surprising, given the close relationship between the mendicant orders and between the cults of these two saints, each of whom was believed to have received the stigmata— Francis visibly, Catherine invisibly—as a seal upon their special closeness to Christ in his suffering and upon their Christlike mission for the Church on earth, which Francis worked to save from corruption, and Catherine from schism. In *The Dialogue*, Catherine's God refers to Francis's reception of the holy wounds as opening up "a path for the others"—a path she herself followed.[39] Although Catherine's rival cult as a stigmatist encountered historical Franciscan resistance,[40] Raymond's point in quietly comparing his Catherine to Bonaventure's Francis is the unity of these and other saints against an apocalyptic background; the suffering endured by the Church is seen in Catherine and Francis to unite the bridal Church all the more closely to its crucified Bridegroom. Raymond explains in the *Life*, quoting Catherine's own words, that the wounds she received during her vision before the altar at Pisa became, for her, a source of virtue: "I can feel strength flowing into me from those wounds, which at first only added to my sufferings" (para. 198).

Whereas Raymond employs the outer frame of the *Life* (the first prologue and the final chapter) to highlight the theme of virtues hidden in the narrative proper, Bonaventure takes the opposite strategy, using the outermost chapters (1–4, 13–15) to narrate the events in Francis's history, and the eight enclosed chapters (5–12) to consider Francis's virtues, one by one.[41] Both Raymond and Bonaventure place, however, an initial emphasis on humility. Bonaventure calls humility "the guardian and ornament of all the virtues," and relates that Francis "strove to build himself up on this virtue," following Christ, who descended from on high "to our lowly estate," in order to "teach humility in both word and example."[42]

In the first prologue, Raymond introduces not only Christ but also Mary Magdalene as a mirror for Catherine in her humility. He quotes Catherine speaking to herself the following words: "These [evils] are the result of your wickedness. Acknowledge yourself, then, for what you are, and weep for your sins. Weep for them like Magdalene at the feet of the Lord until, like her, you hear the words, 'Your many sins have been forgiven you, because you have loved much'" (para. 12).

Raymond's tale of his own conversion from doubt about Catherine's virtues to faith in their genuineness (a conversion in which he hopes his readers will share) involves a Magdalene-like weeping. Early in the *Life* proper, he confesses to having been skeptical about Catherine. Seeking to discern the truth, he devises a fail-proof test. Convinced as a theologian that "a heartfelt contrition for one's sins is a convincing sign of the grace of God" and that "such contrition could come from no one but the Holy Spirit" (para. 87), Raymond playfully asks Catherine to pray that he be granted the experience of compunction for his sins—a tearful experience of remorse that is, in fact, given to him the following day through Catherine's intercession and in her physical presence. This unexpected gift of tears—which Raymond half-jokingly likens to a bull issued by the Roman Curia (para. 87)— effects and authenticates not only Raymond's own conversion from doubt to belief, but also, at least in his eyes, the truth of Catherine's sanctity, the genuineness of her virtues, grounded in humility and interconnected with those of others, in anticipation of her papal canonization.

PATIENT READING: THE *LIFE* AND THE FINAL CHAPTER

Given the emphasis on humility in the prologue and the role played by the penitent Mary Magdalene as Catherine's patron saint and alter ego throughout the *Life*, it is at first surprising that Raymond's epilogue features not Catherine's humility, but her patience. Having stressed the miracles, moral and physical, worked through Catherine during her earthly life and also posthumously, in part 3, chapter 6, Raymond offers a "compendium of the whole of the foregoing work," in which he rereads the entire *Life* as offering proof of "Catherine's patience, lest any reasonable doubt of her sanctity should still persist" (para. 397). Raymond sees this single, infused moral virtue as uniting all of Catherine's virtues: "As I hope to show . . . (the Lord helping me), every part of her life had her patience interwoven with it" (para. 397).

This final chapter calls attention to itself on several grounds. The preview of a *Life* of humility (announced in the prologue) does not (at least superficially) match its review as a *Life* of patience. The choice of patience is, moreover, in itself remarkable, since patience per se is neither a theological virtue nor a cardinal virtue (but it has ties with both charity and fortitude). Most obviously, the final chapter is structurally anomalous. Raymond indicates in his second prologue to the *Life* that it has, in honor of the Blessed Trinity, "three main divisions: *Part One*: Catherine's birth, infancy, and girlhood, up to her espousals to our Lord inclusive; *Part Two*:

the story of her life after she became a public figure, that is, from the time of her espousals to her passing from this world; *Part Three*: her death and the events which led up to it; also a selection of some of the miracles which took place at and after her death" (para. 21). Chapter 6 of part 3, however, falls outside of this scheme. "It is," in the words of Conleth Kearns, "a distinct composition, constituting a kind of appendix to the Life as a whole."[43]

Observing Raymond's own comments concerning it, Kearns spells out in a footnote a threefold purpose for this added chapter, which stands curiously outside the *Life* proper and yet within it: (1) to provide a brief version of the preceding work, (2) to further the cause of Catherine's canonization, and (3) to "introduce some elements which will be new even to readers of all that has preceded it."[44] Kearns highlights new narrative elements that result from Raymond's topical invention under the heading of "patience" — for example, Raymond's detailed account of the Florentine plot to murder Catherine in 1378 and, I would add, Raymond's one and only mention (in passing, and therefore often overlooked by readers) of something for which Catherine is rightly famous: her successful persuasion of Pope Gregory XI to return from Avignon to his proper seat (as bishop of Rome) in Rome.[45]

The final chapter, then, remembers Catherine's life, adding what has been seemingly forgotten in the preceding pages; it does not simply repeat Raymond's *Life*. Does the concluding chapter on the virtue of patience add new *theological*, and also narrative, elements retrospectively to the *Life*? In what follows, I argue that it does. I begin with a comparison of Raymond's respective discussions of virtue in the final chapter and in the preceding *Life*, where Raymond seldom mentions patience and its related virtue, fortitude, and writes, instead, principally of charity. The explicitly marked, dialogical relationship between part 3, chapter 6, on the one hand, and everything that precedes it, on the other, enables, then, the discovery of other intertextual dialogues—in particular, those between and among Catherine, Raymond, and Thomas Aquinas on the topic of martyrdom, humility, and heroic patience.

Raymond displays his sense of humor when he stages the final chapter on Catherine's heroic patience as a temptation for the reader to impatience. "This compendium," he writes, "is meant for those readers who are quickly wearied; for such, namely, as feel an hour longer than a whole day when pious questions are in question, but who feel a whole day shorter than an

Heroic Virtue in Blessed Raymond of Capua's *Life of Catherine of Siena* 163

hour when tales and light reading are concerned" (para. 397). In sharp contrast to the long, preceding, novelistic *Life of Catherine*—a work that has merited the adjective *prolix*—the final chapter is governed by "a rigorous plan, whose very order will cut short all prolixity and ensure brevity of treatment" (para. 397). Defining patience as that virtue that "comes into play in dealing with what runs counter to [one's] welfare," Raymond outlines a "rigorous plan" to examine Catherine's patience as tried by the loss of goods—pleasurable, useful, and seemly—that affected the well-being, first, of her body and, then, of her soul. In so doing, he refers briefly to many incidents he has previously recounted, providing precise cross-references to the respective, earlier chapters in parts 1, 2, and 3.

The cross-references indicate that Raymond does not in fact offer the final chapter as a lazy reader's substitute for the preceding *Life*, but rather, as a commentary upon it, to encourage the reader's study and rereading of the *Life*, in order to notice what the abridged version has omitted and to see in sharp relief what the longer version has obscured. The *Life*, moreover, encourages the reading of Catherine's own writings, to which it refers directly and indirectly. The brevity of the final chapter is meant actually to prolong the already lengthy *Life* by making it an object of retrospective, theological reflection.

Raymond keeps strictly to his announced outline for part 3, chapter 6. With regard to *pleasurable* and *useful* goods, Raymond notes that from her earliest childhood, Catherine vowed her virginity to God, "gave herself to prayer and penance," practicing "abstinence in food and drink" (para. 400). She suffered the lack of these useful goods of bodily sustenance, he explains, as a protection for the perpetual virginity she had vowed at age seven, when she first renounced the pleasurable good of sex (para. 399). Abstaining completely from meat and cooked food by the age of fifteen, she eventually stopped eating "food of any kind" (para. 400), except the Eucharist. Catherine practiced patience—that is, she suffered these bodily hardships, and recurrent illnesses, chronic pain, and occasional physical abuse, without succumbing to sadness and indeed joyfully, Raymond observes.

Her truly heroic patience, however, "came into play," he argues, "in enduring privation with regard to those *seemly* goods" appropriate to her personal calling as a virgin, penitent, mystic, healer, exorcist, and prophetess—namely, "her attachment to continual prayer, her mortification of her body, her work for the welfare of her neighbor" (para. 402). Her parents opposed her desire for contemplation by depriving her, for example, of the "seemly good" of time alone in her own room (para. 401). They tried to persuade her to marry and thus to lose the "seemly good" of her espousal to Christ. Her mother opposed her penances, and her confessor and advisors tried to force her to take food. Her religious superiors sometimes "forbade her to go to places where she had been ordered by divine revelation to go" (para. 404). Some of them blocked her ardently desired reception of the sacraments, of confession and Communion. Her acts of devotion made her "the butt of calumny, obstruction, and persecution" (para. 406). Infuriated with her frequent ecstasies, some even kicked her (para. 407). "All this she bore and put up with without a murmur" (para. 406).

With regard to the patiently endured deprivation of the seemly, spiritual goods of "a good name and holy friendships," Raymond tells how Catherine suffered tongue-lashings and "the accusation of unchastity" (para. 409), which circulated through the town in rumors spread about her by three Sienese women—Cecca, Palmerina, and Andrea—whom Catherine had nursed in their terrible illnesses, contracting leprosy herself from Cecca in the process. Insulted and misunderstood by humans, especially those closest to her, Catherine bore all these sufferings "victoriously by her courageous and ever-vigilant patience" (para. 415), eventually winning the three women's conversions, one by one.

Demons also afflicted her directly, knocking her down, "but all the time," Raymond reports, "she kept a smiling and cheerful countenance, ridiculing the Enemy" (para. 418). Although Catherine suffered terribly at the hands of human instruments, her real tormentors, according to Raymond, were the unseen demons who scourged and beat her, even as they had afflicted Saint Anthony in the desert; it was the demons who stirred up her enemies against her and who eventually martyred her.

At this point in the final chapter of the *Life*, Raymond narrates at length a story he had not previously told in any detail: that concerning Catherine's peace-making missions in Florence in 1376 and 1378, at first at the request of Pope Gregory XI and then on behalf of his successor, Pope Urban VI. Raymond's goal is to show in the life of Catherine a close reenactment of Christ's arrest in Gethsemane and thus her participation in his passion. Confronted in a wooded garden outside Florence by a mob armed

Heroic Virtue in Blessed Raymond of Capua's *Life of Catherine of Siena*   165

"with swords and clubs," Catherine "got ready for the martyrdom she had long desired" (para. 427), saying to the would-be assassins, "I am ready to suffer for Christ and His Church" (para. 427). Like Jesus, who answered the soldiers who sought him with the words "I am He" (John 18:5), Catherine declared to the rioters who had come looking for her, "I am Catherine" (para. 427). Like Jesus, she begged them not to harm her companions. Bitterly disappointed at not being killed that night, Catherine nevertheless suffered as the martyrs had. "Indeed," Raymond relates, "the people of Florence were still so much in fear that, as in the time of the martyrs, no one was willing to receive Catherine into his house" (para. 428). Catherine was, however, eventually successful; she left Florence in 1378 only after a peace treaty between Florence and the Holy See had been "negotiated, concluded, signed, and finally promulgated in the city" (para. 429).

Exhausted, summoned to Rome at the outbreak of the Great Schism, Catherine died there at age thirty-three, Raymond writes, in such a manner "as to put her on a level with the martyrs," after a trial lasting thirteen weeks: "neither the pains nor the motive of martyrdom in the fullest sense were lacking to her" (para. 430). It is as a martyr, Raymond urges, that Catherine deserves to be canonized by "the surest and the shortest way": "In such cases, where the courage that endures martyrdom itself is present, the presence of patience, too, cannot be doubted; the question is not even raised" (para. 430).

MARTYRDOM AND THE QUESTION OF HEROIC PATIENCE

Martyrs were, of course, historically the first group of Christians to be accorded cultic and liturgical recognition by the Church, as their tombs became the sites of prayer, of miracles, and of Eucharistic celebrations on the anniversaries of their deathdays, which were understood to be their *natales*, "birthdays," into eternal joy in heaven.[46] Augustine in *City of God* calls them the Church's "heroes," who, by giving up their lives, bore witness to Christ, who offered himself as a sacrifice "by His humility, manifesting Himself to mortals by the mortality that He assumed."[47] Indeed, for Augustine, "martyrs were preeminently paragons of humility," Peter Iver Kaufman has written.[48]

In arguing for Catherine's status as a martyr or confessor (the confessors were originally understood to be saints who had endured a martyr's persecution but had survived their tortures in prison or in the arena), Raymond sidesteps the problem of having to establish a new category for Catherine as a saint within the ever-growing panoply of saintly types—alongside, for example, the contemporary visionary mystic, Saint Bridget of Sweden (d. 1373), with whom Catherine is often compared;[49] indeed, he challenges in Catherine's case the necessity of the canonization process as it had developed by the fourteenth century, even as he provides a basis, in accord with Thomistic moral theology, for her recognition as a saint precisely through such a process.

In *Summa theologiae* II-II, q. 12, Aquinas defines martyrdom as "an act of virtue" that "consists essentially in standing firmly to truth and justice against the assaults of persecution" (art. 1).[50] More precisely, he names it "an act of fortitude," an infused moral virtue that strengthens a person to hold fast to the truths of the faith and its practice "against dangers of death" (art. 2). Thomas goes on to describe the act of martyrdom as "elicited" by fortitude, "as being its proper motive cause," but "commanded" by the theological virtue of charity, "as its first and chief motive cause"(art. 2). A special virtue, in that it "directs the acts of all other virtues to their last end" and "gives the form to all acts of virtue" (*ST* II-I, q. 23, a. 8), charity finds the "greatest proof of [its] perfection" in "martyrdom" (*ST* II-II, q. 124, a. 3).

Asked whether martyrdom "is an act of the greatest perfection," Thomas answers "no" with respect to "the species of the act," which is death, but "yes" with respect to "its first motive cause," charity (*ST* II-II, q. 124, a. 3). As a scriptural proof, he quotes John 15:13: "Greater love than this no man hath, that a man lay down his life for his friends."

If martyrdom enacts the meeting point of charity and fortitude as theological and moral virtues, the same may be said of martyrdom as an act of patience. As Thomas acknowledges, "martyrs are also praised for their patience" (*ST* II-II, q. 124, a. 2), which he defines elsewhere in the *Summa* as "a quasi-potential part of fortitude" (*ST* II-II, q. 136, a. 4). Braving the danger of death, the martyrs must also be ready to endure it, to suffer it patiently, out of love for God and neighbor. Quoting 1 Corinthians 13:4, "Charity is patient," Thomas describes patience as "a virtue . . . caused by charity" (*ST* II-II, q. 136, a. 3).

The thought of Thomas on the interconnectedness of all the infused virtues, on their basis in charity, and on charity's enacted perfection in martyrdom thus provides Raymond with an authoritative means to understand Catherine's life as whole, a "unity in diversity." Raymond's specific emphasis on patience remains surprising, however. Thomas himself has relatively little to say about patience per se, which, he says, "is not the greatest of the virtues, but falls short, not only of the theological virtues, and of prudence and justice . . ., but also of fortitude and temperance" (*ST* II-II, q. 136, a. 2). The object with which patience contends, according to Thomas, is hardship—an object not connected directly either to a theological good nor necessarily to overcoming a great obstacle to such a good.

In reply, Raymond admits that "patience in itself [is not] the noblest virtue or the queen of virtues," but he finds it "in constant attendance on that virtue which . . . is the greatest of them all, never passes away, and never ceases for its activity," namely, charity (para. 395). Greater than "signs and wonders" (as Gregory the Great bears witness in his *Moralia in Job* and in his *Dialogues*),[51] patience is "the first condition of charity" for Raymond, since "charity is [first of all] patient" (1 Cor. 13:4); patience is the virtue that enables perseverance in charity and in every other virtue (since it enables one to endure obstacles and daily hardships); and, finally, patience is the virtue by which one suffers the martyrdom that fortitude braves (para. 396).

What this brief analysis, given by Raymond in the concluding chapter of his *Life of Catherine of Siena*, fails to make explicit is that Raymond's choice of patience in particular as Catherine's virtue par excellence derives from her own strong teaching on this virtue in *The Dialogue*. There she, conscious of the revelations that God has imparted to her, draws support from the book of Revelation, from which she quotes.[52] Christ's words to her echo Revelation 2:10, telling her that "perseverance is the virtue that receives glory and the crown of victory."[53] Even more instructive in this context is the apocalyptic reference to the "patience of the saints" (*patientia sanctorum*) who keep the faith (Rev. 14:12) and the divine assurance that follows: "Blessed are the dead who die in the Lord" (Rev. 14:13).

According to Catherine, "All the virtues can at times simulate perfection when they are actually imperfect, but they cannot deceive patience. For if this gentle patience, the very heart of charity, is present in the soul, she shows that all the virtues are alive and perfect" (*Tutte le virtù si possono alcuna volta occultare e mostrarsi perfette essendo imperfette, eccetto che a te non si possono nascondere; che se questa dolce pazienzia, mirollo di carità, è nell'anima, ella dimonstra che tutte le virtù sono vive e perfette).*[54]

In another passage, which confirms the singular proof that patience gives to the life of virtue, Catherine records the words of Christ to the soul:

On insult shines patience, the queen who reigns over all the virtues because she is the heart of love. She is the sign and signal of the soul's virtues, showing whether or not they are rooted in me, eternal Truth. She conquers and is never conquered. Her companions are courage and perseverance, and she returns home victorious.

[. . . nella ingiuria riluce la pazienzia, reina, che tiene la signoria e signoreggia tutte le virtú, perchè ella è il mirollo della carità. Ella dimostra e rassegna le virtú nell'anima; dimostra se elle sono virtú fondate in me, Verita eternal, o no. Ella vince e non è mai vinta; ella è accompagnata da la fortezza e perseveranzia, come ditto è; ella torna a casa con la vittoria.][55]

Clearly, Catherine thinks and speaks about patience in a manner qualitatively different from Aquinas. Whereas he sees charity as causing patience, Catherine places it at charity's very heart. When a person knows him- or herself to be beloved by God, "the soul catches fire with unspeakable love, which in turn brings continual pain. Still, this is not a pain that troubles or shrivels up the soul. On the contrary, it makes her grow fat. For she suffers because she loves me, nor would she suffer if she did not love me."[56] In relation to the infinite, undeserved love of God, the soul's love in return suffers, as it were, under its own limits, which it desires to overcome.

It suffers, too, from an awareness of its own sinfulness, for which it desires to make atonement, not on its own, but in union with Christ's atoning love. "Guilt is not atoned for by any suffering, simply as suffering," Catherine explains, "but rather by suffering borne with desire, love, and contrition of heart. The value is not in the suffering, but in the soul's desire."[57] Considering herself "worthy of punishment and unworthy of reward," Catherine's soul welcomes the opportunity to "suffer with patience and so make atonement,"[58] not only for herself but for others.[59]

Catherine's doctrine of patience thus acknowledges both a foundation in love-filled humility and an unfolding of patience from and through charity's very heart. In his first prologue to the *Life*, Raymond calls special attention, as Catherine's confessor, to her pronounced sense of guiltiness, which undergirds her bond of charity with sinners and her purgatorial patience in suffering: "She accused herself as guilty before the Lord, on behalf of all others and beyond all others," regarding herself in some mysterious sense "as the cause of all the wrongdoing that was committed by sinners" (para. 13).

"The soul's love in divine charity is so joined with perfect patience that the one cannot leave without the other," Catherine's Christ instructs her in *The Dialogue*. "The soul, therefore, who chooses to love me must also choose to suffer for me anything at all that I give her. Patience is not proved except in suffering, and patience is one with charity."[60] Eager to be one with Christ in his work of saving souls, Catherine hears the Lord's promise: "I will fulfill your desire by giving you much to suffer, and your patience will spread light [*gittando lume la pazienzia vostra*] into the darkness in all the world's evil. Do not be afraid. . . . I am at your side."[61]

Patience, then, is a virtue with which she identified herself and her mission, even as Saint Francis identified himself especially with poverty. For Raymond of Capua, Catherine of Siena was patience embodied, a personification of that patience which Catherine herself describes as the "queen who stands guard upon the rock of courage" (*pazienzia è reina, posta nella rocca della fortezza*).[62] In his *Life of Catherine of Siena*, he bears personal witness to the singular, enduring power of Catherine's patience: "That patience of hers was a greater source of support to myself than any other thing I ever heard of or saw in her way of living and acting, be they miracles or anything else, however impressive. She was a steadfast pillar, . . . [grounded] in a charity so firmly based that she could not be moved . . . by any tempest" (para. 415).

Raymond's final chapter, in which he systematically reviews Catherine's life as evincing heroic patience, enables him to link together in a single chain/*catena* the many scattered references to different virtues in the preceding chapters: Catherine's charity, humility, obedience, purity, justice, fortitude, and wisdom. Catherine's patience, moreover, links her to other souls—Raymond himself among them—who struggle for sanctity in the present life, and to those saints before her (above all, Mary Magdalene) who have already triumphed through patience. Steadfast, Catherine in her patience becomes for Raymond an ecclesial and a Petrine image, rock-like in her enduring firmness, "for she was founded on the solid rock," closely united "to Christ himself the supreme Rock" (para. 415).

One might wish that Raymond had explicitly invoked Catherine's own doctrine of patience in the final chapter of the *Life* and that he had more self-consciously echoed her language, instead of presenting her "primary virtue" in a Scholastic way, somewhat at odds with her own understanding of it. In choosing patience, however, Raymond was true to Catherine's own high evaluation of a virtue regarded by Thomas Aquinas as a lesser, indeed deficient, virtue, and he sought to show its true greatness in her. Raymond's concern was to win Catherine's canonization and thus to give her writings, her prophetic voice, a hearing in the wide circles of the Church. Therefore he translated not only her native, Tuscan dialect into Latin, but also her virtue of heroic patience, as she understood and practiced it, into an idiom more familiar to the moral theologians of his day. Raymond did so dialogically, cross-referencing previous chapters, where he invites his readers to open Catherine's own *Book* and collected *Letters*. In this way he confesses that no translation is perfect, even as he bears witness through it to perfected virtue. What he writes in the first prologue, he might have repeated at the end the *Life* as a whole: "The above incomplete but veracious sketch of her perfections will be enough to enlist your sympathy and your interest for the story [of Catherine's life]. But if only you could have been with me and witnessed for yourself what I saw and heard" (para. 16).

In his study of the historical development of the canonization process, Kenneth Woodward has pointed to the historical existence of two different hagiographic discourses: on the one hand, a narrative theology, reflective of monastic tradition, in which the evidence of sanctity arises from the story of the saint's virtuous life and miracles, related chronologically; on the other hand, a topical, Scholastic, and juridical mode of hagiography, grounded in moral theology. Raymond of Capua's *Life of Catherine of Siena* offers a rare instance of the combination of the two discourses. The two hagiographic modes are in undeniable tension, Woodward notes, but "in imaginative hands, narrative and proof of virtue can be made to mesh."[63]

In this chapter, I have focused on the tension between the prologue and the epilogue of Raymond of Capua's *Life of Catherine of Siena*, each of which interprets her story as a whole from the viewpoint of a single virtue, which is described as interconnected with others. Catherine's humility—the theme of the prologue—is seen to be perfected, in the end, in the martyrdom of patience that is the theme of the epilogue. Charity—especially that figured in the fearless and generous love of the much forgiven Magdalene, Catherine's alter ego in the *Life* proper—mediates between the two in Raymond's narrative theology, so that the epilogue does not contradict but rather reaffirms, albeit in a Scholastic style, what Raymond's prologue proclaims. The linked "chain" of the hagiographer's book thus offers in its own way the "chain" of the apocalyptic angel (Rev. 20:1–2), who is Catherine herself.

CHAPTER SEVEN

MARY MAGDALENE AND THE EUCHARIST

Reading Jacobus de Voragine's *Legenda aurea* with Catherine of Siena, Raymond of Capua, and Osbern Bokenham

A thirteenth-century masterwork, Jacobus de Voragine's *Legenda aurea* (*Golden Legend*) (ca. 1260) had a long and wide reception. This chapter focuses attention on three well-known, late medieval auditors of Jacobus de Voragine's work: Saint Catherine of Siena (1347–80); her hagiographer, Blessed Raymond of Capua (1330–99); and Osbern Bokenham (ca. 1393–ca. 1464), the Austin friar who translated the *Legenda aurea* in its entirety into Middle English for Cecily Neville (1415–95), Duchess of York, and, prior to that, its legend of Mary Magdalene into poetry for Isabel Bouchier (1409–84), Duchess of Essex.[1] Because Mary Magdalene as a biblical saint figures within Jacobus's *Legenda aurea* in both the "temporale" chapter on Easter Sunday and in the "sanctorale" chapters for her own feast and that of her sister Martha,[2] the example of the Magdalene safeguards a holistic approach to Jacobus's *Legenda aurea*, even as it highlights its structural dualism and anagogical emphasis. The latter features presented challenges for late medieval readers of the *Golden Legend* as its audience widened. Catherine imitated the Magdalen in prayer, preaching, fasting, and Eucharistic feasting; Catherine's hagiographer used Jacobus's Mary Magdalene to defend the Sienese saint's unusual Eucharistic practices; and Bokenham strove to tie the Magdalen's legend back to a mundane, practical, Christian piety, founded on biblical meditation and sacramental reception.

A biblical saint whose legend goes beyond what the Gospels narrate about her, Mary Magdalene reflects the time-ending, anagogic, and liturgical cast of Jacobus's hagiographies in their peculiar, general transcendence of history, biblical and secular. That transcendence had implications for the imitability of the saints. It required hermeneutical invention by preachers, who used Jacobus's work as a resource, and by the vernacular translators and editors of the *Legenda aurea*, who modified it in order to enhance the moral and catechetical lessons to be learned from the saints, while fostering their readers' hope of heaven.[3]

Catherine of Siena took Mary Magdalene, consciously and ardently, as her model, giving equal credit to the biblical and the extrabiblical parts of the saint's legend. This credence of hers gave Raymond of Capua considerable concern because of Catherine's fasting practices, for which only the legendary and extrabiblical Magdalene offered a precedent. The particular case of the reception of Mary Magdalene's story by Catherine and her Scholastic hagiographer, however, also shows a theological sophistication belying any sharp distinction between vernacular and clerical religiosity in the later Middle Ages. Catherine and Raymond both regard Jacobus de Voragine's expository and narrative theology in the *Legenda aurea* as kindred to that of his great Dominican contemporary, Thomas Aquinas (1225–74), whose Eucharistic doctrine helps them, in turn, to interpret Jacobus's "Saint Mary Magdalene." For Catherine herself, as elucidated by her own writings and suggested by William Flete's, however, this Thomistic interpretation rests, somewhat unevenly, on an Augustinian base.

The composite argument of this chapter proceeds in eight parts, four of them concerning the *Legenda aurea* in its own right and four devoted to its reception by selected readers. The first two sections characterize the place of the *Legenda aurea* within the history of hagiography and in its relation to the senses of sacred scripture. The third section surveys Jacobus's treatment of Mary Magdalene within several different chapters of the *Legenda aurea*, and the fourth section pays particular attention to Eucharistic themes in his "Saint Mary Magdalene." In the fifth, I turn to Catherine of Siena's devoted reception of Jacobus's legendary Magdalene within an Augustinian framework; in the sixth, to Raymond of Capua's Thomistic defense of Catherine's Eucharistic practice in imitation of Jacobus's Magdalene. The seventh section discusses Jacobus's overall influence upon Raymond's complex portrayal of Catherine as Mary Magdalene's doublet. The eighth and final section features Osbern Bokenham's Augustinian translation of Jacobus's story of Mary Magdalene in his *Legendys of Hooly Wummen* (*Legends of Holy Women*)—a translation into Middle English that revises the presentation of sainthood found both in Jacobus and in his fellow English Austin, William Flete (ca. 1325–ca. 1390), Catherine's early confessor.

THE *LEGENDA AUREA* IN THE HISTORY OF HAGIOGRAPHY

The *Legenda aurea* is a mammoth, enormously influential work by a scholar-bishop.[4] Jacobus, whose work has defined the hagiographic genre for many, self-consciously imitates the *Etymologiae* of Isidore of Seville (560–636), an early encyclopedist, in providing etymologies for the names of the saints. Arranged in accord with the liturgical calendar and probably intended as a reference work for clerics,[5] Jacobus's tremendously popular compilation of saints' *Lives* became an important source for collections of *exempla* used by preachers (an art in which Jacobus himself, archbishop of Genoa, excelled).[6] Between the thirteenth and the sixteenth centuries, it gained translation into Europe's main vernacular languages and was printed in English translation in 1483 by William Caxton.[7]

Best known to its sixteenth-century critics for its preservation of popular legends about the saints, it is in fact a multigenre work by a Scholastic encyclopedist that combines a rich trove of liturgical lore about, and theological commentary upon, the major feasts and seasons of the Church year, on the one hand, with short *Lives* of the saints, on the other. Jacobus took material for the latter mainly from earlier thirteenth-century collections of short *Lives* by fellow Dominicans: Jean de Mailly's *Abbreviatio in gestis et miraculis sanctorum*, Bartholomew of Trent's *Liber epilogorum in gesta sanctorum*, and Vincent of Beauvais's *Speculum maius*.[8] By Eamon Duffy's count, there are 153 saints' legends ("sanctorale" entries) and 23 nonhagiographic chapters ("temporale" entries), "devoted to the systematic exposition of the medieval church's understanding of salvation."[9] Arranged according to the liturgical calendar, the *Legenda aurea* begins with a prologue on the seasons of the liturgical year and a chapter on "The Advent of the Lord," and it concludes with an entry "On the Dedication of a Church," which functions as a fitting, closing symbol for the work as a whole.

Extracted from the liturgical context that the work as a whole provides, the individual, highly abbreviated legends have been roundly criticized as undermining the cult of the saints, casting doubt on their historicity, discouraging their imitation, and departing from the Gregorian tradition of biblical/exegetical hagiography.[10] Luis de Vives (1493–1540), for example, once lamented, "How unworthy of the saints, and of all Christians, is that history of the saints called the Golden Legend."[11] The opinion of the Spanish humanist has been long and widely shared, as Sherry L. Reames demonstrates in her magisterial study of the *Legenda aurea*'s early modern reception. Recent scholarship, however, has also sought to understand Jacobus's work holistically, to account for authorial intention and actual use by its early readers, to grasp its immense appeal for almost three centuries of Christian readers, and thus (to echo Reames) "to gain a more sympathetic perspective on the book than its Renaissance critics had."[12] Robert Seybolt points out that, after all, "the *Legenda Aurea* led the Bible in the number of editions issued in the fifteenth century."[13]

A biblical scholar, a liturgical theologian, and a historian (his *Historia Lombardica* is included in the *Legenda aurea* in its penultimate legend, that of Saint Pope Pelagius), Jacobus developed in the *Legenda aurea* an original way of narrating the stories of the saints, fashioning a verbal medium suitable to an eschatological view of them existing in what Jacques Le Goff calls "sacred time."[14] (Jacobus's circular arrangement of the saints in accord with the liturgical seasons of the year and the dates of their feasts may well have inspired the vision of the saints in the concluding cantos of Dante's *Commedia*, where the saints encircle the throne of God.)[15] As Alain Boureau has argued in a paradigm-shifting book, Jacobus has consistently diminished the individuality of the saints through abridgment in order to heighten an awareness of their communion, their interchangeability, their timeless witness to the Eternal, and the providential ordering of history itself toward this telos.[16] Saintly actions, rapidly narrated, point to God himself (in Thomistic terms) as "Pure Act" (*actus purus*) and to Christ as the "Abbreviated Word" of the Father (*Verbum abbreviatum*).[17] Given this eschatological orientation, martyr saints predominate in the pages of the *Legenda aurea*. "None of Jacobus's saints were ordinary men and women living ordinary lives," writes Eamon Duffy. "[They] are uncomfortable people, insofar as they can be said to be people at all, often at odds with the world around them."[18]

176 THE SAINT'S *LIFE* IN THE SCHOLASTIC AGE

The different senses of scripture—literal/historical, allegorical, tropological, anagogical—are closely aligned to the historical development of saints' *Lives*. The early hagiographers emphasized typological figuration, the wonderment awakened by miracles, and meditative, exegetical discovery; canon lawyers privileged the proof of personal virtue; and Jacobus himself aligned the saintly narrative chiefly with its anagogical and liturgical dimension, inclusive of preaching. In so doing, Jacobus remains a biblical hagiographer, attuned to its different senses, especially the *sensus anagogicus*. "As a general rule Jacobus supports each point he is making with one or several texts from Scripture," William Granger Ryan points out, but he frequently quotes "only the first few words."[19] This abbreviation of scriptural passages accords with Jacobus's general strategy of particular abridgment as a means toward holistic inclusion (the achievement of a useful saintly *summa* mirroring the *communio sanctorum*).

THE *LEGENDA AUREA* AND THE ANAGOGICAL SENSE

André Vauchez and others have noted that the saints featured in the *Legenda aurea* are not the recently canonized saints of Jacobus's own era (the five exceptions to that rule being Peter of Verona, Francis of Assisi, Dominic, Thomas Becket, and Elizabeth of Hungary),[20] but rather long-venerated saints from the Bible and early Church, "above all the martyr saints of the first four centuries."[21] Distantly recalled and short-lived, these martyr saints, apostles, confessors, and hermits are especially suited for Jacobus's experiments in literalized anagogy, his brief meditations on timeless, world-renouncing saints with firm commitments and divine energy, saints whose mortal bodies even in torture and death manifest features associated with the glorified body.

The shortest of Jacobus's legends—that of Saint Praxedes—is just four sentences long in William Granger Ryan's translation. It epitomizes the *Legenda aurea*'s emphasis on eschatology (the time-ending events of death and judgment) and anagogy (the end of heaven or hell): "Praxedes was sister to blessed Prudentiana, and they were sisters of Saints Donatus and Timothy, who were instructed in the faith by the apostles. At a time when persecution was raging, they buried the bodies of many Christians. They also distributed all their goods to the poor. Finally they fell asleep in the Lord about the year of the Lord 165, in the reign of Emperors Marcus and Antoninus II."[22]

Burying martyrs—a corporal work of mercy—provides Praxedes with repeated reminders of her own mortality and call to witness to Christ, perhaps at the cost of her own life. Her charitable dispossession of earthly goods marks a life radically oriented toward the life to come. Her bonds to other saints indicates her destiny to join the saints in glory. Her falling asleep in the Lord declares not simply her death, but her victorious entrance into God's own eternal rest.

Anagogy, the fourth of the traditional senses of scripture, teaches to what end of eternal bliss the earthly path of holy living leads, in accord with God's promises. In his study of the names and number of the biblical senses, Henri de Lubac cites several definitions of "anagogy," among them that of Nicholas of Lyra (ca. 1270–1349) in his prologue to the *Glossa ordinaria*: "If the things signified by the words . . . are referred to so as to signify things that are hoped for in the beatitude to come, this is the anagogical sense."[23] Framing the four senses as marking the ascent of the soul, Gregory the Great in the *Moralia in Job* describes the anagogical sense as a contemplative understanding of scripture: "Sometimes flashing in the midst of the darkness of the present life as a glint from the light of eternity, contemplation holds us in suspense for higher things."[24] Also employing the image of light, Thomas Aquinas explains, "If 'fiat lux' [Gen. 1:3] be said as meaning, 'Let us be led into glory through Christ,' this pertains to the anagogic sense."[25]

Summarizing an array of such formulations, de Lubac notices that anagogy is always "forced to be last" in the numbering of the four senses (literal, allegorical, tropological, anagogical), because it points to the *telos* of Christian hope, which is fulfilled in the life to come: "Mystical or doctrinal, taught or lived, true anagogy is therefore always eschatological."[26] De Lubac identifies two different anagogical traditions—that of Pseudo-Dionysius's *Celestial Hierarchies* and that of Origen's mystical exegesis— between which there were "struggles for influence and . . . attempts at synthesis" throughout the Middle Ages.[27] The synthetic "meeting of mystical exegesis" and of "mystical contemplation," de Lubac observes, occurs "at the endpoint; and this point is anagogy."[28] In the Dionysian tradition, however, "a disassociation tended to develop between *invisibilia* and *futura*, as between the mystic life and the meditation on Scripture."[29]

This disassociation, in turn, put both eschatology (as a theological orientation) and the unity of the biblical senses at risk, according to de Lubac, who cites in support the telling observation of Jean Leclercq, "Eschatology occupies practically no place in the teaching of Abelard."[30] Leclercq famously contrasts the theological styles of monastic and Scholastic theology, emphasizing the former's stress on the organic unity of the biblical senses, secured by the twinned importance of history and eschatology. For his part, de Lubac focuses study on the twelfth and thirteenth centuries, when biblical mystagogy first began to suffer disintegration, but he prognosticates the further loss of the eschatological sense in late Scholastic theology and the resultant separation of the biblical senses. When "theology no longer [had] the form of an exegesis," he opines, "a state of mind was created that affected exegesis itself and the theory of the four senses, affecting everything, especially the definition of anagogy."[31]

Jacobus's definition of anagogy in the *Legenda aurea* takes its cue not primarily from the Bible but from the liturgy and from what Le Goff calls "sacred time,"[32] in its arrangement according to the liturgical year, with its annual reminders of the Last Judgment to come and of eschatological hope (notably in the Feasts of All Saints and All Souls). The liturgical cycle includes the daily remembrance of saints and martyrs, whose individual feasts are celebrated, whose names are invoked in the canon of the Mass, and whose stories were included in the night Office. The relics and icons of the saints were and are venerated in the churches and on their altars, where the Eucharist is celebrated. The Eucharist is the eschatological center, the "food of martyrs" and the place of encounter with the Lord and Judge.[33] Echoes of hymns and antiphons punctuate the *Legenda aurea*. Jacobus refers again and again to John Beleth's *Summa de ecclesiasticis officiis* (1162).[34]

Jacobus writes, moreover, at the same time that his fellow bishop William Durandus of Mende (1230–96) is composing his *Rationale divinorum officiorum*. Durandus famously interprets the liturgy symbolically, applying to its outward signs and actions the exegetical levels of interpretation familiar to biblical commentators: "The [rationale of the high priest] was embroidered with four colors and golden thread, and now, as I stated above, the reasons for the variety of the ecclesiastical offices and rites can be said to correspond to these four colors and are understood through four senses: namely, the historical, allegorical, tropological, and anagogical: with faith [i.e., the gold] at the center of all the colors."[35] Durandus does not extend his approach to hagiography, but his exegetical turn to the liturgy invites comparison with Jacobus's less overtly exegetical work in its encyclopedic combination of "sanctorale" with "temporale."

The biblical/exegetical extension of Durandus and the eschatological foreshortening of Jacobus in their respective liturgical theologies may each in their own way reflect and respond to changes in biblical study in a Scholastic age, when the unity of the biblical senses, long secured through *lectio divina*, was being affected and weakened by new methods of study and eschatology deemphasized. Jacobus's encyclopedic inclusiveness exceeds in its sheer quantity and diversity that of Beleth and Durandus and requires, by its very vastness, the abridgment of the individual entries. Jacobus's emphatic, liturgical interest in eschatology—mirrored in the abbreviated tales of martyrs, virgin saints, and confessors—may be understood as his attempt to provide a conservative, liturgical counterbalance to the erosion of the eschatological in the academic theology of his day.

JACOBUS'S MARY MAGDALENE IN "THE RESURRECTION OF THE LORD" AND AMONG THE LEGENDS

The saints' *Lives* in the *Legenda aurea* are seldom related in explicitly biblical language, but they depend for their interpretation on the "temporale" entries, rich in biblical citations, marking the great feasts of Christ and the Church and the liturgical seasons within which the saints' feasts are celebrated: the "time of deviation" (from Septuagesima to Easter), the "time of reconciliation" (from Easter to Pentecost), the "time of pilgrimage" (from the octave of Pentecost to Advent), the "time of renewal" (from Advent through Christmas).[36] In these "temporale" chapters, Jacobus provides an abundance of biblical quotations and references, generally used as proof texts, taken from the Gospels, Psalms, Acts, the Epistles of Saint Paul, and Isaiah, among other books of the Bible.

The first of Jacobus's references to Mary Magdalene in the *Legenda aurea* appears, fittingly, in the entry for Easter Sunday, "The Resurrection of the Lord." The entry provides a striking example of Jacobus's status as a Scholastic theologian. Duffy notes, "Most of [the] expository chapters differ markedly from the chapters devoted to the lives of the saints," in that the former offer "a dense doctrinal and symbolic analysis of the main features of the Christian faith," and exhibit the "scholastic urge to order, systematize, tabulate, and analyze."[37]

In Jacobus's practice, the starting point is not the Bible approached exegetically (wherein scripture itself poses questions), but rather a question, to which he replies, using selected biblical verses as proofs. Presupposing familiarity with the Gospels for Easter, for example, Jacobus begins "The Resurrection of the Lord" not with the exegesis of a pericope from the lectionary, not with the evangelical accounts of Christ's resurrection, but with seven questions abruptly posed:[38] "First [1], how is it true to say that the Lord lay in the tomb for three days and nights and rose on the third day? Second [2], why did he not come to life immediately after dying instead of waiting until the third day? Third [3], how he rose. Fourth [4], why he hurried his rising rather than wait for the general resurrection. Fifth [5], why he rose. Sixth [6], how many times he appeared after the resurrection. Seventh [7], how he brought out the holy fathers who were in limbo and what he did there."[39] Three of Jacobus's questions (1, 2, 4) concern the timing of the Resurrection. One question (3) concerns the manner of Christ's rising. Another (5) concerns the reasons for Christ's rising. Two concern the manifestations of Christ's resurrection—that is to say, his appearances on earth and in limbo (6,7).

These seven questions may well be compared to the four questions (53–56) concerning the Resurrection found in *Summa theologiae* III, q. 53 ("Whether it was necessary for Christ to rise again"), which includes four articles: 1, Why it behooved Christ to rise again; 2, Whether it was fitting for Christ to rise again on the third day; 3, Whether Christ was the first to rise from the dead; 4, Whether Christ was the cause of his own resurrection. Question 54 (in four articles) addresses a set of questions about the quality of Christ's risen body. Question 55 ("The Manifestation of the Resurrection") in six articles takes up issues concerning Christ's appearances, including the appropriateness of women as witnesses to, and preachers about, Christ's resurrection (*ST* III, q. 55, a. 1). Question 56, subdivided into two articles, considers the causal effect of Christ's resurrection on humankind.[40]

Jacobus's seven questions and their arrangement clearly differ from those of Aquinas, but there is also considerable overlap in content. Thomas's articles about the when and why of Christ's rising (*ST* III, q. 53, a. 1 and 2) roughly match Jacobus's first, second, fourth, and fifth questions. Thomas's quaestio 55, concerning the manifestations of the Resurrection, accords with Jacobus's two questions regarding Christ's appearances. Jacobus's question about the "how" of Christ's rising jibes with articles in Thomas's quaestio 53 and quaestio 54. The philosophical cast of Thomas's responses to the two articles in quaestio 56 also finds a correspondence in Jacobus: "[Christ's] resurrection is the efficient, exemplary, and sacramental cause of our resurrection."[41]

Jacobus proceeds to answer his seven questions one by one, referring in the process to thirty biblical proof texts; to the *Glossa ordinaria*; to patristic authorities: Augustine, Ambrose, Bede, Gregory, Dionysius, Sedulius, Leo the Great, and Gregory of Nyssa; to medieval scholars: Peter of Ravenna and Peter Comestor; and to the Gospel of Nicodemus (for its dramatic account of the harrowing of hell, which Jacobus narrates). He answers the respective questions in a paratactic fashion by listing five reasons why Christ did not rise immediately; seven ways Christ rose; three reasons why Christ did not wait to rise until the general resurrection; four benefits for humankind of Christ's rising; thirteen post-Resurrection appearances (ten explicitly mentioned in the Gospels, plus three that Jacobus insists may be assumed: to James of Alpheus, to Joseph of Arimathea, and to the Virgin Mary).

"The first of [Christ's] apparitions was to Mary Magdalene," writes Jacobus, "as in John 20:1–18 and in Mark 16:9: 'Rising early on the first day of the week, he appeared first to Mary Magdalene,'"[42] Jacobus goes on to give five reasons, each with a biblical proof text, for this singular distinction given to Mary, who "represents all repentant sinners" (*que typum gerit penitentium*).[43] Jacobus's first, second, and third reasons clearly show that he identifies Mary Magdalene with the unnamed, sinful woman who washed Christ's feet with her tears at the house of Simon the Leper (Luke 7:36–50): "The first, that she loved him more ardently. . . . The second, in order to show that he had died for sinners; Matt. 9:13. . . . The third, because harlots go ahead of the wise in the kingdom of heaven; Matt. 21:31."[44] His fourth reason, referencing the *Glossa ordinaria*, finds it fitting that a woman should "announce life," reversing Eve's role as "messenger of death."[45] His fifth, quoting Romans 5:20, contrasts the abounding of sin with superabounding grace.[46]

The last of the etymologies that Jacobus provides at the start of the legend "Saint Mary Magdalene" strikingly also recalls Romans 5:20: "After her conversion she was magnificent in the superabundance of grace, because where trespass abounded, grace was superabundant."[47] Jacobus provides three meanings for "Mary" and three for "Magdalene." The former set of glosses ("bitter sea, or as illuminator, or as illuminated") are decidedly anagogical in their meanings, each of which points to the "better part" (of three parts) that the contemplative Mary has chosen (Luke 10:42): "As she chose the best part of heavenly glory, she is called illuminated."[48] The latter set of etymologies ("'remaining guilty,' or . . . armed, or unconquered, or magnificent"), by contrast, emphasize the Magdalene's tripartite history, pointing "to what manner of woman she was before, at the time of, and after her conversion."[49]

Taken together, the two sets of glosses juxtapose time and eternity, contemplative ascent and chronological change. Comparable in function but not in form to the *accessus ad auctores* that introduce the primary texts read in the schools,[50] Jacobus's etymologies serve to preview the story that follows and hint at the lessons to be learned from it. The two sets of three glosses depend, moreover, on the Ambrosian and Gregorian tradition that conflates three figures: the sinful woman of Luke 7:36–50, Mary of Bethany, and Mary of Magdala into one representative character whose life story thus reflects three spiritual stages of development: purgation (the sinful but repentant woman, moved by love), illumination (the contemplative woman sitting at Jesus's feet), and union (the strong woman at the cross, witness to the Resurrection, sharer in Christ's glory).[51]

The composite legend of Mary Magdalene, known to the Middle Ages in its fullest form in the *Legenda aurea*, imaginatively combines into a single *Life* episodes involving the unnamed sinful woman of Luke 7:36–50, who washed Jesus's feet with her tears, anointed them, and dried them with her hair; Mary of Bethany, who sat at Jesus's feet (John 11:38–42), witnessed the resurrection of her brother Lazarus (John 11:1–44), and anointed Jesus's head (Matt. 26:6) and/or feet (Mark 14:3, John 12:1–8) prior to his betrayal by Judas; and Mary of Magdala, a leading woman disciple of Jesus (Luke 8:1–3; Mark 16:9), present at his crucifixion (John 19:25, Mark 15:40, Matt. 27:56), mentioned by name among the women who brought spices to the tomb (Mark 16:1, Luke 24:10), and singled out by John as the first to encounter the risen Christ (John 20:1–18). It also extends the Magdalen's story beyond the biblical references, to tell of her preaching, missionary activity, and miracles at Marseilles, her thirty-year contemplative withdrawal to the wilderness, her death and burial, the discovery of her tomb at Aix, and the transferal of her relics to the Abbey of Vézelay.[52]

Most of Jacobus's legend begins, in fact, "some fourteen years after the Lord's passion and ascension into heaven,"[53] extending well beyond the biblical accounts of Mary Magdalene to narrate episodes in her later life as fervent evangelist and mystically gifted hermit. Citing "Brother Albert" (almost certainly Albert the Great), Jacobus also interjects a vigorous rebuttal of the story (with attendant complications) that Mary Magdalene, prior to her conversion, had originally been engaged to marry the apostle John: "These tales are to be considered false and frivolous."[54] The miracle stories told by Jacobus retell events symbolically apt to a saint who was privileged to "announce life" on the day of the Lord's resurrection:[55] the romance-like restoration to life of a mother and child, long supposed to be dead after a storm at sea; the revival of a knight who had (it seems) been killed in battle; the safe delivery of babies; the conversion of sinners.

JACOBUS'S EUCHARISTIC LEGEND OF MARY MAGDALENE

Like the Israelites fed by manna from heaven, Jacobus's Mary Magdalene, in the legend well known to Raymond of Capua and to Catherine Benincasa herself,[56] goes off to an "empty wilderness," taking up her solitary dwelling "in a place made ready by the hands of angels."[57] In this barren landscape, lacking streams of water, grass, and trees, the saint is sustained "not with earthly viands but only with the good things of heaven."[58] Carried aloft by angels at the seven canonical hours, the Magdalen's ecstatic levitation in prayer—whether it be physical, spiritual, or quasi-physical—is accompanied by her hearing "with her bodily ears . . . the glorious chants of the celestial hosts."[59]

In its contemplative rather than penitential emphasis, this portion of the Magdalen legend builds upon the identification of Mary of Bethany as the exemplar of the contemplative life and only superficially resembles the legend of Saint Mary of Egypt, with which it is often compared.[60] Jacobus's language more closely recalls the flight of the apocalyptic woman "into the desert, where she had a place prepared by God" (Rev. 12:6)—a text applied to the Church, but also to the Virgin Mary, whose body was assumed into heaven. Indeed, Joana Antunes observes, "Mary Magdalene's [bodily] elevation [by angels]," her "physical assumption," made it "necessary [for late medieval Christians] to create an effective way to distinguish between her assumption and that of the Virgin Mary."[61]

In a Cistercian life of Mary Magdalen that predates the *Legenda aurea*, the saint dies in simple ecstasy at the coming of the Lord, who appears to her in the wilderness.[62] In the *Legenda aurea*'s rendition of the life of Saint Mary of Egypt, the penitent Mary, a converted prostitute, dies alone in the desert on Holy Thursday, shortly after receiving the Eucharist from a priest, who returns a year later to the spot, finds her body, and buries it there, near the bank of the Jordan.[63] The *Death of the Magdalene* by Sebastian Conca (1680–1764) (see plate 7.1) similarly depicts Mary Magdalene's death as occurring alone in a cave, where the saint, holding her crucifix, passes from this life into the company of the angels.[64]

The explicitly Eucharistic account of the Magdalene's death, preserved in Jacobus de Voragine's major source, the *Speculum historialis* (part of *Speculum maius*) of Vincent of Beauvais, belongs, as Jacobus explains, to an alternative version of her legend narrated by "Hegesippus (or, as some books have it, Josephus)."[65] According to James E. Cross, who has transcribed three Latin texts belonging to that tradition, "the 'Narrat Josephus' variant was extant certainly before the late ninth century."[66]

Jacobus's Magdalen does not die in solitary ecstasy at Christ's appearance to her in the wilderness, after having long feasted on the manna-like bread of angels, nor does she pass from this world in the wilderness after receiving Holy Communion from a traveling priest or visiting angel. Jacobus, like Vincent of Beauvais before him, turns in his *Legenda* to an alternate "Narrat Josephus" source for the ending and imagines instead the saint, accompanied by angels and uplifted by them, first returning from the wilderness to the church in town, as she had promised a wandering priest she would, exactly on the day of the Lord's resurrection.[67] There she dies in visible oneness with the human community of the faithful, after receiving the Eucharistic host from the hand of Bishop Maximin in the presence of gathered clergymen: "Blessed Mary Magdalene, shedding tears of

Plate 7.1. Sebastian Conca, *The Death of the Magdalene*, 1700–1764, oil on copper. Raclin Murphy Museum of Art, University of Notre Dame. Mr. and Mrs. Al Nathe Fund, 1990.003.

joy, received the Lord's Body and Blood from the bishop. Then she lay down full length before the steps of the altar, and her most holy soul migrated to the Lord."[68]

In Jacobus's Latin, the "corpus" of the Lord is echoed by the "corpusculo" of the saint, prostrate before the altar.[69] Her tears of joy evoke and transform the tears she had once shed for her sins and later in her grief at Christ's death. Just as those tears had at first blinded her to the presence of the risen Christ in the garden (John 20: 11–15), now her tears bear witness to her recognition of the Lord in the Eucharist (1 Cor. 11:29). Witnessing to the Lord's resurrection, to his glorified body in the Host, she—ever an apostle to the apostles—dies a martyr's death before the altar at the hour of matins, early on the day of the Lord's rising from the dead. The sweet fragrance that pervades the church and the "aromatic lotions"[70] with which Maximin embalms her body powerfully recall the spices and perfumed oils carried by the holy women to Christ's tomb (Luke 24:26), and also Mary's prophetic anointing of Jesus at Bethany, in preparation for his death (John 12:3).

Jacobus's "Legend of Saint Martha" records that Martha and Mary died a week apart from each other, both witnessing to the Resurrection and to the Eucharist. Martha "heard the angelic choirs bearing her sister's soul to heaven," immediately called the community together to share her joy, and voiced a prayer to her sainted sister: "O my beautiful and beloved sister [*o pulcherrima et mihi dilecta soror*], may you live in the blessed abode with him who was your master and my guest [*hospite meo*]!"[71] At the hour of her own death, Martha sees her sister again, this time "carrying a torch with which she lighted all the candles and lamps [*cereos et lampades*]," in preparation for Christ's coming to Martha to offer her his own eternal hospitality: *Veni, dilecta hospita mea* ("Come, my beloved guest").[72]

CATHERINE OF SIENA AS DEVOTEE OF MARY MAGDALENE

Not only Raymond of Capua's *Life of Catherine of Siena*,[73] but also Catherine's *Letters* attest to her multifaceted devotion to Mary Magdalene,[74] whose composite biography in the *Legenda aurea* Catherine knows and accepts. In one of her earliest letters, dated before May 1374, Catherine encourages her spiritual daughter, Monna Agnesa, to imitate "the blazing love" of "that loving apostle Magdalen," who humbly "sat at the Lord's feet," fearlessly "ran and embraced the cross," "preached in the city of Marseilles," and persevered in her tearful quest for Jesus until she found him.[75] Another concludes with a petition begging "the gentle Magdalen, so in love," for a share in her contrition and "self-contempt."[76] Writing in Lent 1376, Catherine exhorts Monna Bartolomea of Lucca, "Turn in affectionate love, with the dear loving Magdalen, and embrace the sweet venerable cross."[77] Self-forgetful, drunk with love for Jesus, Catherine's Magdalen in this and other letters is fearless of the Roman soldiers, utterly detached from the world, its pursuits, and its vanities, free to follow her master to the cross.[78]

Catherine's writings show further variation on the theme, however. In a letter dating from 1377, she exhorts a sinner to repentance, allegorizing Mary Magdalene's visit to Christ's tomb in Mark 16:3–5: "Go into the tomb of self-knowledge, and with Magdalen ask, 'Who will roll back the stone from the tomb for me?'"[79] Interpreting the two angels of the Resurrection account in John 20:12 as the twinned virtues of "true hope and lively faith," "holy love and reverence for God" and "hatred" for sin, Catherine counsels her spiritual son to remain in the tomb of self-knowledge until he finds Christ "risen in [his] soul by grace."[80] Then he is to announce the good news to his brothers—namely, "the true, solid, lovely virtues" with whom he is to abide.[81]

In her *Dialogue*, Catherine draws a similar parallel between the stages in the soul's growth in love and the life of the apostles, who first gathered in hiding in the upper room and then, when the Holy Spirit descended at Pentecost, "left the house and fearlessly preached [God's] message by proclaiming the teaching of the Word."[82] So too the soul (Catherine's own soul) stayed at home in "the house of self-knowledge," and then "rose up in contempt of that imperfection and in love for perfection" to serve her neighbors with Christ's love and "in perfect union" with God.[83] William Flete's *Documento spirituale* (1377) records Catherine's own account to the hermit friar of how she conquered self-love through dwelling in the "cell" of self-knowledge, the "knowledge of [her] own sins."[84] Michael Benedict Hackett cites this document alongside Catherine's earliest letters as proof that Catherine has deeply grasped "what is known as classic Augustinian interiority."[85]

Evoking the *noli me tangere* of John 20:17, addressed to Mary Magdalene, Catherine foresees for the penitent the reward of virtue: "Christ lets you touch him in continual humble prayer by appearing to your soul in a way you can feel."[86] The mysterious words of the risen Christ to Mary—*Noli me tangere*, "Do not touch me," "Do not cling to me," "Do not hold on to me"—have inspired various interpretations. In his *Commentary on the Gospel of John*, Thomas Aquinas points to two mystical explanations, both of which take their bearing from Jesus's own stated reason, "for I have not yet ascended to the Father" (John 20:17). According to the first, Mary Magdalene stands here as a figure for the Gentiles, who are to be joined to Christ's mystical body, the Church, only after the great commission given to the apostles at Christ's ascension to "make disciples of all nations" (see Matt. 28:19; Mark 16:15, 20; Luke 24:46–52). According to the second, Mary's faith in Jesus Christ had not yet advanced to the "point of believing that he was equal to the Father"—a grace she received at his ascension to the Father.[87]

Alluding to Saint Augustine's teaching in *De Trinitate*, Aquinas calls "touch . . . the last stage of knowledge."[88] By this definition, Mary Magdalene came to touch, to know, the Lord more perfectly after his ascension. The Eucharistic implications of this become apparent when one pairs the risen Lord's words to Mary Magdalene with those spoken in John 6, where Jesus names himself "the bread that came down from heaven" (John 6:33, 41, 50–51, 58). There Jesus pointedly associates his Eucharistic presence with his divinity, manifested in his ascension. "Does this shock you? What if you were to see the Son of Man ascending to where he was before?" (John 6:62).

Through prayer, adoration of the elevated host (the touch of the eyes), and Communion, Catherine, like Mary Magdalene, could come into a vital contact with Christ, the Son of God and source of all virtues. The language of Catherine's last mentioned letter—in which she hails the Lord's appearance to the soul; his inward, palpable touch; and the fortifying of the virtues—approximates the diction of her book, *The Dialogue*, in which there is no direct mention of Mary Magdalene, but manifold, intertextual allusions to her.

By the time Catherine dictates the *Dialogue*, she has arguably become so completely an *altera Magdalena* that the *Dialogue*'s preaching and teaching—its exposition of different kinds of tears and of stages in love (correspondent to bodily zones: the feet, the side, the mouth), its stress on the "house of self-knowledge" (*casa del cognoscimento di sé*),[89] its angelic doctrine, its discourse on the table of the cross, the Eucharist, and the virtues—is as much the Magdalene's as it is Catherine's own and God's. In the end, the Father summarizes his teaching in words reminiscent of the legendary Magdalen: "I told you about the virtue of those who live as angels [*come angeli*], at the same time touching upon the excellence of the sacrament [*della eccellenzia del sacramento*]. . . . I described for you four stages of tears [*Di quattro stati di lagrime*]. . . . Now I invite you to weep [*Ora Io t'invito ad pianto*], you and my other servants."[90]

Although the *Dialogue* does not mention the Magdalen by name, it does refer explicitly to a holy hermit, Saint Dominic (1170–1221), and Saint Agnes of Montepulciano (1268–1317) in a context evocative of the legendary Magdalen, fed by angels in the desert—a context that also recalls both Catherine's own inedia and her Eucharistic devotion. Speaking about his providential care for the bodily needs of his servants, God the Father explains that he usually feeds the hungry through inspiring others to perform corporal works of mercy. Sometimes, however, he acts directly, without a human intermediary. To illustrate this, the Father points to three examples from the lives of the saints. In the first, God sends an angel to heal and feed a holy hermit: "His body had the help it needed, and his soul experienced wonderful joy and delight in the angel's company."[91] In the second, two angels come to feed Saint Dominic and his friars "with the whitest of bread" (*con pane bianchissimo*).[92]

In the third, Saint Agnes and her companions, establishing a new monastery at a "place [that] had been a brothel [*luogo di peccatrici*],"[93] go breadless for three days, eating only greens that miraculously sufficed for their nourishment. When Catherine objects, "the human body cannot live on nothing but greens" (*perché pure dell'erba non vive il corpo*), the Father replies that he can, and sometimes does, alter the human body to make it "amenable" to unusual means of nourishment, adding, "And you know that this is so because you have experienced it yourself" (*E tu sai che egli è così, ché l'ài provato in te medesima*).[94]

RAYMOND OF CAPUA'S THOMISTIC DEFENSE OF CATHERINE

Catherine of Siena's inedia—her "holy anorexia" (to use the words of Rudolf Bell)—was clearly a scandal to her contemporaries, a grave problem to herself, and a potential block to her canonization.[95] Her disturbing inedia, which Catherine herself named an afflicting weakness (*infirmitas*),[96] arguably entailed manifold vices: a lack of conformity with the example of Christ, who came "eating and drinking" (Luke 7:34); disobedience to Christ's express command to his disciples (Luke 10:8, "And into whatsoever city you enter, . . . eat such things as are set before you"); a scandalous singularity in refusing food—a practice that prohibits imitation by others;[97] excess in fasting, as a violation of temperance; inability to discern the devil's destructive deceit in tempting her to that excess; and possibly her own fraud in pretending not to eat and drink, while doing so in secret.[98] Catherine's progressive inability to eat led to her early death.

When Raymond of Capua composed his *Life of Catherine of Siena* (*Legenda maior*) (1385–95), he clearly hoped for Catherine's canonization,[99] ending the *Life* with the words: "From all that has been written in this work the final conclusion to be drawn is that it is a fitting thing that this holy Virgin and Martyr should be enrolled by the Church Militant in the catalogue of the Saints."[100] Raymond knew full well that he needed to answer Catherine's detractors on these and other charges.

Raymond devotes four long paragraphs to a systematic rebuttal of the specific charges regarding Catherine's inedia.[101] He notes Christ's approval of John the Baptist's fasting and calls attention to the revered example of the Desert Fathers and Mary Magdalen, who fasted in the wilderness. He refers to Catherine's humble submission to God's will in giving her an exceptional vocation and an unusual suffering. Denying the devil's power over her, Raymond points to the evident fruits of the Spirit (Gal. 5:22–23) in Catherine's life—charity, joy, and peace—and he warns Catherine's slanderers of the price to be paid for calumny. Most importantly, Raymond insists that Catherine's inedia is mysteriously connected to her frequent reception of the Eucharist and thus to her martyr's witness to Christ's glorified body, present in the sacrament, and to the unity of the Church.[102]

Raymond makes this case following two convergent lines: Thomas Aquinas's teaching on the Eucharist and its effects, on the one hand, and Jacobus de Voragine's legend of Mary Magdalen, on the other. Raymond's citations of Thomas and of Jacobus's *Legenda aurea* have drawn the separate attention of scholars, but the logical convergence between these two thirteenth-century Dominican sources in Raymond's employ of them has not received the study it deserves.[103] Putting these two sources into conversation with each other greatly expands the theological significance of Raymond's repeated, explicit, and implicit comparisons of Catherine to the Magdalen, whom Thomas names "the apostle to the apostles,"[104] the witness to the resurrected Christ. Like Raymond, who identifies Catherine both with Mary Magdalene and with the Bride of the Song of Songs, Thomas, in his *Commentary on the Gospel of John*, likens Mary Magdalene on Easter morning to the Bride, searching for her beloved.[105] In this way, both Thomas and Raymond renew an ancient Christian tradition, studied long ago by Jean Danielou, which sees the Song of Songs as prophetic of baptism and the Eucharist.[106]

Replying to those who object to Catherine's frequent reception of communion, Raymond cites various authorities, among them "the renowned Saint and Doctor, Thomas Aquinas," who encourages the faithful who are properly disposed to receive the sacrament often, even daily, "for it is certain that a soul in the proper dispositions [e.g., of belief, reverence, and charity] receives immense graces from the reception of this wonderful and precious Sacrament."[107] "This is the mind and the view of Saint Thomas," Raymond adds, "a Doctor whose teaching Catherine followed in practice."[108] Raymond particularly alludes here to Thomas's *respondeo* in *Summa theologiae* III, q. 80, a. 10, but Catherine's hagiographer also turns to Aquinas elsewhere — for instance, on the question of the truth of Catherine's unfulfilled prophecy of a crusade.[109] Raymond's dictum that Catherine followed Thomas's Eucharistic teaching "in practice" surely has a broader meaning in the *Life*.[110]

Enumerating the many saints — Paul, Dominic, John the Evangelist, Agnes of Montepulciano, and Mary Magdalene — who appeared to Catherine, Raymond mentions that "often enough Saint Thomas Aquinas" also visited Catherine.[111] In the *Dialogue*, Catherine herself (or rather, God the Father, speaking to Catherine) refers several times to Thomas Aquinas, praising him as a contemplator and teacher of divine Truth: "With his mind's eye he contemplated my Truth ever so tenderly and there gained light beyond the natural and knowledge infused by grace."[112] As someone who "learned more through prayer than through human study,"[113] Thomas was a model Dominican for Catherine. Catherine echoes Thomas's Eucharistic poetry in her *Dialogue*.[114]

Her debt to Thomas (as to other theologians) is diffuse,[115] and her theological style differs markedly from his in the *Summa*, but Catherine sometimes makes a Scholastic distinction in the *Dialogue*, consistent with Thomas's own—as, for example, when she reports the Father's teaching that the Eucharist can be received either "virtually" (*virtualmente*), through desire and reverence, or "sacramentally" (*sacramentalmente*), through reception of the consecrated host.[116] In either case, the one who lovingly communes with Christ experiences the gracious effect of the sacrament: "And so the soul is inebriated and set on fire and sated with holy longing, finding herself filled completely with the love of [God] and of her neighbors."[117]

Raymond reports the words of Jesus to Catherine, at the start of her public life: "I intend to flood your soul with such an abundance of divine grace that its effects will brim over upon your very body, which will begin to take on an abnormal way of life, totally different from the common run of men. Besides this, your heart will now be so filled with burning zeal for the salvation of souls that you will lay aside the conventional restraints imposed upon women, and mingle freely in the company of men, as well as women. . . . Indeed, you are to plunge boldly into public activity of every kind."[118]

In that same chapter we read: "It was at this juncture that, inspired by our Lord himself, she took on the practice of frequent Communion. . . . [H]er longing for more and more frequent Communion was so intense that when she could not receive it her very body felt the deprivation, and her forces seemed to droop. For as her body shared the overflow of the energies of her spirit, so it could not but be weakened when her spiritual vitality flagged for lack of the Bread of Life."[119] When Catherine's desire and need to receive Communion sacramentally was thwarted, Christ gave himself in the sacrament to her,[120] as depicted in Giovanni di Paolo's painting, *The Miraculous Communion of Saint Catherine of Siena* (1447–65) (see plate 7.2). Raymond goes so far as to assert that Catherine's inedia, her inability to eat normally, was an involuntary effect of her Eucharistic reception. The "torrent of heavenly graces and consolations [that] flooded her soul," especially when she received the sacrament, "were so abundant," Raymond writes, "that their effects brimmed over upon her body also, checking the natural flow of its vital juices, and so altering the action of her stomach that it could no longer assimilate food."[121]

The language of spiritual overflow affecting the body—energizing it virtuously, but also depriving it of earthly sustenance—recalls the teaching

Plate 7.2. Giovanni di Paolo, *The Miraculous Communion of St. Catherine of Siena*, 1447–1465. The Metropolitan Museum of Art, New York. https://www.metmuseum.org/art/collection/search/436511.

of Thomas on the glorified, resurrected body, joined at the *Parousia* to the once-separated soul, but also Thomas's teaching on the Eucharist, the food of martyrs. Discussing the tales of martyrs in Jacobus's *Legenda aurea*, Caroline Walker Bynum provides a Thomistic gloss: "Indeed, Thomas Aquinas, writing just as James [i.e., Jacobus] was compiling his *Golden Legend*, explained that the martyrs bear up under pain exactly because the beatific vision flows over naturally into their bodies."[122]

Describing the effects of the Eucharist in the *Summa*, Thomas similarly begins with the life-giving power of the sacrament, which he links to Christ himself, sacramentally present in the hypostatic union. Quoting John 6:58, "He that eateth Me, the same also shall live by Me," Thomas emphasizes the effect of Christ's living human body, present in the Host, on the very bodies of communicants: "Hence Cyril says on Luke 22:19: 'God's life-giving Word by uniting Himself with His own flesh, made it to be productive of life. For it was becoming that He should be united somehow with bodies through His sacred flesh and precious blood, which we receive in a life-giving blessing in the bread and wine.'"[123] Consumed under the appearance of bread and wine, "the sacrament does for the spiritual life all that material food does for the bodily life, namely, by sustaining, giving increase, restoring, and giving delight."[124]

Distinguishing between the sacrament as such (that is, the outer sign), the "thing" (*res*) of the sacrament (that is, its inner grace), and the effect of the sacrament, Thomas evaluates the different Old Testament prefigurations of the Eucharist (e.g., the bread and wine offered by Melchizedek, the Passover lamb, etc.), concluding that the manna by which the Israelites were fed in the desert is the "chief figure" of the sacrament with "regard to its effect"—manna "'having in it the sweetness of every taste' (Ws 16:20), just as the grace of this sacrament refreshes the soul in all respects."[125] A soul so strengthened necessarily also affects the living body to which the soul is joined. The effect of the sacrament can even now, therefore, anticipate the effect of the soul in glory upon the resurrected body. On this point, Thomas quotes Augustine: "As Augustine says (*Ep. ad Dioscor.* cxviii): 'God made the soul of such powerful nature, that from its fullest beatitude the fullness of health overflows into the body, that is, the vigor of incorruption.'"[126]

Aquinas's Eucharistic doctrine of transubstantiation, famous for its employ of Aristotelian terms and concepts, is carefully wedded to his teaching on the senses of the scriptures. Thomas's treatment of the "form" of the sacrament (that is, the words of institution voiced at Mass at the consecration of the "matter" of the sacrament, bread and wine) focuses attention on the biblical and sacramental *sensus litteralis*. He notes the exact wording: Jesus said, "*This* is my body" (Luke 22:19, *Hoc est corpus meum*), not "*bread* is my body,"[127] or "*here* is my body."[128] Thomas's commentary in part III of the *Summa theologiae* on the threefold signification of the sacrament of the Eucharist correlates closely, moreover, with the three spiritual senses of scripture, as he describes them in *Summa theologica* I, q. 1.[129] The sacrament goes by various names, Thomas observes. As the "memorial" of Christ's "sacrifice" on the cross, which fulfills all the sacrifices of the Old Law, especially that of the Paschal lamb, the Eucharist points (allegorically) to the past.[130] As "holy communion," the Eucharist points in the present to its virtuous (tropological) effect, the "unity of the mystical body" in the bond of charity.[131] As "viaticum," the Eucharist (anagogically) anticipates the future and "foreshadows the divine fruition, which shall come to pass in Heaven."[132]

RAYMOND'S CATHERINE AS DOUBLET OF JACOBUS'S MARY MAGDALENE

In his *Life of Catherine of Siena*, Raymond presents Catherine as a complex doublet of Mary Magdalene, whom Jesus himself gives to Catherine to be her mother and teacher.[133] Raymond's narrative of this dream-vision first shows Catherine crouched, weeping at Christ's feet as a penitent—a posture reminiscent of the Magdalen herself (identified with the sinner of Luke 7:36–50); then Catherine turns her eyes, gratefully and confidently, to the saint whom she accepts as her mother, even as the apostle John, standing with Mary Magdalene at the cross, had once accepted the Virgin Mary as his mother (John 19:26–27). Raymond immediately follows this narrated "peak point"[134] in the relationship between Catherine and Mary Magdalene with a paragraph (one of at least five similar paragraphs in the *Life*)[135] in which he highlights his own discovery of a mystic parallel between Catherine's Eucharistic nourishment and the Magdalen's raptures in the desert. Both saints lived for years without ordinary food. Like Mary Magdalene, lifted up in her ecstasies by angels, Catherine too "heard the secret things of God"[136]—a phrase echoing Paul's account of his own ecstatic experience in 2 Corinthians 12:1–4.

Raymond reinforces the theme of Catherine's mystical union with God with key citations of the Song of Songs,[137] oft applied to the Virgin Mary and to Mary Magdalene. Aquinas, for example, writes, "Before daybreak, she [Mary Magdalene] came to the tomb, incited by her exceedingly great love: 'Its flashes,' the flashes of love, 'are flashes of fire' (Sg 8:6)."[138] Indeed, Raymond glosses the tripartite division of the *Life of Catherine of Siena* with a single verse of the Song, divided into three phrases: "Who is she that comes up out of the desert, abounding in delights, leaning on her Beloved?" (Sg 8:5).[139] "Without sleep and without food," Raymond remarks, "[Catherine] was 'stayed up with flowers,' (as the *Canticle* says), that is, with those thoughts and words of love which ever kept aspiring upwards to her Spouse."[140]

Critics of Raymond take him to task for emphasizing so strongly this particular parallel between the two women saints at the seeming expense of others—for example, their active preaching, their zealous devotion to the crucified Christ, their ardent compunction and penitence.[141] Raymond, intent upon Catherine's canonization, is no doubt interested in foregrounding in the Magdalen legend a saintly precedent for what is particularly scandalous to many: Catherine's inedia and Eucharistic practice. For Raymond and for Catherine herself, however, the Eucharist—the sacrament of sacraments—and its virtuous effects are indeed mysteriously central to the saint's whole experience. For them, too, Mary Magdalen is a saint especially associated with Eucharistic devotion. Bynum notes, citing the work of Victor Saxer, "The saints most frequently depicted on Eucharistic tabernacles were the Virgin, Magdalen, Christopher, and little Saint Barbara, as she was known from the *Golden Legend*."[142] Womblike and tomblike, the tabernacle was a site to be visited by other Marys in search of the Lord Jesus, present in the Eucharist.

Raymond names Catherine "Virgin and Martyr," even though she did not die, as many of Jacobus's martyr-saints do, at the hands of pagan persecutors of the faith. In claiming the title of "martyr" for Catherine, Raymond emphasizes through the *Life* her patient endurance of suffering, her willingness to die for Christ—for example, during a period of civil strife in Florence—and her invisible bearing of Christ's stigmata.[143] What might be added to this is her martyr's witness to Christ's glorified body in the Eucharist. Like the Virgin Mary, who suffered a spiritual martyrdom standing at Christ's cross and then, assumed into heaven, shared bodily in Christ's resurrection, the Magdalen, present with Mary and John at the cross, bore a singular witness to the resurrected Christ both in the Gospel accounts and in her legendary manner of death, after receiving the Eucharist on the day of Christ's rising. Catherine, the Magdalene's twin, similarly died on a Sunday, April 29, 1380, after receiving the Blessed Sacrament.

Playing upon the close identification he sees between Catherine and Mary Magdalene as witnesses to the risen Lord, Raymond casts himself in the contrastive position of another apostolic witness, Saint Thomas the Twin. A careful theologian and initially a doubter in Catherine's virtue, exceptional gifts, and mission, Raymond confesses his faith in Catherine's sanctity, paraphrasing the words of the apostle, "My Lord and my God!" (John 20:28): "This other doubter . . . now cries out: 'Truly the spouse, truly the disciple, of my Lord and my God'!"[144]

By the end of the *Life*, however, Raymond, preacher and hagiographer, finds himself also to be another Mary Magdalene, greeted by Catherine in the very words of the risen Christ. At the time of Catherine's death in Rome, Raymond was away. "I was in Genoa," he writes, "[preparing] to go by sea to Pisa."[145] Passing a statue of the Virgin Mary on his way to the dormitory, he paused for an Ave, when "all at once [he] heard a voice. . . . whose words were more clearly perceptible to [his] soul than any words spoken to [his] bodily ears."[146] At this moment Catherine spoke to Raymond, who did not recognize her immediately: "Fear absolutely nothing. I am here for you. I am in heaven for you. I will protect and defend you. Do not be anxious; do not be afraid; I stand here for you."[147] At this typological moment in the *Life*, Genoa becomes the garden, and Raymond hears Catherine, as the mourning Magdalene once heard the still living Christ: "Fear not" (Matt. 28:5).

Reading Jacobus de Voragine's "Saint Mary Magdalene" alongside Catherine of Siena, and with the gloss provided by Thomas's Eucharistic theology, Raymond found a way of reading the life of the challenging saint whose *Life* he was then able to write. Imitating the fast of a legendary saint and participating, like her, in the visionary ecstasies and Holy Communion that fueled her preaching, Catherine herself found a model and friend in

Mary Magdalene, but also in Aquinas, Jacobus, Raymond, and William Flete. The last, an Augustinian hermit residing in a cave of Lecceto, must have been for Catherine a living counterpart to the Magdalen in her contemplative withdrawal to the wilderness. Few saints may be said to have read the *Legenda aurea* with a hermeneutical exigency comparable to Catherine's, but the wide audience of the *Legenda aurea* gives reason to believe that many late medieval Christians were inventive in discerning not only its tropological application to themselves, but also its anagogical thrust toward the glory that awaits the faithful disciple in the company of all the saints.

OSBERN BOKENHAM'S AUGUSTINIAN READING OF JACOBUS DE VORAGINE'S MARY MAGDALENE

Tracing the dissemination of Catherinian texts in England, Steven Rozenski remarks that they were promoted "by members of a variety of religious orders: the Carthusians (especially Stephen Maconi), the Dominicans, and Augustinian connections via her English confessor, William Flete."[148] Flete's *Remedies against Temptation*, and "Cleanness of Soul" (a translation of Catherine's *Documento spirituale*, dictated to Flete) circulated widely in England, in the company of such texts as Walter Hilton's *The Mixed Life* and Richard Rolle's *The Form of Living*.[149] Although he has not previously been named, the Austin friar-poet Osbern Bokenham may have been one of those Augustinian connections in England for Catherine. Cecily, Duchess of York (1415–95), for whom Bokenham translated the *Legenda aurea* in the years between 1443 and 1449,[150] discussed Catherine of Siena (and Mechthild of Hackeborn and Bridget of Sweden) with her friends at table.[151]

In many ways, Bokenham's personality seems quite distant from Flete's. Both Augustinian friars studied at Cambridge University—Flete in the 1350s, Bokenham in the 1420s. Flete, a *baccularius* who had lectured on Peter Lombard's *Sentences*, renounced the opportunity to incept as a master in 1358, choosing instead to set sail for Italy, where he was determined to live an observant, eremitical life. Bokenham, by contrast, completed the higher degree, was known by the title "master," and enjoyed the privileges at Clare Priory afforded by that rank. Bokenham also traveled extensively, making two trips to Italy and going on pilgrimage to the Shrine of Saint James in Compostela in 1455, whereas Flete strictly maintained his residence in Lecceto, close to Siena. In three letters Flete composed in 1377 for his fellow Augustinians in England, he called urgently for the order's reform and warned, in particular, against the spiritual dangers for monks of travel and of using the title "master."[152] In their autobiographical remarks, moreover, Flete and Bokenham present divergent profiles—Flete's soaring and prophetic; Bokenham's jovial and gregarious.

Bokenham, devoted to saints and saints' shrines, may well, however, have taken pride as an Augustinian in Friar William of England's reputation for holiness and in his association with Catherine of Siena, revered (but not yet canonized) as a saint. To some extent, Bokenham may even have aspired to imitate Flete in the spiritual formation of the devout lay readers, men and women, for whom he wrote hagiographies in English, transforming Jacobus de Voragine's *Legenda aurea* and fitting it to the needs of a new generation. As Bokenham relates in the prolocutory to the *Life*, Lady Isabel Bouchier commissioned Bokenham's poetic translation of Jacobus's legend of Mary Magdalene because, as she told the friar, she had "a synguler deuocyoun" born "of pure affeccyoun" to that holy woman, "of apostyls þe apostyllesse," a sinner whom Christ had made "pure & clene."[153]

Sheila Delany describes the Magdalene legend as "conceptually central to Bokenham's aesthetic and doctrinal concerns," noting that its biblical heroine "possesses an aura not shared by [the] other saints"; that Bokenham has given her tale a central location in his *Legendys of Hooly Wummen*; and that it is the only one in that collection to have a tripartite structure: the prolocutory (lines 4981–5262), the prologue (lines 5263–66), and the *Life* proper (lines 5367–6311).[154]

Bokenham's tripartite structure transforms Jacobus's legend of Mary Magdalene in the *Legenda aurea* by detaching it from its original setting and moving it into a different framework, wherein the hagiographer himself appears on stage (in the prolocutory), in company with the saint with whom Bokenham and his reader(s) engage, not only by hearing her speak and pray from within the *Life* proper, but also through the poet's inserted prayers addressed to God and to the saint herself. These include Bokenham's prayers for Elizabeth de Vere, Countess of Oxford (lines 5056–61), his prayer to the Trinity (lines 5143–5262), his prayers to Mary Magdalene (lines 5351–66, 5740–44, 6305–11), Mary Magdalene's prayer to Jesus (lines 5444–57), the prince's prayers to the Magdalen (lines 5997–6014, 6081–94), and the princess's prayer of thanksgiving to her (lines 6100–6108).

Bokenham transforms Jacobus's legend further by deleting some of the recounted miracles and, importantly, by narrating in full the biblical episodes involving Mary to which Jacobus merely refers. In expanding the explicitly biblical material, Bokenham anticipates a strategy of addition that William Caxton will later use in his printed translation of the *Legenda Aurea* (1483). Karen Winstead points out, "Of Caxton's 250 chapters, about 70 are not found in Jacobus's collection, and more than 40 are not found in either of the prior Middle English translations. . . . Perhaps most surprisingly, Caxton includes the 'lives' of thirteen Old Testament figures whose stories are translated from scripture with little embellishment."[155] At least in England, the fifteenth century saw what Winstead and others describe as experimentation and innovation in the composition of hagiographies.[156] Among the translators of Jacobus's work, Bokenham and Caxton "both attest to the stature and sustained influence of Jacobus's *Legenda aurea* as a hagiographic classic *and* signal a resistance to its vision" by supplementing or replacing "Jacobus's hagiographies with texts that are inimical to his austere and antiworldly model of sainthood."[157]

Bokenham uses the prologue to translate into Middle English verse Jacobus's etymologies for Mary Magdalene's name, but also to instruct his reader that the following story "both of þe gospel, þat kan not ly, / And of hyr legend to-gydyr is bounde" (lines 5347–48), so that it might more effectively teach the Pauline lesson mentioned by Jacobus, namely, "wher wrechydly / Syn regnyd, grace doth superhabounde" (lines 5349–50; cf. Rom. 5:20–21).[158] Bokenham's poetic, biblical narrations in the *Life* are not, however, literal translations of the Gospels, but imaginative meditations upon the Gospel stories traditionally associated with the person of Mary Magdalene, composed in an affective style akin to that found in Nicholas Love's popular *Mirror of the Blessed Life of Jesus Christ* (ca. 1400).[159] The poet moves the emotions through the Magdalen's tears and love. Bokenham carefully marks his departures from, and his return to, Jacobus's text with explicit references to his source, "Ianuence" (lines 5387, 5734, 5748), as "legenda aurea doth specyfye" (line 5273). The juxtaposition of "Gospel" and "legend" in this case works to identify Jacobus's *Legenda* only with the legendary material.

Delany rightly points to Augustine's *De doctrina Christiana* as an important context for Bokenham's preacherly poetics.[160] Reading Bokenham's tripartite legend alongside Flete's works, however, other Augustinian and Catherinian intertexts also come readily to mind—notably, Augustine's *De Trinitate* and his commentaries on the creation story in Genesis.

The prolocutory includes a long prayer to the Blessed Trinity that explicates that sublime Christian mystery (lines 5143–54),[161] praises the Triune God for God's works in creation (lines 5154–62), and points to the creation of humankind in God's image, according to the three faculties of mind, reason, and will (lines 5163–70), and as possessing also God's similitude through preternatural gifts (lines 5171–76) and through mankind's governance of the other creatures (lines 5177–82). The prayer then praises the Trinity for the saving work of the incarnate second person, who by his blood ransomed and refashioned humanity (lines 5182–5213). Bokenham's prayer finally turns into a petition as the poet, refusing to invoke the pagan muses, seeks both God's inspiration for his work and God's grace for his patroness, Lady Isabel (lines 5214–62).

Remarkable for the catechetical clarity and comprehensiveness of its Christian doctrine, the prayer shows its indebtedness to Augustine at every turn, stressing the great difference between God's eternity, fullness of being, and goodness, on the one hand, and the creature's nothingness in itself, on the other. God "me made of nought," Bokenham recalls, even as God "Both heuene & erthe hast made of nouht" (lines 5142, 5155). Saint Catherine's fundamental spiritual understanding, as imparted to William Flete in the *Documento spirituale*, was similarly built upon a threefold rock.[162] First, she considered creation and knew "that she had no being of herself, but depended totally on God both for her coming into being and for her preservation: it was the Creator who did all this and did it of his own free gift."[163] Second, she considered how God, freely and lovingly, "by his own blood has restored the life of grace."[164] Third, she considered her own postbaptismal sins and need for conversion.

Reversing Jacobus's abridgment, Bokenham narrates Mary Magdalene's biblical tale of sin, conversion, and transformation through grace, but he also retains from Jacobus the postbiblical legend wherein the apostolic Magdalen brings about the conversion and transformation of the people of Marseilles, starting with the prince and princess. In this way, the saint whose *Life* Bokenham tells is not only an example to be followed, but also an agent of God's grace, who, from within the legend, speaks to Bokenham and his audience, calling them to convert and inspiring their hope in her miraculous intercession for them.

The framing device of the prolocutory sets the contemporary scene of the Epiphany party in 1445 (presumably at Clare Castle) adjacent, as it were, to the luxuries enjoyed at "a castel callyd Magdalum" (line 5384), where Mary—rich, young, and beautiful—lives at the start of the *Life*. Bokenham's naming of classical gods, goddesses, planets, poets (Ovid), and philosophers (Plato) in the prolocutory stands rhetorically near to the narrated idolatry of the childless royal couple who sacrifice to the goddess Diane, tyrannize over the poor, and resist Mary Magdalene's sermons. Delany has argued that Bokenham's classical language entails not only an allusion to his fellow poets Chaucer, Gower, and Lydgate, who used similar diction, but also a Christian critique of what Bokenham regards to be an insidious, contemporary idolatry of fame and privilege: "[Bokenham shows] that he can write in an aureate fashion if he wishes to, but [he] has chosen another style deliberately."[165]

By its length and central placement in the *Life*, the romantic, far-flung legend of the conversion of this couple and thus of the city of Marseilles (lines 5801–6143) far outweighs the concluding account (146 verses) of Mary Magdalene's solitary sojourn in the wilderness, her final reception of Holy Communion, and her burial (lines 6151–6297). Isabel Bouchier is not expected to imitate the solitary, ascetic saint. Bokenham's contemplative Magdalene is already, it seems, living the ascended afterlife, raised by angels above this earth, but his active, apostolic Magdalene in the legend of Marseilles lives contrastively, as it were, the afterdeath of the resurrected life.

Through her agility—*agilitas* being a property of Christ's glorified body—Mary Magdalene exhibits in the legend what appears to be powers of bilocation. She preaches to the prince and his wife recurrently, even in their dreams; she performs a midwife's service to the prince's wife when she gives birth during a violent storm at sea; she preserves incorrupt the body of the dead wife, who, in a state of suspended animation, continues to breastfeed her child while she also travels mysteriously in spirit with her husband to Saint Peter's in Rome; the saint also cares for the child for two years until the husband returns, finds the boy alive, and witnesses his wife's return to life.

A wondrous tale of resurrection fitting to Mary Magdalene's biblical witness to Christ's, her legend is replete with symbols suggestive of the sacraments. The baptism finally received by the converted couple is presaged by sea voyage, childbirth, death, and rising.[166] The Eucharist is mysteriously announced by the breastfeeding mother.[167] Marriage itself shows its threefold, Augustinian goods in the remarkable chastity, loving fidelity, and procreation of the couple.[168] The anagogy of these sacraments is the eternal wedding feast heralded in the scriptures.

Through his imaginative retelling of the Gospel stories of Mary Magdalene's composite life (316 verses; lines 5415–5731) right before the legend (342 verses) of the couple's conversion, Bokenham has thus coupled Gospel truth, which does not lie, with a legend of conversion rich in sacramental symbolism. That coupling warrants for his poetic *Life* of Mary Magdalene as a whole both religious faith and, with regard to the legendary portion, what Samuel Taylor Coleridge (1772–1834) will later call "poetic faith," "the willing suspension of disbelief."[169] Bokenham's hierarchical distinction between the biblical and legendary texts and between their levels of signification allows for their fruitful, devotional yoking through images.

An illumination from Marguerite d'Orléans's Book of Hours (ca. 1430), roughly contemporary with Bokenham's work, makes this point (see plate 7.3).[170] Central to the image is an abbreviation of John 12:3, "Maria ergo Magdalene unxit pedes Ihesu et extersit capillis suis et tota domus impleta est ex odore unguenti" (Mary Magdalene therefore anointed the feet of Jesus and dried them with her hair, and the whole house was filled with the fragrance of the ointment). The verse recalls Mary's anointing of Jesus at Bethany six days before Passover—an expensive anointing that anticipates the burial of Jesus's body. Above the verse, a red-mantled Magdalene reclines in the desert at her own death, still holding the vial of ointment that she had carried to Jesus's empty tomb (Luke 24:1, 10). Above her, six angels appear, lifting up Mary Magdalene as she continues to hold the vial, the iconographic symbol of the extravagant act of worship for which Jesus praises her in Bethany, prophesying her remembrance "wherever this gospel is preached in the whole world" (Matt. 26:13). As scripture comments upon scripture, the perfume of the oil that fills the whole house in Bethany signifies the universal proclamation of the gospel: "Your name is oil poured out" (Sg 1:3).

Plate 7.3. Horae ad usum romanum, ca. 1430.
Bibliothèque nationale de France, Paris. BN Ms. lat. 1156B, fol. 174r.

Mary's own story similarly overflows its bounds. In the narrative border, the flowing of the fragrance spilled forth in John 12:3 is transformed into the flowing waves of the Mediterranean, upon which boats and ships are launched, recalling Mary's legendary voyage, together with Martha and Lazarus and Maximin, as missionary to Marseilles, and recalling the adventurous sea voyages taken by the prince and his pregnant wife. The camels on the winding road into the desert symbolize the far reach of the Gospels, even as they evoke the prophesied young camels of Isaiah 60:6, who bear their gifts of gold and frankincense "to proclaim the praises of the Lord."

PART 3

The Saint's *Life* in Modernity

CHAPTER EIGHT

THE ENDS OF HAGIOGRAPHY

Erasmus's *Jerome*, Harpsfield's *Life of More*, and More's Epitaph

Even his [Thomas More's] tomb in the old church there [in Chelsea], with its long plain inscription, is hidden in darkness, almost as though he had died a death of shame.

— P. S. Allen, 1918

Scholars of the history of hagiography regularly point to the sixteenth century as a watershed moment, citing Protestant and Catholic critique of Jacobus de Voragine's *Legenda aurea* and the Reformers' attacks against the cult of the saints, but also Desiderius Erasmus's new-style *Life of Saint Jerome* (*Hieronymi Stridonensis vita*) (1516) and related writings produced in humanist circles. Among the latter, the *Life of Thomas More* (ca. 1556) by Nicholas Harpsfield (1519–75), a devotee of Erasmus and More, deserves special attention. Hailed as "the first scholarly biography in English,"[1] Harpsfield's book places its author at an exact point of literary beginnings and endings. "Although the first modern biographer, he can also be regarded as almost the last Englishman (of a long succession) to write, on English ground, a treatise upon the life of a saint," R. W. Chambers writes.[2] Chambers refers to Harpsfield's book as "a complete biography" and a "hagiography,"[3] but without probing the creative tension implied in that dual generic identification.

"Ro. Ba.," the author of *The Lyfe of Syr Thomas More, Sometimes Lord Chancellor of England* (1599), credits both Nicholas Harpsfield and Thomas

Stapleton (1535–98) as his chief sources. Writing "To the courteous reader," "Ro. Ba." places his work squarely within a long hagiographic tradition: "It hath bene as ancient and a commendable cvstome in the Church of god, and noe lesse laudable then profitable, always to haue had a special care that the liues and deaths of godes sainctes and martyrs should be with care and fidelitie registred and recorded to all faithfull posteritie."[4] The author, who calls himself "a young beginner," cites patristic authorities and hagiographers to demonstrate the importance of writing saints' *Lives* as a means both to preserve Christian unity "in the same rule of faith" (*in eadem fidei regula*) and to inspire virtuous imitation: "The example of others is very forcible, yea, it vseth secret violence to drawe mans nature to good or euell."[5] Acknowledging that this hagiographic tradition stands in great need of repair through new Latin editions of the early sources—for example, the six-volume *Vitae sanctorum* of Laurence Surius (1570)—and suitable vernacular translations, "Ro. Ba." offers his *Life of More* as a remedy for his fellow Englishmen, a concise compendium of the whole tradition of saints' *Lives*. All the virtues may be found in More, whom "Ro. Ba." names "a Confessour, Doctour, and Martyr."[6]

Helen C. White presents an ambiguous argument in her attempt to place within a long, hagiographic tradition the successive sixteenth-century *Lives* of More, namely, William Roper's memoir of his father-in-law (composed approximately twenty years after More's death); Harpsfield's *Life and Death of Sir Thomas More* (commissioned by Roper and dedicated to him); Thomas Stapleton's *The Life and Illustrious Martyrdom of Sir Thomas More* (in his *Tres Thomae*, 1588); and the *Life* by "Ro. Ba., otherwise unidentified."[7] Charting changes in hagiography as a genre over time, from its first beginnings in the passion accounts of early Christian martyrs to William Caxton's 1483 edition of the *Golden Legend*, White acknowledges the sixteenth-century reaction against medieval hagiography, even as she proposes the Tudor martyrologies, both Catholic and Protestant, as renewing the hagiographic tradition from its sources. Accordingly, she describes Roper's memoirs, at the base of all subsequent *Lives* of More, as both "hagiographic" and "prehagiographical."[8] She detects a hagiographic "pattern" in Roper's assembled notes, on the one hand, but she also discerns in the successive *Lives* of More a steady movement from historical eyewitness to hagiography, on the other: "It is possible by going a little way into the next century to recapitulate in the development of the More legend the development of the whole of the preceding martyrological tradition from what might be called the prehagiographic record to the edge of the *Legenda Aurea*."[9] Warren Wooden comments that White "seems unsure how the life of More is related to the hagiographic tradition."[10]

This chapter argues that Harpsfield's *Life*, building upon Roper's *Life* (known to Harpsfield in manuscript, but first published in Paris in 1626, under the title *The mirrour of vertue in worldly greatnes, or the life of Syr Thomas More*), follows the revisionary model set by Erasmus in his *Life of Saint Jerome* (1516). That model transfers to the writing of a saint's *Life* principles traditionally employed in biblical interpretation, but disturbed by contemporary battles over the senses of scripture, starting with the *sensus litteralis*, and related issues of human and divine authorship. The difficulty in writing and reading More's *Life* as hagiography is thus inextricably tied to related, confessional difficulties in translating and interpreting the Bible. Erasmus's philological approach to the scriptures, which famously privileges Jerome's grammatical command of the ancient languages over Augustine's theological reception of the sacred texts written in them,[11] lays a foundation, willy-nilly, for modern, form-critical biblical studies,[12] even as his *Life of Saint Jerome* propels the early modern saint's *Life* in the direction of documentary biography. Erasmus's editions of Jerome's works and of the New Testament in Greek were both published in 1516. Ironically, in Erasmus's retelling of his story, Saint Jerome (ca. 347–420), who authored the fabulous *Life of Saint Paul the First Hermit* (*Vita Sancti Pauli primae eremitae*), and other hagiographies,[13] and who translated the Hebrew scriptures into Latin, thus becomes instrumental in distancing the Bible from sacred biography.

HAGIOGRAPHY *EX SCRIPTURIS*: SAINT JEROME'S *LIFE* OF PAUL OF THEBES

Scholars often note autobiographical elements in Jerome's legend of the hermit Paul, whose asceticism and seclusion mirrors that of Jerome himself, who (by Erasmus's account) "withdrew far into the wild desert, . . . uninhabited except by wild beasts and serpents and here and there a group of monks."[14] In the *Vita Pauli*, Jerome refers directly to his own experience in the wilderness, where he encountered monks like Paul.[15] Hilmar Pabel observes, "His lives of the holy monks Paul, Hilarion, and Malchus are not simply essays in hagiography; they serve to present Jerome as the living embodiment of ascetic virtue."[16] Similarly, the *Life of the Eminent Doctor Jerome of Stridon Composed Mainly from His Own Writings* by Desiderius Erasmus of Rotterdam (1516) argues for Erasmus's status as a latter-day Jerome, renewing his books and sharing in the saint's "aura," which (in the words of Lisa Jardine) "modulated into that of the exemplary scholar-translator."[17] Pabel notes the resemblance between the self-fashioning of the two men of letters: "In Erasmus, as with Jerome, self-promotion and Christian literary labour were not at cross-purposes."[18]

In the biography of Jerome that prefaces the first volume of his edited letters, Erasmus makes no explicit mention of Jerome's enormously popular and beautifully written *Life* of Paul of Thebes,[19] but he does include that text among the "pieces of moral instruction by exhortation and example" in Jerome's literary corpus.[20] Obviously intended as an artful companion piece to Athanasius's *Life of Antony* (ca. 360), Jerome gave a copy of the *Vita Pauli* in 374 to Paul of Concordia.[21]

Composed near the dawn of Christian hagiography, Jerome's short *Life of Paul the First Hermit* helped to define the genre in its intimate relationship to the scriptures. Combining Virgilian, mythic, biblical, and Jewish sources,[22] Jerome's *Vita Pauli* focuses on the beginning and the end of the hermit's long life in the wilderness. Fleeing into the wilderness during a time of persecution (graphically narrated by Jerome), the young Paul accomplishes what Stefan Rebenich calls the transformation of "the bloody martyrdom of persecution into a bloodless martyrdom of asceticism."[23] The pagan pleasure garden (*locus amoenissimus*) where one young confessor, a bound prisoner, has suffered sexual assault stands in sharp contrast to the new paradise Paul finds in the mountains—a safe refuge, supplied with a spring, a spacious cave, and palm trees. There he lives out his solitary life, his whereabouts known only to God, his battles with demons left untold to his contemporaries (and to Jerome's readers).

The climax of the story is the wondrous meeting of Paul with Antony of Egypt, who has searched for the true first hermit and been miraculously directed to Paul's distant cave by mythic creatures: a centaur, a satyr, and a she-wolf. Paul unbars his door at Antony's persistent knocking and pleading.

The two holy men, brothers in Christ, embrace and break together a loaf of bread, which a raven has supplied. At Paul's request, Antony then leaves Paul in order to fetch the cloak given him by Athanasius, with which he is to bury Paul's body. Returning quickly, he finds Paul dead, his body still kneeling in prayer. Antony is without a spade, but two lions helpfully appear to dig with their claws the grave of the saint and then to receive Antony's blessing before departing. Antony then honors Paul's memory by donning the hermit's palm-leaf tunic, an eschatological symbol of victory (Rev. 7:9), on the feasts of Easter and Pentecost. The story ends with Jerome's exhortation to his readers to choose heavenly over worldly riches, even as he, "the sinner Jerome," endeavors to "choose Paul's tunic."[24]

Through the narrated appearance of mythological creatures, quotations from Virgil's *Aeneid*, and allusions to other classical sources (Florus, Seneca, Cicero, Ovid, Sallust, and Tacitus), Jerome as a hagiographer accomplishes several ends. He appeals to the imagination of readers, Christian and non-Christian, who are familiar with the Latin classics. He presents the Christian saint as a hero whose greatness surpasses the heroes of the pagans, whose piety exceeds that of Aeneas. He imitates Saint Paul, who quotes from the Greek poets in his address to the Athenians (Acts 17:22–31), in order to make a theological case that God has not entirely withheld the knowledge of God from previous generations; rather God has manifested himself, albeit in hidden and mysterious ways, even to the pagans. Finally, through the skillful melding of short, Virgilian passages with the plain style of his own, biblically infused prose, Jerome accomplishes the creation of a new Christian eloquence, enriched (so to speak) with the spoils of the Egyptians.[25]

The *Vita Pauli* contains only one verbatim biblical quote (1 John 4:18), but the short text is replete with biblical echoes, close paraphrases, and typologies. Counting conservatively, Carolinne White identified twelve scriptural intertexts.[26] In his critical edition, Bazyli Degórski has since identified thirty-nine biblical paraphrases.[27] To White's and Degórski's lists of biblical evocations, I would add echoes of the Song of Songs in the *Life of Paul*'s imagery of lilies, roses, bed, and kisses — imagery that prepares for the evocation of Song of Songs 5:2–6 as a type-scene. Jerome's *Life of Paul* allusively joins the seeking and knocking of Matthew 7:7–8 to that of the Song in such a way that Antony's persistent knocking at Paul's bolted door until the sixth hour (the hour of Jesus's crucifixion) offers a narrative commentary on the Bridegroom's nocturnal knocking at his beloved's latched entrance. The searching Antony, declaring his readiness to die on the doorstep, becomes an *alter Christus*, figured as the passionate Bridegroom whose hair, wet with dew, reminded Christian commentators of Christ's thorn-crowned head, wet with blood.[28]

The biblical passages echoed in Jerome's *Life of Paul* as part of its letter reflect all four senses of scripture: historical (1 Kings 17:3–6; Mark 9:23; 1 Sam. 24:8), tropological (1 John 4:18; Matt. 7:7; Luke 11:9; 1 Cor. 13:5, 7; Eccles. 3:7), allegorical (Sg 5:2–6), and anagogical (2 Tim. 4:7–8; Rev. 14:4–5). The temporal and epistemological gaps in the hagiographic narration, the evident symbolism of things, and the shimmering interplay of different biblical senses through intertextual citation ensure that the literal narrative of the *Vita Pauli* cannot, and should not, be read at a single level of historical signification; its meaning must be searched out through the Bible to which it refers and finally discovered there.

This close, intertextual relationship with the scriptures means that the human author of hagiographies such as Jerome's *Life of Paul* is inherently at the service of the Bible's own divine author. We saw in chapter 4 of this book how Hugh of Saint Victor regarded the writings of the Fathers of the Church, including their hagiographies, as so closely united to the canonical books of the Bible and to the apostolic deposit of faith as to constitute a third part of (an addendum of sorts to) the New Testament.[29] Just as scripture interprets scripture, the writings of the Fathers—albeit not with the same, absolute inerrancy—are upheld as authoritative guides, led by the Holy Spirit to illuminate the scriptures.

Ian Christopher Levy explains that the doctrine of the unity of the scriptures, of the different senses of scripture, and of the practice, heralded by Origen and Augustine, of using scripture to interpret scripture, depends on the Church's belief in the divine authorship of the Bible.[30] "What made Holy Scriptures unique among all texts for the medieval exegetes," Levy remarks, "was precisely that, beyond the human author, there remained the divine author, who did intend the many spiritual senses of the text to be recovered."[31] Given "a divine author who comprehends all meaning within his intellect simultaneously,"[32] and guided by that author's intent to teach charity,[33] exegetes used scripture to illuminate scripture across the two testaments, interpreting difficult passages in the light of those verses whose meaning is plain. Schooled by Origen and Ambrose, Augustine could affirm: "The Holy Spirit has magnificently and wholesomely modulated the Holy Scriptures so that the more open places present themselves to hunger and the more obscure places may deter a disdainful attitude."[34] Balancing text with text, the exegetical practice affirmed a fundamental principle: "Holy Scripture is its own interpreter."[35]

Hagiography is not scripture per se, but by its intertextual participation in, and imitative extension of, the scriptures, a saint's *Life* such as Jerome's *Vita Pauli* bears witness to what the Bible reveals and demands. The biblical medium is a good part of hagiographical message.[36] Just as God is the author of the two books of Creation and the Bible—each necessary to the other's proper understanding[37]—so too is God through God's grace the privileged author of the saint, whose sanctity bears witness to God's own: "Be holy as I am holy" (1 Pet. 1:16). Composing a saint's *Life* in biblical language conveys the theological doctrine that God himself is the author of a saint's holiness, the Word who has impressed the divine image and established God's likeness in the saint. The saint (to the extent that he or she is a saint) is the "author" of his own life only secondarily, in collaboration with the divine author and dependent on God's grace, even as the human writers of the scriptures are authors in a secondary sense, their work inspired by God's Spirit.

The early Church and the Middle Ages recognized the mysterious joining of the divine author and the holy human authors (*auctores*) of the scriptures. In the early Christian affirmation of the unity of the two testaments against the heresy of Marcion (ca. 85–ca. 160), the divine author who gave the scriptures their authority (*auctoritas*) stands so much in the foreground that scripture is called "Word of God" (on the authority of scripture itself)[38] and likened to the Incarnate Word (John 1:1, 14) in its revelatory power. The doctrine of biblical inerrancy follows from the primacy of God as author and from the understanding of the scriptures as divinely inspired (see 2 Tim. 3:16–17).

Whereas the Fathers of the Church emphasize the marvelous condescension of God in speaking to humans through the human words of the prophets and through God's incarnate Son (see Heb. 1:1), modern commentators stress the diminishment of independent human agency in this patristic doctrine of the scriptures. Hailing God as the divine author of the book of Job, Gregory the Great, for instance, treats as superfluous the question of the human author, whom he compares to a pen moved by the Spirit.[39] Alastair Minnis describes it thus, "The notion of the [human] *auctor* as an agent engaged in literary activity was submerged; the truth of the Bible was maintained at the expense of its human contributors."[40] Indeed, "God was believed to have controlled human authors in a way that defied literary description."[41]

This description of patristic doctrine is debatable to the extent that it implies a mantic possession of the human authors of scripture by the Holy Spirit, but Minnis does demonstrate an apparent historical shift in the understanding of the divine–human interaction during the Middle Ages. Building upon the new emphasis placed on the literal/historical sense of the scriptures in the twelfth century, and influenced by Aristotelian notions of causality, the human *auctores* of the Bible — their lives, historical intentions, and choices — received more attention during the Scholastic period. Theologians of the thirteenth, fourteenth, and fifteenth centuries spoke in various ways of a duplex literal sense, reflective of both human and divine intentions;[42] of the scriptures' *forma tractatus* and *forma tractandi*;[43] of double or triple or quadruple efficient causality;[44] of extrinsic and intrinsic material;[45] of immediate and remote final causes.[46] Thanks to the teaching of Thomas Aquinas and others, observes Minnis, "the fact of the divine inspiration of Scripture no longer interfered with thorough examination of the literary issues involved" in the Bible's composition.[47]

Concomitant with this increased, Scholastic attention to the human *auctores* of the Bible as agents came an increased tendency to compare them to respected non-Christian authors — philosophers Aristotle, Plato, and Seneca; poets Homer, Virgil, and Ovid — and to elevate Christian *auctores* (biblical and nonbiblical) above other sorts of writers: scribes, translators, compilers. Humanists such as Erasmus certainly quarreled with the Scholastic theologians, but they also furthered these tendencies.[48] Seeking through an advanced knowledge of the ancient languages to restore the texts of classical, biblical, and patristic authors to their pristine purity, purging them of the dross of accumulated scribal errors and mistranslations, the humanists claimed for themselves a share in the ancient writers' original, charismatic *auctoritas*.

Under the mantle of Jerome (but also in competition with him as translator), Erasmus directed himself in the years between 1510 and 1516 both to producing a bilingual, Greek and Latin edition of the New Testament (as a basis for correcting textual errors in the *Biblia vulgata*) and to editing the letters of Saint Jerome. The first project—issued in five editions between 1516 and 1535—enabled the respective, vernacular translations of the Bible by Martin Luther (1522) and William Tyndale (1526), into German and English, respectively. From a methodological perspective, Erasmus the humanist "approached the Bible text as if it were a pagan classical text,"[49] in order to establish an authoritative edition. Dismayed at the outcries from his critics who protested against his correction of the Gospels as "rank sacrilege," Erasmus wrote to Henry Bullock in 1516, "Why are we in greater distress over a difference in reading in Scripture than over a difference of interpretation?"[50] His critics "have lost nothing," Erasmus insists, "and have gained something worth having. The text they love they will henceforth read more accurately and understand more correctly."[51]

Without intending to do so, Erasmus's editions risked undermining belief in the inerrancy of scripture itself through highlighting the possibility of human error in the literal sense of the Bible as the faithful had received it in the *Biblia vulgata* and were receiving it in the vernacular translations of Luther and Tyndale, among others. Changes in the letter of the scriptures were seen to destabilize the long tradition of doctrinal exegesis based on the *sensus litteralis*.[52] Erasmus's critics—Catholics and Protestants alike—voiced a growing chorus of concern that his individual editorial decisions, translations, and annotations served to undermine belief in the Trinity and Christ's divinity,[53] in marriage as a sacrament,[54] and in liturgical expression; finally, his critics sensed that his methods, taken as a whole, challenged the inerrancy of the scriptures by treating them as historical artifacts subject to philological corrections independent of the Church's traditional exegesis and rule of faith (*regula fidei*). Erasmus and the pious Christian humanists of his age themselves practiced a fourfold exegesis of the Bible—Thomas More's *De Tristia Christi* (*On the Sadness of Christ*, 1535)[55] is an exquisite example of this kind of meditative commentary— but biblical study itself was altered at its foundation through Erasmus's biblical project. In the strong words of Henk Nellen and Jan Bloemendal, "[Erasmus's] legacy irreversibly inspired researchers to a hermeneutical approach that in the end could not but result in irrefutable attacks on the self-evidence, sufficiency, and complete inerrancy of Holy Writ."[56]

In the related project of the edition of Jerome's writings, Erasmus similarly placed emphasis on the historical, human authorship of Jerome at the expense of considerations of the divine author of the saint, transforming the hagiography of Jerome into Jerome's biography. Erasmus lambastes previous hagiographies of the saint from Stridon as unworthy of the man and sets out to correct them on the basis of Jerome's trustworthy self-report, demythologizing the saint's legend in the process. Neglecting mention of the *Vita Pauli* in his biography of Jerome, Erasmus also avoids naming Jerome among the ancient Christian hagiographers, who (he suggests) went too far in catering to the "extraordinary credulity" of the "common man" through their illuminating "by the miraculous the glory of saintly men."[57] Deeply self-identified with Jerome as a biblical scholar, Erasmus tactfully resists calling attention to this particular point of difference between them, even as he imitates Jerome in narrating the life of a saint after whom he has modeled himself and whom he desires in some sense even to surpass.

HEIRONYMUS EX HEIRONYMO: ERASMUS'S BIOGRAPHY OF SAINT JEROME

Transforming Jerome into his own likeness, Erasmus announces his preferred task: to present the well-educated person with a factual *Life* of Saint Jerome, stripped bare of "ridiculous tales of miracles and stories of the most shameless falsity."[58] The scholar from Rotterdam declares, "I find it distasteful to say anything at all about his miracles, which are widely known, whatever the pleasure this kind of tale gives to some."[59] Erasmus thus cursorily dismisses, for example, the famous story of Jerome and the lion so often cited in iconography.[60] For Erasmus, Jerome's own person outshines every other wonder: "To me the greatest miracle is the miracle of Jerome as he expresses himself to us in his many books of lasting and pre-eminent quality."[61] During Jerome's own lifetime, Erasmus avers, the many notable Christians who visited him in Bethlehem—Augustine's friend Alypius among them—accomplished a double pilgrimage to a holy place and to a living saint.[62]

In his letter dedicating the volume to William Warham (1450–1532), archbishop of Canterbury, Erasmus lauds "the books of great men, in which they live on for the world at large even after their death"; he calls the books written by the Church Fathers "relics of the mind," lamenting that they have suffered sad, textual neglect, in contrast to their material relics, which receive veneration: "the slippers of the saints and their drivel-stained napkins we put to our lips."[63]

Redefining "miracle" and "relic," Erasmus's *Life of Jerome* is generally acknowledged to be (in the words of Eugene Rice) "a saint's life written to an unprecedented standard of accuracy and critical skepticism and a turning point in Renaissance hagiography."[64] Pabel emphasizes points of continuity between Erasmus and Quattrocentro humanist hagiographers, but he too concludes, "Erasmus's life of Jerome achieved a goal that had eluded humanists for a century."[65] Structured in the manner of a forensic speech defending the saint and praising him, the *Life* begins with an exordium in which Erasmus announces his intention to present a new sort of saint's story, that portrays "the saints just as they actually were," inclusive of their human imperfections, in order to inspire the imitation of them by others.[66] Unembellished by miracles and "without resort to sackcloth, hair shirts, prodigious fasts, and incredible vigils," a saint's story should provide a "skillful expression" of an "image" that reflects "the meaning of Christian piety."[67]

Peter Bietenholz observes that "Erasmus positively envisaged a historical science and proceeded to demonstrate its methods in the life of Jerome."[68] Lamenting that Jerome has been ill-served by previous hagiographers, Erasmus explains in his exordium that he has chosen to reconstruct the series of events in Jerome's life in a scientific way, reducing "to narrative form" material gathered "from scattered parts of his writings."[69] Erasmus has indeed consulted a variety of other sources (Prosper, Severus, Orosius, Rufinus), but "above all," he has based his "inquiry into Jerome's life on the works of Jerome himself."[70] "For who," Erasmus asks, "would have a better knowledge of Jerome than Jerome himself? Or who would give a truer picture?"[71]

The narrative that follows this exordium begins with Jerome's birth in Stridon and proceeds chronologically. Erasmus accompanies every factual assertion with textual evidence to discount alternative reports. A scholar of languages, Erasmus does not disdain the classical and medieval practice of providing explanatory etymologies. Noting that Jerome's father was named

Eusebius, Erasmus remarks: "This is not without significance for the future: it is very fitting that a hero of 'saintly name' (this is what Jerome means in Greek) be the offspring of a 'pious man.'"[72] Dwelling upon Jerome's education in grammar and rhetoric under the tutelage of the best teachers, Erasmus describes it as preparatory for Jerome's mission "to refute the pagans who viewed Christians with contempt for their lack of eloquence and style."[73]

Commenting indirectly upon the shortfalls of sixteenth-century monasticism, Erasmus observes that the monastic life Jerome chose for himself was not characterized by the "petty rules of men" and "ceremonial formality," but by "the practice of the original, free, and purely Christian life."[74] In the wilderness, Jerome studied the Hebrew, Chaldean, and Syriac languages in order to be able to understand scripture and devoted himself to a scholarly life: "He reread his entire library, renewing the memory of his old studies; he learned Holy Scripture word for word. He meditated on the prophets, most alert in searching out the hidden meaning of their prophecies. From the Gospels and the apostolic letters as from the purest springs he drew the philosophy of Christ."[75]

Combining his praise of Jerome with defense against Jerome's detractors, Erasmus takes up, one by one, the controversial points in Jerome's life: his "divinely sent" (*diuinitus immisso*) dream,[76] in which Christ the judge berates him for being a Ciceronian rather than a Christian;[77] the rumors of unchastity that circulated about him in Rome; his quarrel with Rufinus and the Origenists; his testy relationship with Augustine; his reputation for having a sharp tongue and an angry disposition. To each charge, Erasmus gives a robust, particular answer, but the common theme of his defense is that Jerome suffered a "martyrdom" of "insults,"[78] leveled against him by jealous detractors. Erasmus flatly denies that Jerome was ever elected a cardinal.[79] Based on Jerome's own words, Erasmus is willing to grant that the saint lost his virginity in his youth, before his baptism: "Jerome had his lapses."[80] Taken in context, however, Erasmus insists that even Jerome's imperfections witness to his striving for holiness and ultimately magnify his greatness.

Erasmus's treatment of Jerome's dream is especially important to his argument about the scholarly saint. Erasmus mentions the dream briefly in the narration of Jerome's life and then returns to it, as previously announced, in the section of the *Life* devoted to refutation. Against the charge that Jerome was indeed a Ciceronian who cared more for eloquence than Christian doctrine—who was, in short, guilty as charged in his dream and rightly beaten as punishment—Erasmus cites his own previous defense of Jerome in the *Antibarbari* and the defenses made by "the most learned men Lorenzo Valla and Angelo Poliziano."[81] He adds, moreover, that Jerome himself gives two, contrary accounts of the dream. Writing as a youth to Eustochium, Jerome ascribes a supernatural origin and visionary quality to the dream, which served to fortify his Christian commitment; as an old man instructing a young pupil, however, Jerome recalls the dream as a sort of warning nightmare to which overzealous students, subject to test anxiety, are prone. "It was not a dream, wrote the youth; it was a dream, wrote the old man."[82] Given disparate accounts of the experience, Erasmus interjects, readers "have to decide whether they prefer to believe an old man or a youth."[83]

Erasmus's own choice is clear. Allowing that the dream was "divinely sent" and had a properly chastening effect upon the young Jerome, Erasmus nonetheless sides with the old man Jerome that it was only a dream and not "an actual experience [of Christ], that is, a vision."[84] Why? For the obvious reason that the saint did not, in fact, renounce his secular books (as he had reportedly vowed in the vision he would),[85] but continued to use them throughout his life, putting them to Christian service. Dismissing the whole topic as "childish and ridiculous," Erasmus declares that he "would prefer to be flogged with Jerome than to be anointed with honey in the company of those who are so obviously terrified by the dream of Jerome that they very piously abstain from all classical literature."[86]

Erasmus defends Jerome both against those who regard him as too Ciceronian and against those fellow humanists who find his rhetoric insufficiently Ciceronian. The latter defense is important because of the obvious discrepancy in style between the rhetoric of the Bible, to which Jerome devoted his grammatical study, and that of the Roman orator, whom Jerome emulated, albeit in a manner suited to his different subject matter.[87] "If Cicero speaks eloquently about his gods, what prevents a Christian from also speaking eloquently about holiness and true religion?" Erasmus asks.[88]

In his closing peroration, Erasmus imitates the historical Jerome, embroiled in controversies, by lambasting also the Scholastic theologians who have underappreciated Jerome's excellence as a theologian. Erasmus has in mind those who have turned the sacred discipline of theology "into something Sophistic or Thomistic or Scotistic or Occamistic"; who have descended into "juvenile quibbles" and "paltry questions"; and who know too little of the scriptures and the Fathers to be able to refute heresies.[89] But he also quarrels with those theologians who have wrongly belittled Jerome in comparison to Augustine. Erasmus argues to the contrary: "Jerome surpassed Augustine in dialectics no less than he outstripped him in eloquence and . . . he was no less Augustine's superior in learning than he was in excellence of style."[90]

Mocking the theologians' use of the number four to reduce the number of the Fathers of the Church and to match them to the four biblical senses, Erasmus summarizes: "To Gregory they assign tropology, to Ambrose allegory, to Augustine anagogy, and to Jerome, to assign him something, they leave the literal and grammatical sense."[91] In Erasmus's view, however, this apparently lowly assignment is in fact a backhanded tribute to Jerome's greatness, given the foundational character of the letter of the scriptures. More than any other, Jerome deserves the name "theologian," according to Erasmus, because "he preferred to give utterance to divine truth rather than human nonsense, because he preferred to walk amid Scripture's verdant meadows rather than to struggle through the spiny thickets of these modern theologians."[92] "Many have lacked the knowledge of languages, some purity of faith, and certain ones integrity of life," writes Erasmus, but "Jerome and Jerome alone has exhibited all these qualifications."[93]

As Erasmus himself foresaw, his edition of Jerome's writings excited both praise and blame. In the wake of Martin Luther's Theses (1517), Catholic critics discovered in Erasmus's annotations on Jerome's works manifold doctrinal errors, indicative of the Dutch scholar's Lutheranism.[94] For his part, Luther, through a "myopically selective" reading of Jerome, claimed him in support of the Reformers' attack on the papacy.[95] Pope Adrian VI used Jerome's example to urge Erasmus to write against Luther.[96] Scholastic theologians and fellow humanists alike, offended by Erasmus's criticism of them at the conclusion of the *Hieronymi Stridonensis vita*, pointed out the famous editor's own theological and grammatical errors.[97] Writing in 1517, Luther protested at Erasmus's evaluation of Jerome over Augustine: "I see that not everyone is a truly wise Christian just because he knows Greek and Hebrew. St. Jerome with his five languages cannot be compared with Augustine, who knew only one language. Erasmus, however, is of an absolutely different opinion on this. But the discernment of one who attributes weight to one's will is different from that of him who knows nothing else but grace."[98]

Luther was no defender of hagiography, but his Augustinian critique of Erasmus's portrayal of Jerome as lacking in grace rings true. In the ancient and medieval tradition of hagiography, the agency of God and of God's grace is expressed in calls, miracles, visions, and conversions and attested by a providential design that links the dates, places, actions, and sufferings in the saint's life with those found in the scriptures. Stripping miracles, visions, and voices from his *Life* of Jerome, Erasmus has removed the expected signs of divine agency and makes the saint's (apparently unaided) human agency central. Jerome's scholarly vocation appears innate to him, a matter of choice, but not the result of God's direct call. Jerome's life in the Holy Land inevitably recalls the places and events of the Gospels, but Erasmus's factual narration pays minimal attention to this sacramentality of place. Erasmus's Jerome practices an austere life and studies the scriptures, but he does not echo the scriptures in his own reported speech, nor is he overheard at prayer. Erasmus presents his readers with a Jerome who embodies an ideal type of scholar-saint, who imbibes the philosophy of Christ, who engages in historical events, and who sets an imitable example of virtue and of striving for virtue amidst troubles, but whose personal engagement with God (and God's with him) is obscure.

Erasmus's methodological decision to interpret Jerome as Jerome has written about himself (*Hieronymus ex Hieronymo*) replays in another key what Levy names a basic, constant principle of biblical interpretation from the time of the Fathers through the Renaissance, namely, that the scriptures are self-interpreting.[99] Because Erasmus only references Jerome's autobiographical comments, however, the effect is radically different. Rather than a *Life* written and read at different levels of signification, Erasmus's biography of Jerome is purely historical in its very letter. Erasmus uses Jerome selectively to establish facts and to defend Jerome against his critics' charges, not to reveal the saint's inner life of devotion. The method has the strange effect of making Jerome the author of his own *Life*, whereas hagiography as a genre emphatically presents the saints as the works and instruments of God, whose agency is manifest in, with, and through them. The author of the saint's *Life* is, properly speaking, the God revealed in the scriptures, in Christ Jesus, and in the saint. To this divine author, the hagiographer plays a servant's role. The biographer, by contrast, serves the self-fashioned life.[100]

HARPSFIELD'S ERASMANIAN *LIFE AND DEATH OF SIR THOMAS MORE*

Caught between the two, Nicholas Harpsfield's *Life and Death of Sir Thomas More* falls on the side of biography, however much Harpsfield may have wished that biography's own end would be hagiographical. As we shall see, More's self-authored Epitaph, conspicuously located at the structural midpoint of Harpsfield's book, between More's "Life" and "Death," symbolizes this dilemma within Harpsfield's narrative and only partly serves to resolve it. What finally marks Harpsfield's *Life* of More as Erasmanian is not merely its direct borrowings from Erasmus's epistolary portrait of More and its frequent invocations of Erasmus's name, but also and more importantly its reliance upon the research method Erasmus pioneered in his *Life of Saint Jerome*. That method constructs the story of More's life not from the scriptures, but from More's own writings, in combination with textual evidence from other sources, especially William Roper's *Lyfe of Sir Thomas Moore, Knighte*.

Bietenholz has cast doubt on the influence of Erasmus's *Life of Jerome* upon the history of biography, noting that Erasmus himself "never again availed himself of the model here created."[101] Erasmus's lively portrait of Thomas More in his 1519 letter to Ulrich von Hutten, for example, is neither a documentary nor a complete biography, composed as it is sixteen years before More's death.[102] Erasmus's *Life of Origen* (1536) also falls short of the mark set in the *Life of Jerome*.[103] The first complete and scholarly biography composed in England, Harpsfield's *Life* of More, counters Bietenholz's doubt, however, proving that Erasmus's biographical principles, announced in his *Life* of Jerome, did indeed affect the history of biography and, with it, hagiography.

In the dedicatory letter addressed to William Roper (ca. 1496–1578), Nicholas Harpsfield presents the completed biography as "a paper newyeres gifte,"[104] given in grateful return for Roper's earlier gift of his own assembled memoirs of his father-in-law. Harpsfield acknowledges Roper's notes to be his main source, which he has supplemented with additional information. Roper's *Lyfe*, in turn, is indebted not only to his personal memories of conversations with More twenty years earlier, but also to More's extant correspondence, episodes from which Roper retold with dramatic flare.[105] Roper, in short, narrated according to the Erasmanian biographical principle, "Hieronymus ex Hieronymo," in describing "More from More."[106]

The opening sentence of Roper's *Lyfe* echoes Erasmus's praise of More: "FORASMUCHE as Sir Thomas Moore, knighte, sometime lorde Chauncelor of England, a man of singular virtue and of a cleere vnspotted consciens, *as witnessethe Erasmus*, more pure and white then the whitest snowe, and of such an angelicall witt, as England, he saith, neuer had the like before, nor neuer shall againe, . . . was in his dayes accompted a man worthy of perpetuall famous memory."[107] Harpsfield's *Life* includes a verbatim quote in Latin of the passage from Erasmus to which Roper alludes.[108] Harpsfield's dedicatory letter to Roper picks up, moreover, on Roper's salutation of Erasmus by echoing Erasmus's letter to Ulrich von Hutten (July 23, 1519), in which the scholar from Rotterdam declares himself no more able "to produce a portrait of More than one of Alexander the Great or Achilles," since "such a sitter demands the skill of an Appelles."[109] Harpsfield similarly declares himself inadequate to the task Roper has assigned to him, invoking the example of Appelles, who alone might worthily paint the image of Alexander.[110]

Unlike Roper, however, who makes no further mention of Erasmus, Harpsfield calls up the witness of the Dutch humanist repeatedly by name and quotes from his writings concerning More. Echoing Erasmus's portrait of More in the letter to Ulrich von Hutten, Harpsfield describes More's charitable works, his pleasant and witty manner of speech, his first and second wife, his physical appearance, and his menagerie of animals.[111] Attesting to More's children's knowledge of Greek and Latin, Harpsfield cites "the renowned Clerke also, Erasmus Roterodamus, who receaued from them sundry letters."[112] Harpsfield quotes "the saide Erasmus," who, donning the *persona* of Jerome, praised More's daughter Margaret as "our Eustochium."[113] Echoing Erasmus, Harpsfield describes the More household as a Christian version of Plato's Academy.[114] He credits Erasmus, "Brixius great frende," with convincing More to withdraw from his controversy with Germanus Brixius.[115] He points to Erasmus's friendship with More: "The saide Erasmus of all men in the world [most] delighted in the companye of Sir Thomas More, whose helpe and frendshipp he muche vsed when he had any affaires with king Henry the eight."[116] Erasmus's praise of More's wit elicits Harpsfield's own praise of "the great excellent Clerke, Erasmus Roterodamus, of fine and excellent wittes a meete and conuenient Judge, as one that of all other, I suppose, of our time, after this our worthy man [Thomas More], had himselfe a most singular pregnant witt."[117]

Harpsfield's sole criticism of Erasmus is that he lacked More's humility in admitting and retracting errors, even after More had counseled him to do so. Had Erasmus followed More's advice, Harpsfield suggests, "I trowe his books would be better liked of our posteritie, which perchaunce shal be faine either vtterly to abolishe some of his woorkes, or at least to redresse and reforme them."[118] This telling admission points to a fall in Erasmus's reputation among English Catholics—a fall that may have tempted Harpsfield to distance More's memory from that of the Dutch humanist (as did recusant Catholics in years to come). Harpsfield steadfastly resists that temptation, advancing instead the view that More's friendship with Erasmus, together with their shared humanist commitments and Catholicism, remained intact to the end.[119]

Harpsfield's biography of More is structured according to the classical "sandwich" pattern established by Suetonius (ca. 69–ca. 122) in his biographies of the twelve Caesars. The first part chronicles More's public life, ending with his resignation of the chancellorship and his composition in 1532 of his own epitaph, which is then engraved on his tomb. (To this topic we will return.) The middle section of the *Life* interlaces discussion of More's private life at home and his familial relations (part 2), his writings (part 3), and the esteem in which he was held by learned friends (part 4). The final section returns to the point in time where part 1 ended, More's resignation of the chancellorship. Part 5 chronicles the dramatic events leading up to More's imprisonment, trial, and death. In part 6, Harpsfield offers his own interpretation of More's life, meditating on his Christian vocation and his martyrdom for the unity of the Catholic Church. This Suetonian structure is, in turn, subsumed into the two-part structure spelled out in the biography's title, *The Life and Death of Sir Thomas More*, and anchored by Harpsfield's use of More's self-authored epitaph.

Part 3, on More's writings, is located centrally in Harpsfield's biography. This focuses attention on More's polemical writings against heresies and in particular against William Tyndale's "adulterate and vitiate" translation of the New Testament.[120] Unlike hagiography as a genre, which frequently echoes the scriptures through quotation, allusion, and paraphrase, Harpsfield's documentary biography seldom employs biblical language; this is true even (and perhaps especially) in part 3, where biblical translation and exposition is precisely at issue. Describing More's polemic against

Tyndale, Harpsfield enumerates the English translations of individual words to which More objected as being inaccurate and theologically tendentious, but Harpsfield also charges Luther and Tyndale more broadly with sacrilege against the scriptures: "these good brethren partly denye the verye texte it selfe and whole books of the sacred Scripture. . . . they haue of a sett purpose peruerted and mistranslated the saide holy Scripture."[121] Harpsfield makes no mention of Erasmus's Greek and Latin edition of the New Testament, upon which the Reformers drew, thus setting the work of the Dutch humanist silently apart from theirs.

Harpsfield's survey of More's polemical writings includes his response to Tyndale's writing on "The Supper of our Lorde," in which the author argues that the sacrament of the Eucharist is "but for a memorial onely bare breade and wine."[122] This sacramental controversy is also an exegetical one. As More reminds Tyndale and others, allegorical interpretations depend upon acknowledging the literal sense of the scriptures, but "if with anye of your allegoricall exposicions, you denye the very literall sense beside, and say that the body of our sauiour is not really vnder the fourme of bread in the sacrament, than say we that in your such expowning, you playn expowne it false."[123]

Scriptural controversy is part of More's story in yet another sense, since it was of issue in the matter of Henry VIII's marriages to Catherine of Aragon (1509–33) and Anne Boleyn (1533–36). Henry's first wife had been married at a young age in 1501 to his brother Arthur, who died five months later; the marriage had no issue and was perhaps never consummated. With a papal dispensation from the pertinent canon law, Henry married his brother's widow, who bore him a daughter, Mary, the only long-term survivor of Catherine's six (or more) pregnancies. Growing unhappy in his marriage, which had failed to produce a male heir, and enamored of Anne Boleyn, Henry turned to the scriptures to seek a basis for an annulment, citing Leviticus 18:16 (prohibiting incest) and Leviticus 20:21 (prophesying a curse of childlessness for incestuous unions) — texts countered by Deuteronomy 25:5–10, which obliges Levirate marriage.

Harpsfield relates that the king, seeking More's support for an annulment, showed him "certaine places of Scripture that somewhat seemed to serue his appetite."[124] More's reluctantly undertaken study of these passages, taken in context, and of patristic commentary upon them, led More to conclude that no annulment was warranted. Knowing More's view, the king revisited the issue with him a second time, "And incontinently layde the Byble open before him, and there read such words as moued him and other learned persons" to think otherwise.[125] A canon lawyer, Harpsfield provides no detailed description of More's reasoning in the *Life*, reserving discussion of that matter for his own *Treatise on the Pretended Divorce of King Henry VIII from Queen Catherine of Aragon*.[126]

Given the controversies in which the scriptures are themselves submerged, direct biblical quotation, close paraphrase, and explicit allusion are relatively rare in Harpsfield's lengthy *Life* of More. The scriptures are the objects of narrative (among many other objects), but they seldom enter into the narrative voice. Other sources than the Bible itself—Erasmus's letters, More's writings, Roper's memoirs, Hall's Chronicle, the account of More's trial published in the Paris Newsletter, the Indictment—are Harpsfield's material of choice. The biographer alludes to More's practice of praying the Psalms, but he does not quote from them.[127] Commenting on More's quick-witted rejoinder to his wife, Alice, when she beseeches him in prison to be reasonable and relent in his resistance to the king, Harpsfield likens her to the biblical temptresses, Job's wife and Eve, but the comparison is broad and almost humorously presented.[128] Making another Joban comparison, Harpsfield writes that More endured false accusation "as blessed St. Job was falslye and wrongfully noted of Eliphas."[129]

Twice Harpsfield seizes upon an image with biblical resonance in order to establish a metaphoric similitude. The stretched comparisons resemble the conceits of the Metaphysical poets. The coal with which More writes his last letters from prison, his *Dialogue of Comfort against Tribulation*, and his treatise on Christ's passion, for instance, reminds Harpsfield of the purifying coal that burned the lips of the prophet Isaiah: "For albeit he wrote these books with a deade blacke coale, yet was there another and a most hot burning coale, suche a one, I say, as touched and purified the lippes of the holy prophete Esaias, that directed his hande with the deade coal, and so inflamed and incensed his heart."[130] The severed, parboiled head of More, mounted on a pole, reminds Harpsfield of More's witness to the headship of the pope as Christ's vicar over the Church, a headship Henry VIII has severed in order to place "St. Peter's head . . . vpon his owne shoulders," an "vggly sight to beholde."[131]

The characterization of Harpsfield's *Life* of More as hagiographic stems not from its literary genre and narrative style, which is decidedly biographical and biblically distant, but from its frequent invocation, especially in parts 5 and 6, of the names and examples of the saints whom More sought to imitate. Before his arrest and imprisonment, More speaks to his wife and children "of the liues of the holy martyrs, of their greeuous martyrdoms, of their meruailous patience, of their passion[s] and deathes that they suffred rather then they would offende God."[132] From his prison cell in the Tower of London, More sees three Carthusian monks on their way to the place of execution, hailing them as "blessed fathers . . . cheerefully going to their death as bridegromes to their marriage."[133] Sentence having been passed against him at his trial, More forgives his enemies, invoking the example of "the blessed Apostle St. Paul" who consented to the death of Saint Stephen, "and yet be they nowe both twaine holy Saintes in heauen."[134] On the morning of his death, More sends a gold coin to his executioner "after the example of that holy Martyr Saint Ciprian."[135] Harpsfield compares Thomas More as a martyr to "the blessed martyrs St. Thomas of Douer and St. Thomas of Caunterbury."[136]

Above all, of course, More is implicitly likened to the Saint of Saints, Jesus Christ, through the sheer process of his imprisonment, his well-kept silence (resembling Christ's before Pilate), the false testimony of Master Rich, More's unjust condemnation, and his forgiveness of his enemies. Harpsfield tells his readers that More is writing his line-by-line meditative exposition of the Gospel accounts of Christ's passion (the unfinished work "On the Sadness of Christ") during his time in the Tower, but the biographer nowhere echoes the text either of the Gospels or of More's commentary. The historical resemblance of More's martyrdom to Christ's passion and death is so evident that Harpsfield only relates the facts of the proceedings.

MORE'S EPITAPH AND THE ENDS OF HAGIOGRAPHY

In anticipation of his death, More wrote his own epitaph in Latin in 1532 and had it engraved on his tomb inside the parish church in Chelsea (Old Chelsea Church), placing it on the north side of the altar. That same year saw Henry VIII's acceptance of his resignation as lord high chancellor of

England, an office he held from October 1529 to May 1532; his father, Sir John More, had died not long before, in 1530, instilling Thomas's own mindfulness of death.

The epitaph mentions London as the city of Thomas More's birth, alludes modestly to his education, praises King Henry VIII as "Defender of the Faith" and notes the unique and well-deserved honor given with that title, and lists in chronological order the various civil offices More has held (member of the king's Council, undertreasurer of England, chancellor of the Duchy of Lancaster, lord chancellor of England, speaker of the Parliament, foreign ambassador). It highlights More's role, together with that of Cuthbert Tunstall, bishop of London, in the historic peace treaty negotiated at Cambrai. The epitaph praises Tunstall's extraordinary learning, wit, and virtue. It describes More's own conduct as well esteemed by his prince, the nobles, and all the people, except the "thieves and murderers [and heretics]" whom More prosecuted. It sings the praises of Judge John More, Thomas's father, whose memory Thomas honors with devotion. It describes the personal bonds to family, the ill-health, and the process of aging that moved More to petition the king to be released of the chancellorship and to be allowed to withdraw from worldly affairs in order to spend his last years as a private citizen, preparing his soul for death and the afterlife. The inscribed tomb itself should keep him mindful, while still alive, of death's approach and heaven's hope. By it, too, More petitions that others may join in prayer for him. The epitaph concludes with Latin verses honoring More's first and second wives, Jane and Alice, both of whom are to share the tomb with him as last resting place.

Peter Sherlock describes it as a humanist work, designed to discourage displays of grief, "to perpetuate the fame of the dead and the city-state."[137] Sherlock notes, too, that the epitaph was "unusually long for the period" and served a number of different purposes.[138] Countering the thesis of Nigel Llewellyn, Sherlock argues that "the texts inscribed on many tombs" were "focused on conveying messages to the future, and . . . more concerned with the sacred than most scholars have hitherto acknowledged."[139] Monumental inscriptions shaped the memory of the past and aimed at controlling the historical narrative, changing the present, and securing a better future. This narrative control sometimes "involved censorship, even fabrication," and "could be profoundly controversial."[140]

More's composition of his own epitaph was a highly unusual act and indeed a topic of controversy. Explaining his resignation of the chancellorship, More tells Erasmus in a letter dated June 14, 1532, that he has been suffering worrisome chest pains and rejoices in the possibility of a return to private life.[141] More makes no mention of his other motives for resignation, namely, his unwillingness to accept the king's supremacy over the Church in England, his inability to approve Henry's marriage to Anne, and his increasingly dangerous, conflicted relationship with the king. Writing again to Erasmus in June 1533, More explains that he has prepared his own epitaph to put to rest the rumors flying about that he had been forced to resign the chancellorship by the king whose displeasure he had supposedly incurred, when in fact he had other, personal motives for his request to be relieved of his office—a request that had been granted graciously and benevolently by the king.[142] More foresees that the rumors may have the effect of tainting his reputation and thus dulling the force of his writings against heresies; the self-defensive epitaph thus serves the faith.[143] The epitaph also seeks to recall the king to his own youthful stance as Defender of the Faith, remind him of More's long, loyal service, perpetuate the king's good graces toward him, and enable More's peaceful withdrawal from public life.

The epitaph's petition for prayers for More, both in 1532 and after his foreseen death, also directs the future and shapes its outcome. Confirming the doctrine More expounds in *The Soul's Supplication* (1529),[144] it expresses More's religious faith in life after death and his hope to be spared suffering in purgatory through the prayers of others and through his own sincere repentance, penance for past sins, and patient suffering of God's will in this life.

More reports to Erasmus that the same critics who first spread rumors of the king's disfavor with him—rumors the epitaph sought to put to rest— now accuse him of vainglory for having recorded his own accomplishments on his tomb.[145] In his letter to Johannes Faber, bishop of Vienna, dating from late 1532, Erasmus forwards to him a copy of the text of More's epitaph and echoes it in praising both More and King Henry; Erasmus takes care also to praise the humility of More, "who preferred to leave to his heirs the love of piety rather than the honour of insignia."[146] Against More's self-description as one grievous to heretics,[147] Erasmus praises his "extraordinary clemency," reporting (incorrectly) that "under his chancellorship no one was put to death for condemned beliefs."[148]

The accusation of vainglory suggests the relative novelty of More's self-authored and self-fashioning epitaph, which, in good part, reads like a *curriculum vitae*. The studies of Llewellyn, Sherlock, and others demonstrate significant changes in how the dead were memorialized in post-Reformation England, but the research of Philippe Ariè, Erwin Panofsky, and Paul Binski outlines a much longer history of change.

Binski notes, "The greatest early Christian sarcophagi erase the narrative of the person—the subject of the old eulogistic formulae—by means of the narrative of the Faith."[149] Biblical scenes replaced images of the deceased person, whose very life was understood to have been incorporated into the life of Christ and of the Church. During the Middle Ages, however, "narrative elements, . . . especially those drawn from the Bible, withered in almost all of western Europe."[150] The effigy of the deceased became "a key means of asserting selfhood and history."[151] Epitaphs and votive inscriptions marked medieval Christian tombs, as did emblems of the trades practiced by the deceased.[152] The inscribed tombs named the deceased, urged prayers for them, and reminded the still-living of their own mortality and judgment to come. "In theory, though not [always] in practice, humility was more appropriate to an epitaph than grandiloquence," Binski notes; the common practice, especially in the case of vernacular epitaphs, was indeed "to place a simple inscription."[153]

More's self-authored epitaph clearly posed a problem for Harpsfield as the biographer of a man whom he numbers among the saints and martyrs. Unlike Roper, who does not refer explicitly to the epitaph, Harpsfield attaches importance to More's autobiographical "Summarie and effectuall discourse of his life,"[154] following the Erasmanian principle of narrating "Morus ex Moro." The opening paragraph of Harpsfield's *Life* takes its cue from the first sentence of the epitaph, which mentions London and More's familial lineage: "This excellent and peerlesse man . . . was beautified . . . by the place of his birth, being borne at London, the chiefe and notable principall Citie of this our noble Realme, [as] by the heritage and woorshipfull familie whereof he sprange."[155] Harpsfield allows More's *curriculum vitae* of his public life to order the events related in part 1 of the *Life*. He takes More's understated reference to his education (*IN LITERIS VTCVNQ[VE] VERSATUS*) as a license for a more expansive, biographical treatment of it. More's pious praise of his father, John More, inspires Harpsfield's (and Roper's) remembrance of scenes where the younger More showed himself a devoted son. The negotiations at Cambrai, highlighted in the epitaph, are similarly emphasized in the *Life*.

Most importantly, Harpsfield places discussion of the epitaph and narrates its inscription at the very end of part 1. It thus marks the closing of the public phase of More's life in a manner foreboding of his death. Harpsfield follows closely the argument presented in More's letter to Erasmus, indicating that More had composed the epitaph for the tomb to quell vicious rumors that "he was against his will thrust out of the Chauncellourshipp."[156] When that rumor had been squelched, More's enemies "beganne, causelesse, to prattle and talke against his saide Epitaphe as very vaineglorious."[157] Harpsfield admits that "some spice of vaineglory often times crepeth"[158] into the hearts of gifted and successful men, but he declares More to be innocent of such vice. Harpsfield insists that More's sole motive for writing the epitaph was to further "God's cause and religion," since false rumors of the king's displeasure with him would besmirch his reputation and impair his effectiveness in defending the faith in "open books" against the Protestants.[159] Praising the king under his title "Defender of the Faith" and declaring the king's benevolence, the epitaph thus serves to support More's past and continued work in God's cause.

Harpsfield's very careful arrangement of material places More's self-authored epitaph at the end of part 1 in counterpoint to his own interpretation of More's life in part 6. There Harpsfield sets aside his role as biographer *in sensu stricto* and plays, in effect, the part of a canon lawyer defending More's cause in a process of canonization. (Canon law was, in fact, Harpsfield's professional field of expertise.) Doing so, however, requires and enables him to establish lines of continuity and consistency between part 1 of the *Life* and the rest of the narration. Harpsfield seems to have this rhetorical move well planned in advance, since at a key passage in part 1 concerning More's discernment of vocation, Harpsfield actually begins to make his larger argument, reserving further proofs until later: "Of the which our iudgement we shall render you hereafter suche causes as moue vs so to thinke."[160]

At issue is a Morean mystery. Harpsfield, following Roper, indicates that the young Thomas More spent four years at the Charterhouse (1499–1503) in London before deciding to marry.[161] Erasmus does not mention the Charterhouse, but states that More "applied his whole mind to the pursuit of piety, with vigils and fasts and prayer and similar exercises preparing himself for the priesthood."[162] Harpsfield emphasizes that the monastic path deeply attracted the young lawyer and shaped to some extent the homelife of More and his family in Chelsea, More's wishes for his retirement, and his spirituality in the Tower. Erasmus interprets the youthful decision to abandon thoughts of ordination as an acknowledgment on More's part of his strong sexual desires and inability to be a good monk: "He would rather be a chaste husband than an unchaste priest."[163] Harpsfield, by contrast, interprets the decision as a broad, freely taken choice for the active life of the laity, lived out in the world, over the contemplative life of the Carthusians, lived in a state of withdrawal from world affairs.[164]

But what motivated that decision? Given that the contemplative life is objectively higher (as the "better part" chosen by Mary of Bethany; cf. Luke 10:42) and that More also felt strongly inclined toward it, Harpsfield imagines a reader marveling why More "did not follow, embrace, and pursue the saide inclination."[165] To which Harpsfield replies, first, that Christ leaves each one free to choose the higher, but "no man is precisely bounde so to doo."[166] Harpsfield's second response is speculative: "*Were it so* that he had such propension and inclination [to a monastic life], God himself *seemeth* to haue chosen and appointed this man to another kinde of life, to serue him therein more acceptably to his diuine honour, and more profitably for the wealth of the Realme and his owne soule also."[167]

The idea that God himself may have intervened and directed More's vocational decision for the active life introduces the suggestion of a quasi-hagiographic, divine agency into Harpsfield's *Life* of More, but the biographer lacks a testimony from More himself to that effect; God's action, if God indeed acted, remains a hypothesis to the writer, hidden to the reader, and it may have been hidden to More himself in those years when he seems to have been "in some doubt and deliberation with himself what kind and trade of life he should enter, to folowe and pursue all his longe life after."[168]

When Harpsfield returns, as promised, to this issue in part 6, the *Life*'s two citations of the Carthusians work together to confirm his hypothesis. More spent four years with the Carthusians in his youth, when he discerned his vocation. From his prison cell in the Tower, he saw three Carthusian monks on their way to be executed for the same crime with which he himself had been charged, and he hailed their happy martyrdom in anticipation of his own.[169] Associated with these religious in his death, More fulfills his double vocation as a married layman, monk-like in his devotion. Harpsfield sees his hypothesis of a divine intervention in More's early decision to leave the Charterhouse confirmed by this association of martyrs, wherein More fulfills a destined role as representative of the laity: "Which notable part to playe, and to be therein his messenger for the laitie, it seemeth that God did purposely choose and reserue him, though for the time he were propense and inclined to some lyking towarde a solitarye and religious life."[170]

Witnessing to the unity of the laity and the religious in the one faith, More also stands in Harpsfield's argument as a martyr for the faith, giving his life for the article in the Apostles' Creed that declares belief in one, holy, catholic, and apostolic Church. Harpsfield declares: "He was the first of any whatsoeuer laye man in Inglande that dyed a martyr for the defence and preseruation of the vnitie of the Catholike Churche."[171]

Harpsfield's epitaph (so to speak) for Thomas More, which unifies the parts of More's life within a divine plan, contrasts with, and serves as a structural counterbalance to, More's own epitaph, which emphasizes a disjuncture between his active, public life and that of his retirement, when he at last, in fulfillment of that "which he had almost always desired from his earliest years," may turn "from the affairs of this life and meditate on the eternity of the life to come."[172] If More suffered any anxiety that he, like Pico della Mirandola (1463–94), had left his true calling unfulfilled, he must have welcomed his loss of public office and his martyrdom as an earthly purgatory.[173] Harpsfield's *Life* suggests otherwise, namely, that More's active life, which ultimately led to his martyrdom, was from beginning to end a true vocation, not an avoidance of one, a means of purification and growth in virtue, oriented toward an eschatological goal.

In 1522, More composed an unfinished treatise on the four last things: "deth, dome, pain, and ioy"—a meditative exposition of Sirach 7:40, "Remember . . . thy last thinges, and thou shalte neuer sin in this world."[174] The epitaph he composed was (among other ends) to serve that end. Departing from Harpsfield's arrangement, "Ro. Ba." concludes his *Lyfe of Syr Thomas More* with an English translation of More's epitaph, as if it speaks plainly enough for itself and served its purpose well: "he hath caused this tomb to be made for himselfe . . . that might every day put him in [memory] of death."[175] Substituting More's self-authored epitaph for the biblical verse that partly inspired it, "Ro. Ba.," no less than Harpsfield, signals the end of hagiography in biography, even as he celebrates a martyr's eschatological conclusion.

CHAPTER NINE

MODERN LITERARY EXPERIMENTS IN BIBLICAL HAGIOGRAPHY

The candle stub had long since burned down in the twisted candleholder, dimly illuminating in this impoverished room the murderer and the prostitute.

—Dostoevsky, *Crime and Punishment*

Is it possible (to echo the language of Emmanuel Levinas) for the "Said" of the biblical hagiography—a literary genre of former ages, now superseded by biography or bio-hagiography—to become again a "Saying," an utterance that calls to, and moves, its readers, inviting their intensified dialogue with the scriptures? In "On the Jewish Reading of Scriptures" (1979), Levinas suggests that the coal fire of the ancient Talmudic writings, burnt low and seemingly extinguished, can be rekindled through the fan of living breath upon the coals, which "light up by being blown upon."[1] Is the "brief candle" of the saint's *Life*, once burnt out, able to be relit as a means for biblical illumination?

Despite this book's narrative of a gradual disassociation of Bible and hagiography and of the related literal/historic and spiritual senses, the answer remains inconclusive. Saints continue to appear on the scene whose own experience of mystical illumination vis-à-vis the scriptures defines their hours of conversion, of vocation, and of mission—so much so that their life stories, even when told in the form of documentary biography or as a dossier in the canonization process, inevitably draw others back to the Bible and stimulate a renewed, theologically enriched exegesis. One thinks, for example, of the Servant of God Chiara Lubich (1920–2008), whose life as foundress of the Focolare was defined by her profound understanding, together with her cofounders, of John 17:21 ("that they may all be one") and of Jesus's cry of dereliction from the cross in Matthew 27:46, "My God, my God, why hast thou forsaken me?"[2] Or of the Servant of God Dorothy Day, cofoundress with Peter Maurin of the *Catholic Worker*, who meditated daily upon the scriptures and whose lifework in service to the poor was framed in response to the Sermon on the Mount.[3] Schoenstatt's founder, the Servant of God Father Joseph Kentenich (1885–1968), orphaned in his childhood, took as his watchword Jesus's words from the cross, "Behold, your mother" (John 19:27).[4] The sudden illumination of John 1:14, "And the Word became flesh," moved the Servant of God Father Luigi Guissani (1922–2005) at age fifteen and later inspired his founding of the Communion and Liberation movement.[5]

Perhaps such candidates for beatification and canonization will inspire newly biblical ways of relating their life stories.[6] At present, however, biography—chronologically arranged, carefully researched, well documented—remains the dominant genre for the public narration of a saint's life; "hagiography" (that is, bio-hagiography), in turn, has become virtually synonymous with a biased reporting of the facts, a "construction" of things at odds with a saint's more complicated, historical existence. Both biography and bio-hagiography are sufficiently distanced from the Bible as to awaken the desire for new, experimental, artistic forms capable of melding the saint's story together with both the scriptures and history.

In this chapter, I look briefly at three such experiments in historical fiction: Dostoevsky's portrayal of Father Zosima in *The Brothers Karamazov* (1879–80), Willa Cather's depictions of the priest-heroes in *Death Comes for the Archbishop* (1927), and Franz Werfel's *Song of Bernadette* (1941). All three works are remarkable for their integration of multiple senses of signification, at once biblical and hagiographic, arising from their "storylike," historical sense. This integration derives not only from the "willing suspension of disbelief" regularly operative in the reading of fiction[7] or from the recognized historical basis of the story and its characters, but also from the biblical intertextuality itself.

DOSTOEVSKY'S BIBLICAL HAGIOGRAPHY

Saved from execution by a firing squad, Fyodor Dostoevsky (1821–81) subsequently spent four years (1850–54) in a Siberian prison camp, where the New Testament—a gift to him and his fellow prisoners from the Decembrist wives—was the only reading material allowed to him. As Dostoevsky recalls, he kept this book under his pillow, read it himself, and sometimes read passages aloud to others.[8] According to Geir Kjetsaa, who has studied Dostoevsky's marginalia and underlining in the book, "the marked passages are distributed over 21 of the 27 books of the New Testament, [but] Dostoevsky decidedly preferred the writings of St. John."[9] The passages that drew Dostoevsky's interest were clearly invested for him with "present-day relevance."[10] Fueled by that sense of relevance, Dostoevsky's imagination discovered new links between the Bible and everyday life as it was being experienced in nineteenth-century Russia. "From the mid-1860s," writes Kjetsaa, "one can observe in Dostoevsky an increasingly strong urge to see human beings and their actions in the divine perspective of the Bible. Every single 'natural' thing seems to have its special spiritual and divine counterpart."[11] For this reason and others, Henri de Lubac does not hesitate to name the Russian novelist a "prophet."[12]

In *Crime and Punishment* (1866), Dostoevsky mirrors his own experience to some degree in that of Raskolnikov, the student whose crime of a double murder leads him eventually to a Siberian prison camp. Long before his confession and sentencing, however, Raskolnikov's crime has itself become his punishment, haunting his conscience, sickening him, and inspiring thoughts of suicide. In an artistically daring scene, Dostoevsky depicts the distraught Raskolnikov in conversation with the saintly young prostitute Sonya, who, he learns, had received the gift of a New Testament from Lizaveta, one of his victims. Raskolnikov insists that Sonya read aloud to him the story of Lazarus's death and rising from the dead (John 11:1–45).[13] Dostoevsky includes the entire text of the lengthy Gospel passage in the novel, punctuating it with short descriptions of Sonya's voice, breathing, and emotions as she reads aloud, and as she glimpses the relevance of the story to Raskolnikov and herself.[14] The characters fall silent at the end of Sonya's reading, and Dostoevsky frames the scene with an image of light, metaphorically appropriate, of course, to Christ, the raiser of Lazarus and the healer of the blind, but also to the novelist's own biblically hagiographic art: "The candle stub had long since burned down in the twisted candleholder, dimly illuminating in this impoverished room the murderer and the prostitute, strangely united for the reading of the eternal book."[15]

Dostoevsky's *The Brothers Karamazov* (1880) has on the dedication page another Johannine passage: "Verily, verily, I say unto you, Except a corn of wheat fall into the ground and die, it abideth alone: but if it die, it bringeth forth much fruit" (John 12:24).[16] Shortly before his death, the elder Zosima recites this same verse to his young disciple, Alyosha Karamazov, and exhorts him to remember it in connection with the foreseen suffering of his brother Dimitri, soon to be accused of murder.[17] Later, Father Zosima relates a dramatic episode from his youth in which he takes the Gospel from the table and shows John 12:24 to a man who has committed a terrible murder fourteen years ago, urging him to confess publicly what he did and thus to plant the seed of truth in the ground.[18] In answer to the man's bitter question about who wrote the books of the Bible, "Who wrote them, were they human beings?" Zosima replies, "The Holy Spirit wrote them."[19]

Compiling the dying Zosima's memories of his life, Alyosha (otherwise known as Alexei Fydorovich Karamazov) wrote "The Life of the Hieromonk and Elder Zosima, Departed in God," which Dostoevsky's first-person narrator inserts into book 6 of the novel as its hagiographic heart. That "Life" features a chapter titled "Holy Scripture in the Life of Father Zosima." In it the dying monk recalls precious memories from his childhood, memories that include "memories of sacred history,"[20] the Bible stories he heard, loved, and understood. At age eight he heard a reading from the book of Job during Holy Week with a sudden understanding of it: "For the first time in my life I consciously received the first seed of the word of God in my soul. . . . For the first time in my life I understood what was read in God's church."[21] Against the protests of pastors who say that they cannot competently teach the Word of God, Zosima urges them to read the scriptures lovingly aloud to children and then to the children's parents, beginning with Bible stories from the Old Testament that never fail to captivate the imagination: "Read to them of Abraham and Sarah, of Isaac and Rebecca, . . . of how Jacob went to Laban and wrestled with the Lord in his dream. . . . Read to them, and especially to the children, . . . of the dear youth Joseph."[22]

Together with the scriptures, Zosima recommends readings "from the Lives of the Saints, at least the life of Alexei, the man of God, and of the greatest of the great, the joyful sufferer, God-seer, and Christ-bearer, our mother Mary of Egypt."[23] Read aloud by their pastor to small groups of the faithful, these "simple tales," biblical and hagiographic—each like a "tiny seed"—will pierce the hearts and yield abundant fruit, Zosima insists.[24] The monk witnesses to this piercing of the heart through his own tears as he reads, and remembers reading, the scriptures.

The saintly Father Zosima's teaching in Dostoevsky's novel organically unites the book of the scriptures with the lives of the saints and with the Book of Creation, all of them authored by God, each of them illuminating the other. Indeed, the chapter on scripture concludes with a celebration of creation's beauty as seen by Zosima on a beautiful, remembered night in July, when he lay awake on a riverbank, talking with a young fisherman "about the beauty of this world of God's."[25] The young man's heart "was burning" at this revelation of the world's beauty,[26] which Zosima explains theologically: "For the Word is for all, all creation and all creatures, every little leaf is striving toward the Word, sings glory to God, weeps to Christ, unbeknownst to itself, doing so through the mystery of its sinless life."[27] Zosima's praise of the goodness and beauty of creation ("for everything is perfect, everything except man is sinless") at the end of the chapter thus echoes his earlier interpretation of the revelation given to Job: "Here the Creator, as in the first days of creation, . . . looks at Job and again praises his creation."[28]

Father Zosima is Dostoevsky's fictional character, but he reflects two saints in the Russian Orthodox canon, Saint Tikhon Zadonsky (1724–83), well known for his love of the scriptures,[29] and especially Saint Nil of Sora (1433–1508), devoted to the Holy Writings and to Hesychastic prayer. Mourning the death of his son Alexei, Dostoevsky visited the Optina Pustyn monastery, famous for its effort to revive the Hesychastic tradition in Russian Orthodoxy. Nel Grillaert has argued persuasively that "in his hagiography of the 'pure, ideal Christian,'" represented in Father Zosima, Dostoevsky "attempted to create an alternative to the paralyzed Russian church" of his time "by infusing . . . echoes of a Russian Orthodox consciousness, theology, and spirituality that had been pushed into the margins of the Russian church."[30]

Although Father Zosima is revered by many as a living saint, he also has critics—people envious of his reputation for holiness, suspicious of his behavior, and opposed, more generally, to the revival of the Hesychastic tradition of elders, which they regard as a dangerous innovation. Dostoevsky uses a naturalistic departure from hagiographic convention—namely, the stench of Zosima's corpse during the wake in summer's heat—to bring to the surface this critical current, which precipitates open division in the monastery and a spiritual crisis in Alyosha, Father Zosima's young devotee.

That crisis is brilliantly resolved in a scene that, like a similar scene in *Crime and Punishment*, involves the reading aloud of the scriptures. After a crucial encounter with Grushenka, a would-be temptress turned angel, and Rakitin, a tempter overcome, Alyosha returns at night to the hermitage where the body of Father Zosima lies in an open casket. There Father Paissy, keeping vigil, is reading aloud the Gospel according to John. Alyosha enters just as the monk reads the story of the wedding feast at Cana (John 2:1–11). Dostoevsky incorporates the biblical passage verbatim into the novel, interspersing between the verses Alyosha's thoughts as he listens.

Alyosha interprets the Gospel's story of marriage and miracle as tropologically relevant to his recent, joyful experience with Grushenka and to the remembered words of Father Zosima about Jesus's love: "He who loves men, loves their joy."[31] Grushenka's eschatological folktale of the onion given to the poor becomes for him a brief candle, as it were, to illumine the gospel. He imagines the scene of the wedding feast vividly, picturing the guests, and, as he does so, Alyosha's literal meditation suddenly turns into a revelatory, allegorical dream-vision. He sees Father Zosima among the guests, arising from the dinner table to greet and to welcome him also to the feast: "We are rejoicing, . . . we are drinking new wine, the wine of a new and great joy."[32] The dream-vision announces the anagogy of the biblical text, its foretelling of the eternal banquet, at which (Alyosha learns from a radiant Zosima) Christ the merciful judge will be the gracious host: "He is waiting for new guests, he is ceaselessly calling new guests, now and unto ages of ages."[33]

Sharing in Zosima's experience, Alyosha, whose illumined understanding of the scriptures has altered his perception of the world, leaves the hermitage and the still-unburied corpse to go outside. Dostoevsky signals Alyosha's personal integration as a cosmic hierarchy: "the mystery of the earth touched the mystery of the stars."[34] Overcome with the awareness of love, beauty, and forgiveness, Alyosha prostrates himself on the ground, weeps as he kisses the earth, and arises from it as one reborn.

CATHER'S BIBLICAL BORDERLANDS

Willa Cather's masterpiece *Death Comes for the Archbishop* (1927) chronicles the adventures of Father Jean Latour and Father Joseph Vaillant, French missionaries at work in nineteenth-century New Mexico, Mexico, Arizona, and Colorado. Cather stays close to her chief historical source for biographical information about her models for the two priest characters—namely, Father Jean-Baptiste Lamy (1814–88), the first bishop of New Mexico, and Father Joseph Projectus Machebeuf (1812–89), who became the first bishop of Denver and Utah.[35]

Like Dostoevsky, Cather consciously incorporates biblical and hagiographical material into her unusual, frankly experimental novel.[36] According to her own testimony, she drew inspiration for her style and approach from the New Testament,[37] from Jacobus de Voragine's *Golden Legend*,[38] and from Puvis de Chavannes's frescoes of the life of Saint Genevieve that she had seen in Paris in 1902.[39] Likening the lives of the French missionaries in her novel to those of the saints in the *Golden Legend*, Cather explains in a letter to Fanny Butcher, "Legend is a sort of interpretation of life by Faith. It was that background of order and discipline that gave the lives of those missionaries proportion and measure and accent, like a work of art."[40]

The hagiographic style and content of Cather's historical fiction has been studied from various perspectives: its direct allusions to local saints' cults (Santiago, Joseph),[41] its incorporation of little stories from the *Lives* of saints (e.g., the apparitions to Junipero Serra and to Juan Diego),[42] its sacramental treatment of setting,[43] the theme of miracles,[44] the episodic structure of the novel as a whole, and its peculiar temporality, distanced from the measures of calendric time.[45]

The biblical intertextuality of the novel has, by contrast, attracted little scholarly interest. Unlike Dostoevsky, who incorporates lengthy quotations from scripture at key moments in the narrative, Cather disperses short biblical echoes throughout the novel, making very rare use of direct quotation. The effect of the biblical echoes is not merely to characterize the priest missionaries as imitators of Saint Paul, spreading the gospel, but also to thematize the theological interface between the books of the Bible, of creation, and of human experience, all of which serve to illumine each other. Confronting a new world, the priests understand scripture in a new way, even as the scriptures instruct their view of that world.

Saint Paul is clearly the chief model for Cather's French missionaries. Father Vaillant, we are told, "was like the saints in the early church, literally without personal possessions."[46] In the reader's first glimpse of Father Latour, he is on horseback, alone, without water, lost in a desert landscape of conical red hills; there he pauses to pray, kneeling at the foot of a cruciform juniper tree. Father Latour's thirst reminds him not only of Christ's physical thirst on the cross (John 19:28), but also of his thirst for souls, and that of the first missionaries to the region, centuries ago: "They thirsted in the deserts, starved among the rocks, climbed up and down its terrible canyons on stone-bruised feet, broke long fasts by unclean and repugnant food. Surely these endured *Hunger, Thirst, Cold, Nakedness*, of a kind beyond any conception St. Paul and his brethren could have had."[47] Exposed to the elements, to accidents, and to the diseases that also plague the Native Americans (smallpox, measles, and cholera), the French missionaries, like their Spanish predecessors, are not infrequently in danger of death. After death, the priests hope to have "stars in [their] crowns" (cf. Rev. 12:1).[48]

The priests themselves, not surprisingly, understand their activity in terms of biblical parables. They water the once sown "seeds" of the gospel (Matt. 13:5–6); they unearth the "buried treasure" (Matt. 13:44) of the faith still held by the Indigenous people long after the departure of the Spanish missionaries to the region.[49] They are evangelized and converted, in turn, by the people they serve, who have entered the kingdom of heaven like "little children" (Matt. 18:3), the "least" of whom "shall be the first" (cf. Matt. 23:11; Luke 9:48).[50] Spiritually renewed and reborn in the New World, Bishop Latour speaks of "that wind that made one a boy again" (cf. John 3:8). A garden becomes the scene of Bishop Latour's "re-creation" in the multiple senses of that word.[51] In that garden, too, a transformed Magdalena greets the priests, bearing witness to her own resurrection and theirs.[52] The "today–today" of the bishop,[53] childlike in memory and expectation in the days before his death, recalls the Easter psalm: "This is the day the Lord has made" (Ps. 118:24).

Whereas Dostoevsky's great strength as a novelist is dialogue, Cather's is description, especially the description of landscapes and scenes as the characters see them. The novelist seamlessly blends the natural imagery of the Southwest with biblical imagery. Weak and thirsty, Latour stumbles upon a paradisal place, *Agua secreta* (Hidden Water), where he finds a warm welcome, baptizes children, sanctifies marriages. The literal place-name, like many in the Southwest, thus gains sacramental, biblical significance. The "earthen thrashing floor" there reminds him of the winnowing of "the children of Israel";[54] the whiteness of the Angoras gathered in "great flocks of goats" (cf. Sg 6:4) reminds the priest of "the whiteness of them that were washed in the blood of the Lamb" (Rev. 8:4);[55] before his eyes "the smoke of burning piñon logs rose like incense to Heaven" (cf. Rev. 8:4).[56]

Later, atop the mesa where the Ácomas dwell, the young Bishop Latour envisions the rocky fortress as a symbol of the universal human desire for something stable, protective, "without shadow of change" (James 1:17), "their Rock" in the desert giving fresh meaning to "Rock" as God's biblical name (cf. Ps. 18:2; Deut. 3:24; 1 Cor. 10:4).[57] Later in life, Latour discovers the rock, the stone, the hill, from which he builds his cathedral in Santa Fe, literalizing the biblical word, "Upon this rock I will build my church" (Matt. 16:18).[58] The name and color of the Sangre de Cristo mountains, visible at a distance, similarly recalls to his mind the blood of Christ shed at Calvary, but also "the dried blood of saints and martyrs in the old churches in Rome" that sometimes liquefy.[59]

Cather clearly contrasts Bishop Latour's beautiful cathedral in Santa Fe (the outward sign of a church built of "living stones" (1 Pet. 2:5) with the gloomy fortress church built by the tyrannical Friar Baltazar Montoya on the mesa at Ácoma in the early 1700s. The "Legend of Fray Baltazar" stands in the novel as antitype of a saint's legend. The friar, Bishop Latour learns, demanded slave-service from the Ácomas in order to enjoy a garden and good meals atop the mesa; he "lived more after the flesh than after the spirit" (cf. Rom. 8:5).[60] His tyrannical behavior and his orchestration of an elaborate feast, to which he invites the local clergy, inevitably recall King Belshazzar's feast in the book of Daniel, chapter 5, and the Chaldean king's sudden death. Baltazar similarly dies on the very night of the feast. After he accidentally kills a Native American serving boy with an angrily thrown cup, Baltazar is himself executed by the Ácomas, thrown down from the top of the mesa.

Apart from the two French missionaries, no single character is ever a focus of attention for a long time. They come to the fore, and then disappear from view. This episodic treatment supports Cather's artistic decision to sustain a moral approach to characterization, based on outwardly observable, characteristic behavior. Beginning in book 2, chapter 2, "Missionary Journeys," the priests meet a series of characters that resemble "Vice" figures from medieval morality plays.[61] Cather in this way follows a tradition traceable to Origen, who interpreted the Israelites' conquest of the Canaanite tribes as an allegory of spiritual battle against Wrath, Pride, Avarice, Fornication, and other sins.[62]

Buck Scales, the inhospitable American host who plans to kill the two priests traveling "on the lonely road to Mora" (67), is the very embodiment of Wrath. Motivated by vengeance, Don Manuel Chavez is another wrathful character, who, in Cather's memorable phrase, "not only [has] a story, but seem[s] to have become his story" (184). The chief vice of Doña Isabella Olivares is her "vanity" (194). Sloth and gluttony are embodied in the corpulent figure of Trinidad Lucero, a nephew of Padre Lucero at Arroyo Hondo. Padre Lucero is notorious for his avarice and hoarding. His friend Padre Antonio José Martinez is characterized by a Luciferian pride that gives him a dictatorial control over "all the parishes in northern New Mexico and the native priests at Santa Fé" (139); he exhibits in classic form, however, all three principal lusts: "the lust of the flesh, the lust of the eyes, and the pride of life" (1 John 2:16).

In a brilliant reworking of Jesus's parable of the foolish rich man, surprised by death (Luke 12:16–18), and of multiple biblical passages comparing death to a thief in the night,[63] Cather relates that the miserly Padre Lucero kills a would-be robber who has broken into his house at night. Traumatized by the event, the old priest's health breaks, and he sets his affairs in order on his deathbed, where he receives the sacraments. His last days and hours provide a memorable foil for those of Archbishop Latour. They also anchor the novel's indebtedness to Dante, for the old priest's dying words are reputed to convey his vision of a Luciferian Padre Martinez in hell: "Eat your tail, Martinez, eat your tail!" (174).[64]

The friendship—indeed, the brotherhood—between the two French missionaries contrasts with the self-interested bond between the rebel priests, Martinez and Lucero, who break away from the authority of Bishop

Latour to establish a schismatic church. Riding a pair of twin mules on their shared and separate missionary journeys, Father Vaillant and Father Latour have forged an unbreakable bond from their youth in the seminary, albeit one costly with self-sacrifice. Here, too, Cather shows herself an astute reader of the *Legenda aurea*, whose catalogue of saints includes many paired saints who ministered, and were martyred, together.[65] In the case of Cather's priestly heroes, their twosomeness veils a triune relationship to Christ, to Christ's Church, and to the Virgin Mary, to whom both priests are tenderly devoted. Turning the familiar, novelistic, lovers' triangle on its head, Cather's hagiographic novel thus bears witness to the communion of saints.[66] As Bishop Latour lies dying, he remembers the decisive, early morning train ride he and Father Vailliant took together in their youth to leave their homeland and go together to the New World; the memory becomes a symbol for his earthly departure heavenward in spiritual company with his stalwart friend.

WERFEL'S APOCALYPTIC *SONG OF BERNADETTE*

Saint Bernadette Soubirous (1844–79) was canonized in 1933, the year of Hitler's rise to power in Germany. The following year, Franz Werfel's book about the Armenian genocide, *The Forty Days of Musa Dagh* (1934) was banned in Germany, where it was understood to be a coded protest against the anti-Semitism of the Third Reich. Werfel fled from Austria to France after the *Anschluss* in 1938 and later spent weeks in hiding, together with his wife, in Lourdes, France, after the German invasion of France in 1940. There he read Henri Lassere's *Notre Dame de Lourdes* (1869), which he later used as his major historical source. A Jewish novelist, playwright, and poet, Franz Werfel vowed to write the story of Bernadette, should he find a safe escape to the United States. He fulfilled that vow in 1941, writing *Das Lied von Bernadette* (*The Song of Bernadette*) immediately upon his arrival in Hollywood.

Far from an escapist work, *Song of Bernadette* is a biblical hagiography, not because direct quotation or frequent echo of the letter of scripture can be found on its pages, however, but because of its allegorical linkage of what Werfel calls the "mystic basic facts" of biblical revelation: "creation of the world, fall of man, incarnation, resurrection, etc." to a "simple tale," re-

Modern Literary Experiments in Biblical Hagiography 247

alistically narrated.[67] The structure of the novel, in short, mirrors the structure of scripture and conveys in a relatively hidden way what the Bible teaches, both openly and figuratively. Part of the novel's secret is an allegory about Jewish suffering and eschatological salvation.[68]

Song of Bernadette is divided into five books, each with ten chapters. The numerical correspondence to the rosary's mysteries in sets composed of five decades is made explicit in the title of chapter 50, "The Fiftieth Ave." The mysteries of the rosary—joyful, sorrowful, glorious—are precisely what Werfel calls the "mystic basic facts"[69] found in the Gospels: the Annunciation, the Visitation, the Nativity, and so on upon which the pray-er meditates while repeating the Hail Mary, the Our Father, the Glory Be.[70] In book 1 of *Song of Bernadette*, the apparition of the beautiful Lady to the young girl recalls the appearance of the angel to Mary and, at yet another level of signification, the election of each of God's chosen ones, an election that entails suffering.

Completely absent from the award-winning 1943 film *Song of Bernadette*, based on Werfel's international bestseller, are the numerous invocations of the theme of the demonic in the novel. Werfel's description of the grotto at Massabielle, the site of the Marian apparitions, emphasizes that it is initially a filthy, accursed place, where pigs rout, snakes slither, garbage is dumped, and bones are unearthed. The Virgin's unseemly descent to this place "of rubble, swine, and snakes" is, therefore, virtually a descent into an earthly hell.[71] The bare feet of the beautiful Lady on the rock at Massabielle are at once historical—that is, Bernadette professes to see them—and biblical, recalling the Lord's prophecy to the serpent in the proto-Gospel, "I will put enmity between you and the woman, and between your seed and her seed; (s)he shall bruise your head" (Gen. 3:15).[72] Exegetical tradition glosses that verse from Genesis with the vision in Revelations 12 of the woman "clothed with the sun, with the moon under her feet," crowned with twelve stars—the woman "pursued" by the dragon, out of whose open mouth "water like a river" pours, to sweep the woman away "with the flood" (Rev. 12:1, 13, 15).

Substituting for the traditional wordplay "Ave/Eva," which contrasts Mary's salvific role as the true "mother of the living" with Eve's as fallen humanity's genetrix (Gen. 3:20), Werfel plays instead with "Ave/Gave," contrasting between the "Ave" addressed to Mary with the name of the river flowing near the grotto. The serpentine river becomes, in fact, Werfel's main, expressionist symbol for the demonic as it intrudes upon Bernadette's encounters with the Lady. The chapter "Of a River's Rage and Woe" immediately precedes the chapter in book 1 recounting the Lady's first appearance to Bernadette.

Left alone by her sister Marie and their friend Jeanne Abadie, Bernadette has a strange, acoustic experience: "The Gave River has changed its tune."[73] It suddenly sounds like a busy, public road, crowded with "a hundred open carts and wagons and omnibuses and landaus and victoria-chaises," their drivers and passengers raising a "shrill confusion of voices, . . . sharp cries of woe" and audible curses: "Flee while you can! To hell with you!"[74] The scene recalls Werfel's "Personal Preface" to the book, where he describes the general panic, hunger, anger, and despair of motorists who clogged the roads when the Nazi troops occupied the border town of Hendaye, closing the border to Spain in June 1940, after the French collapse to the Germans: "The Pyrenean *départements* had turned into a phantasmagoria—a very camp of chaos. . . . In endless lines stood the cars of the fugitives, piled mountain-high with household gear, with mattresses and beds; there was no gasoline to be had."[75]

Werfel repeats this imagistic pattern, which evokes the horsemen of the Apocalypse, at key moments in the novel. When a chorus of voices begins to pray the rosary piously at the grotto during one of the apparitions, Bernadette suddenly hears an opposite sound, "a rout in panic terror" that seems "to race across the [Gave] river" on "galloping horses and rattling vehicles," with voices heard to cry out, "Flee, flee. . . . Avaunt from here!"[76] Turning her eyes in the direction of the river, the Lady silently commands its silence and brings "the immemorial rumbling and foaming of the Gave . . . to [her] heel like a daunted wolf."[77] When a confused Bernadette thinks that the Lady wants her to drink from the Gave, rather than the (still undiscovered) spring, the Lady speaks to correct her, thus rejecting the river, "the playground of hostile forces," as "not fit" for her purposes.[78]

After miracles of healing begin to occur at the spring and the first series of Marian apparitions comes to an end, demonic activity displays itself rebellious in paranormal phenomena near the site,[79] including a child's glimpse of a "demon" in the water of the Gave.[80] Bernadette's former teacher, Sister Marie Thérèse Vauzous, has a recurrent dream of the grotto at Massabielle as a hell's mouth, "a mawlike abyss," next to which flowed "a gray river," on the banks of which "stood hundreds of figures with filthy bandages, leaning on canes and crutches."[81] In her final, excruciating illness, Bernadette herself suffers demonic attacks in various, shape-shifting forms, including one in which the devil "embodied as the Gave," growls his curse at her: "Away from here! . . . Flee while you may!"[82]

The ancient, biblical enmity between the woman and the serpent, between the New Eve and the devil, grounds this strong image pattern, wherein Bernadette is the protagonist of Mary, the Immaculate Conception, unstained by original sin. At the same time, Werfel's apocalyptic sense of history discerns the old enemy of humankind at work in the radical evil of twentieth-century war, anti-Semitism, and genocide. Against the Nazi drive to purge society of the Jews and the mentally and physically handicapped, the Virgin at Lourdes had opened a spring of healing for body and soul through the hand of a chosen child, herself afflicted with asthma, poverty, and ignorance. In Werfel's vision, the trainloads of invalids, "the grievously sick from all parts of the world" who travel to Lourdes seeking healing,[83] are a divine counter, given in advance, to the Nazi deportation trains en route to the death camps. What happened at Lourdes that had provoked the devil's attacks was, in short, prophetic of happenings to come. Werfel's last chapter places on the lips of Pius XI, the pope who canonized Bernadette in 1933, this same interpretation of Lourdes as a "very rock" against the "demonic sway" that was already in Bernadette's time "threatening to plunge the human spirit into bloody madness."[84]

Werfel's novel is, by his own testimony, "full of meaning,"[85] theologically symbolic in ways that few among his readers will recognize.[86] Little studied by literary critics, it contains not only a timely interpretation of Revelations 12, but also an allegory of Jewish election, suffering, and witness that is keyed in, first, by Werfel's comparison of the spring at Lourdes to a baptismal font,[87] in the basin of which the Bouhouhorts baby is cured through immersion,[88] and then by the cancer-stricken Bernadette's declaration, "The spring isn't for me."[89] Werfel's "Theologoumena," composed in the United States between 1942 and 1944, spells out a wealth of connections left hidden in the novel.[90]

From within the novel itself, however, the possibility of illumination is affirmed by the experience of characters who suddenly gain insight. The partially blinded stonemason Bouriette has "an uncommon thought" that leads him to test the healing power of the moistened earth at Massabielle.[91] The "lightning of cognition" pierces the heart of the distraught Madame Bouhouhorts when she witnesses the death agony of her child and suddenly understands that the "dipping and laving" in the spring water, commanded by the Lady and performed by Bernadette, are purposeful and meant to be enacted by her in her distress.[92] At the sight of Bernadette's tumor, which reveals to her the visionary's secret suffering, the nun Vauzous understands "its meaning in a sudden overwhelming flash of illumination," a "terrifying grace."[93]

In Werfel's novel, the lit candles carried in procession to the grotto and held in the hands of people at prayer become the symbol of a progressive illumination. The narrator notes the "first candle to burn at Massabielle,"[94] the "crowd with its burning candles,"[95] the candle in the entranced Bernadette's own outstretched right hand, which (to the amazement of the observant physician, Dr. Douzous) licks the fingers of her left hand, leaving it miraculously "painless and unharmed."[96] Returning to Lourdes after an absence of twenty years, Hyacinthe Lafite comes to the grotto at twilight. His hour of conversion occurs in dimming daylight, but also in the light of the "great iron stand in front of the niche in the grotto, a strange palm of candles, quiver[ing] with its hundred flames."[97]

The large Lourdes mural (1887) by Luigi Gregori (1819–96) in the Basilica of the Sacred Heart at the University of Notre Dame shows a kneeling Bernadette holding a tall candle and looking up at the beautiful Lady who has appeared to her (see plate 9.1). Perhaps the "brief candle" of hagiography in its capacity to illumine the scriptures—the Bible's letter and its veiled mysteries—is burning still, after all, but at a greater distance from the "eternal book"[98] read aloud by Dostoevsky's Sonya and Father Zosima and memorized by the medieval hagiographers. Biblically evocative and sustained throughout by its apocalyptic prophecies, Werfel's *Song of Bernadette* quotes the Bible directly only once, when a priest intones the Song of Songs (5:2) as part of the prayers for the dying saint: "I was asleep, but my heart waked. It is the sound of my beloved that knocketh, saying: Open to me, my sister, my love, my dove, my undefiled; for my head is filled with dew, and my locks with the drops of night."[99] Solomon's Song of Songs, the allegory of allegories, discloses the "mystic basic facts" of all the saints' *Lives*,[100] including Werfel's *Song of Bernadette*.

Plate 9.1. Luigi Gregori, *Lourdes Mural*, 1887, Basilica of the Sacred Heart, University of Notre Dame. Photograph courtesy of Nancy Cavadini.

CHAPTER TEN

HISTORICAL TRUTH, BIBLICAL CRITICISM, AND HAGIOGRAPHY

The saint's *Life* as a broadly defined literary genre (inclusive of hagiography and biography) has never entirely lost its early function of illumining the Gospels, much as a reflective foil magnifies a light.[1] It suffered an eclipse, nonetheless, in the early modern period that strangely foreshadows what Hans Frei (1922–88) has called "the eclipse of biblical narrative" in modernity, when the organically interconnected levels of premodern scriptural signification—literal, allegorical, tropological, anagogical—became increasingly separated from each other. Focusing on biblical scholarship, Frei finds "the seeds of disintegration" present already in the seventeenth century, when a shift and reversal of perspective begins to occur.[2] Increasingly, the truth of the Bible, grounded in its historical sense, is no longer the standard for the world's realities, calling them into judgment, but rather the world's realities—known to the world through scientific and historical research, political exercise, and jurisprudence—test the Bible's. The question becomes, "Do the stories and whatever concepts may be drawn from them describe what we apprehend as the real world?"[3]

In Frei's analysis, "Realistic, literal reading of the biblical narratives found its closest successor in the historical-critical reconstruction of specific events and texts of the Bible," the guiding question for the moderns being, "How reliable are the texts?"[4] Concerned with "specific texts and specific historical circumstances," such scholars have discerned no literal basis, however, for reading the Bible as a divinely inspired unity or for using scripture across the canon to interpret scripture.[5]

The "figural reading" of patristic and medieval exegesis, which bore witness to the unity of the Old and New Testaments,[6] has "found its closest successor," according to Frei, "in an enterprise called biblical theology," which argues for the Bible's unity either through tracing common theological themes and concepts throughout the scriptures or by highlighting successive episodes "within a single, gradually developing and cumulative *history*," the metanarrative of salvation history.[7]

The tropological (moral and ethical) sense of premodern exegesis extended the Bible's historical narratives, typology, and teaching into each one's life. In Frei's view, this scriptural sense has been greatly undermined for modern readers by the disassociation of literal and figurative meanings, but it remains somewhat in force because of the inescapable realism and "history-like" quality of biblical narrative.[8] This "history-like" *sensus litteralis* is acknowledged, Frei marvels, even by those Biblicists who question, in positivist terms, the historical accuracy of the biblical stories.

The same threefold pattern of disassociation (literal/historical, figural, moral/ethical) that Frei discerns in modern biblical scholarship is clearly evident in modern hagiographical scholarship. Exactly in the seventeenth century—the same period in which Frei perceives the first "seeds of disintegration" in biblical interpretation—the critical study of the *Lives* of the saints began. The combined efforts of the Jesuit researchers known today as the Bollandists—Heribert Rosweyde, S.J. (1569–1629), John van Bolland, S.J. (1596–1665), Godfrey Henschen, S.J. (1601–81), and Daniel von Papenbroeck, S.J. (1628–1714), and others—eventually resulted in the monumental *Acta sanctorum*, published in fifty-three folio volumes between 1643 and 1794.

The quest of the Bollandists, which continues to this day, and which gave rise to Hippolyte Delehaye's 1905 *Legends of the Saints*, is to test the historical accuracy and reliability of the extant *Lives* against one another and against various external sources of documentation, to provide a critical apparatus helpful in resolving apparent contradictions, and thus to protect the cult of the saints from the discredit that arises from error. Thomas Heffernan affirms: "[Delehaye's] motivation was to provide a solid historical foundation for those saints whom the church worshipped [*sic*]."[9] Partly because of the vituperative charges leveled by Edward Gibbon (1737–94), who found "a total disregard of truth and probability" in many early martyrdom accounts,[10] Delehaye and his fellow Bollandists were "concerned to authenticate a canon of texts that had some claim to historical authenticity."[11]

In this effort, the natural allies of the Bollandists were and are historians who, for their own reasons, seek to know, understand, and describe the medieval cult of the saints as a fact with cultural, sociological, economic, and political consequences. To this task historians in growing numbers have dedicated themselves, ever since the innovative, Marxist, Czech historian František Graus (*Volk, Herrscher, und Heiliger im Reich der Merowinger: Studien zur Hagiographie der Merowingenzeit*, 1965) demonstrated the usefulness of hagiographic sources for social history. The work of three scholars in the 1980s has proven pivotal: Peter Brown (*The Cult of the Saints: Its Rise and Function in Latin Christianity*, 1981), Caroline Walker Bynum (*Holy Feast and Holy Fast*, 1987), and André Vauchez (*Sainthood in the Later Middle Ages*, 1981). Since then, there has been a flood of important hagiographic studies by historians.[12]

This combined hagiographical enterprise by Bollandists and social historians plainly parallels the modern impulse in biblical criticism to test, verify, and interpret the Bible's "letter" not principally by the Church's rule of faith (*regula fidei*), but historically in time and place as a human work, a cultural product. Much knowledge has been gained by this. By its procedural bracketing, however, of the theological questions of divine inspiration, authorship, and intervention, biblical "higher criticism" casts them into doubt (a process signaled by the "demythologizing" of Rudolf Bultmann), even as its "lower criticism" of the text undermines traditional exegesis based (according to the findings of modern scholarship) on errors in transmission, faulty translation, or the verbal concordance of biblical words and phrases stemming from diverse authors, chronological periods, and cultural idioms.

Not surprisingly, therefore, modern historians who narrate the life of a medieval saint resemble biblical scholars in search of the Historical Jesus. Augustine Thompson's recent *Francis of Assisi: A New Biography*, for example, uses the earliest sources to construct a minimalist, demythologized account of the founder of the Franciscans. Thompson says of his own work, "The similarity to Historical Jesus studies is obvious."[13] The "Historical Francis" that emerges from Thompson's biography is not, however, the "real Francis."[14] "My 'Historical Francis' . . . is 'historical,'" writes Thompson, "in that the picture I have painted is the result of historical method, not theological reflection or pious edification."

Everywhere Thompson draws a sharp divide between history and hagiography.[15] Although several early sources report that Francis was baptized John (Giovanni), a common Christian name, and renamed or nicknamed Francesco ("Frenchy"), Thompson declares himself "very suspicious of its historicity," for no other reason than "the biblical typology that controls the saint's name change" and the related, subsequent hagiographic comparisons of Francis to his putative namesake, John the Baptist.[16] Thompson similarly omits from his biography of Francis the "famous speaking crucifix that gave Francis a mission to 'rebuild my church'"—an event that the Dominican historian terms "theological elaboration, and not historical," even though (and indeed because) it "explain[s] theologically what appears to be random behavior (church repair)" and presents "a prophecy of Francis's future role" for the Church as a whole.[17] Finally, to cite a third example of the biographer's antihagiographic bent, Thompson omits the well-known story of Francis's taming of the wolf of Gubbio—a miracle story that may well have been literally intended by the early hagiographers (and understood by their readers) as a parable or allegory and that has inspired imitation by present-day peacemakers.[18]

"SACRED BIOGRAPHY" AND "BIBLICAL THEOLOGY"

If the critical program of the historian biographers and Bollandists is akin to biblical criticism, the generic project of "sacred biography" can be likened to that which Frei ascribes to "biblical theology." Reconstructive approaches to salvation history have preserved a semblance of the premodern figurative sense and of the Bible's inspired unity, albeit at the expense of a loosened tie to the Bible's literal sense as *historia*. For such interpreters, the Bible's "letter" *is* its "meaning" for the people of God. Similarly, Thomas Heffernan's important *Sacred Biography: Saints and Their Biographers in the Middle Ages* (1988) endeavors to correct Delehaye's *Legends of the Saints*, first, by including a consideration of some of the classic, biblically inflected *Lives* the Jesuit Bollandist had excluded, and, second, by advancing a theological argument for the meaningfulness to all medieval Christians, clerical and lay, of hagiographic convention, which presents the saint to view in his or her conformity to Christ and in communion with other saints. Heffernan thus unites the two hagiographical strands, learned and popular, that Delehaye, suspicious of convention, had separated.

In upholding hagiographic convention, however, Heffernan finds it difficult to acknowledge and to account for the distinctive features of an individual *Life* and for changes in hagiographic writings across time. He argues that a different kind of truth than that privileged by the modern historian is conveyed by medieval hagiography—a timeless truth. "Although these lives were written under different circumstances at different times about individuals from vastly different social backgrounds," he observes, "the conservative ethos of the genre (inherent in its rhetoric and its theology) tends to play down differences while extolling socially accepted paradigms of sanctity."[19]

Heffernan argues, further, "that we can establish the tradition that brings this diversity together," a tradition that stems from two quite different models and harmonizes them: "Greco-Roman biography on the one hand and Hellenized-Jewish character sketches on the other."[20] From the former, according to Heffernan, Christian hagiography derives and adapts its own "interplay of *praxeis* and *ethos*" in the presentation of the saint as simultaneously truly exceptional (in his or her intimacy with God) and imitable (in virtuous deeds).[21] From the latter, hagiography derives its conventional concern with the miraculous, the wondrous deeds wrought by God through the saints.[22] In combination, the two sources give rise to a distinctive kind of narrative, a human life characterized by "virtuous" deeds in the double sense of moral goodness and divine power.[23] Heffernan emphasizes "the primacy of the dramatic deed in medieval saints' lives" and its paradigmatic usefulness in teaching "the faithful to imitate actions" that recall "Christ's behavior in the Gospels."[24]

BIBLICAL TROPOLOGY, MORAL TEACHING, AND HAGIOGRAPHY

If the *sensus historialis* of medieval hagiography has inspired the work of modern historians and its figural meaning that of literary scholars such as

Heffernan, the moral implications of saint's lives have excited the interest of philosophers, most notably Edith Wyschogrod, Paul Ricoeur, and Alasdair MacIntyre, who in *After Virtue* asserts, "The chief means of moral education is the telling of stories."[25] Wyschogrod's *Saints and Postmodernism: Revisioning Moral Philosophy* points in particular to the saint's life, describing it in phenomenological terms as a narrative characterized by a threefold temporality (that of the saint, the hagiographer, and the reader); by composition in an imperative, rather than indicative, mode; and by a social formation that expresses and reinforces a communion of saints: "The life that is recounted is shaped in conformity with social expectations connected with saintly acts."[26] Although very unlike a "fable or purely didactic story," which exists to illustrate a moral lesson, the hagiographic narrative, aimed at the reader's imitation, often has an "upshot" that is "bound up with a moral point."[27] Inspired in part by the philosophy of Emmanuel Levinas, who emphasizes the ethical force of biblical commandment and the power of Talmudic tales, Wyschogrod defines hagiography as "a narrative linguistic practice that recounts the lives of saints so that the reader or hearer can experience their imperative power."[28] By this definition the scandalous lack of historical accuracy (in positivist historical terms) in hagiography is overcome. "Some factual biographies of saints may not be hagiographic," Wyschogrod insists, "whereas some works of fiction may be at least partially so, especially if the narrative is recast to exhibit the compelling force of a life."[29]

Wyschogrod's ethical and moral retrieval of hagiography, medieval and modern, may be placed parallel to philosophical and theological readings of the Bible that emphasize its status as a morally instructive narrative: for example, Stanley Hauerwas's *A Community of Character* (1991), Rufus Black's *Christian Moral Realism* (2000), Paul Nelson's *Narrative and Morality* (2010), and Alexander Lucie-Smith's *Narrative Theology and Moral Theology: The Infinite Horizon* (2007). As Lucie-Smith usefully points out, however, advocates of narrative theology (biblical or hagiographic) as a provocative and rebellious form of moral teaching, aimed at disrupting a mundane and customary morality, often seem too quick to dismiss altogether the value of authoritative moral teaching, biblical commandment, and communal practice, separating what should be joined together.[30]

The pattern of disassociation between and among the three approaches to hagiography I have just described mirrors that which Frei discerns in biblical studies. The historians bracket the question of the truth of miracles, theologically considered, even as they analyze the stories of miracles in saints' lives and study the reports of miracles at particular saints' sites as offering documentary evidence of a local people's religious practice and experience. The exponents of hagiography as sacred biography confirm on literary and rhetorical grounds a hagiographic unity, conventionality, and figurative truth that historians would question as "historical." Finally, the moral philosophers see in the hagiographic narrative itself, whether factual or fictive, a spur to saintly action in the present. All three groups of scholars make many similar observations about the *Lives* of saints, but they each reason from their own starting point, instead of building upon a shared assumption about the historical existence, the reality, of the saint *qua* saint, in his or her relationship to other historical realities, past and present.

HAGIOGRAPHIC AND BIBLICAL NARRATIVE

Is this threefold correspondence between modern biblical and hagiographic studies a pure coincidence that tells us more about modernity than about any actual family resemblance between hagiography and the Bible? Recall that Frei traces the breakdown of the premodern coherence of the literal, allegorical, and tropological senses to a crisis in the understanding of *historia* itself and to modern doubt about the historicity (in positivist terms) of the Bible's *sensus litteralis*. Drawing upon the brilliant comparative work of Erich Auerbach in *Mimesis*, Frei seeks to retrieve the older understanding of the biblical *sensus litteralis* as "history-like" in its "plain sense" meaning and thus to reground the figurative and tropological senses in the biblical letter. From Auerbach, Frei derives the following distinctive features of biblical narrative in the Old and New Testaments: the "device of chronological sequence," the insistent setting of "characters or individual persons, in their internal depth and subjectivity, . . . in the context of the external environment," the constant intermingling of "nonmiraculous and miraculous accounts and explanations," and the regular juxtaposition of "serious effect" and "didactic elements" with "what is casual, random, ordinary, and everyday."[31] Auerbach discovers in the deliberate, artful sparseness of the biblical narrative, in its gaps, silences, and "fragmentary speeches," a "call for interpretation" and personal application.[32] Citing Karl Barth, Frei similarly advocates a revival of a multilayered exegesis of biblical narratives appropriate to *lectio divina* and to the text's own "call for interpretation": "(1) *explication* . . . (2) *meditation* . . . (3) *applicatio*."[33]

The *applicatio* of a biblical episode to one's own life might suggest at least the beginning of a link in Frei's own thought between biblical and hagiographic reading. Judging by his guarded comments about the "realism" of biblical miracle stories, however, and by his insistence (echoing Auerbach) that the narrated past of biblical characters provides a realistic "background" for their recorded actions in the present,[34] I suspect that Frei himself—no student of medieval hagiography and a postliberal theologian more at home in modern systematics than in medieval exegesis—would probably have resisted any association of hagiography with biblical narrative and argued instead for an alignment of hagiography with myth. After all, the imperfect past of saints (when recorded at all) is much less the "background" to their *Lives* than is the grace and glory of God, which surrounds them, empowers them, and illumines them even in their weakness (like the golden background of an icon).

Such a distancing of a saint's *Life* from biblical story would be mistaken, however, on at least three scores. First of all, as Robert Alter has written, Auerbach's description of biblical style in Genesis 22 would have to be "seriously modified" in application to narratives in other books of the Bible, for example, the David cycles and the book of Job.[35] Similarly, what Auerbach discovers so brilliantly in the Markan account of Peter's denial of Jesus cannot be found everywhere alike in the Gospels, in Acts, and in Revelation. Not every biblical narrative is "fraught" in the same way with (Auerbachian) "background."[36] A fuller accounting of biblical narrative features and episodic examples arguably allows for a greater affinity and overlap between the biblical and the saintly story.

Second, such a distancing fails to address the richness and diversity of the hagiographic tradition and to account for the uses of scriptural quotation and typology within it. Scriptural intertext arguably establishes a bridge between an individual saint's *Life* and biblical story so strong that an individual hagiography, echoing scripture, might serve as a kind of biblical commentary upon or illumination of that passage or set of passages and a witness to historical exegesis. Similarly, the liturgical use of saintly *exempla* (often extracts from *Lives*) in sermons to illumine biblical stories and to submit the lives of the listeners to their tropology attests to the "history-like" quality of both.[37] Explicitly contrasting hagiography to myth, Wyschogrod writes, "Saints' lives, even when punctuated by miraculous interventions and rhetorical strategies reflecting specific literary contexts, appear to be informed by a will to historicity. . . . Hagiographic discourse purports to disclose a life" and to be "lived forward" in that of others.[38]

Third, aligning hagiography with myth and against the Bible follows Delehaye's lead in *Legends of the Saints*—a book that, as Sherry L. Reames observes, "points in the wrong direction" by presenting "the typical saint's legend [as] just a kind of Christian folklore," reductive of "historical characters and events to a few, simple, predictable patterns."[39] Delehaye accomplishes this greatly misleading introduction to hagiography by purposely excluding from consideration hagiographies representing what Reames calls "real excellence in the genre,"[40] such as Gregory the Great's *Life of Saint Benedict*, in the *Dialogues*, book 2.[41]

Gregory's *Life of Saint Benedict* provides, in fact, clear and explicit guidance about how to read that *Life* in relation to the biblical stories and teachings it so clearly evokes.[42] As the title *Dialogues* indicates, Gregory's narration of the *Life* is interrupted at key points by questions posed to him by his interlocutor, Peter—questions that Matthew Dal Santo has argued reflected contemporary anxieties about the rising cult of the saints and thus served an apologetic function.[43] The human context of trusting community, within which questions can be honestly raised and answered, wonderment expressed, conversation enjoyed, makes the sharing of the *Life of Saint Benedict* an expression of, and a means for, the communion of saints that unites the Church in glory with that still struggling below *in via*. Though they serve as an exemplar of a distinctive, late antique literary genre,[44] the fictionalized exchanges in Gregory's *Dialogues* had a model character for households and communities throughout the Middle Ages who gathered for the reading aloud and discussion of books.[45]

The exchanges between Peter and Gregory demonstrate the potential for saints' *Lives* to stimulate and to reflect biblical study and theological investigation. At the literal level, Peter shows himself attentive to repeated phrases and variation upon them. Noticing that Benedict is said to have "returned to himself" (a phrase that echoes Acts 12:11 and Luke 15:17) and then to have "dwelt with himself, in the sight of the Creator," Peter asks about the meaning of the latter expression, which prompts Gregory's use of scripture to comment upon scripture and his brief unfolding of a doctrine of repentance, ecstasy, and contemplative *stabilitas* in virtue.[46] Puzzled by Benedict's foreknowledge of a man's predestined fall from grace, Peter questions Gregory about the saint's access to such divine knowledge, citing pertinent biblical passages that appear to be contradictory (1 Cor. 2:9–12; Rom. 11:33–34; Ps. 118 [119]:13), to which Gregory replies, citing affirmative passages (1 Cor. 6:17, 2:9–12) and harmonizing the texts: "Wherefore the saying of David and Saint Paul agree together."[47] When Benedict is said to have obtained the release of two departed souls from a state of excommunication, Gregory calls Matthew 16:19 ("whatever you loose on earth shall be loosed in heaven") to Peter's attention.[48]

Many of Peter's comments concern the repetition in the *Life of Saint Benedict* (albeit with variation) of miracles recorded in the Bible. Peter and Gregory thus highlight the figural quality of the hagiographic episodes. "The things you report are strange, and much to be marveled at," observes Peter. "In making the rock to yield water, I see Moses; and in the iron, which came from the bottom of the lake, I behold Elisha; in the walking of Maurus on the water, I perceive Peter; in the obedience of the crow, I contemplate Elias; and in lamenting the death of his enemy, I acknowledge David: and therefore, in my opinion, this one man was full of the spirit of all good men."[49] Echoing John 1:16, Gregory responds by identifying this spirit with "the spirit of the one true God," of whose "fullness we have all received"[50]

Gregory's reply associates the power of miracles with moral transformation. But how? Gregory goes on to offer a concise, theologically rich account of the meaning and purpose of miraculous signs. From the Holy Spirit, he explains, God's servants receive God's grace, gifts, and virtues—spiritual endowments that only God can give and that the saints cannot pass on directly to others. The signs of miracles give evidence of these spiritual gifts, however, in the sight of God's friends and enemies alike, closing the hearts of the proud to the "sign of Jonas" (Matt. 12:40) and opening those of the humble who, "against death, lay hold of [Christ's] power and might."[51] The meaning of all miracles worked through and by the saints is to awaken faith, hope, and love by pointing to the greatest miracles of all, the Incarnation and Resurrection: "He died in the sight of the proud, to rise again before the eyes of the humble."[52]

In answer to Peter's request, "Tell me . . . whether holy men can do all such things as they please, and obtain at God's hands whatsoever they desire," Gregory replies with a tale that seems to illustrate the dictum of Augustine: "Love, and do what you will."[53] In it, Scholastica, Benedict's sister, obtains her wish from God against Benedict's contrary desire, because hers is the greater love, the more perfect charity, and (Gregory reminds Peter) "God is charity" (1 John 4:8).[54]

The devil, frustrated by Benedict's virtuous life, his zeal in spreading the kingdom of God, and his destruction of idols, appears to the holy man after calling out his name, "Benedict, Benedict," and asking, "Why do you persecute me?"[55] Adalbert de Vogüé notes that "by an astonishing transposition," the conversion of Paul on the road to Damascus (Acts 9:1–9) is "mirrored in this demonic episode," which likens the saint to Paul the persecutor and assigns to Satan "the place of the glorious Christ."[56]

What de Vogüé fails to mention is that the related episodes of divine and demonic appearances are tied to basic principles of biblical interpretation, namely, the first and the last Rules of Tychonius, preserved in Augustine's *De doctrina Christiana* (*On Christian Doctrine*): "Of the Lord and His Body" (revealed to Saint Paul) and "Of the Devil and His Body."[57] The saint's *Life* composed by Gregory the Great is to be read as scripture is read, as its hermeneutical translation. We've seen how late medieval hagiographers strained to apply these Rules of Tychonius to the *Lives* of controversial saints—Anselm of Canterbury, Francis of Assisi, Catherine of Siena—contemporary to themselves in apocalyptic times.

HAGIOGRAPHY AS NARRATIVE BIBLICAL COMMENTARY

Lost to the historical record are the many conversations, similar to that between Peter and Gregory, that the reading aloud and communal sharing of saint's *Lives* must have occasioned. Extant hagiographies by medieval theologians bear witness, however, to a complex intertextuality between the saint's *Lives*, the Bible, and the biblical commentary tradition—an intertextuality so rich and strong that the *Lives* themselves may be seen to offer a commentary upon the Bible in a narrative form.

Herein, we have studied selected hagiographies written between the eighth and the seventeenth centuries by well-educated, biblically literate, and exegetically gifted writers. We have seen (in chaps. 1–3) the close relationship between biblical commentary and saintly narrative in hagiographies composed by monastic writers: Felix of Croyland, Aelred of Rievaulx, and Bernard of Clairvaux. In Eadmer of Canterbury's *Life of Anselm* and its companion piece, the *Historia novorum*, discussed in chapter 4, we have witnessed a startling, new, pre-Scholastic distinction between hagiography and history—a distinction roughly contemporaneous with Hugh of Saint Victor's attempt in the *Didascalicon* (ca. 1125) to defend the Bible's literal meaning as a "historical" sense supportive of a multilayered interpretation. Hugh sought to fend off both an apocalyptic literalism that saw biblical prophecies fulfilled in current events, on the one hand, and an academic approach that delighted in disputed questions, on the other.

Increasingly unmoored from its historical foundation in scripture and reflecting anxiety about that unmooring, hagiography during the Scholastic period mirrors the disassociation of the traditional biblical senses in Scholastic disputation. We saw in chapters 5–7 that hagiographies composed by three Scholastic writers—Bonaventure, Raymond of Capua, and Jacobus de Voragine—exhibit a variety of "dualist" features: the "outer" life set apart from the "inner" life; the saint's observed bodily experience contrasted with his or her ecstatic, mystical experience; the saint's contested virtues and refuted vices; the hagiographer's careful referrals to divergent sources, opinions, and traditions; the answering of disputed questions, including the question of the saint's sanctity.

The dawn of modern biblical study in Erasmus's sixteenth-century editions coincides with the novelty in humanist circles of saint's *Lives* written as biographies, rather than biblical commentaries. Harpsfield's Erasmanian *Life of More*, discussed in chapter 8, exemplifies this close, methodological linkage between documentary hagiography (if it can still be called hagiography) and the historical-critical approach to the Bible. The outing of the "brief candle" of hagiography, traditionally conceived to be the Bible's visual aide, thus eerily foreshadows Frei's "eclipse of biblical narrative" in modernity.

Can the outed candle of hagiography as biblical illumination be relit? Chapter 9 surveys the works of three novelists—Fyodor Dostoevsky, Willa Cather, and Franz Werfel—who aimed consciously at such a revival in their historical fictions, and who did so with remarkable success. These saint's *Lives* vary in their relationship to the Bible, in accord with their respective emphases upon its different senses, but they all endeavor to illumine its literal meaning, seen afresh and anew in the reflective mirror of saintly experience. Amid calls for a new resourcing of biblical exegesis based both on the historical-critical method and on the living tradition of biblical reception by the faithful, these novelists have made their own call for a restoration of hagiography that is at once historical, tropological, allegorical, and anagogical because profoundly biblical.

NOTES

INTRODUCTION

1. From digitalgallery.nypl.org. See https://www.pinterest.com/pin/psalm-26-historiated-initial-david-holding-candle-blessed-by-lord--269230883946583034/.

2. *The Book of Legends, Sefer Ha-Aggadah: Legends from the Talmud and Midrash*, ed. Hayim Nahman Bialik and Yehoshua Hana Ravnitzky, trans. William G. Braude (New York: Schocken, 1992), 3.

3. The codex is now housed in Trinity Library, Dublin.

4. Unless otherwise indicated, I use *The Holy Bible*, Revised Standard Version (San Francisco: Ignatius, 1966), for English quotations; for Latin, I use *Biblia sacra vulgata*, 5th ed., ed. Robert Weber and Roger Gryson (Stuttgart: Deutsche Bibelgesellschaft, 2007).

5. Athanasius, *The Life of Antony and the Letter to Marcellinus*, trans. Robert C. Gregg (Mahwah, NJ: Paulist, 1980), 31.

6. Augustine, *Confessions*, trans. Henry Chadwick (Oxford: Oxford University Press, 2008), 8.12 (29), 153.

7. Bonaventure, *The Life of St. Francis*, trans. Ewert Cousins (Mahwah, NJ: Paulist, 1978), 199.

8. For a useful introduction, see Duncan Robertson, *Lectio Divina: The Medieval Experience of Reading* (Collegeville, MN: Cistercian Studies, 2011). Robertson does not discuss the application to hagiography.

9. On the use of saints' *Lives* in the Divine Office, see Simon Ditchfield, *Liturgy, Sanctity, and History in Tridentine Italy: Pietro Maria Campi and the Preservation of the Particular* (Cambridge: Cambridge University Press, 2002); Michael Kwatera, "A Critique of Vatican II's Directives Regarding the Hagiographical Readings in the Liturgy of the Hours" (Master's thesis, University of Notre Dame, 1980).

10. See Beverly Maayne Kienzle, Edith Wilks Dolnikowski, Rosemary Dragle Hale, Darleen Pryds, and Anne T. Thayer, eds., *Models of Holiness in Medieval Sermons: Proceedings of the International Symposium* (Louvain-La-Neuve: Fédération Internationale des Instituts d'Études Médiévales, 1996). Thomas L. Amos points out, "The *Homilies on the Gospels* of Gregory the Great circulated widely throughout Carolingian Europe and taught about saints with the same air of wonder that his

Dialogues created"; see Amos, "Early Medieval Sermons and the Holy," in Kienzle et al., eds., *Models of Holiness in Medieval Sermons*, 34.

11. On the importance of iconography in the ongoing cult of saints, see David Williams, *Saints Alive: Word, Image, and Enactment in the Lives of the Saints* (Montreal and Kingston: McGill-Queen's University Press, 2010).

12. For the legend of Saint Margaret, see Jacobus de Voragine, *The Golden Legend: Readings on the Saints*, trans. William Granger Ryan (Princeton, NJ: Princeton University Press, 2012), 368–70.

13. Gregory the Great, *Homiliae in Hiezechihelem prophetam*, ed. M. Adriaen, CCSL (Turnhout: Brepols, 1971), 142:163: "in sanctorum Patrum uita cognoscimus quid in sacrae Scripturae uolumine intelligere debeamus" (1.10.38). I thank Fr. Andrew Hofer, O.P., for this reference.

14. Hugh of St. Victor, *The "Didascalicon" of Hugh of St. Victor: A Medieval Guide to the Arts*, trans. Jerome Taylor, Records of Western Civilization (1961; repr. New York: Columbia University Press, 1991), 5.7, 128–29.

15. Hugh of St. Victor, *The "Didascalicon,"* 5.7, 128–29.

16. This schema, spelled out in *Didascalicon* 4.2, is original with Hugh, *The "Didascalicon,"* 217n2. Hugh recognizes, of course, that the writings of the Fathers do not belong to the biblical canon per se, as is clear from his listing of the books of the Bible in *Didascalicon* 4.2. On this expansiveness in Hugh, see Craig Tichelkamp, *The Mystified Letter: How Medieval Theology Can Reenchant the Practice of Reading* (Minneapolis, MN: Fortress, 2023).

17. Thomas Aquinas cites the Glossator's explanation of the term "Nazarite" as meaning "the saint of saints"; see Aquinas, *Catena Aurea: Commentary on the Four Gospels*, trans. John Henry Newman (Oxford: J. H. Parker, 1842–1845), 3:24. The angel tells Mary, "The child to be born will be called holy [*sanctum*], the son of God" (Luke 1:35). The imagery of the overshadowing Spirit at the hour of the Annunciation recalls the filling of the tabernacle and of the inner sanctuary (holy of holies) with God's glory in Exodus 40:34–35. Saint Peter extends the call to holiness to all those adopted in Christ as God's children, quoting the words "Be holy as I am holy" (1 Pet. 1:16).

18. See Carol Piper Heming, *Protestants and the Cult of Saints in German-Speaking Europe, 1517–1531*, Sixteenth Century Studies 65 (Kirksville, MO: Truman State University Press, 2003); Lee Palmer Wandel, *Voracious Idols and Violent Hands* (Cambridge: Cambridge University Press, 1995); Eamon Duffy, *Stripping of the Altars: Traditional Religion in England, 1400–1580* (1992; repr. New Haven, CT: Yale University Press, 2005).

19. Quoted in John MacQueen, *Numerology: Theory and Outline History of a Literary Mode* (Edinburgh: Edinburgh University Press, 1985), 18.

20. See Sherry L. Reames, *The "Legenda aurea": A Reexamination of Its Paradoxical History* (Madison: University of Wisconsin Press, 1985), 61.

21. Eric Waldram Kemp, *Canonization and Authority in the Western Church* (Oxford: Oxford University Press, 1948), 110–11; see Hostiensis, *In Tertium Decretalium Librum Commentaria*, on X.3.45 (*De reliquis* 1; *Audivimus*), Venice edition of 1581, facsimile (Torino: Bottega d'Erasmo, 1965), 172–73.

22. Hippolyte Delehaye, S.J., *The Legends of the Saints: An Introduction to Hagiography*, trans. V. M. Crawford (1907; repr. Notre Dame, IN: University of Notre Dame Press, 1961).

23. For a discussion of this *Life*, which Erasmus edited, see chapter 8 of this book.

24. Delehaye, *Legends of the Saints*, 60.

25. This "two-tier" understanding has been sharply called into question by the work of Peter Brown, *The Cult of the Saints: Its Rise and Function in Latin Christianity* (Chicago: University of Chicago Press, 1981).

26. Delehaye, *Legends of the Saints*, 61.

27. Despite the clarion call of Hans Urs von Balthasar to regard the lives of saints as wellsprings for theology, the reluctance of contemporary theologians to engage hagiographic materials (much less write a saint's *Life*) is striking. Ironically, the genre deemed properly "theological" by historians is virtually unstudied by professional theologians today. For recent exceptions to that rule, see Balthasar, "Theology and Sanctity," in *Explorations in Theology I: The Word Made Flesh* (San Francisco: Ignatius, 1989), 181–209; Marie Anne Mayeski, "New Voices in the Tradition: Medieval Hagiography Revisited," *Theological Studies* 63, no. 4 (2002): 690–710; Danielle K. Nussberger, "Saint as Theological Wellspring: Hans Urs von Balthasar's Hermeneutic of the Saint in a Christological and Trinitarian Key" (PhD diss., University of Notre Dame, 2007).

28. Augustine, *Confessions* 8.11 (27), trans. Chadwick, 151.

29. On the antinomy as "biographical dualism," see Thomas J. Heffernan, *Sacred Biography: Saints and Their Biographers in the Middle Ages* (New York: Oxford University Press, 1988), 30–31.

30. Alastair J. Minnis, *Medieval Theory of Authorship: Scholastic Literary Attitudes in the Later Middle Ages*, 2nd ed. (Philadelphia: University of Pennsylvania Press, 2010), 72, 58.

31. Minnis, *Medieval Theory of Authorship*, 21–22, 77, 102, 145–59.

32. On this point, see Peter Brown, "The Saint as Exemplar in Late Antiquity," in *Saints and Virtues*, ed. John Stratton Hawley (Berkeley: University of California Press, 1987), 3–14.

33. See, for example, Jacobus de Voragine, *Golden Legend*, trans. Ryan, 30–31, 88, 168, 275, 277, 281, 369, 382, 404, 449, 453, 468, 714.

34. See Nigel Hamilton, *Biography: A Brief History* (Cambridge, MA: Harvard University Press, 2007).

35. See Alison Knowles Frazier, *Possible Lives: Authors and Saints in Renaissance Italy* (New York: Columbia University Press, 2005); David J. Collins, *Reforming*

Saints: Saints' Lives and Their Authors in Germany, 1470–1530, Oxford Studies in Historical Theology (Oxford: Oxford University Press, 2008).

36. Collins, *Reforming Saints*, 8; David Collins, "A Life Reconstituted: Jacobus de Voragine, Erasmus of Rotterdam, and Their Lives of St. Jerome," *Medievalia et Humanistica*, n.s., 25 (1998): 31–51.

37. See Robert Kolb, *For All the Saints: Changing Perceptions of Martyrdom and Sainthood in the Lutheran Reformation* (Macon, GA: Mercer University Press, 1987).

38. See Brad S. Gregory, *The Unintended Reformation: How a Religious Revolution Secularized Society* (Cambridge, MA: Belknap Press of Harvard University Press, 2012).

39. George Eliot translated Strauss's book into English as *The Life of Jesus, Critically Examined*, published in London in 1846, arousing considerable controversy.

40. Ernst Renan, *The Life of Jesus*, trans. Charles E. Wilbour (New York and Paris: Carleton, Michel Lévy frères, 1864), 38–39.

41. Hans W. Frei, *The Eclipse of Biblical Narrative: A Study of Eighteenth and Nineteenth Century Hermeneutics* (New Haven, CT: Yale University Press, 1974).

42. M. D. Chenu, *Nature, Man, and Society in the Twelfth Century: Essays on New Theological Perspectives in the Latin West*, ed. and trans. Jerome Taylor and Lester K. Little (1957; repr. Chicago: University of Chicago Press, 1968), 162–201.

43. Kevin L. Hughes, "Chapter Five: Living the Word," in *The Oxford Handbook of Mystical Theology*, ed. Edward Howells and Mark MacIntosh (Oxford: Oxford University Press, 2020), 117.

CHAPTER ONE. Psalm Use, Prayer, and Prophecy in the *Lives* of Saint Guthlac

1. Throughout this chapter, I use *Felix's "Life of Saint Guthlac,"* ed. and trans. Bertram Colgrave (Cambridge: Cambridge University Press, 1956), a facing-page, Latin/English edition. For the Old English prose translation, I use *The Anglo-Saxon Version of the Life of St. Guthlac*, ed. and trans. Charles Wycliffe Goodwin (London: John Russell Smith, 1848), a facing-page Old English/English edition, based on Cotton Vespasian MS. D.xxi.

2. Sally Musseter, "Type as Prophet in the Old English *Genesis B*," *Viator* 14 (1983): 41–58.

3. For an excellent, comprehensive study of the *Enarrationes in psalmos* under the aspect of the theme of the "whole Christ," see Michael Fiedrowicz, *Psalmus vox totius Christi: Studien zu Augustins "Enarrationes in Psalmos"* (Freiburg im Breisgau: Herder, 1997). Fiedrowicz's extensive introduction (1:13–66) to the complete English-language translation in six volumes of the *Enarrationes in psalmos* by Maria Boulding (see note 5, below) reflects the insights of his 1997 monograph.

4. Jean Danielou, S.J., *The Bible and the Liturgy* (1951; repr. Notre Dame, IN: University of Notre Dame Press, 1956), 115.

5. See Augustine, *Expositions of the Psalms* (*Enarrationes in psalmos*), 6 vols., trans. Maria Boulding, O.S.B., ed. Boniface Ramsey, intro. Michael Fiedrowicz (Hyde Park, NY: New City Press, 2004). Boulding chiefly bases her translation upon D. Eligivs Dekkers and Johannes Fraipont, ed., *Enarrationes in psalmos*, CCSL 38–40 (Turnhout: Brepols, 1956), but she also takes more recent critical work on the extant manuscripts into account.

6. Musseter, "Type as Prophet," 50.

7. Paul Bradshaw, *Reconstructing Early Christian Worship* (Collegeville, MN: Liturgical Press, 2010), 117 (italics original). Cf. William L. Holladay, *The Psalms through Three Thousand Years: Prayerbook of a Cloud of Witnesses* (Minneapolis, MN: Fortress Press, 1996), 115: "By one count, there are fifty-five citations of the Psalms in the New Testament, counting parallels in the Gospels as individual items; and these are found in all sections of the New Testament. . . . Functionally, then, the Psalms are treated as Scripture."

8. Bradshaw, *Reconstructing Early Christian Worship*, 118.

9. Bradshaw, *Reconstructing Early Christian Worship*, 123.

10. Bradshaw, *Reconstructing Early Christian Worship*, 123.

11. See Athanasius, *The Life of Antony and the Letter to Marcellinus*, ed. and trans. Robert C. Gregg (New York: Paulist, 1980), 101–29.

12. Danielou, *Bible and the Liturgy*, 315.

13. Danielou, *Bible and the Liturgy*, 315.

14. Sigmund Mowinckel, *The Psalms in Israel's Worship*, trans. D. R. Ap-Thomas (Oxford: Blackwell, 1962), 1:62–63, 69.

15. Mowinckel, *Psalms in Israel's Worship*, 1:218. Mowinckel points to such oracles in Psalms 12:6; 60:8–10; 108:8–10.

16. Mowinckel, *Psalms in Israel's Worship*, 1:218.

17. Mowinckel, *Psalms in Israel's Worship*, 1:218–19.

18. 1 Samuel 10:5–6, 10. See Mowinckel, *Psalms in Israel's Worship*, 2:54, 66.

19. For Mowinckel's discussion of psalmic prophecy and prophetic psalms, see Mowinckel, *Psalms in Israel's Worship*, 2:53–73.

20. Jonathan Black, "Psalm Uses in Carolingian Prayer Books: Alcuin and the Preface to *De psalmorum usu*," *Mediaeval Studies* 64 (2002): 3.

21. Black notes: "In a 1936 article, André Wilmart determined that *De psalmorum usu* and *Officia per ferias*, two major collections of private devotion printed in editions of Alcuin's works, were in fact compiled during the half-century after Alcuin's death in 804" (Black, "Psalm Uses," 1). See André Wilmart, "Le manuel de prières de saint Gaulbert," *Revue bénédictine* 48 (1936): 236–65.

22. Black, "Psalm Uses," 5.

23. Gregory the Great, *Homiliae in Hiezechihelem prophetam*, ed. M. Adriaen, CCSL 142 (Turnhout: Brepols, 1971), 1.1.15, 12.

24. I quote Jonathan Black's translation.

25. Black, "Psalm Uses," 7.

26. See Jordan Wales, "'Sacrifice' in the Theology of Gregory the Great" (PhD diss., University of Notre Dame, 2014); on compunction, see Jean Leclercq, *The Love of Learning and the Desire for God: A Study of Monastic Culture*, trans. Catherine Misrahi (New York: Fordham University Press, 1974), 39.

27. See Adalbert de Vogüé, "One Last Trace of Psalm-Prayers?," in *Praise No Less Than Charity: Studies in Honor of M. Chrysologus Waddell*, ed. E. Rozanne Elder (Kalamazoo, MI: Cistercian Publications, 2002), 17–30.

28. Black, "Psalm Uses," 7.

29. Black, "Psalm Uses," 1–2.

30. See [Alcuin], *De psalmorum usu*, PL 101:465–508; Black, "Psalm Uses," 1.

31. Black, "Psalm Uses," 7.

32. Black, "Psalm Uses," 8, 60.

33. For biblical quotes in this chapter, I use *Biblia Sacra Iuxta Vulgatam Versionem*, ed. Roger Gryson (Stuttgart: Deutsche Bibelgesellschaft, 2007); *The Holy Bible* (RSV), Catholic ed. (San Francisco: Ignatius, 1966).

34. See Bertram Colgrave, "Introduction," in *Felix's "Life of Saint Guthlac,"* 16–19.

35. Colgrave, "Introduction," 57.

36. To view these roundels, digitized and in the public domain, see https://www.bl.uk/collection-items/guthlac-roll.

37. Colgrave, "Introduction," 12–14.

38. Colgrave, "Introduction," 14n2.

39. Colgrave, "Introduction," 14. On the tradition associating Guthlac with psalm use, see also Jane Roberts, "An Inventory of Early Guthlac Materials," *Mediaeval Studies* 32 (1970): 193–233, esp. 224–25.

40. *Felix's "Life of Saint Guthlac,"* chap. 22, 84/85; *Anglo-Saxon Version*, chap. 2, 18: "þa girnde he his sealmas to leornianne."

41. *Felix's "Life of Saint Guthlac,"* chap. 22, 84/85. The Old English translation does not render this ornate sentence.

42. *Felix's "Life of Saint Guthlac,"* chap. 23, 86/87; *Anglo-Saxon Version*, chap. 2, 18: "ða hæfde he his sealmas geleornod and canticas, and ymnas, and gebeda æfter cyriclicre endebyrdnysse."

43. *Felix's "Life of Saint Guthlac,"* chap. 27, 90/91; *Anglo-Saxon Version*, chap. 3, 24: "mid þam strælum þæs halgan sealmsanges."

44. *Felix's "Life of Saint Guthlac,"* chap. 29, 96/97; *Anglo-Saxon Version*, chap. 4, 28: "and efne swa witedomlice muþe þæt he sang and clypode to Gode, and cwæð: In tribulatione mea invocavi Dominum, et reliqua. Þæt ys on englisc:

Min Drihten on minre geswincnysse ic þe to clypige, ac gehyr þu me and gefultuma me on minum earfeðum."

45. Felix's "Life of Saint Guthlac," chap. 29, 96/97. The Old English version does not include Guthlac's use of Psalm 117.

46. Felix's "Life of Saint Guthlac," chap. 29, 96/97, with italics added; *Anglo-Saxon Version*, chap. 4, 30: "and him sona his heorte and his geþanc eall wæs onlihtod." The translator omits Felix's use of Psalm 17.

47. Felix's "Life of Saint Guthlac," chap. 28, 94/95; *Anglo-Saxon Version*, chap. 4, 26: "he nawiht ne onbyrigde buton berenne hlaf and wæter; and þonne sunne wæs on setle, þonne þigede he þa andlyfene þe he bigleofode." The Old English text does not translate the Latin word *ortonomia*, meaning "rule"; it simply indicates Guthlac's resolution ("Þa geþohte he . . .") thus to regulate his eating. On the monastic and eremitical regulation of food practices, see Sarah Downey, "Too Much of Too Little: Guthlac and the Temptation of Excessive Fasting," *Traditio* 63 (2008): 89–127, esp. 106–21.

48. Felix's "Life of Saint Guthlac," chap. 30, 100/101; *Anglo-Saxon Version*, chap. 5, 32/33.

49. Felix's "Life of Saint Guthlac," chap.30, 100/101; *Anglo-Saxon Version*, chap. 5, 32/34: "þa aras he sona and to Gode clypode, and hyne gebæd and þus cwæð: Syn mine fynd, min Drihten God, á on-hinder gecyrde."

50. Felix's "Life of Saint Guthlac," chap. 30, 100/101; *Anglo-Saxon Version*, chap. 5, 34: "Þa sona æfter þam wordum se awyrigeda gast efne swá smic beforan his ansyne áidlode."

51. Augustine, "Exposition of Psalm 55," in Augustine, *Expositions of the Psalms*, trans. Boulding, 3:95–96.

52. Felix's "Life of Saint Guthlac," chap. 31, 102/103; *Anglo-Saxon Version*, chap. 5, 36: "ac he mid witegiende muðe þus cwæð: Drihten me ys on þa swyþran healfe, forþon ic ne beo oncyrred fram þe."

53. Felix's "Life of Saint Guthlac," chap. 31, 106/107. Chapter 5 of the Old English translation refers to Guthlac as a "blessed man" ("se eadiga Guthlac," "se eadiga wer Guthlac").

54. Felix's "Life of Saint Guthlac," chap. 33, 108/109; *Anglo-Saxon Version*, chap. 5, 40: "ða comon him togeanes haligra gasta heap, and hi ealle sungon and þus cwædon: Ibunt de virtute in virtutem, et reliqua. Ðæt ys on englisc: Halige men gangeð of mægene on mægen."

55. Felix's "Life of Saint Guthlac," chap. 31, 108/109; *Anglo-Saxon Version*, chap. 5, 42: "Ða æfter þam wordum hi gewiton ða awyrgedan gastas efne swá smic fram his ansyne."

56. Felix's "Life of Saint Guthlac," chap. 34, 110/111; *Anglo-Saxon Version*, chap. 6, 44: "and [he] þone sealm sang: Exurgat deus et dissipentur, et reliqua." The translator here omits any equivalent expression for the Latin phrase "velut prophetico ore."

57. Felix's *"Life of Saint Guthlac,"* chap. 34, 110/111; *Anglo-Saxon Version,* chap. 6, 44: "þa gewiton hi saw swa smíc fram his ansyne."
58. Felix's *"Life of Saint Guthlac,"* chap. 36, 114/115; *Anglo-Saxon Version,* chap. 8, 46/47–48/49.
59. Felix's *"Life of Saint Guthlac,"* chaps. 37–40, 116–27; *Anglo-Saxon Version,* chaps. 9–11, 48/49–56/57.
60. Felix's *"Life of Saint Guthlac,"* chap. 35, 110/111; *Anglo-Saxon Version,* chap. 7, 44/45–46/47.
61. Felix's *"Life of Saint Guthlac,"* chap. 43, 132/133; chap. 44, 136/137; *Anglo-Saxon Version,* chaps. 14–15, 62/63–66/67.
62. Felix's *"Life of Saint Guthlac,"* chap. 46, 142/143; *Anglo-Saxon Version,* chap. 13, 60: "Eac se eadiga were Guðlac witedomlice gaste weox and fremede."
63. Felix's *"Life of Saint Guthlac,"* chap. 48, 148/149; *Anglo-Saxon Version,* chap. 18, 74/75–76/77.
64. Felix's *"Life of Saint Guthlac,"* chap. 50, 154/155; *Anglo-Saxon Version,* chap. 20, 80: "forþon þan eahtoþan dæge bið ende þære minre mettrumnysse."
65. Felix's *"Life of Saint Guthlac,"* chap. 49, 148/149; *Anglo-Saxon Version,* chap. 29, 76: "ic bæd God þæt he . . . þe gefultomode; and he þa mine béne gehyrde."
66. Felix's *"Life of Saint Guthlac,"* chap. 49, 150/151; *Anglo-Saxon Version,* chap. 29, 78: "forþon Drihten þe bið on fultume." Colgrave cites the following echoes of the Psalms: Ps. 27:7 (*Dominus adiutor*); Ps. 26:9 and Ps. 20:12 (*ne declines in consilium quod non potest stabiliri*); Ps. 89:9 (*dies defecerunt*); Ps. 143:4 (*dies illius velut umbra*); and Ps. 72:28 (*spem suam in Domino posuit*).
67. Felix's *"Life of Saint Guthlac,"* chap. 52, 164/165; *Anglo-Saxon Version,* chap. 21, 94. The translation abridges Aethelbald's prayer in such a way that the psalmic echoes are lost.
68. Felix's *"Life of Saint Guthlac,"* chap. 52, 164/165; *Anglo-Saxon Version,* chap. 21, 94. Again, the translation lacks the biblical echoes found in the Latin.
69. Felix's *"Life of Saint Guthlac,"* chap. 52, 166/167; *Anglo-Saxon Version,* chap. 21, 96. The translation of this episode ends with Guthlac's prophecy of Aethelbald's future kingdom and lacks the confirming sign of the food provision, but it does mention "signs" (*tacna*) wrought through Guthlac.
70. Felix's *"Life of Saint Guthlac"* chap. 29, 96/97; *Anglo-Saxon Version,* chap. 4, 28.
71. In endnotes to his edition of Athanasius's *Life of Antony,* Robert C. Gregg identifies citations of Pss. 117, 26, 67, 117, 89, 49, 38, 1, 19, 37, 9, and 124; see Athanasius, *The Life of Antony and the Letter to Marcellinus,* ed. and trans. Robert C. Gregg (New York: Paulist, 1980), 134–44. For a comparative study, see B. P. Kurtz, "From St. Anthony to St. Guthlac: A Study in Biography," *Modern Philology* 12 (1926): 103–46.

72. See Athanasius, *The Life of Antony*, ed. and trans. Gregg, para. 6, 35; para. 13, 41.

73. The Roman Rite for exorcism includes the following psalms: 53, 90, 67, 69, 117, 34, 30, 21, 3, 10, and 12; see *The Roman Ritual in Latin and English*, ed. and trans. Philip T. Weller (Milwaukee: Bruce Publishing Co., 1952), 2:158–229. For an ancient background study, see Craig A. Evans, "Jesus and Psalm 91 in Light of the Exorcism Scrolls," in *Celebrating the Dead Sea Scrolls: A Canadian Contribution*, ed. Peter W. Flint, Jean Duhaime, and Kyung S. Baek, Early Judaism and Its Literature 30 (Atlanta: Society of Biblical Literature, 2011), 541–55.

74. Roberts, "An Inventory of Early Guthlac Materials," 203. See also Kurtz, "From St. Anthony to St. Guthlac," 113.

75. See M. P. Ciccarese, "Le visioni di S. Fursa," *Romanobarbarica* 8 (1984–85): 232–303; Marina Smyth, "The Origins of Purgatory through the Lens of Seventh-Century Irish Eschatology," *Traditio* 58 (2003): 91–132, esp. 109–16; Marina Smyth, "The Body, Death, and Resurrection: Perspectives of an Early Irish Theologian," *Speculum* 83, no. 3 (2008): 531–71, esp. 553–54.

76. Bede, *The Ecclesiastical History of the English People*, ed. Judith McClure and Roger Collins, trans. Bertram Colgrave (Oxford: Oxford University Press, 1999), 140.

77. For a useful introduction, see Brian Daley, S.J., "Finding the Right Key: The Aims and Strategies of Early Christian Interpretation of the Psalms," in *Psalms in Community: Jewish and Christian Textual, Liturgical, and Artistic Traditions*, ed. Harold W. Attridge and Margot E. Fassler (Atlanta: Society of Biblical Literature, 2004), 189–206.

78. Walter Brueggemann, *The Prophetic Imagination*, 2nd ed. (1978; repr. Minneapolis, MN: Fortress, 2001), 2.

79. *Felix's "Life of Saint Guthlac,"* chap. 23, 86/87; *Anglo-Saxon Version*, chap. 2, 18/19.

80. Jesse D. Billett, *The Divine Office in Anglo-Saxon England, 597–c.1000* (London: Henry Bradshaw Society, 2014), 11.

81. Billett, *Divine Office in Anglo-Saxon England*, 108; for references to Aelfwald, see 103, 108; to Aethelbald, see 99. For the thesis of consolidation, Billett finds support in Catherine Cubitt, *Anglo-Saxon Church Councils, c. 650–c.850* (London: Leicester University Press, 1995), 125–52. Cubitt draws the same conclusion: "The evidence for Roman customs indicates that the canons of Clofesho should be seen as consolidating Romanization and not introducing it" (148).

82. Billett, *Divine Office in Anglo-Saxon England*, 108.

83. See Billett, *Divine Office in Anglo-Saxon England*, chart 2.1, 16–17. Amalarius is famous for his typological interpretation of the Mass and Office; see Amalar of Metz, *On the Liturgy*, Vol. 1, *Books 1–2*, and *On the Liturgy*, Vol. 2, *Books*

3–4, ed. Eric Knibbs, Dumbarton Oaks Medieval Library (Cambridge, MA: Harvard University Press, 2014). Knibbs builds upon the 1948 edition of Amalarius's *Liber Officialis* by J. Hanssens.

84. See Billett, *Divine Office in Anglo-Saxon England*, 32–36.
85. Billett, *Divine Office in Anglo-Saxon England*, 48, 112–13.
86. *Felix's "Life of Saint Guthlac,"* chap. 50, 153.
87. *Felix's "Life of Saint Guthlac,"* chap. 50, 152. See Billett, *Divine Office in Anglo-Saxon England*, 115–16.
88. Peter Lucas interprets this light as a symbolic reference to the Easter candle and the Holy Saturday vigil; see Lucas, "Easter, the Death of St. Guthlac, and the Liturgy for Holy Saturday in Felix's *Vita* and the Old English *Guthlac B*," *Medium Aevum* 61 (1992): 1–16.
89. *Felix's "Life of Saint Guthlac,"* chap. 50, 158/159.
90. See Franz-Rudolf Weinert, *Christi Himmelfahrt. Neutestamentliches Fest im Spiegel alttestamentlicher Psalmen: Zur Entstehung des römischen Himmelfahrtsoffiziums* (St. Ottilien Archabbey, Emming, Germany: Editions of St. Ottilien, 1987), 153–70.
91. Danielou, *Bible and the Liturgy*, 311.
92. Danielou, *Bible and the Liturgy*, 308, 311–12.
93. See *Felix's "Life of St. Guthlac,"* chaps. 30, 31, and 34.
94. Douglas Farrow, *Ascension Theology* (New York: T&T Clark, 2011), 64. See also Farrow, *Ascension and Ecclesia: On the Significance of the Doctrine of the Ascension for Ecclesiology and Christian Cosmology* (Grand Rapids, MI: William B. Eerdmans, 1999).
95. *Felix's "Life of Saint Guthlac,"* chap. 50, 154/155. The Latin text echoes Gregory the Great's *Dialogues*.
96. Peter Lucas argues that Felix's *Vita Sancti Guthlaci* evokes the Easter candle in the imagery of light that filled the hermitage at Guthlac's death during Easter Week; see Lucas, "Easter, the Death of St. Guthlac, and the Liturgy for Holy Saturday," esp. 8–11.
97. See Jane Roberts, ed., *The Guthlac Poems of the Exeter Book* (Oxford: Clarendon, 1979). On hagiography and the Office, see Thomas Heffernan, "The Liturgy and the Literature of Saints' Lives," in *The Liturgy of the Medieval Church*, 2nd ed., ed. Thomas J. Heffernan and E. Ann Matter (Kalamazoo, MI: Medieval Institute Publications, 2005), 65–94.
98. Stephan Borgehammar, "A Monastic Conception of the Liturgical Year," in Heffernan and Matter, eds., *The Liturgy of the Medieval Church*, 16n5. For a good introduction to the topic, see Joyce Bazire and James E. Cross, "Introduction," in *Eleven Old English Rogationtide Homilies*, ed. Joyce Bazire and James E. Cross (Toronto: University of Toronto Press, 1982), xv–xxxii. See also Joyce Hill,

"The *Litania maiores* and *minores* in Rome, Francia, and Anglo-Saxon England: Terminology, Texts, and Traditions," *Early Modern Europe* 9 (2000): 211–46.

99. John Harper, *The Forms and Orders of Western Liturgy from the Tenth to the Eighteenth Century* (Oxford: Clarendon, 1991), 152.

100. See Stephen J. Harris, "The Liturgical Context of Ælfric's Homilies for Rogation," in *The Old English Homily: Precedent, Practice, and Appropriation*, ed. Aaron Kleist (Turnhout: Brepols, 2007), 165.

101. Michael Lapidge, ed., *Anglo-Saxon Litanies of the Saints* (London: Henry Bradshaw Society, 1991), 12–13.

102. Michel Andrieu, ed., *Les ordines Romani du Haut Moyen Age* (Louvain: Spicilegium Sacrum Lovaniense, 1961), 5:317.

103. Harris, "The Liturgical Context of Ælfric's Homilies for Rogation," 163.

104. Roberts, "An Inventory of Early Guthlac Materials," 220.

105. Samantha Zacher, *Preaching the Converted: The Style and Rhetoric of the Vercelli Book Homilies* (Toronto: University of Toronto Press, 2009), 268, 229.

106. For the annotated Old English text, see *Vercelli Homilies IX–XXIII*, ed. Paul E. Szarmach (Toronto: University of Toronto Press, 1981), 97–101; for a modern English translation, see "Vercelli Homily XXIII," trans. Francis M. Clough, in *The Vercelli Book Homilies: Translations from the Anglo-Saxon*, ed. Lewis E. Nicholson (Lanham, MD: University of America Press, 1991), 155–59. Omitting the fourth temptation, the vision of the Britons, Homily 23 lacks the direct quotation of Psalm 67:1.

107. *Vercelli Book Homilies: Translations*, 159; *Vercelli Homilies IX–XXIII*, 99. Although the homiletic quality of the closing words is unmistakable, the translated excerpt from Felix's hagiography of Guthlac conspicuously lacks many other familiar homiletic features. Sarah Downey notes, however, that the demons' temptation of Guthlac to excessive fasting in chapter 30 of Felix's *Vita Sancti Guthlaci* parodies homiletic exhortations to fast in extant sermons for Lent and Rogationtide and uses the same biblical examples; see Downey, "Too Much of Too Little," 95–106.

108. See Michael Fox, "Vercelli Homilies XIX–XXI, the Ascension Day Homily in Cambridge, Corpus Christi College 162, and the Catechetical Tradition from Augustine to Wulfstan," in *New Readings in the Vercelli Book*, ed. Samantha Zacher and Andy Orchard (Toronto: University of Toronto Press, 2009), 254–79.

109. The poem *Elene* also exhibits homiletic features; see Éamonn Ó Carragáin, *Ritual and the Rood: Liturgical Images and the Old English Poems of the "Dream of the Rood" Tradition* (Toronto: Toronto University Press, 2005); Charles D. Wright, "The Pledge of the Soul: A Judgment Theme in Old English Homiletic Literature and Cynewulf's *Elene*," *Neuphilologische Mitteilungen* 91 (1990): 23–30.

110. Black, "Psalm Uses," 7.

276   Notes to Pages 38–40

CHAPTER TWO. Hexaemeral Miracles in Saint Aelred of Rievaulx's *Life of Ninian*

1. Marsha L. Dutton, "Introduction to Walter Daniel's *Vita Ælredi*," in Walter Daniel, *The Life of Ælred of Rievaulx*, trans. F. M. Powicke, Cistercian Fathers 57 (Kalamazoo, MI: Cistercian, 1994), 42. Cistercian Fathers series hereafter abbreviated as "CF."
2. See John MacQueen, *St. Nynia: A Study of Literary and Linguistic Evidence* (Edinburgh: Oliver and Boyd, 1961); Winifred W. MacQueen, "Miracula Nynie Episcopi," in *Transactions of the Dumfriesshire and Galloway Natural History and Antiquarian Society, 1959–1960* (Dumfries: Council of the . . . Society, 1961), 21–57. I thank Jean Truax for first directing me to these studies.
3. John MacQueen, "The Literary Sources for the Life of St. Ninian," in *Galloway: Land and Lordship*, ed. Richard D. Oram and Geoffrey P. Stell (Edinburgh: Scottish Society for Northern Studies, 1991), 17.
4. Winifred MacQueen, "Miracula Nynie Episcopi," 23.
5. See Aelred of Rievaulx, *The Life of Ninian*, in *The Lives of the Northern Saints*, trans. Jane Patricia Freeland, ed. Marsha L. Dutton, CF 71 (Kalamazoo, MI: Cistercian, 2006), chap. 8. Hereafter I cite the *Life* by chapter number. For the Latin text, see *Pinkerton's Lives of the Scottish Saints*, rev. W. M. Metcalfe (Paisley, Scotland: Alexander Gardner, 1889), 1:9–39.
6. Aelred, *Life of Ninian*, prologue.
7. Aelred, *Life of Ninian*, prologue.
8. See Charles Dumont's note 1 in Aelred of Rievaulx, *The Mirror of Charity*, trans. Elizabeth Connor OCSO, CF 17 (Kalamazoo, MI: Cistercian, 1990), 302.
9. Aelred, *Mirror of Charity*, 1.32.90–92, 142–44. For the Latin text, see Aelred of Rievaulx, *De speculo caritatis*, in *Opera Omnia*, Vol. 1, *Opera ascetica*, ed. A. Hoste, O.S.B., and C. H. Talbot, CCCM 1 (Turnhout: Brepols, 1971). The *Mirror of Charity* is conventionally regarded as Aelred's first literary work, but the *Life of Ninian* may, in fact, predate the *Mirror*; see Brian Patrick McGuire, *Brother and Lover: Ælred of Rievaulx* (New York: Crossroad, 1994), xvii, 42–43, 45. McGuire notes the absence of the *Life of Ninian* from the list of Aelred's works given by Walter Daniel in the *Vita Ailredi* and argues that it was excluded from the list because composed at King David's court, before the beginning of Aelred's life as a Cistercian. The exact dating of the *Mirror* is a difficult matter, however, as Charles Dumont has shown; see Dumont, "Ælred of Rievaulx: His Life and Works," in Aelred, *Mirror of Charity*, 11–66. If begun while Aelred was a young novice master (ca. 1142–43), its composition continued over a period of ten years. That extended range of time would encompass the later date usually ascribed to the *Life of Ninian* (ca. 1154), on the basis of Aelred's prologue to the *Life*, which suggests

its commissioning by a bishop or lord of Galloway, perhaps for an episcopal ordination at Whithorn.

10. See Marco Carlos Emerson Hernández, "Augustine and the Seeds of Creation and Recreation," chap. 1, in "The Seeds of Creation and New Creation: St. Thomas Aquinas and His Predecessors on the Generative Principles of Natural and Supernatural Life" (PhD diss., University of Notre Dame, 2014), 21–69. Emerson Hernández traces the influence of Augustine's thought upon, and its development by, subsequent theologians, who distinguished a wonder (*mirabilia*) from a miracle (*miraculum*) and disagreed with Augustine and with one another about whether or not God's work of creation was, strictly speaking, miraculous. See also Robert M. Grant, *Miracle and Natural Law in Graeco-Roman and Early Christian Thought* (Eugene, OR: Wipf and Stock, 2011).

11. Augustine, *De utilitate credendi/Über den Nutzen des Glaubes*, trans. Andreas Hoffman (Freiburg: Herder, 1992), chap. 34: "Miraculum, voco, quicquid arduum aut insolitum supra spem vel facultatem mirantis adparet" (180).

12. Augustine acknowledges that magicians and evil spirits can also perform wonders, but these do not concern us here. See John Hardon, S.J., "The Concept of Miracle from St. Augustine to Modern Apologetics," *Theological Studies* 15 (1954): 229–57, esp. note 2.

13. Augustine, *Confessions*, trans. Henry Chadwick (Oxford: Oxford University Press, 2008), 13.21 (30), 290.

14. Augustine, *The City of God*, trans. Marcus Dods (New York: Modern Library, 1950), 22.8, 819.

15. *City of God* 10.12, 318.

16. *City of God* 10.29, 336.

17. *City of God* 21.9, 780.

18. Augustine, *The Literal Meaning of Genesis*, 2 vols., trans. John Hammond Taylor, Ancient Christian Writers 41–42 (New York: Newman, 1982), 9.18.34, 42:94. See the insightful discussion of this remarkable passage in Emerson Hernández, *The Seeds of Creation and New Creation*, chap. 1.

19. *City of God*, 22.8.

20. *Conf.* 9.7 (16), 165.

21. *Conf.* 13.21 (30), 290.

22. On this point, see Hardon, "Concept of Miracle," 231; Peter Harrison, "Miracles, Early Modern Science, and Rational Religion," *Church History* 75, no. 3 (2006): 493–510, esp. 495–99.

23. *City of God*, 21.8, 776.

24. *City of God*, 21.8, 776.

25. Walter Daniel, *The Life of Ælred of Rievaulx*, trans. F. M. Powicke, CF 57 (Kalamazoo, MI: Cistercian, 1994), chap. 42.

278   Notes to Pages 42–44

26. Daniel, *Life of Ælred of Rievaulx*, chap. 51.
27. Daniel, *Life of Ælred of Rievaulx*, chap. 51.
28. Marsha L. Dutton, "Friendship and the Love of God: Augustine's Teaching in *Confessions* and Ælred of Rievaulx's Response in *Spiritual Friendship*," *American Benedictine Review* 56 (2005): 7.
29. See Aelred, *Mirror of Charity*, 1.28.79, 134 (where Aelred quotes *Conf.* 8.11.26) and 1.34.113, 157 (where *Conf.* 9.13.34 is quoted).
30. Dutton, "Introduction to Walter Daniel's *Vita Ælredi*," in Daniel, *Life of Ælred of Rievaulx*, 42.
31. Aelred, *Life of Ninian*, chap. 1; Daniel, *Life of Ælred*, chap., 2.
32. Aelred, *Life of Ninian*, chap. 1; Daniel, *Life of Ælred*, chap. 4.
33. Aelred, *Life of Ninian*, chap. 2; Daniel, *Life of Ælred*, chap. 14.
34. Aelred, *Life of Ninian*, chap. 2. The letter from Saint Bernard to Aelred that prefaces the *Mirror of Charity* shows the abbot's familiarity with Aelred's personal history at King David's court. Aelred probably met Bernard for the first time at Clairvaux while on his trip to Rome (Daniel, *Life of Ælred*, chap. 14).
35. Daniel, *Life of Ælred*, chap. 38; Aelred, *Life of Ninian*, chap. 6.
36. Aelred reports that Ninian brought masons with him from the Continent (Aelred, *Life of Ninian*, chap. 3).
37. The Bible describes the Israelites' building of the sanctuary in Exodus at God's command in language that recalls God's own work of creation in Genesis 1. See Everett Fox, trans., *The Five Books of Moses* (New York: Schocken, 1997), 484.
38. MacQueen, "Literary Sources for the Life of St. Ninian," 20.
39. John C. Eby, "Bringing the Vita to Life: Bede's Symbolic Structure of the Life of St. Cuthbert," *American Benedictine Review* 48 (1997): 316–38; Walter Berschin, "*Opus deliberatum ac perfectum*: Why Did the Venerable Bede Write a Second, Prose Life of St. Cuthbert?," in *Saint Cuthbert, His Cult, and His Community to AD 1200*, ed. Gerald Bonner, David Rollason, and Clare Stancliffe (Woodbridge, Suffolk: Boydell and Brewer, 1989), 95–102.
40. *City of God* 11.30, 375. See also Augustine, *On Christian Doctrine*, trans. D. W. Robertson Jr. (New York: Macmillan, 1968), 2.16.25: "An ignorance of numbers also causes many things expressed figuratively and mystically in the Scriptures to be misunderstood" (51).
41. MacQueen, "Literary Sources for the Life of St. Ninian," 21.
42. John MacQueen, *Numerology: Theory and Outline History of a Literary Mode* (Edinburgh: Edinburgh University Press, 1986), 58; *City of God* 11.30, 474–75. See also Ernst R. Curtius, *European Literature and the Latin Middle Ages*, trans. William R. Trask (New York: Pantheon, 1953), 501–9.
43. Aelred, *Mirror of Charity*, 1.20.57, 119–20.
44. Aelred, *Mirror of Charity*, 1.32.90–92, 142–44.

45. The *Miracula Nynie Episcopi* has only four of the six miracles found in book 1 of Aelred's *Life of Ninian*. John MacQueen admits that the fifth and sixth miracles may be "later additions" not found in the earliest source, but he suggests that the *Miracula* writer may simply have chosen to omit two miracles found in the original prose source (MacQueen, "Literary Sources for the Life of St. Ninian," 21). Aelred either discovered a biblical significance in the six miracles present in his source, or he added two miracles to an original four in order to establish and to develop a correlation in the *Life* to the days of creation.

46. Augustine, *Literal Meaning of Genesis*, 6.6.10–11, 41:184–85. Augustine concludes that humanity was created invisibly, as in a seed, on the sixth day; visibly (in sexed bodies, suitable for propagation) on the seventh.

47. Dorothy Glass, "*In Principio*: The Creation in the Middle Ages," in *Approaches to Nature in the Middle Ages*, ed. Lawrence D. Roberts, Medieval and Renaissance Texts and Studies 16 (Binghamton, NY: Center for Medieval and Renaissance Studies, 1982), 68.

48. Hugh of Saint Victor, *On the Sacraments of the Christian Faith*, trans. Roy J. Deferrari (Cambridge, MA: Medieval Academy of America, 1951), 1.10.8, 179.

49. Emile Mâle, *The Gothic Image: Religious Art in France of the Thirteenth Century*, trans. Dora Nussey (New York: Harper and Row, 1958), 29.

50. Glass, "*In Principio*," 71. See also Johannes Zahlten, *Creatio Mundi: Darstellungen der sechs Schöpfungstage und naturwissenschaftliches Weltbild im Mittelalter*, Stuttgarter Beiträge zur Geschichte und Politik 13 (Stuttgart: Klett-Cotta, 1979).

51. Glass, "*In Principio*," 73.

52. David L. Simon, "Comment," in Roberts, ed., *Approaches to Nature in the Middle Ages*, 105–6.

53. See Augustine, *Literal Meaning of Genesis*, 4.20, 37, 41:127–28.

54. Augustine's commentaries on Genesis—*De Genesi contra Manichaeos* (389), books 11–13 of *Confessions* (400–401), and *De Genesi ad litteram* (400–415)—return again and again to the questions of time and eternity and to the challenge of reconciling Sirach 18:1 and Genesis 1:1 with the counting of successive days in Genesis 1:3–2:4. On Augustine's engagement with Sirach 18:1, see Michael Gorman, "The Unknown Augustine: A Study of the Literal Interpretation of Genesis (*De Genesi ad litteram*)" (PhD diss., University of Toronto, 1974), 9–10.

55. Glass takes a somewhat different position vis-à-vis artistic representation in keeping with Augustine's doctrine of a simultaneous creation; see Glass, "*In Principio*," 72.

56. Glass, "*In Principio*," 79–82. This famous tapestry, perhaps originally intended for a dome, depicts the works of the six days in eight, not six, sections that encircle the Christ-Logos. A dove symbolizing the Spirit-Creator fills the section of

the circle directly above the Christ-Logos; beneath Christ appear an abundance of birds and fish, the creatures of the fifth day. This arrangement visually connects the prelude to the first day in Genesis 1 to Jesus's baptism at the Jordan and the start of his public ministry. The work of the sixth day (the creation of Adam, Adam's naming of the animals, and Eve's creation from Adam's side) is represented in two sections, one on the right and the other on the left. Two angels, representing the separation of light from darkness, occupy sections at opposite sides of the dove. Beneath the angel of light, a section depicts the separation of the waters above and below the firmament. At the opposite side of the circle, below the angel of darkness, the firmament appears amidst the waters.

57. Hildegard von Bingen wrote to Bernard of Clairvaux, who replied with a letter of encouragement and who apparently brought her writings to the attention of Pope Eugenius III (a Cistercian) in 1147, the same year when Aelred became abbot of Rievaulx.

58. The Rupertsberg Manuscript of *Scivias* has been lost, but the illuminations have been reconstructed, using photographs of the original; see Adelgundis Führkötter, *The Miniatures from the Book "Scivias"—"Know the Ways"—of St. Hildegard of Bingen from the Illuminated Rupertsberg Codex* (Turnhout: Brepols, 1977). See also *Hildegardis Bingensis "Scivias,"* ed. Adelgundis Führkötter, OSB, with the help of Angela Carlevaris, OSB, CCCM 43 and 43A (Turnhout: Brepols, 1978). I thank Bart Janssens for his assistance in the reproduction here of tabula 10 from that volume.

59. Hildegard of Bingen, *Scivias*, trans. Mother Columba Hart and Jane Bishop (New York: Paulist, 1990), 150.

60. On Hildegard and the hexaemeron, see Margot E. Fassler, *Cosmos, Liturgy, and the Arts in the Twelfth Century: Hildegard's Illuminated "Scivias"* (Philadelphia: University of Pennsylvania Press, 2023), 93–157. An alternative, horizontal arrangement (not depicted by Hildegard, but recommended by my colleague Daniel Machiela) would pair the creation of light on the first day with that of the sun and the moon on the fourth; the separation of the waters above and below the dome on the second day with the flying of created birds and the swimming of created fish on the fifth; and the separation of land and sea on the third day with the creation of land animals on the sixth.

61. Hildegard of Bingen, *Scivias*, 149.

62. Hildegard of Bingen, *Scivias*, 150.

63. I thank Mary J. Zore for permission to use this photograph of her artwork, which she kindly supplied.

64. The artist confirms this interpretation in her email message (June 15, 2021) to me: "Reflecting on the nature of the 'rest' of the Sabbath Day, I find it to be essentially a 'communing with God.' I felt the Bleeding Pelican served to foreshadow the Eucharist as a meeting place between God and man—a meeting place

given by the providential love of the Father, as well as through the self-sacrificing love of Christ, who creates and also re-creates through His sacrifice, which is renewed in the Mass."

65. On the interplay between the many saints and the one Christ, see Thomas Heffernan, *Sacred Biography: Saints and Their Biographers in the Middle Ages* (New York: Oxford University Press, 1988), 7.

66. Aelred, *Life of Ninian*, chap. 4; *Conf.* 3.8 (16), 46–47; 10.30 (41); 10.29 (64), 203–17.

67. *Conf.* 13.2 (3), 274.

68. Aelred, *Life of Ninian*, chap. 4.

69. Aelred, *Life of Ninian*, chap. 4.

70. *Conf.* 13.18 (22), 285.

71. Aelred, *Mirror of Charity*, 1.32.90, 142.

72. Aelred, *Mirror of Charity*, 1.32.90, 142.

73. *Conf.* 11.9 (11), 227.

74. Aelred, *Life of Ninian*, chap. 5.

75. Aelred, *Life of Ninian*, chap. 5.

76. MacQueen, "Miracula Nynie Episcopi," 23.

77. Aelred, *Life of Ninian*, chap. 5.

78. Aelred, *Life of Ninian*, chap. 5.

79. *Cassell's Latin Dictionary*, 5th ed. (New York: Macmillan, 1968), 303.

80. Augustine, *Sermons on the Liturgical Seasons*, trans. Mary Sarah Muldowney, RSM (New York: Fathers of the Church, 1959), 6.

81. Augustine, *Sermons on the Liturgical Seasons*, 13.

82. Augustine, *Sermons on the Liturgical Seasons*, 19.

83. Augustine, *Sermons on the Liturgical Seasons*, 25.

84. Aelred, *Mirror of Charity*, 1.32.91, 143.

85. Aelred, *Life of Ninian*, chap. 5; *City of God* 21.8, 776.

86. For a recent study, see Jacek Olesiejko, "Heaven, Hell and Middangeard: The Presentation of the Universe in the Old English *Genesis A*," *Studia Anglica Posnaniensia: International Review of English Studies* 45, no. 1(2009): 153–62, https://go.gale.com/ps/i.do?p=LitRC&u=googlescholar&id=GALE|A216412190&v=2.1&it=r&sid=LitRC&asid=e991dbaa.

87. Aelred, *Life of Ninian*, chap. 7.

88. *Conf.* 13.17 (20), 285.

89. Aelred, *Mirror of Charity*, 1.32.90, 142.

90. *Webster's Ninth New Collegiate Dictionary* (Springfield, MA: Merriam-Webster, 1988), 216.

91. *Cassell's Latin Dictionary*, 429.

92. *Conf.* 13.19 (24), 287.

93. *Conf.* 13.19 (24), 287.
94. *Conf.* 13.22 (32), 291–92.
95. *Conf.* 13.21 (31), 291.
96. *Conf.* 13.21 (31), 291.
97. Aelred, *Mirror of Charity*, 1.32.91, 143.
98. Aelred, *Life of Ninian*, chap. 9.
99. Aelred, *Life of Ninian*, chap. 9.
100. Aelred, *Life of Ninian*, chap. 9. I cite *Biblia Sacra iuxta Vulgatam Versionem*, 5th ed., ed. Robert Weber and Roger Gryson (Stuttgart: Deutsche Bibelgesellschaft, 2007).
101. *Conf.* 13.15 (16), 282.
102. *Conf.* 13.15 (18), 283.
103. *Conf.* 13.15 (16), 282.
104. Aelred, *Mirror of Charity*, 1.32.90, 142.
105. MacQueen, "Literary Sources for the Life of St. Ninian," 21.
106. Curiously, a version of this miracle occurs in Walter Daniel's *Letter to Maurice*, where we read that not a drop of rain fell upon Aelred when he slept for six or seven nights under a leaky roof in a hovel in Galloway (Daniel, "Letter to Maurice," in *Life of Ælred of Rievaulx*, 153–54). Daniel offers no interpretation of this phenomenon, apart from the witness it gives to Aelred's virtue in the last stage of his life.
107. Aelred, *Mirror of Charity*, 1.32.91, 142.
108. Aelred, *Mirror of Charity*, 1.32.91, 142–43.
109. Aelred, *Life of Ninian*, chap. 10.
110. Following and developing Augustine's idea of Sabbath rest, Aelred connects the stages in the growth of charity to three Sabbaths in *Mirror of Charity*, 3.2.3: "Let love of self, then, be man's first Sabbath, love of neighbor the second, and love of God the Sabbath of Sabbaths" (223).
111. *Conf.* 13.8 (9), 277.
112. *Conf.* 13.9 (10), 278.
113. MacQueen, "Literary Sources for the Life of St. Ninian," 21.
114. Aelred, *Life of Ninian*, chap. 10.
115. Aelred, *Life of Ninian*, chap. 10.
116. Augustine, *Expositions of the Psalms, 121–50*, trans. Maria Boulding, O.S.B., ed. Boniface Ramsey (Hyde Park, NY: New City Press, 2004), 6:511.
117. Augustine, *Expositions of the Psalms, 1–32*, trans. Maria Boulding, O.S.B., ed. John E. Rochelle, O.S.A. (Hyde Park, NY: New City Press, 2000), 1:67–70; Ambrose of Milan, *Commentary of Saint Ambrose on Twelve Psalms*, trans. Ide M. NiRiain (Dublin: Halcyon Press, 2000), 1–35.
118. *Conf.* 13.20 (26), 288.

119. *Conf.* 13.20 (28), 289.
120. *Conf.* 13.21 (29), 290.
121. Aelred, *Life of Ninian*, chap. 11.
122. Aelred, *Life of Ninian*, chap. 11.
123. Aelred, *Life of Ninian*, chap. 11.
124. *Conf.* 13.38 (53), 304.
125. Aelred, *Life of Ninian*, chap. 11. The short second book (chaps. 12–15) of *The Life of Ninian* recounts four posthumous miracle stories.
126. Aelred, *Life of Ninian*, chap. 11.
127. Aelred, *Life of Ninian*, chap. 6.
128. Aelred, *Life of Ninian*, prologue.

CHAPTER THREE. The Song of Songs and Saint Bernard of Clairvaux's *Life of Saint Malachy*

1. Aelred of Rievaulx, *The Life of Ninian*, in *The Lives of the Northern Saints*, trans. Jane Patricia Freeland, ed. Marsha L. Dutton, CF 71 (Kalamazoo, MI: Cistercian Publications, 2006), chap. 11.
2. Aelred, *Life of Ninian*, chap. 11.
3. Aelred, *Life of Ninian*, chap. 11.
4. Bernard of Clairvaux, *On the Song of Songs 1*, trans. Kilian Walsh, O.C.S.O., CF 4 (Kalamazoo, MI: Cistercians Publications, 1971), Sermon 3.1.1.
5. See Bernard of Clairvaux, *On the Song of Songs 2*, trans. Kilian Walsh, O.C.S.O., CF 7 (1976; repr. Kalamazoo, MI: Cistercian Publications 1983), Sermon 26.
6. Aelred, *Life of Ninian*, chap. 1.
7. Aelred, *Life of Ninian*, chap. 10.
8. Bernard of Clairvaux, *On the Song of Songs 1*, Sermon 1.4.8.
9. Shawn M. Krahmer, "The Virile Bride of Bernard of Clairvaux," *Church History* 69, no. 2 (2000): 323.
10. See John P. Bequette, "Reclaiming the Heritage of the Apostles: *Haereditas* in Bernard's *Life of Saint Malachy*," *Cistercian Studies Quarterly* 44, no. 3 (2009): 279–98; B. W. O'Dwyer, "St. Bernard as Historian: *The Life of St. Malachy of Armagh*," *Journal of Religious History* 10 (1978): 128–41.
11. Bernard of Clairvaux, *The Life and Death of St. Malachy the Irishman*, trans. Robert T. Meyer, CF 10 (Kalamazoo, MI: Cistercian Publications, 1978), chap. 29, para. 66, p. 84; chap. 1, para. 1, p. 15; Bernard of Clairvaux, *Vita Sancti Malachiae*, in *Sancti Bernardi Opera*, Vol. 3, *Tractatus et Opuscula*, ed. J. Leclercq and H. M. Rochais (Rome: Cistercian Publications, 1963), 29.66, 1.1. Hereafter in

284   Notes to Pages 63–65

citations I give the page number in Meyer's translation (CF 10), followed by the chapter and paragraph numbers given both in Meyer's translation and in the Latin edition of the *Vita Malachiae*.

On the historical relationship between Bernard and Malachy, see Marie Thérèse Flanagan, "St. Malachy, St. Bernard of Clairvaux, and the Cistercian Order," *Archivium Hibernicum* 68 (2015): 294–311.

12. Chrysogonus Waddell, "The Two Saint Malachy Offices from Clairvaux," in *Bernard of Clairvaux: Studies Presented to Dom Jean Leclercq*, ed. M. Basil Pennington, Cistercian Studies 23 (Washington, DC: Consortium Press, 1973), 123–50.

13. Bernard of Clairvaux, *Life and Death of St. Malachy*, CF 10:85; *Vita Malachiae* 30.67.

14. Martha G. Newman, "Contemplative Virtues and the Active Life of Prelates," in Bernard of Clairvaux, *On Baptism and the Office of Bishops*, CF 67 (Kalamazoo, MI: Cistercian Publications, 1974), 19.

15. Martha G. Newman, *Boundaries of Charity: Cistercian Culture and Ecclesiastical Reform, 1098–1180*, Figurae Reading Medieval Culture (Stanford, CA: Stanford University Press, 1996), 115, 169.

16. Bernard of Clairvaux, *On the Conduct and Office of Bishops*, in *On Baptism and the Office of Bishops*, trans. Pauline Matarasso, 77; Bernard of Clairvaux, Epistola 42, "Ad Henricium Senonensem archiepiscopum," in *Sancti Bernardi Opera*, Vol. 7, ed. Jean Leclercq and H. M. Rochais (Rome: Editiones Cisterciensis, 1974), 9.33.

17. Bernard of Clairvaux, *Five Books on Consideration: Advice to a Pope*, trans. John D. Anderson and Elizabeth T. Kennan, CF 37 (Kalamazoo, MI: Cistercian Publications, 1976), 104, 106; Bernard of Clairvaux, *De consideratione ad Eugenium papam tertiam libri quinque*, in *Sancti Bernardi Opera*, Vol. 3, *Tractatus et Opuscula*, ed. Jean Leclercq and H. M. Rochais (Rome: Editiones Cisterciensis, 1957), 3.5.19; 3.5.20.

18. Bernard of Clairvaux, "On the Conduct and Office of Bishops," CF 67:51; Letter 42, 3.11.

19. Bernard of Clairvaux, "On the Conduct and Office of Bishops," CF 67:51; Letter 42, 3.12.

20. Bernard of Clairvaux, "On the Conduct and Office of Bishops," CF 67:51; Letter 42, 3.11.

21. See Friedrich Ohly, *Hoheleid-Studien: Grundzüge einer Geschichte der Hoheliedauslegung des Abendlandes bis um 1200* (Frankfurt am Main: F. Steiner, 1958), 94–109; E. Ann Matter, *The Voice of My Beloved: The Song of Songs in Western Medieval Christianity* (Philadelphia: University of Pennsylvania Press, 1990), 86–122; Ann W. Astell, *The Song of Songs in the Middle Ages* (Ithaca, NY: Cornell University Press, 1990), 50–60.

22. See Ernst H. Kantorowicz, *The King's Two Bodies: A Study in Medieval Political Theology* (Princeton, NJ: Princeton University Press, 1957), 212–13, 215, 217; Uta-Renate Blumenthal, *The Investiture Controversy: Church and Monarchy from the Ninth to the Twelfth Century* (Philadelphia: University of Pennsylvania Press, 1988).

23. Megan McLaughlin, "The Bishop as Bridegroom: Marital Imagery and Clerical Celibacy in the Eleventh and Early Twelfth Centuries," in *Medieval Purity and Piety: Essays on Medieval Clerical Celibacy and Religious Reform*, ed. Michael Frassetto (New York: Garland, 1998), 229. McLaughlin cites the work of Robert L. Benson, *The Bishop-Elect: A Study in Medieval Ecclesiastical Office* (Princeton, NJ: Princeton University Press, 1968); George Duby, *Medieval Marriage: Two Models from Twelfth-Century France* (Baltimore: Johns Hopkins University Press, 1966); Jean Gaudemet, "Note sur le symbolisme medieval: Le marriage de l'evêque," *L'année canonique* 22 (1978): 71–80; James L. Brundage, *Law, Sex, and Christian Society in Medieval Europe* (Chicago: University of Chicago Press, 1987).

24. Bernard of Clairvaux, *Life and Death of St. Malachy*, CF 10:33–34; *Vita Malachiae* 8.16.

25. Bernard of Clairvaux, *Life and Death of St. Malachy*, CF 10:38; *Vita Malachiae* 10.19.

26. Bernard of Clairvaux, *Life and Death of St. Malachy*, CF 10:35; *Vita Malachiae* 8.17.

27. Bernard of Clairvaux, *Life and Death of St. Malachy*, CF 10:39; *Vita Malachiae* 10.20.

28. Bernard of Clairvaux, *Life and Death of St. Malachy*, CF 10:39; *Vita Malachiae* 10.21.

29. Bernard of Clairvaux, *Life and Death of St. Malachy*, CF 10:39; *Vita Malachiae* 10.20.

30. Bernard of Clairvaux, *Life and Death of St. Malachy*, CF 10:40; *Vita Malachiae* 10.21.

31. Bernard of Clairvaux, *Life and Death of St. Malachy*, CF 10:42; *Vita Malachiae* 12.24.

32. Bernard of Clairvaux, *Life and Death of St. Malachy*, CF 10:43; *Vita Malachiae* 12.25.

33. McLaughlin, "The Bishop as Bridegroom," 210–11.

34. Bernard of Clairvaux, *Life and Death of St. Malachy*, CF 10:50; *Vita Malachiae* 14.34.

35. Bernard of Clairvaux, *Life and Death of St. Malachy*, CF 10:50; *Vita Malachiae* 14.34.

36. On the latter, see Paul Beaudette, "'In the World but not of It': Clerical Celibacy as a Symbol of the Medieval Church," in Frassetto, ed., *Medieval Purity and Piety*, 23–46. According to Beaudette, "The definitive legislation of priestly

celibacy took place in the first half of the twelfth century in the canons of the First and Second Lateran Councils" (23).

37. Mary Carruthers, *The Craft of Thought: Meditation, Rhetoric, and the Making of Images* (Cambridge: Cambridge University Press, 2000), 117–18.

38. Carruthers, *The Craft of Thought*, 168, 130.

39. Bernard of Clairvaux, *Life and Death of St. Malachy*, CF 10:28; *Vita Malachiae* 5.11.

40. Fiona Griffiths, "Siblings and the Sexes within the Medieval Religious Life," *Church History* 77, no. 1 (2008): 35.

41. Griffiths, "Siblings and the Sexes," 53.

42. On this issue, Griffiths cites the work of Pearse Aidan Cusack, "St. Scholastica: Myth or Real Person?" *The Downside Review* 92 (1974): 145–59.

43. Bernard of Clairvaux, *Life and Death of St. Malachy*, CF 10:21; *Vita Malachiae* 3.6.

44. Bernard of Clairvaux, *Life and Death of St. Malachy*, CF 10:21; *Vita Malachiae* 3.6.

45. Bernard of Clairvaux, *Life and Death of St. Malachy*, CF 10:28; *Vita Malachiae* 5.11.

46. Bernard of Clairvaux, *Life and Death of St. Malachy*, CF 10:28; *Vita Malachiae* 5.11.

47. Bernard of Clairvaux, *Life and Death of St. Malachy*, CF 10:28; *Vita Malachiae* 5.11.

48. Bernard of Clairvaux, *Life and Death of St. Malachy*, CF 10:28; *Vita Malachiae* 5.11.

49. Bernard of Clairvaux, *Life and Death of St. Malachy*, CF 10:28; *Vita Malachiae* 5.11.

50. Bernard of Clairvaux, *Life and Death of St. Malachy*, CF 10:28; *Vita Malachiae* 5.11. "Since it was not his sister's soul but her sin he hated . . ."

51. Bernard of Clairvaux, *Life and Death of St. Malachy*, CF 10:28; *Vita Malachiae* 5.11.

52. See Bernard of Clairvaux, *Life and Death of St. Malachy*, CF 10:59, 61–62; *Vita Malachiae* 20.45–46; 21.47.

53. See Ann W. Astell, *Eating Beauty: The Eucharist and the Spiritual Arts of the Middle Ages* (Ithaca, NY: Cornell University Press), 27–61.

54. Bernard of Clairvaux, *Life and Death of St. Malachy*, CF 10:68–69; *Vita Malachiae* 25.54.

55. Bernard of Clairvaux, *Life and Death of St. Malachy*, CF 10:68–69; *Vita Malachiae* 25.54.

56. Bernard of Clairvaux, *Life and Death of St. Malachy*, CF 10:68–69; *Vita Malachiae* 25.54.

Notes to Pages 73–75   287

57. Bernard of Clairvaux, *Life and Death of St. Malachy*, CF 10:57; *Vita Malachiae* 18.42.

58. Bernard of Clairvaux, *Life and Death of St. Malachy*, CF 10:57; *Vita Malachiae* 19.43; CF 10:58; *Vita Malachiae* 19.44.

59. Bernard of Clairvaux, *Life and Death of St. Malachy*, CF 10:69–70; *Vita Malachiae* 25.55–56.

60. Bernard of Clairvaux, *Life and Death of St. Malachy*, CF 10:69; *Vita Malachiae* 25.55.

61. Bernard of Clairvaux, *Life and Death of St. Malachy*, CF 10:69; *Vita Malachiae* 25.55.

62. On Gregory the Great as the "Doctor of Compunction," see Bernard McGinn, *The Growth of Mysticism: Gregory the Great through the 12th Century*, Vol. 2 of *The Presence of God: A History of Western Christian Mysticism* (New York: Crossroad, 1994), 48–50.

63. Gregory the Great, *Dialogues* 3.34, *PL* 77:300; Gregory the Great, *Morals on the Book of Job* (Oxford: John Henry Parker, 1844), 3:1 (pt. 5), 56: "The one emotion excites tears of pain and sorrow, the other tears of joy."

64. See Gregory the Great, *Moralia in Iob* (Pt. 5), bk. 24, chap. 6.10–12, *PL* 76:291D–293B.

65. Gregory subdivides the lower and the higher streams of compunction each into two, for a total of four. See Gregory the Great, *Moralia in Iob* (Pt. 5), bk. 23, chap. 21.41–43, *PL* 76:275–77: "De quatuor modis justi in compunctione afficiuntur."

66. Bernard of Clairvaux, *On the Song of Songs 2*, Sermon 40:2–3, 200–201.

67. See Newman, *Boundaries of Charity*, 108: "By using the same descriptive language for their own monasteries as for Christian society as a whole, the Cistercians implied that the sense of caritas that they had developed within their communities could be extended to encompass all of Christendom."

68. Bernard of Clairvaux, *Life and Death of St. Malachy*, CF 10:47; *Vita Malachiae* 14.31.

69. Bernard of Clairvaux, *On the Conduct and Office of Bishops*, CF 67:50; Letter 42, 11 (emphasis added).

70. Bernard of Clairvaux, *On the Conduct and Office of Bishops*, CF 67:49; Letter 42, 9.

71. Bernard of Clairvaux, *On the Conduct and Office of Bishops*, CF 67:49; Letter 42, 10.

72. Bernard of Clairvaux, *On the Conduct and Office of Bishops*, CF 67:51; Letter 42, 11.

73. Bernard of Clairvaux, *On the Song of Songs 2*, Sermon 40:2–3, 200–201.

74. Bernard of Clairvaux, "Preface," in *Life and Death of St. Malachy*, 13.

288   Notes to Pages 75–80

75. Bernard of Clairvaux, Letter 343, to Pope Eugenius, in *The Letters of St. Bernard of Clairvaux*, trans. Bruno Scott James (Kalamazoo, MI: Cistercians Publications, 1998), 420.

76. Bernard of Clairvaux, *On the Song of Songs 3*, CF 31:122–23, Sermon 59, 2.3.

77. Bernard of Clairvaux, *On the Song of Songs 3*, CF 31:124–25, Sermon 59, 2.5–3.6.

78. Bernard of Clairvaux, *Life and Death of St. Malachy*, CF 10:82; *Vita Malachiae* 29.65.

79. Bernard of Clairvaux, *Life and Death of St. Malachy*, CF 10:82–83; *Vita Malachiae* 29, 65.

80. Bernard of Clairvaux, *Life and Death of St. Malachy*, CF 10:34; *Vita Malachiae* 8.16.

81. Bernard of Clairvaux, *Life and Death of St. Malachy*, CF 10:34; *Vita Malachiae* 8.16.

82. Bernard of Clairvaux, *Life and Death of St. Malachy*, CF 10:34; *Vita Malachiae* 8.17.

83. Bernard of Clairvaux, *Life and Death of St. Malachy*, CF 10:34; *Vita Malachiae* 8.16.

84. Bernard of Clairvaux, *On the Song of Songs 4*, trans. Irene Edmonds, CF 40 (Kalamazoo, MI: Cistercian Publications, 1980), Sermon 84.6, 192.

85. Bernard of Clairvaux, *On the Song of Songs 4*, Sermon 84.5.

86. Bernard of Clairvaux, *On the Song of Songs 4*, Sermon 76.3.7, 115.

87. Bernard of Clairvaux, *On the Song of Songs 4*, Sermon 76.3.7, 116.

88. Bernard of Clairvaux, *On the Song of Songs 4*, Sermon 76.3.8–4.9, 116–18.

89. Bernard of Clairvaux, *On the Song of Songs 4*, Sermon 77.1, 122.

90. Bernard of Clairvaux, *On the Song of Songs 4*, Sermon 77.4, 124–25.

91. Bernard of Clairvaux, *Life and Death of St. Malachy*, CF 10:34; *Vita Malachiae* 8.16.

92. See Bernard of Clairvaux, *Life and Death of St. Malachy*, 135n63.

93. Bernard of Clairvaux, *On Loving God*, CF 13B (Kalamazoo, MI: Cistercian Publications, 1995), 12; Bernard of Clairvaux, *De diligendo Deo*, in *Sancti Bernardi Opera*, Vol. 3 (Rome: Editiones Cistercienses, 1963), 3.10. Bernard refers his readers explicitly to this passage in Sermon 51.3.5, in *On the Song of Songs 3*, CF 31:44. In that sermon he gives a different interpretation, associating the left hand with the holy fear of punishment and the right hand with the hope of reward.

94. Bernard of Clairvaux, *On Loving God*, CF 13B:15; *De diligendo Deo*, 4.12.

95. Bernard of Clairvaux, *On the Song of Songs 1*, Sermon 10.4.6, 64–65.

96. Bernard of Clairvaux, *On the Song of Songs 1*, Sermon 12.1.1, 77.

97. Bernard of Clairvaux, *On the Song of Songs 1*, Sermon 12.1.1, 78.

98. Robert Meyer notes the *maneo/manus* pun in Bernard of Clairvaux, *Life and Death of St. Malachy*, 13n85.

99. Bernard of Clairvaux, *Life and Death of St. Malachy*, CF 10:16; *Vita Malachiae* 1.1.
100. Bernard of Clairvaux, *Life and Death of St. Malachy*, CF 10:16; *Vita Malachiae* 1.2.
101. Bernard of Clairvaux, *Life and Death of St. Malachy*, CF 10:41; *Vita Malachiae* 11.22.
102. Bernard of Clairvaux, *Life and Death of St. Malachy*, CF 10:64; *Vita Malachiae* 23.50.
103. Bernard of Clairvaux, *Life and Death of St. Malachy*, CF 10:67; *Vita Malachiae* 24.53.
104. Bernard of Clairvaux, *Life and Death of St. Malachy*, CF 10:68; *Vita Malachiae* 25.54.
105. Bernard of Clairvaux, *Life and Death of St. Malachy*, CF 10:91; *Vita Malachiae* 31.73.
106. Bernard of Clairvaux, *Life and Death of St. Malachy*, CF 10:92; *Vita Malachiae* 31.75.
107. Bernard of Clairvaux, "Sermon on the Passing of Saint Malachy, the Bishop," in *Life and Death of St. Malachy*, 99, para. 3.
108. Bernard of Clairvaux, "Sermon on the Passing of Saint Malachy, the Bishop," in *Life and Death of St. Malachy*, 99, para. 3.
109. Bernard of Clairvaux, *Life and Death of St. Malachy*, CF 10:85; *Vita Malachiae* 30.67.
110. Bernard of Clairvaux, *Life and Death of St. Malachy*, CF 10:88; *Vita Malachiae* 31.70.
111. Bernard of Clairvaux, *Life and Death of St. Malachy*, CF 10:11.
112. Bernard of Clairvaux, *Life and Death of St. Malachy*, CF 10:11.
113. Bernard of Clairvaux, *Life and Death of St. Malachy*, CF 10:12.
114. Bernard of Clairvaux, *Life and Death of St. Malachy*, CF 10:13.
115. Bernard of Clairvaux, *Life and Death of St. Malachy*, CF 10:13.
116. Bernard of Clairvaux, *Life and Death of St. Malachy*, CF 10:13.
117. Bernard of Clairvaux, *On the Song of Songs 1*, Sermon 3.1.1, 16. See also Sermon 1.5.9–10; 1.6.11.

CHAPTER FOUR. Eadmer's Parabolic *Life* and *History* of Saint Anselm of Canterbury

1. R. W. Southern, *Saint Anselm and His Biographer: A Study of Monastic Life and Thought, 1059–c.1130* (Cambridge: Cambridge University Press, 1963), 301. Added later (ca. 1119–25) by Eadmer, books 5 and 6 of the *Historia novorum* describe the dispute between Ralph d'Escures (archbishop of Canterbury, 1114–22)

and Thurstan (archbishop of York, 1119–40), over the primacy of their respective archiepiscopal sees.

2. As Southern reconstructs the composition process, Eadmer added the two posthumous miracle accounts to the first recension after making some stylistic changes to the *Life*. Fourteen years later, he added a book of *Miracles* to the *Life* as his "last tribute to Anselm" (Southern, *Saint Anselm and His Biographer*, 316, 318–19).

3. Eadmer, *The Life of St. Anselm, Archbishop of Canterbury, by Eadmer*, ed. and trans. R. W. Southern, Oxford Medieval Texts (Oxford: Clarendon, 1972), 1.

4. Southern, *Saint Anselm and His Biographer*, 333.

5. Charles C. Rozier, "Between History and Hagiography: Eadmer of Canterbury's Vision of the *Historia novorum in Anglia*," *Journal of Medieval History* 45, no. 1 (2019): 1.

6. Sally N. Vaughn, "Eadmer's *Historia novorum*: A Reinterpretation," in *Anglo-Norman Studies 10: Proceedings of the Battle Conference 1987*, ed. R. Allen Brown (London: Boydell Press, 1988), 260.

7. Rozier, "Between History and Hagiography," 1.

8. M. D. Chenu, *Nature, Man, and Society in the Twelfth Century: Essays on New Theological Perspectives in the Latin West*, ed. and trans. Jerome Taylor and Lester K. Little (1957; repr. Chicago: University of Chicago Press, 1968), 162–201.

9. Vaughn, "Eadmer's *Historia novorum*: A Reinterpretation," 288.

10. Eadmer, "Preface," in *Life of St. Anselm . . . by Eadmer*, 2.

11. Southern, *Saint Anselm and His Biographer*, 299, 300.

12. Southern, *Saint Anselm and His Biographer*, 300.

13. Southern, *Saint Anselm and His Biographer*, 301, 315.

14. Rozier, "Between History and Hagiography," 12.

15. Vaughn, "Eadmer's *Historia novorum*," 259–260, 283. It is unclear exactly what Vaughn imagines Eadmer to have destroyed and recopied—all the notes he had assembled, or only those he first separated out for future use in the *Life*?

16. Vaughn, "Eadmer's *Historia novorum*," 263.

17. See Vaughn, "Eadmer's *Historia novorum*," 263–69.

18. Rozier, "Between History and Hagiography," 10. Rozier finds "among the texts collected at Christ Church during Eadmer's lifetime" the following histories: the A and F versions of the Anglo-Saxon Chronicle, Josephus's *De antiquitate Iudacia*, Eusebius's *Historia ecclesiastica*, Orosius's *Historiae adversus paganos*, Eutropius's *Brevarium historiae* [plus surely Bede's *Historia ecclesiastica*] (9).

19. Rozier, "Between History and Hagiography," 9.

20. Antonia Gransden, *Historical Writing in England c. 550 to c. 1307* (Ithaca, NY: Cornell University Press, 1974), 129.

21. Southern, *Saint Anselm and His Biographer*, 330.

22. Gransden, *Historical Writing in England*, 132.

23. Gransden, *Historical Writing in England*, 133.

24. Southern, *Saint Anselm and His Biographer*, 334–36.
25. Michael Staunton, "Eadmer's *Vita Anselmi*: A Reinterpretation," *Journal of Medieval History* 23, no. 1 (1997): 2.
26. Thomas J. Heffernan, *Sacred Biography: Saints and Their Biographers in the Middle Ages* (New York: Oxford University Press, 1988), 31.
27. Jerome Taylor, "Introduction," in *The "Didascalicon" of Hugh of St. Victor: A Medieval Guide to the Arts*, trans. Jerome Taylor, Records of Western Civilization (1961; repr. New York, NY: Columbia University Press, 1991), 4.
28. Martin Grabmann, *Die Geschichte der scholastischen Methode* (Freiburg im Breisgau: Herdersche, 1909), 1:7.
29. See Alex J. Novikoff, "Anselm, Dialogue, and the Rise of Scholastic Disputation," *Speculum* 86 (2011): 387–418.
30. Hugh of Saint Victor, *"Didascalicon" of Hugh of St. Victor* 5.6, 140.
31. Hugh of Saint Victor, *"Didascalicon" of Hugh of St. Victor*, 5.6, 127.
32. See Lesley Janette Smith, *The Glossa Ordinaria: The Making of a Medieval Bible Commentary* (Leiden and Boston: Brill, 2009).
33. Hugh of Saint Victor, *"Didascalicon" of Hugh of St. Victor*, 5.7, 128–29.
34. Augustine, *On Christian Doctrine*, trans. D. W. Robertson Jr. (Indianapolis: Bobbs-Merrill, 1958), 1.36.40: "Whoever, therefore, thinks that he understands the divine Scriptures or any part of them so that it does not build the double love of God and of our neighbor does not understand it at all" (p. 30); 3.10.15: "But Scripture teaches nothing but charity, nor condemns anything except cupidity, and in this way shapes the minds of men" (p. 88).
35. Hugh of Saint Victor, *"Didascalicon" of Hugh of St. Victor* 5.7, 128.
36. Hugh of Saint Victor, *"Didascalicon" of Hugh of St. Victor* 5.7, 128.
37. Hugh of Saint Victor, *"Didascalicon" of Hugh of St. Victor* 4.2, 103.
38. This schema is original with Hugh; see Hugh of Saint Victor, *"Didascalicon" of Hugh of St. Victor*, 217n2.
39. Hugh of Saint Victor, *"Didascalicon" of Hugh of St. Victor* 4.2, 103–4.
40. Anselm first uses the expression "faith seeking understanding" (*fides quaerens intellectum*) in *Proslogion* 2–4.
41. Eadmer, *The Life of St. Anselm . . . by Eadmer*, 10. Southern provides facing-page Latin and English, counting the facing pages with a single page number. Hereafter quotes from the *Life* are cited parenthetically by abbreviation (*VA*) and page. For biblical quotes, I either follow Southern's translation of the *Holy Bible* as quoted in the *Life* or use the Douay-Rheims translation (Baltimore: John Murphy, 1899).
42. Eadmer, *Eadmer's "History of Recent Events in England" (Historia Novorum in Anglia)*, trans. Geoffrey Bosanquet (Philadelphia: Dufour, 1965), 2.103. Hereafter direct quotes from Bosanquet's translation are cited parenthetically by abbreviated title (*HN*) and the page number found in Eadmer, *Historia Novorum in Anglia*, ed. Martin Rule, Rolls Series (Wiesbaden: Kraus Reprint, 1965). Bosanquet's

translation cites in the margins the corresponding page in Rule's edition of the Latin text, from which I occasionally quote bracketed words and phrases.

43. Southern, "Introduction," in Eadmer, *The Life of St. Anselm . . . by Eadmer*, xii.

44. Southern, "Introduction," in Eadmer, *The Life of St. Anselm . . . by Eadmer*, xii. For the story, see *Life of Saint Anselm . . . by Eadmer*, 167–68.

45. Hugh of Saint Victor, *"Didascalicon" of Hugh of St. Victor*, 6.4, 140.

46. Hugh of Saint Victor, *"Didascalicon" of Hugh of St. Victor* 6.3, 135–36.

47. Hugh of Saint Victor, *"Didascalicon" of Hugh of St. Victor* 6.4, 141–42.

48. Hugh of Saint Victor, *"Didascalicon" of Hugh of St. Victor* 6.4, 141.

49. Beryl Smalley, *The Study of the Bible in the Middle Ages* (1952, 1964; repr. Notre Dame, IN: University of Notre Dame Press, 1978), 89.

50. Henri de Lubac, S.J., *Medieval Exegesis: The Four Senses of Scripture*, 3 vols., trans. Marc Sebank (Vol. 1), E. M. Macierowski (Vols. 2 and 3) Ressourcement: Retrieval & Renewal in Catholic Thought (Grand Rapids, MI: Wm. B. Eerdmans, 1998–2009), 3:222.

51. Chenu, *Nature, Man, and Society in the Twelfth Century*, 168. Gillian Evans concurs: "Increasingly, philosophical and historical theology went their separate ways"; see Evans, "St. Anselm and Sacred History," in *The Writing of History in the Middle Ages: Essays Presented to Richard William Southern*, ed. R. H. C. Davis and J. M. Wallace-Hadrill (Oxford: Clarendon, 1981), 209.

52. See Chenu, *Nature, Man and Society in the Twelfth Century*, 177–93; Bernard McGinn, *Visions of the End: Apocalyptic Traditions in the Middle Ages*, 2nd ed. (New York: Columbia University Press, 1998); Marjorie Reeves, *The Influence of Prophecy in the Later Middle Ages: A Study in Joachism* (1969; repr. Notre Dame, IN: University of Notre Dame Press, 1994). Among the apocalyptic interpreters of special concern here are Anselm of Havelberg (1100–1158), Gerhoh of Reichersberg (1093–1169), Rupert of Deutz (1075–1129), perhaps even Hildegard of Bingen (1098–1179) and Honorius Augustodunensis (ca. 1080–ca. 1151). Joachim of Fiore (ca.1135–1202) brings this trend to its florescence.

53. Kevin L. Hughes, "Chapter Five: Living the Word," in *The Oxford Handbook of Mystical Theology*, ed. Edward Howells and Mark MacIntosh (Oxford: Oxford University Press, 2020), 117–18.

54. Chenu, *Nature, Man, and Society in the Twelfth Century*, 166.

55. de Lubac, *Medieval Exegesis*, 2:201.

56. Hughes, "Chapter Five: Living the Word," 117.

57. On Hugh's adaptations of Gregory's image, see Hugh of Saint Victor, *"Didascalicon" of Hugh of St. Victor*, trans. Taylor, 223nn3, 9, 14; Franklin T. Harkins, *Reading and the Work of Restoration: History and Scripture in the Theology of Hugh of St. Victor* (Toronto: Pontifical Institute of Mediaeval Studies, 2009), 179.

58. Hughes, "Chapter Five: Living the Word," 118.
59. Hughes, "Chapter Five: Living the Word," 118.
60. Heffernan, *Sacred Biography*, 97.
61. On this rite, see James Monti, *A Sense of the Sacred: Roman Catholic Worship in the Middle Ages* (San Francisco: Ignatius, 2012), 186–89, 195.
62. Michel Andrieu, ed., *Le Pontifical romain au moyen-âge*, Vol. 3, *Le pontifical de Guillaume Durand*, Studi e testi 88 (Vatican City: Biblioteca Apostolica Vaticana, 1940), 386; cited in Monti, *Sense of the Sacred*, 195.
63. The most famous New Testament positive example is found in Acts 1:23–26, where lots are cast to choose either Mathias or Barsabbas to take the place of Judas. A negative example, seen as a fulfillment of the prophecy in Psalm 22:18, is the soldiers' casting of lots for the robe of Jesus at Calvary. Proverbs 18:18 recommends the use of lots for the solving of disputes.
64. See William E. Klingshirn, "Defining the *Sortes Sanctorum*: Gibbon, Du Cange, and Early Christian Lot Divination," *Journal of Early Christian Studies* 10, no. 1 (2002): 77–130.
65. One might also recall Jesus's opening of the scroll of the prophet Isaiah at the start of his public ministry, reading it aloud at Nazareth and declaring its fulfillment (Luke 4:16–21; Isa. 61:1–2, 58:6). On the importance of the eighth verse of Psalm 39 to its Christological reception in Hebrews, see Wolfgang Kraus, "Ps 40 (39):7–9 in the Hebrew Bible and the Septuagint, with Its Reception in the New Testament (Heb. 10:5–10)," in *XVI Congress of the International Organization for Septuagint and Cognate Studies: Stellenbosch, 2016*, ed. Gideon R. Kotzé, Wolfgang Kraus, and Michael N. van der Meer (Atlanta: Society of Biblical Studies, 2019), 119–32.
66. Ernst R. Wendland, "'Blessed is the man who will eat at the feast in the Kingdom of God' (Lk 14:15): Internal and External Intertextual Influence on the Interpretation of Christ's Parable of the Great Banquet," *Neotestamentica* 31, no. 1 (1997): 180.
67. Wendland, "Blessed is the man who will eat at the feast," 165. The roughly parallel parable in Matthew 22:1–14 adds eschatological significance. It specifies that the host is a king and the feast a wedding banquet for the king's son; it adds a third part, in which one of those who have been invited is expelled, because he lacks a wedding garment.
68. For a description of this rite and of the meaning of the pallium, see Monti, *Sense of the Sacred*, 202–3.
69. For the scholarly quarrel about Anselm's actions and motives at this crucial point in his career, see Richard W. Southern, "Sally Vaughn's Anselm: An Examination of the Foundations," *Albion* 20, no. 2 (1988): 181–204; Sally N. Vaughn, "Anselm: Saint and Statesman," *Albion* 20, no. 2 (1988): 205–20.

70. Grandsen agrees: "Eadmer's principal defence of Anselm was the picture he gave of his sanctity" (Grandsen, *Historical Writing in England*, 134).

71. Wendland notes: "The central theme of 'eating at a divinely hosted banquet'... is rather common in the Old Testament" (Wendland, "Blessed is the man who will eat at the feast," 171).

72. Southern notes this repetition and the "sense of the miraculous" (Eadmer, *Life of St. Anselm ... by Eadmer*, 7).

73. See, for example, Matthew 16:5–12, where Jesus warns his disciples about the "yeast of the Pharisees and Sadducees" after the miracles of multiplication of bread.

74. Chapter 37 of the Benedictine Rule allows for this occasional substitution, but Anselm makes "a full and habitual use of this liberty"; see Southern's note, Eadmer, *Life of St. Anselm ... by Eadmer*, 73.

75. Staunton, "Eadmer's *Vita Anselmi*," 8. For Anselm's own remarks on concession and the granting of permission, see Anselm of Canterbury, "Philosophical Fragments," in Anselm, *The Major Works*, ed. Brian Davies and G. R. Evans (Oxford: Oxford University Press, 2008), 475–76.

76. See Luke 5:1–11; John 21:1–14; Matt. 17:24–27.

77. The following chapter in the *Vita Anselmi* (1.18) also relates a wondrous catch of fish foreseen by Anselm.

78. Staunton, "Eadmer's *Vita Anselmi*," 6.

79. Southern, in Eadmer, *Life of St. Anselm ... by Eadmer*, 68n1.

80. Southern, in Eadmer, *Life of St. Anselm ... by Eadmer*, 68n1.

81. Staunton, "Eadmer's *Vita Anselmi*," 8.

82. Staunton, "Eadmer's *Vita Anselmi*," 13.

83. See *HN* 83–91.

84. Anselm lists four meanings of the verb "to will" and explains, "he who wills in the *permissive* manner, neither *effectuates* nor *approves* nor *concedes* that which he wills, but merely *permits* it in a non-approbative manner" (Anselm, "Philosophical Fragments," in *Major Works*, 476).

85. Staunton, "Eadmer's *Vita Anselmi*," 7.

86. The idea of being tested by fire is biblical. See, for example, 1 Pet. 1:7 and 1 Cor. 3:13. On a related theme, scripture speaks of gold being refined by fire; see Rev. 3:18 and Zech. 13:9.

87. Recall Southern's theory that Anselm must have discovered Eadmer's secret work on the hagiography in 1100 and commanded him to destroy it. Eadmer himself confesses the event and his only superficial obedience in the final chapter of the *Vita Anselmi*.

88. Thomas Becket as archbishop of Canterbury does indeed accept Anselm's archiepiscopate as setting the pattern and announcing the principles for his

own defense of the Church against the king's control. See the final section of this chapter. John of Salisbury bases his *Life of Anselm* on Eadmer's and goes on to write a *Life of Thomas Becket*, pairing the two saints, even as Eadmer groups Anselm with Saints Dunstan and Elphege—all of them archbishops of Canterbury.

89. The verses that include the apocryphal prayer of Azariah (that is, Abednego), the sung praises of the three, and an expanded description of what happens to them in the furnace are regarded by present-day scholars as later additions to the book of Daniel that were inserted between verses 3:23 and 3:24.

90. Eric Waldram Kemp, *Canonization and Authority in the Western Church* (London: Oxford University Press/Geoffrey Cumberlege, 1948), 62.

91. Kemp, *Canonization and Authority in the Western Church*, 67–69, 70.

92. On the development of this process, see Leonardas V. Gerulaitis, "The Canonization of Saint Thomas Aquinas," *Vivarium* 5, no. 1 (1967): 25–46.

93. Jay Rubenstein, "Liturgy against History: The Competing Visions of Lanfranc and Eadmer of Canterbury," *Speculum* 74, no. 2 (1999): 298.

94. Vaughn, "Eadmer's *Historia novorum*," 260; Southern, "Introduction," in Eadmer, *Life of Anselm . . . by Eadmer*, ix–xxiv.

95. See John of Salisbury, *Anselm and Becket: Two Canterbury Saints' Lives by John of Salisbury*, trans. Ronald E. Pepin (Turnhout: Brepols, 2009).

96. Southern, *Saint Anselm and His Biographer*, 338.

97. Kemp, *Canonization and Authority in the Western Church*, 83. See also E. W. Kemp, "Pope Alexander III and the Canonization of Saints," *Transactions of the Royal Historical Society* 27 (1945): 13–28.

98. Southern, *Saint Anselm and His Biographer*, 342.

99. Kemp, *Canonization and Authority in the Western Church*, 110–11; see Hostiensis, *In Tertium Decretalium Librum Commentaria*, on X.3.45 (*De reliquis* 1; *Audivimus*), Venice edition of 1581, facsimile (Torino: Bottega d'Erasmo, 1965), 172–73.

100. Donald S. Prudlo, *Certain Sainthood: Canonization and the Origins of Papal Infallibility in the Medieval Church* (Ithaca, NY: Cornell University Press, 2015).

CHAPTER FIVE. Saint Francis of Assisi as "New Evangelist" in Thomas of Celano's *Vita prima* and Bonaventure's *Legenda maior*

1. Gregory IX, *Mira circa nos*, in *Francis of Assisi: Early Documents* [*FA:ED*], ed. Regis Armstrong, J. A. Wayne Hellmann, and William Short (New York: New City Press, 1999–2001), 1:567. See Regis J. Armstrong, O.F.M., Cap., "*Mira Circa Nos*: Gregory IX's View of Saint Francis of Assisi," *Laurentianum* 25 (1984): 385–414.

2. Dominique Poirel, "L'écriture de Thomas de Celano: Une rhétorique de la rupture," *Franciscan Studies* 70 (2012): 73–99.

3. Matthew William Kozlowski, "The Man of Perfect Virtue: Bonaventure's *Legenda maior* in the Tradition of Hagiography" (PhD diss., Catholic University of America, 2020), 186 (emphasis original).

4. Thomas of Celano, *The Life of Saint Francis*, in *FA:ED*, 1:259, 266; *Analecta Franciscana*, 10:68, 74: "de toto corpore fecerat linguam." For references to the *Vita prima*, I use *Analecta Franciscana sive Chronica aliaque varia documenta ad historiam Fratrum Minorum spectantia*, Vol. 10, ed. College of St. Bonaventure (Quaracchi: Collegium S. Bonaventurae, 1926–1941); cited as *Analecta Franciscana*.

5. Dominic Monti notes that Francis never speaks of "the Bible" or "holy Scripture," in the sense of a book containing a collection of inspired writings. Rather, he speaks of "the Word of God," or of "the most holy words of the Lord," or "God's holy written words"; see Monti, "Do the Scriptures Make a Difference in Our Lives?" in *Franciscans and the Scriptures: Living the Word of God*, ed. Elise Saggan, OSF. (St. Bonaventure, NY: The Franciscan Institute, 2005), 4.

6. See Theophile Desbonnets, "The Franciscan Reading of the Scriptures," in *Francis of Assisi Today*, Concilium (series) 149, ed. Christian Duquoc and Casiano Floristan (New York: The Seabury Press, 1981), 37–45; Ignace Schlauri, "Saint François et la Bible: Essai Bibliographique de sa Spiritualité Évangélique," *Collectanea Franciscana* 40 (1970): 365–437; James P. Scullion, O.F.M., "A Love Supreme: The Writings of Francis of Assisi and the Gospel of John," in Saggan, ed., *Franciscans and the Scriptures*, 19–32.

7. "The Later Rule," in *FA:ED*, 1:99–100.

8. Bonaventure, *The Major Legend of Saint Francis*, in *FA:ED*, 2:559; *Opera omnia*, 8:516. For the Latin text of Bonaventure's writings, I use the Quaracchi edition, *Doctoris Seraphici S. Bonaventurae opera omnia*, 10 vols., edita studio et cura Collegii a S. Bonaventura, ad plurimos codices mss. emendate, anecdotis aucta, prolegomenis scholiis notisque illustrate (Quaracchi, Italy: Collegium S. Bonaventurae, 1882–1902).

9. John W. Coakley, "The Conversion of St. Francis and the Writing of Christian Biography, 1228–1263," *Franciscan Studies* 72 (2014): 27–71.

10. The editors' introduction to Celano's *Life of Saint Francis* asserts: "His knowledge of the monastic literary tradition as well as his theological acumen supports the opinion that he studied theology, perhaps at Monte Cassino, Rome or Bologna" (*FA:ED*, 1:171). The editors further speculate that Celano studied the liberal arts "possibly at the Benedictine monastery of Saint John the Baptist near Celano" (*FA:ED*, 1:171).

11. These parallels are duly footnoted by the editors of *FA:ED*. See also Sean Kincella, "Athanasius' *Life of Anthony* as Monastic Paradigm for the *First Life of St.*

Francis by Thomas of Celano: A Preliminary Outline," *Antonianum* 72 (2002): 541–56; Michael W. Blastic, "Francis and the Hagiographical Tradition," in *The Cambridge Companion to Francis of Assisi*, ed. Michael Robson (Cambridge: Cambridge University Press, 2012), 68–83. Since Bonaventure's *Legenda maior* borrows heavily from Thomas of Celano's *Vita prima*, the same typologies can also be found in the later work; see William Cook, "Tradition and Perfection: Monastic Typology in Bonaventure's *Life of St. Francis*," *American Benedictine Review* 33 (1982): 1–20; Luigi Pellegrini, "A Century Reading the Sources for the Life of Francis of Assisi," *Greyfriars Review* 7 (1993): 323–46; Emanuela Prinzivalli, "A Saint to be Read: Francis of Assisi in the Hagiographic Sources," *Greyfriars Review* 15 (2001): 253–98; Kozlowski, "Man of Perfect Virtue."

12. *FA:ED*, 1:183; *Analecta Franciscana*, 10:6. On the Augustinian quality of Celano's *Life of Saint Francis*, see Francis de Beer, *La conversion de St. François* (Paris: Éditions franciscaines, 1963).

13. Augustine in his youthful pride initially disdains the Bible for its lack of Ciceronian eloquence; then, as a Manichaean, he faults the Bible for its scandalous examples and supposedly false teaching.

14. See Augustine, *Conf.* 8.12 (29), 9.4 (8).

15. *FA:ED*, 1:293; *Analecta Franciscana*, 10:98–99.

16. *FA:ED*, 1:295; *Analecta Franciscana*, 10:101.

17. *FA:ED*, 2:648; *Opera omnia*, 8:548–49. Unlike Celano, who describes the canonization itself in a detailed, emotive manner, Bonaventure simply references "a great and solemn ceremony . . . too long to describe" (*FA:ED*, 2648; *Opera omnia*, 8:548–49).

18. *FA:ED*, 1:215; *Analecta Franciscana*, 10:29.

19. *FA:ED*, 1:221; *Analecta Franciscana*, 10:34.

20. Jacques Dalarun discovered in 2014 a manuscript (BnF nouv. Ac. Lat. 3245) of *The Life of Our Blessed Father Francis* (or *Vita brevior/Shorter Life*) by Thomas of Celano. See Dalarun, *The Rediscovered Life of St. Francis of Assisi*, ed. Jacques Dalarun, trans. Timothy J. Johnson (St. Bonaventure, NY: The Franciscan Institute, 2016); Sean L. Field, "New Light on the 1230s: History, Hagiography, and Thomas of Celano's 'The Life of Our Blessed Father Francis,'" *Franciscan Studies* 74 (2016): 239–47; Jacques Dalarun, "The New Francis in the Rediscovered Life (*Vita brevior*) of Thomas of Celano," in *Ordo et Sanctitas: The Franciscan Spiritual Journey in Theology and Hagiography. Essays in Honor of J. A. Wayne Hellmann, O.F.M. Conv.*, ed. Michael F. Cusato, Timothy J. Johnson, and Steven J. McMichael (Leiden: Brill, 2017), 32–46.

Another early text, *The Legend for Use in the Choir* (1230), has long been attributed to Thomas of Celano, but recent scholarship casts doubt upon his authorship. See Elenora Rava and Filippo Sedda, "Sulla trace dell'autore della *Legenda ad usum chori* beati Francisci: Analisi lessicografica e ipotesi di attribuzione," *Archivum Latinitas Medii Aevi* 69 (2011): 109–68.

21. Changing intended audiences and purposes affected Celano's successive hagiographic works. See Field, "New Light on the 1230s"; Jacques Dalarun, *The Misadventure of Francis of Assisi: Toward a Historical Use of the Franciscan Legends*, trans. Edward Hagman, O.F.M. Cap. (St. Bonaventure, NY: Franciscan Institute, 2002).

22. For a comparative study of two of Celano's *Vitae* of Francis, see Barbara Newman, "*Innova dies nostros, sicut a principio*: Novelty and Nostalgia in Thomas of Celano's First and Second Lives of St. Francis," *Franciscan Studies* 81 (2023). I thank Newman for sharing the text of her work with me before its publication.

23. Bonaventure, *Disputed Questions on Evangelical Perfection*, ed. Robert J. Karris, O.F.M., trans. Thomas Reist, O.F.M., and Robert J. Karris, O.F.M., Works of St. Bonaventure 13 (Saint Bonaventure, NY: The Franciscan Institute, 2008), 141; *Opera omnia*, 5:150 (emphasis added).

24. Bonaventure, *Disputed Questions*, 93; *Opera omnia*, 5:136.

25. Bonaventure, *Disputed Questions*, 148; *Opera omnia*, 5:152.

26. On Bonaventure's contribution to the doctrine of papal infallibility, see Brian Tierney, *Origins of Papal Infallibility, 1150–1350: A Study in the Concepts of Infallibility, Sovereignty, and Tradition in the Middle Ages* (Leiden: Brill, 1988), 82–92. On the intertwined issues of biblical and papal authority, see Ian Christopher Levy, *Holy Scripture and the Quest for Authority in the Later Middle Ages* (Notre Dame, IN: University of Notre Dame Press, 2012); Levy, *Introducing Medieval Biblical Interpretation: The Senses of Scripture in Premodern Exegesis* (Grand Rapids, MI: Baker Academic, 2018), esp. 263–79.

27. For another approach to this topic, see John V. Apczynski, "What Has Paris to Do with Assisi? The Theological Creation of a Saint," in *Finding Saint Francis in Literature and Art*, ed. Cynthia Ho, Beth A. Mulvaney, and John K. Downey (New York: Palgrave Macmillan, 2009), 79–93.

28. Robert J. Karris, O.F.M., "Introduction," in Bonaventure, *Disputed Questions*, 19. Karris does not expand upon this insight beyond noting the apocalyptic theme in the *Legenda maior* of Francis as the angel of the sixth seal (Rev. 7:2) (*FA:ED* 2:527; *Opera omnia*, 8:504) as being related to the theme of the *viri spirituales* ("spiritual men") in Bonaventure, *Disputed Questions*.

29. Karris lists eighteen references to Matthew, chapters 5 and 6. Bonaventure cites Jesus's instructions to his disciples in Matthew 10 five times; see Bonaventure, *Disputed Questions*, 338.

30. Wayne Hellmann, O.F.M., Conv., "A Theology of Preaching—A Theology of Transformation: The *Life of St. Francis* by Thomas of Celano," in *Franciscans and Preaching: "Every Miracle from the Beginning of the World Came about through Words,"* ed. Timothy J. Johnson (Leiden: Brill, 2012), 59–69.

31. *FA:ED* 1:201; *Analecta Franciscana*, 10:19.
32. *FA:ED*, 1:202; *Analecta Franciscana*, 10:19.
33. *FA:ED*, 1:202; *Analecta Franciscana*, 10:19.
34. *FA:ED*, 1:187–88; *Analecta Franciscana*, 10:9.
35. In a similar change, Bonaventure relates that Christ himself speaks directly to Francis from the cross at San Damiano, telling him to repair the church (*FA:ED*, 2:536; *Opera omnia*, 8:508). In Celano's *Vita prima*, by contrast, Francis simply begins to repair the dilapidated church, "aided by the grace of the Most High" (*FA:ED*, 1:196–97; *Analecta Franciscana*, 10:16–17).
36. Curiously, neither Thomas of Celano nor Bonaventure mentions that Francis previously served as a soldier and suffered as a prisoner of war in Perugia. They refer to Francis's long illness as instrumental in his process of conversion, but they offer no explanation for its onset. Modern historians diagnose Francis's illness, at least in part, as post-traumatic stress syndrome (PTSD). See Augustine Thompson, O.P., *Francis of Assisi: A New Biography* (Ithaca, NY: Cornell University Press, 2012), 9–11, 176–78. Francis's troubling dream of weapons piled up in his father's storehouse—a dream refashioned and given allegorical significance by Bonaventure—has a nightmarish quality in Celano's telling that suggests Francis's memory of wartime experiences. Francis misinterprets the dream as an omen of his future success as a soldier.
37. *FA:ED*, 2:533; *Opera omnia*, 8:506.
38. *FA:ED*, 1:185; *Analecta Franciscana*, 10:8.
39. *FA:ED*, 1:187; *Analecta Franciscana*, 10:9.
40. Coakley, "Conversion of St. Francis," 29.
41. *FA:ED*, 2:542; *Opera omnia*, 8:510 (italics appear in the quoted translation).
42. *FA:ED*, 2:543; *Opera omnia*, 8:510.
43. *FA:ED*, 1:210; *Analecta Franciscana*, 10:25.
44. *FA:ED*, 2:544; *Opera omnia*, 8:510.
45. *FA:ED*, 2:631; *Opera omnia*, 8:542; *FA:ED*, 1:262–63; *Analecta Franciscana*, 10:71.
46. *FA:ED*, 2:547; *Opera omnia*, 8:511.
47. *FA:ED*, 2:547; *Opera omnia*, 8:512.
48. *FA:ED*, 1:204; *Analecta Franciscana*, 10:22. Cf. *FA:ED* 2:612–13; *Opera omnia*, 8:535.
49. *FA:ED*, 2:612–13; *Opera omnia*, 8:535–36.
50. *FA:ED*, 1:251–52; *Analecta Franciscana*, 10:61–62.
51. *FA:ED*, 1:248; *Analecta Franciscana*, 10:57.
52. *FA:ED*, 1:248; *Analecta Franciscana*, 10:57.
53. *FA:ED*, 1:250–51; *Analecta Franciscana*, 10:59–60. Celano relates that Francis extended this reverence to words and individual letters found in different

sources (e.g., correspondence, admonitions, pagan texts), since they also — as he understood — bore a fragmentary witness to the biblical Word of God, to the holy name, and to the very power (God-given) of human thought and expression.

54. *FA:ED*, 2:590; *Opera omnia*, 8:527.

55. *FA:ED*, 2:534; *Opera omnia*, 8:507; cf. *FA:ED*, 1:195; *Analecta Franciscana*, 10:16.

56. *FA:ED*, 1:254; *Analecta Franciscana*, 10:63.

57. *FA:ED*, 1:255; *Analecta Franciscana*, 10:63.

58. *FA:ED*, 1:256; *Analecta Franciscana*, 10:64.

59. *FA:ED*, 1:256; *Analecta Franciscana*, 10:64.

60. *FA:ED*, 2:610; *Opera omnia*, 8:535.

61. Monti, "Do the Scriptures Make a Difference in Our Lives?," 12.

62. *FA:ED*, 1:262–63; *Analecta Franciscana*, 10:71.

63. *FA:ED*, 2:631; *Opera omnia*, 8:542.

64. *FA:ED*, 1:264; *Analecta Franciscana*, 10:72.

65. *FA:ED*, 2:632; *Opera omnia*, 8:543.

66. *FA:ED*, 2:634; *Opera omnia*, 8:543.

67. *FA:ED*, 1:277–78; *Analecta Franciscana*, 10:85.

68. *FA:ED*, 2:643; *Opera omnia*, 8:547.

69. *FA:ED*, 1:284–86; *Analecta Franciscana*, 10:91–92.

70. *FA:ED*, 2:644–45; *Opera omnia*, 8:547.

71. See André Vauchez, "The Stigmata of St. Francis and Its Medieval Detractors," *Greyfriars Review* 13 (1999): 66–89; Octavian Schmucki, *The Stigmata of St. Francis of Assisi: A Critical Examination in Light of Thirteenth-Century Sources* (St. Bonaventure, NY: The Franciscan Institute, 1991).

72. See Bernard McGinn, "Apocalypticism and Church Reform, 1100–1500," in *The Continuum History of Apocalypticism*, ed. Bernard J. McGinn, John J. Collins, and Stephen J. Stein (New York: Continuum, 2003), 273–98; Penn R. Szittya, *The Antifraternal Tradition in Medieval Literature* (Princeton, NJ: Princeton University Press, 1986), 11–61.

73. Robert Karris notes that in *De periculis*, William of Saint-Amour pointedly challenges the credentials of "those who preach on the basis of the authority of the Lord Pope," arguing that the mendicants have not been "sent" to preach (Rom. 10:15) either by the bishops as successors of the apostles or by the parish priests, who are successors of the seventy-two disciples of Luke 10 (see Karris, "Introduction," in Bonaventure, *Disputed Questions*, 11).

74. See David Burr, *Olivi and Franciscan Poverty: The Origins of the "Usus Pauper" Controversy* (Philadelphia: University of Pennsylvania Press, 1989). Olivi's commentary on Apocalypse was condemned by Pope John XXII in 1326, perhaps together with his *Lectura super Matthaeum* (1279–80).

75. According to Bonaventure, the apostles and their disciples preached and worked miracles, thereby destroying idolatry, in the first age; the learned doctors in the second age countered heresies; the lovers of holy poverty, freely chosen, strike against the "avarice that reigns above all at the end of the world" (*Disputed Questions*, 133; *Opera omnia*, 5:147–48).

76. For Bonaventure's refutation of these and other objections, see *Disputed Questions*, 97–158; *Opera omnia*, 5:136–55.

77. William of Saint-Amour, *Quaestio de Mendicitate*, appendix in Bonaventure, *Disputed Questions*, 329.

78. *FA:ED*, 1:201; *Analecta Franciscana*, 10:19; *FA:ED*, 2:542; *Opera omnia*, 8:510.

79. Bonaventure, *Disputed Questions*, 95; *Opera omnia*, 5:136. See also appendix in *Disputed Questions*, 287.

80. See Bonaventure, *Disputed Questions*, 58, 77; *Opera omnia*, 5:125, 131.

81. Bonaventure, *Disputed Questions*, 77–79; *Opera omnia*, 5:131.

82. Bonaventure, *Disputed Questions*, 94; *Opera omnia*, 5:136.

83. Bonaventure, *Disputed Questions*, 97–102; *Opera omnia*, 5:137–39.

84. David A. Clairmont, "Bonaventure on Moral Motivation: Trajectories of Exemplification in His Treatments of Voluntary Poverty," *Journal of the Society of Christian Ethics* 25, no. 2 (2005): 116.

85. See Malcolm Lambert, *Franciscan Poverty: The Doctrine of the Absolute Poverty of Christ and the Apostles in the Franciscan Order, 1210–1323* (London: SPCK, 1961).

86. Kevin Madigan, "Aquinas and Olivi on Evangelical Poverty: A Medieval Debate and Its Modern Significance," *The Thomist* 61 (1997): 584.

87. Kozlowski, *Man of Perfect Virtue*. Kozlowski emphasizes a continuous theme of virtue within hagiographic tradition. Without denying that continuity, I place emphasis on what is distinctive in Bonaventure's theology of justification.

88. On the theo-aesthetic coupling of expression with impression in Bonaventure's *Legenda maior*, see Ann W. Astell, *Eating Beauty: The Eucharist and the Spiritual Arts of the Middle Ages* (Ithaca, NY: Cornell University Press, 2006), 128.

89. On this topic of divine and human authorship, discussed at greater length later in this chapter and in chapter 8 of this book, see Alfred Durand, "Inspiration of the Bible," *The Catholic Encyclopedia* (New York: Robert Appleton Co., 1910), 8:45–50. Durand points to Thomas Aquinas's treatment of prophecy in *ST* II-II, q. 171 and q. 174.

90. See Alastair J. Minnis, *The Medieval Idea of Authorship: Scholastic Literary Attitudes in the Later Middle Ages*, 2nd ed. (Philadelphia: University of Pennsylvania Press, 2012).

91. Gregory the Great, "Preface," in *Morals on the Book of Job* (Oxford: John Henry Parker, 1844), Vol. 1, pts. 1 and 2, 15.

92. See Minnis, *Medieval Idea of Authorship*, 72, 80–81, 94–95, 110–12, 126–27. On the divine inspiration of prophets, see Aquinas, *ST* II-II, qq. 171–74.

93. Coakley, "The Conversion of St. Francis," 28.

94. Coakley, "The Conversion of St. Francis," 28.

95. *FA:ED*, 2:530; *Opera omnia*, 8:506.

96. *FA:ED*, 1:182–83; *Analecta Franciscana*, 10:5–6.

97. *FA:ED*, 1:184; *Analecta Franciscana*, 10:7.

98. *FA:ED*, 2:530; *Opera omnia*, 8:506; *FA:ED*, 1:202; *Analecta Franciscana*, 10:19.

99. Michael G. Lawler, "Grace and Free Will in Justification: A Textual Study in Aquinas," *The Thomist* 35, no. 4 (1971): 604. The actual maxim reads, *facienti quod in se est, Deus non denegat gratiam* ("To the one who does what is in him [meaning: the best he can do], God does not deny grace"). The maxim respects human free will and God's justice, but it does not imply that God is under an external obligation to give grace, which remains God's free gift.

100. Bonaventure, *Breviloquium*, trans. Dominic Monti (St. Bonaventure, NY: The Franciscan Institute, 2005), 5.3.5, 181; *Opera omnia*, 5:255.

101. On the dialogue between Bonaventure and Aquinas on this topic, see Lawler, "Grace and Free Will in Justification."

102. Lawler summarizes the difference of their opinions thus: "Man must prepare himself for justification, Bonaventure taught.... The general rule is that man must dispose himself by a preparation which precedes the act of justification [IV *Sent*. D.17, q. 1, a. 2; q. 3, corp. et ad 1 and 2]. St. Thomas is of another opinion. True, every adult must prepare himself for the grace of justification; but this preparation need not necessarily precede the infusion of grace, it suffices if it accompanies it" (Lawler, "Grace and Free Will," 602).

103. Aquinas, *ST* I-II, q. 114, a. 3 c; quoted in Lawler, "Grace and Free Will," 621.

104. *FA:ED*, 1:217; *Analecta Franciscana*, 10:30.

105. *FA:ED*, 1:282; *Analecta Franciscana*, 10:89–90. For a fine commentary on Celano's moral allegory, see J. A. Wayne Hellmann, O.F.M., Cap., "The Seraph in Thomas of Celano's *Vita prima*," in *That Others May Know and Love: Essays in Honor of Zachary Hayes, O.F.M.*," ed. Michael F. Cusato, O.F.M., and F. Edward Coughlin, O.F.M. (St. Bonaventure, NY: The Franciscan Institute, 1997), 23–41.

106. See Ewert Cousins, *Bonaventure and the Coincidence of Opposites* (Chicago: Franciscan World Press, 1978), 43; Regis J. Armstrong, O.F.M., Cap., "Towards an Unfolding of the Structure of St. Bonaventure's *Legenda maior*," *The Cord* 39 (1989): 3–17; Richard K. Emmerson and Ronald B. Herzman, "The *Legenda maior*: Bonaventure's Apocalyptic Francis," in *The Apocalyptic Imagination in Me-*

dieval Literature (Philadelphia: University of Pennsylvania Press, 1992), 36–75; Bernard McGinn, *The Flowering of Mysticism: Men and Women in the New Mysticism, 1200–1350*, Vol. 3 of *The Presence of God: A History of Western Christian Mysticism* (New York: Crossroad, 1998), 94; Astell, *Eating Beauty*, 106–13.

107. *FA:ED*, 2:558–59; *Opera omnia*, 8:516.

108. Jacques-Guy Bougerol, "The Moral Reflection of Saint Francis and Saint Bonaventure," trans. Michael Cusato, O.F.M., with Girard Etzkom, in Cusato and Coughlin, eds., *That Others May Know and Love*, 43.

109. See Rudolf Hofmann, *Die heroische Tugend: Geschichte und Inhalt eines theologischen Begriffes* (Munich: Kösel & Rastet, 1933).

110. For a recent study of the Matthean beatitudes, see William Mattison III, *The Sermon on the Mount and Moral Theology: A Virtue Perspective* (Cambridge: Cambridge University Press, 2017).

111. See Astell, *Eating Beauty*, 106–13.

112. *FA:ED*, 2: 560; *Opera omnia*, 8:516.

113. Aquinas, *ST* I-II, q. 61, a. 5.

114. Aquinas, *ST* I-II, q. 61, a. 5.

115. Aquinas, *ST* I-II, q. 69, a. 1.

116. Bonaventure, *Breviloquium*, 5.4.1, trans. Monti, 183; *Opera omnia*, 5:256. For a helpful discussion, see Antonino Poppi, O.F.M., "The Gifts of the Holy Spirit according to Bonaventure," trans. Solanus M. Benfatti, C.F.R., *The Dunwoodie Review* 35 (2012): 154–72.

117. Bonaventure, *Breviloquium*, 5.4.3; *Opera omnia*, 5:256. See Poppi, "The Gifts of the Holy Spirit," 157–58. For this discussion, Poppi relies on Bonaventure's *Commentary on the Sentences*. See 3 *Sent.*, d. 34, p. 1, a. 1, q. 1 (Bonaventure, *Opera Omnia* 3:735–39) and q. 2 (*Opera omnia*, 3:739–41).

118. *FA:ED*, 2:577; *Opera omnia*, 8:523.

119. Bonaventure, *Breviloquium*, 5.6.2, 191; *Opera omnia*, 5:258.

120. Bonaventure, *Commentary on the Gospel of Luke, Part 1*, ed. and trans. Robert J. Karris, O.F.M., Works of St. Bonaventure 8 (St. Bonaventure, NY: The Franciscan Institute, 2011), 490, 512, 513. Cited as Bonaventure, *Commentary on Luke*.

121. Bonaventure, *Commentary on Luke*, 512. The seven gifts are wisdom, understanding, counsel, fortitude, knowledge, piety, and fear of the Lord.

122. Bonaventure, *Commentary on Luke*, 481–82.

123. Bonaventure, *Commentary on Luke*, 497.

124. Bonaventure, *Commentary on Luke*, 498.

125. Bonaventure, *Commentary on Luke*, 512–13.

126. Bonaventure, *Commentary on Luke*, 535–36, 497.

127. *FA:ED*, 2:638; *Opera omnia*, 8:545. For the referenced visions, see *FA:ED*, 2:532, 534, 536, 545, 556, and 557; *Opera omnia*, 8:506, 507, 508, 511, and 515.

128. *FA:ED*, 2:545; *Opera omnia*, 8:511.
129. *FA:ED*, 2:556; *Opera omnia*, 8:515.
130. *FA:ED*, 2:557; *Opera omnia*, 8:515.
131. Katherine Wrisley Shelby, "*A Christo sub specie Seraph*: Revisiting St. Bonaventure's Theology of the Stigmata," *Cithara* 61, no. 1 (2021): 27.
132. Bonaventure, *Breviloquium*, prologue, 1–3; *Opera omnia*, 5:201.
133. "The tropological meaning lets us know what we should resolutely do; the allegorical meaning, what we should truly believe; the anagogical meaning, what we should desire for our eternal delight" (Bonaventure, *Breviloquium*, prologue, 5; *Opera omnia*, 5:206).
134. Bonaventure, *Breviloquium*, prologue, 4; *Opera omnia*, 5:206.
135. The Spirit's gifts effect (1) the overcoming of vice; (2) the strengthening of natural powers (rational and emotional); (3) the aiding of the cardinal and theological virtues; (4) conformity with Christ in his suffering; (5) effectiveness in action; (6) advancement in contemplation; (7) the combining of action with contemplation (Bonaventure, *Breviloquium*, 5.5.5, 187–90; *Opera omnia*, 5:257–58).
136. Bonaventure, *Breviloquium*, 5.5.5, 188–89; *Opera omnia*, 5:257.
137. Bonaventure, *Commentaria in Quatuor Libros Sententiarum*, 3 *Sent.* III, d. 34, p. 1, a. 2, q. 1; *Opera omnia* 3:744–45. In the second list of pairings, not given in the *Breviloquium*, Bonaventure associates the gifts with different ways of aiding the three theological virtues efficiently: understanding and knowledge both aiding faith; wisdom and piety aiding charity; fear and fortitude aiding hope. To all of these, counsel is superadded as a general aid.
138. Bonaventure, *Breviloquium*, 5.6.2, 192; *Opera omnia*, 5:258.
139. These three vices of concupiscence recall 1 John 2:16: "the lust of the flesh, the lust of the eyes, and the boastful pride of life."
140. Mourning as a love-longing or languishing for eternal union with God is an aspect of the fourfold compunction delineated by Gregory the Great, *Morals on the Book of Job* 3.1:35–38, 56; Bernard McGinn, *The Growth of Mysticism: Gregory the Great through the 12th Century*, Vol. 2 of *The Presence of God: A History of Western Christian Mysticism* (New York: Crossroad, 1994), 2:48–50.
141. *Breviloquium*, 5.6.3, 192; *Opera omnia*, 5:259.
142. *Breviloquium*, 5.6.5, 194; *Opera omnia*, 5:259.
143. *Breviloquium*, 5.6.5, 194; *Opera omnia*, 5:259.
144. The editors of the early documents note that *austeritas* is a rare term in Bonaventure's writings, appearing only in the *Legenda maior*, in his *Commentary on Luke*, and in several sermons (see their footnote, *FA:ED*, 2:560). In a sermon for Quadragesima, Bonaventure calls austerity "the beginning of human reparation" (*Opera omnia*, 9:208).
145. Bonaventure, *Breviloquium*, 5.5.5, 193; *Opera omnia*, 5:259. Bonaventure here links poverty of spirit with humility and the fear of the Lord.

146. See *FA:ED*, 2:581, note a.
147. Poppi, "Gifts of the Holy Spirit," 164. See Bonaventure, *De donis*, collatio 3; *Opera omnia*, 5:468.
148. Astell, *Eating Beauty*, 113.
149. Bonaventure, *Breviloquium*, 5.8.5, 202; *Opera omnia*, 5:262. See Hyacinth Ennis, "The Primacy of the Virtue of Charity in Morality according to Saint Bonaventure," *Antonianum* 50 (1975): 418–56; Krijin Pansters, *Franciscan Virtue: Spiritual Growth and the Virtues in Franciscan Literature and Instruction of the Thirteenth Century* (Leiden: Brill, 2012).
150. Bonaventure, *Breviloquium*, 5.6.5, 193; *Opera omnia*, 5:259.
151. *FA:ED*, 2:612; *Opera omnia*, 8:530.
152. Bonaventure, *Breviloquium*, 5.5.5, 194; *Opera omnia*, 5:259.
153. *FA:ED*, 2:622; *Opera omnia*, 8:539.
154. *FA:ED*, 2:623; *Opera omnia*, 8:539.
155. Bonaventure, *Breviloquium*, 5.5.5, 194; *Opera omnia*, 5:259.
156. Ewert Cousins, "Introduction," in *Bonaventure*, trans. Ewert Cousins, Classics of Western Spirituality (Mahwah, NJ: Paulist, 1978), 43–44.
157. *FA:ED*, 2:635; *Opera omnia*, 8:544.
158. In the prologue to the *Legenda maior*, Bonaventure explicitly likens Francis to the angel of the sixth seal in Revelations 7:2, and he uses angelic imagery elsewhere to describe the saint. Tradition names nine choirs of angels in three ascending sets: angels, guardian angels, principalities, powers, virtues, dominations, thrones, cherubim, and seraphim.
159. *FA:ED*, 2:639; *Opera omnia*, 8:545.
160. Joseph Ratzinger, *The Theology of History in St. Bonaventure*, trans. Zachary Hayes, O.F.M. (Chicago: Franciscan Herald Press, 1971), 68. Ratzinger notes that Bonaventure distinguishes between the divine inspiration of the scriptures and their revelation(s) of divine truth in a manner that differs from modern usage of the two terms, which tends to treat them as synonymous: "The Bonaventurian concept of *revelatio* (and *inspiratio, manifestatio, apertio*) is not immediately compatible with similar concepts in modern theology" (Ratzinger, *Theology of History in St. Bonaventure*, 58).
161. For Bonaventure's teaching on the spiritual senses, see Ann W. Astell, "A Discerning Smell: Olfaction among the Senses in St. Bonaventure's *Long Life* of St. Francis," *Franciscan Studies* 67 (2009): 91–131; Karl Rahner, "The Doctrine of the 'Spiritual Senses' in the Middle Ages," trans. David Morland, O.S.B., in *Theological Investigations* 16:109–208 (New York: Crossroad, 1979); Hans Urs von Balthasar, *The Glory of the Lord: A Theological Aesthetics*, Vol. 2, *Studies in Theological Style: Clerical Styles*, trans. Andrew Louth, Francis McDonagh, and Brian McNeil, C.R.V., ed. John Riches (San Francisco: Ignatius, 1983), 319–25; Stephen Fields, S.J., "Balthasar and Rahner on the Spiritual Senses," *Theological Studies* 57 (1996): 224–41.

162. Ratzinger, *Theology of History*, 7. See collation 2.13–19, in Bonaventure, *Collations on the Six Days*, ed. and trans. José de Vinck, in *The Works of Bonaventure* (Paterson, NJ: St. Anthony Guild Press, 1970), 5:28–31; *Opera omnia*, 5:338–39. See also collation 13.9–13, in *Collations on the Six Days*, 188–91; *Opera omnia*, 5:389–90.

163. Ratzinger, *Theology of History*, 7.

164. Ratzinger, *Theology of History*, 7. See collation 14.17, in Bonaventure, *Collations on the Six Days*, 209; *Opera omnia*, 5:396.

165. Augustine lists the Rules of Tychonius in *De doctrina Christiana*, 3.30.42–3.37.56; see Augustine, *On Christian Doctrine*, trans. D. W. Robertson Jr. (Indianapolis: Bobbs-Merrill, 1958), 104–17.

166. Collation 15.10, in Bonaventure, *Collations on the Six Days*, 222; *Opera omnia*, 5:400.

167. Augustine reconciled the idea of a simultaneous creation of heaven and earth by God with the idea of a progressive unfolding of creatures through the concept of the *rationales seminales*, understood to be germinal principles present already in the formless waste described in Genesis 1:1–2.

168. Ratzinger, *Theology of History*, 7.

169. Ratzinger, *Theology of History*, 71.

170. Ratzinger, *Theology of History*, 68.

171. Collation 15.12, in Bonaventure, *Collations on the Six Days*, 223; *Opera omnia*, 5:400. On Francis and the angel of the sixth seal, see Ratzinger, *Theology of History*, 33–38. On Bonaventure as a Franciscan Joachite, see Marjorie Reeves, *The Influence of Prophecy in the Later Middle Ages: A Study in Joachimism* (1969; repr. Notre Dame, IN: University of Notre Dame Press, 1993), 180; Ratzinger, *Theology of History*, 14.

172. Hugh of Saint Victor, *The "Didascalicon" of Hugh of St. Victor: A Medieval Guide to the Arts*, trans. Jerome Taylor (New York: Columbia University Press, 1991), 4.2 (103–4).

173. Ratzinger, *Theology of History*, 81.

CHAPTER SIX. Heroic Virtue in Blessed Raymond of Capua's *Life of Catherine of Siena*

1. Raymond of Capua, *The Life of Catherine of Siena*, trans. Conleth Kearns, O.P. (Wilmington, DE: Michael Glazier, 1980), 19; Raymond of Capua, "De S. Catharina Senensi, virgine de poenitentia S. Dominici," in *AASS*, ed. Godefridus Henschenius and Daniel van Papenbroeck, editio novissima, ed. Joanne Carnandet (Paris: V. Palmé, 1866), Vol. 12 (Aprilis III): 858.

2. Raymond's exegesis of verses from the Song of Songs with reference to Catherine is relatively scant in comparison to that of William Flete, whose long panegyric (1382) in praise of Catherine on the second anniversary of her death concludes with many citations of the Song, along with a rich array of other biblical passages; see William Flete, "Sermo in reverentiam B. Catherinae de Senis," trans. Michael Benedict Hackett, in Michael Benedict Hackett, O.S.A., *William Flete, O.S.A., and Catherine of Siena: Masters of Fourteen Century Spirituality* (Villanova, PA: Augustinian Press, 1992), 185–221.

3. Catherine of Siena's revelations were approved by Pope Gregory XIII (1572–85), as being in conformity with the Church's doctrine. A. Poulain explains, "There are two kinds of revelations: (1) universal revelations, which are contained in the Bible or in the *depositum* of Apostolic tradition transmitted by the Church. These ended with the preaching of the Apostles and must be believed by all; (2) particular or private revelations which are constantly occurring among Christians" (Poulain, "Revelations, Private," in *The Catholic Encyclopedia* (New York: Robert Appleton Co., 1912), 13:5.

4. Silvia Nocentini, "The *Legenda maior* of Catherine of Siena," in *A Companion to Catherine of Siena*, ed. Carolyn Muessig, George Ferzoco, and Beverly Mayne Kienzle (Leiden: Brill, 2012), 343.

5. Conleth Kearns, O.P., "Introduction" to Raymond of Capua, *Life of Catherine of Siena*, lviii.

6. In 1376, Catherine herself actively promoted Jacobus's cult in plague-stricken Varagine. On this point, Suzanne Noffke, O.P., cites Blessed Raymond of Capua, *Opuscula et Litterae* (Rome, 1895), 25–30.

7. Kenneth L. Woodward, *Making Saints* (New York: Simon and Schuster, 1996), 68: "The Avignoise popes (1309–1377) transformed the Roman Curia into an efficient bureaucracy. Under their canonical reforms, the procedures for canonization took on the explicit form of a full-blown legal trial between the petitioners, represented by an official procurator, or prosecutor of the cause, and the pope, represented by a new curial official, the 'Promoter of the Faith,' eventually to be more popularly known as 'the Devil's Advocate.'" See also Eric Waldram Kemp, *Canonization and Authority in the Western Church* (London: Geoffrey Cumberlege, 1948).

8. Nocentini, "The *Legenda maior* of Catherine of Siena," 344.

9. Nocentini, "The *Legenda maior* of Catherine of Siena," 344.

10. Augustine, *The City of God*, trans. Marcus Dods (New York: Modern Library, 1950), 10.21 (326).

11. Woodward, *Making Saints*, 393. For the Aristotelean *locus classicus*, see *Nicomachean Ethics* 7.1, where Aristotle, quoting Homer, opposes "brutishness" to "superhuman virtue, a heroic and divine kind of nature"; see *The Basic Works of Aristotle*, ed. Richard McKeon (New York: Random House, 1941), 1036.

12. Aquinas, *ST*, I-II, a. 61, a. 5. Following Macrobius and Plotinus, and departing somewhat from Aristotle, Thomas distinguishes four kinds of moral virtues. The "exemplar virtues" are those found in the mind of God. The "social virtues" belong to humans in accord with their nature as social animals. In between these two sets of virtues—divine and naturally human—are two additional kinds of virtues: the "perfecting" or "cleansing" virtues, on the one hand, and those of the "perfect" or "purified" souls, on the other. The former are the virtues of those "on their way" toward God and "tending towards the Divine similitude"; the latter belong to contemplative souls, whose thoughts are directed to God alone.

13. By the time of the Renaissance, "heroic virtue" was a technical term for the degree of holiness requisite for beatification and canonization. According to Woodward, "The official procedures for canonization established in 1642 by Pope Urban VIII solidified a genuine paradigm shift in the way that holiness was to be understood and accepted. . . . Among other requirements, Urban stipulated that candidates for sainthood must be shown to have practiced the classic Christian virtues, as these had been defined and codified by Aquinas and other Scholastic theologians" (Woodward, *Making Saints*, 225). Prospero Lambertini (later Pope Benedict XIV) composed the standard work on the criteria for canonization: *De beatificatione Servorum Dei et de Beatorum canonizatione* (Bologna, 1734–38). See K. V. Truhlar, "Virtue, Heroic," in *New Catholic Encyclopedia*, 2nd ed. (Washington, DC: Catholic University of America Press, 2002), 14:554–55. For a study of heroic virtue in Renaissance literature, see John M. Steadman, "Heroic Virtue and the Divine Image in *Paradise Lost*," *Journal of the Warburg and Courtauld Institute* 22, no. 1/2 (1959): 88–105.

14. Edith Wyschogrod, *Saints and Postmodernism: Revisioning Moral Philosophy* (Chicago: University of Chicago Press, 1990), highlights precisely this provocative quality in the lives of saints such as Catherine.

15. Raymond takes up these four charges systematically in part 2, chapter 5, paras. 172–77, but passing references to her critics occur throughout the *Life*.

16. Raymond of Capua, "De S. Catharina Senensi, virgine de poenitentia S. Dominici," pt. 1, chap. 9, para. 91, in *AASS*, 12:875; trans. Kearns, 83. Hereafter I refer to Raymond's *Life of Saint Catherine* parenthetically by paragraph number. The numbering of paragraphs is continuous throughout the *Life*. Kearns's translation, which I use in this book, conveniently preserves the numbering in the *Legenda maior* of Saint Catherine, as found in *AASS*, Vol. 12.

17. For references to Mary Magdalene in the *Life*, see paras. 12, 45, 64, 126, 173, and 185.

18. See Ingrid Maisch, *Mary Magdalene: The Image of a Woman through the Centuries*, trans. Linda M. Maloney (Collegeville, MN: Liturgical Press, 1998); Jacobus de Voragine, *The Golden Legend: Readings on the Saints*, trans. William Granger Ryan (Princeton, NJ: Princeton University Press, 1993), 1:376. Jacobus

summarizes Saint Ambrose's composite account of Mary Magdalene's life, based on the Gospels.

19. See chapter 7 in this book on Raymond and Catherine as readers of Jacobus's *Legenda aurea*.

20. The extent to which Catherine's theology and spirituality is properly called either Augustinian or Thomistic is a matter of scholarly debate; see Hackett, *William Flete, O.S.A., and Catherine of Siena*, esp. 107–18.

21. At the fountainhead of the historical critique is Robert Fawtier, *Sainte Catharine de Sienne: Essai de critique des sources*, 2 vols. (Paris: E. de Boccard, 1921–1930); Robert Fawtier and Louis Canet, *La double expérience de Catherine Benincasa* (Paris: Gallimard, 1948).

22. See, esp., Karen Scott, "St. Catherine of Siena, 'Apostola,'" *Church History* 61 (April 1992): 34–46; Scott, "'Io Catarina': Ecclesiastical Politics and Oral Culture in the Letters of Catherine of Siena," in *Dear Sisters: Medieval Women and the Epistolary Genre*, ed. Karen Cherewatuk and Ulrike Wiethaus (Philadelphia: University of Pennsylvania Press, 1993), 87–121; Scott, "Catherine of Siena and Lay Sanctity in Fourteenth-Century Italy," in *Lay Sanctity, Medieval and Modern: A Search for Models*, ed. Ann W. Astell (Notre Dame, IN: University of Notre Dame Press, 2000), 77–90.

23. See Sofia Boesch Gajano and Odile Redon, "La *Legenda maior* di Raimondo da Capua, costruzione di una santa," in *Atti del simposio internazionale Cateriniano-Bernardiniano, Siena, 17–20 aprile 1980*, ed. Domenico Maffei and Paolo Nardi (Siena: Accademia Senese degli Intronati, 1982), 15–36; Heather Webb, "St. Catherine of Siena's Heart," *Speculum* 80, no. 3 (2005): 802–17; Karen Scott, "Mystical Death, Bodily Death: Catherine of Siena and Raymond of Capua on the Mystic's Encounter with God," in *Gendered Voices: Medieval Saints and Their Interpreters*, ed. Catherine M. Mooney (Philadelphia: University of Pennsylvania Press, 1999), 136–67. F. Thomas Luongo summarizes in broad strokes the basis for this feminist critique: "Raymond's challenge in this long and highly sophisticated work of hagiography was to reconcile Catherine's exceptionally active and public career with the standard expectations of female sanctity"; Luongo, *The Saintly Politics of Catherine of Siena* (Ithaca, NY: Cornell University Press, 2006), 8. Without denying that this reconciliation was a concern of Raymond's—and one that helps to account for some of his narrative strategies—I want to point out that he faced other, specifically theological challenges in portraying Catherine's sanctity.

24. The Church is so described in the Nicene Creed (325 AD).

25. One might add, from a purely literary perspective, that this analysis sheds light on Raymond's construction of the *Life of Catherine of Siena* as a proto-novelistic "unity in diversity" of distinct genres.

26. See Catherine of Siena, *Il Dialogo della Divina Providenza*, ed. Giuliana Cavallini (Rome: Edizioni Cateriniane, 1968), 43, 284, 296; Catherine of Siena,

The Dialogue, trans. Suzanne Noffke, O.P. (New York: Paulist Press, 1980), 54, 219, 227. Hereafter I cite the Italian edition followed by the English edition as translated by Noffke.

27. Catherine of Siena, *Il Dialogo*, 18; trans. Noffke, 37.
28. Catherine of Siena, *Il Dialogo*, 13; trans. Noffke, 33.
29. Catherine of Siena, *Il Dialogo*, 20; trans. Noffke, 38.
30. Catherine of Siena, *Il Dialogo*, 18–19; trans. Noffke, 37.
31. Catherine of Siena, *Il Dialogo*, 18–19; trans. Noffke, 37.
32. Catherine of Siena, *Il Dialogo*, 19; trans. Noffke, 38.
33. Aquinas, *ST* I-II, q. 61, a. 5.
34. Kearns's translation is the first to include it.
35. Benedict of Nursia, *The Rule of St. Benedict, Latin and English*, trans. Luke Dysinger, O.S.B. (1997; repr. Santa Ana, CA: Source Books, 2003), 34/35.
36. See Catherine of Siena, *Il Dialogo*, 4; trans. Noffke, 27.
37. William Flete, "Letter to Brother Raymond, Master of Theology," trans. Michael Benedict Hackett, in Hackett, *William Flete, O.S.A., and Catherine of Siena*, 167, 170.
38. *Bonaventure: The Life of St. Francis*, trans. Ewert Cousins, Classics of Western Spirituality (Mahwah, NJ: Paulist Press, 1978), 180–81.
39. Catherine of Siena, *Il Dialogo*, 459; trans. Noffke, 337.
40. See André Vauchez, *The Laity in the Middle Ages: Religious Beliefs and Devotional Practices*, ed. Daniel E. Bornstein, trans. Margery J. Schneider (Notre Dame, IN: University of Notre Dame Press, 1993), 250.
41. On the structure of Bonaventure's *Legenda maior* of Francis, see Ann W. Astell, *Eating Beauty: The Eucharist and the Spiritual Arts of the Middle Ages* (Ithaca, NY: Cornell University Press, 2006), 99–135.
42. *Bonaventure: The Life of St. Francis*, 228.
43. See Raymond of Capua, *Life of Catherine of Siena*, 360n34.
44. Raymond of Capua, *Life of Catherine of Siena*, 360n34.
45. Raymond of Capua, *Life of Catherine of Siena*, 3.6, para. 422. Gregory XI made his solemn entry into Rome on January 13, 1377.
46. Peter Brown, *The Cult of the Saints: Its Rise and Function in Latin Christianity* (Chicago: University of Chicago Press, 1981), 1–22, 69–85; Lawrence S. Cunningham, *A Brief History of Saints* (Oxford: Blackwell, 2005), 10–27.
47. Augustine, *City of God* 10.21 (326) and 10.24 (328).
48. Peter Iver Kaufman, "Augustine, Martyrs, and Misery," *Church History* 63, no. 1 (1984): 1–14.
49. On this topic, see André Vauchez, *The Laity in the Middle Ages: Religious Beliefs and Devotional Practices*, ed. Daniel E. Bornstein, trans. Margery J. Schneider (Notre Dame, IN: University of Notre Dame Press, 1993), 243–53.

50. Aquinas, *ST*, II-II, q. 124, a. 2 (3:1710). Subsequent citations are given parenthetically.
51. See Gregory the Great, *Dialogues* 1.12, cited by Raymond (para. 395). On the relationship between miracles and moral virtue, see William D. McCready, *Signs of Sanctity: Miracles in the Thought of Gregory the Great* (Toronto: Pontifical Institute of Medieval Studies, 1989).
52. The index to Noffke's translation of *The Dialogue* shows echoes of Revelation 1:5, 2:10, 3:20, 7:16–17, 9:7, 13:8, and 21:6.
53. Catherine of Siena, *Il Dialogo*, 140; trans. Noffke, 107.
54. Catherine of Siena, *Il Dialogo*, 224; trans. Noffke, 178.
55. Catherine of Siena, *Il Dialogo*, 174; trans. Noffke, 144.
56. Catherine of Siena, *Il Dialogo*, 8; trans. Noffke, 30.
57. Catherine of Siena, *Il Dialogo*, 6; trans. Noffke, 29.
58. Catherine of Siena, *Il Dialogo*, 6; trans. Noffke, 29.
59. Catherine of Siena, *Il Dialogo*, 32; trans. Noffke, 46.
60. Catherine of Siena, *Il Dialogo*, 12–13; trans. Noffke, 33.
61. Catherine of Siena, *Il Dialogo*, 44; trans. Noffke, 54–55.
62. Catherine of Siena, *Il Dialogo*, 224; trans. Noffke, 178.
63. Woodward, *Making Saints*, 391.

CHAPTER SEVEN. Mary Magdalene and the Eucharist

1. On Catherine's literacy, see Jane Tylus, *Reclaiming Catherine of Siena: Literacy, Literature, and the Signs of Others* (Chicago: University of Chicago Press, 2009). According to Suzanne Noffke, the *Legenda aurea* and Domenico Cavalca's Tuscan translation of *The Lives of the Fathers* are Catherine's sources for "most of her allusions to anecdotes from the lives of the saints"; see Catherine of Siena, *The Dialogue*, trans. Suzanne Noffke, O.P. (New York: Paulist Press, 1980), 292n28.
2. On Martha as Mary Magdalene's sister, see Ingrid Maisch, *Mary Magdalene: The Image of a Woman through the Centuries*, trans. Linda M. Maloney (Collegeville, MN: Liturgical Press, 1998), 44–45. See Jacobus de Voragine, *The Golden Legend: Readings on the Saints*, trans. William Granger Ryan (Princeton, NJ: Princeton University Press, 2012), 376, where Jacobus refers to the identification of Mary of Bethany with Mary Magdalene.
3. See Karen A. Winstead, *Fifteenth-Century Lives: Writing Sainthood in England* (Notre Dame, IN: University of Notre Dame Press, 2020); Simon Horobin, "Politics, Patronage, and Piety in the Work of Osbern Bokenham," *Speculum* 82, no. 4 (2007): 932–49; Klaus Jankofsky, "*Legenda aurea* Materials in the *South English Legendary*: Translation, Transformation, Acculturation," in *Legenda aurea: Sept siècles de diffusion* (Paris: J. Vrin, 1986), 317–29.

4. More than a thousand medieval manuscripts of the *Legenda aurea* survive in Latin, plus approximately five hundred in vernacular languages. See Robert Francis Seybolt, "Fifteenth Century Editions of the *Legenda aurea*," *Speculum* 21, no. 3 (1946): 327–38. On some Middle English renderings, see Sherry L. Reames, "The Cecilia Legend as Chaucer Inherited It and Retold It: The Disappearance of an Augustinian Ideal," *Speculum* 55, no. 1 (1980): 38–57; Horobin, "Politics, Patronage, and Piety in the Work of Osbern Bokenham"; Jankofsky, "*Legenda aurea* materials in the *South English Legendary.*"

5. See Barbara Fleith and Franco Morenzoni, eds., *De la sainteté a l'hagiographie: Genèse et usage de la Legend dorée* (Geneva: Droz, 2001).

6. On Jacobus as preacher, see Steven A. Epstein, *The Talents of Jacopo da Varagine: A Genoese Mind in Medieval Europe* (Ithaca, NY: Cornell University Press, 2016), 11–65; Stefania Guidetti Bertini, *Sermones di Iacopo da Varazze: Il potere della immagini nel Duecento* (Tavarmuzze [Firenze]: SISMEL, Edizioni del Gulluzo, 1998).

7. See Sister Mary Jeremy, "Caxton's *Golden Legend* and Varagine's *Legenda aurea*," *Speculum* 21, no. 2 (1946): 212–21.

8. See Karl-Ernst Geith, "*Die Abbreviatio in Gestis et Miraculis Sanctorum* von Jean de Mailly als Quelle der *Legenda aurea*," in *Analecta Bollandiana* 105, no. 3–4 (1987): 289–302; Barbara Fleith, "The Patristic Sources of the *Legenda aurea*: A Research Report," in *Reception of the Church Fathers in the West: From the Carolingians to the Maurists*, ed. Irena Backus (New York: E. J. Brill, 1997), 1:237–87.

9. Eamon Duffy, "Introduction to the 2012 Edition," in Jacobus de Voragine, *The Golden Legend: Readings on the Saints*, xii. I use this translation throughout. For the Latin text, I use Iacopo da Varazze, *Legenda aurea*, 2 vols., ed. Giovanni Paolo Maggioni (Florence: SISMEL/Edizioni del Galluzzo, 1998), citing as *LA* by volume and page number.

10. For a thorough survey of historically negative, late medieval and early modern reaction to the *Legenda aurea* in Protestant and Catholic camps, see Sherry L. Reames, *The "Legenda Aurea": A Reexamination of Its Paradoxical History* (Madison: University of Wisconsin Press, 1985), 27–43, 44–70; for Reames's own critical comparison of the *Legenda* to the hagiographies of Gregory the Great, see 71–114.

11. Cited in Reames, *The "Legenda Aurea,"* 52.

12. Reames, *The "Legenda Aurea,"* 114. See Alain Boureau, *La Légende dorée: Le systéme narrative de Jacques de Voragine (†1298)* (Paris: Cerf, 1984); Fleith and Morenzoni, eds., *De la sainteté a l'hagiographie*; Jacques Le Goff, *In Search of Sacred Time: Jacobus de Voragine and "The Golden Legend,"* trans. Lydia G. Cochrane (Princeton, NJ: Princeton University Press, 2014); Steven Epstein, *The Talents of Jacopo da Varagine: A Genoese Mind in Medieval Europe* (Ithaca, NY: Cornell University Press, 2016).

13. Robert Francis Seybolt, "The *Legenda aurea*, Bible, and *Historia Scholastica*," *Speculum* 21, no. 3 (1946): 342.
14. See Le Goff, *In Search of Sacred Time*.
15. See Giovanni Farris, *Significati spirituali nei "Sermones" di Iacopo da Varazze e nella "Divina Commedia"* (Savona: M. Sabatelli, 1998).
16. See Boureau, *La Légende dorée*. In her study of the *Legenda aurea*, published close in time to Boureau's, Reames highlights the psychological richness lost through this process of abridgment.
17. For the term "pure act," see Aquinas, *ST* I, q. 25, a. 1. Glossing Romans 9:28 (*verbum enim consummans et brevians . . . verbum breviatum*), the phrase "abbreviated word," used to name the Incarnate Word, is found in many different patristic and medieval sources.
18. Duffy, "Introduction to the 2012 Edition," xix.
19. William Granger Ryan, "Introduction," in Jacobus de Voragine, *The Golden Legend: Readings on the Saints*, xvi.
20. André Vauchez, "Jacques de Voragine et les saintes du XIII siècle dans la *Légende dorée*," in *Legenda aurea: Sept siècles de diffusion: Actes du colloque international sur le "Legenda aurea," text Latin et branches vernaculaires* (Paris: Vrin, 1986), 27–56.
21. Duffy, "Introduction to the 2012 Edition," xv.
22. Jacobus de Voragine, *The Golden Legend: Readings on the Saints*, 374; *LA*, 1:627. Maggioni's edition includes an etymology of Praxedes's name not given in Ryan's translation: "Praxedis dicta est quasi uiridis a praxim quod est uiride; inde praxedis quia uiruit et floruit flore uirginitatis" (Praxedis is pronounced like [the phrase] 'green from practice,' that is, [by living] 'greenly'; whence [she is named] Praxedis because she greened and flourished with the flower of virginity) (my translation).
23. Quoted in Henri de Lubac, *Medieval Exegesis*, Vol. 2, *The Four Senses of Scripture*, trans. E. M. Macierowski (Grand Rapids, MI: William B. Eerdmans, 2000), 37.
24. de Lubac, *Medieval Exegesis*, 2:33.
25. de Lubac, *Medieval Exegesis*, 2:197. Thomas illustrates all four senses using the single expression "fiat lux" (Gen. 1:3). De Lubac takes the quotation from Thomas's commentary on Galatians (*In Gal.*, chap. 5, lect. 7).
26. de Lubac, *Medieval Exegesis*, 2:197.
27. de Lubac, *Medieval Exegesis*, 2:195.
28. de Lubac, *Medieval Exegesis*, 2:195.
29. de Lubac, *Medieval Exegesis*, 2:194–95.
30. Jean Leclercq, *The Love of Learning and the Desire for God: A Study of Monastic Culture*, trans. Catherine Misrahi (New York: Fordham University Press, 1982), 220.

31. de Lubac, *Medieval Exegesis*, 2:195.

32. See Le Goff, *In Search of Sacred Time*.

33. The literature on the Eucharist and eschatology is vast. See Gregory Dix, *The Shape of the Liturgy* (London: Dacre Press, 1945); Rachel Fulton, *From Judgment to Passion: Devotion to Christ and Mary, 800–1200* (New York: Columbia University Press, 2002); Ann W. Astell, *Eating Beauty: The Eucharist and the Spiritual Arts of the Middle Ages* (Ithaca, NY: Cornell University Press, 2006), esp. 24, 97, 215; Gabriel Radle, "Embodied Eschatology: The Council of Nicaea's Regulation of Kneeling and Its Reception across Liturgical Traditions," Part 1 and Part 2, *Worship* 90 (July and September 2016): 345–71, 433–61.

34. For this work, see *Johannis Beleth: Summa de ecclesiasticis officiis*, CCCM 412 (Turnhout: Brepols, 1976). For a study on Jacobus and Beleth, see Billy Brussell Thompson, "'Plumbei cordis, oris ferrei': La reception de la teologia de Jacobus de Voragine y su *Legenda aurea* en la Península," in *Saints and Their Authors: Studies in Medieval Hispanic Hagiography in Honor of John K. Walsh* (Madison, WI: Hispanic Seminary of Medieval Studies, 1990), 97–106.

35. Durand, *Rationale*, prologue; as translated in Timothy M. Thibodeau, "*Enigmata Figurarum*: Biblical Exegesis and Liturgical Exposition in Durand's 'Rationale,'" *Harvard Theological Review* 86, no. 1 (1993): 72. For the Latin text, see *Guillelmi Duranti: Rationale divinorum officiorum I–IV*, CCCM 140, ed. A. Davril and T. M. Thibodeau (Turnhout: Brepols, 1995).

36. Jacobus so describes the four seasons of the liturgical year in his prologue to the *Legenda aurea*, trans. Ryan, 3–4. Whereas the seasons so ordered follow an order reminiscent of salvation history, the liturgical year (as Jacobus points out) actually begins with Advent and the "time of renewal," recalling creation before the Fall and its re-creation in Christ.

37. Duffy, "Introduction to the 2012 Edition," xiii.

38. *LA*, 1:355: "Circa autem ipsam resurrectionem dominicam septem per ordinem sunt consideranda" (Concerning the lordly resurrection itself seven [questions] are to be considered in order).

39. Jacobus de Voragine, *The Golden Legend: Readings on the Saints*, 216; *LA*, 1:355.

40. For these and all references to the *Summa theologiae*, I use St. Thomas Aquinas, *Summa theologica*, trans. Fathers of the English Dominican Province, 5 vols. (New York: Benziger, 1948, repr. Allen, TX: Christian Classics, 1981).

41. Jacobus de Voragine, *The Golden Legend: Readings on the Saints*, 219; *LA*, 1:361.

42. Jacobus de Voragine, *The Golden Legend: Readings on the Saints*, 219–20; *LA*, 1:361. This sentence misremembers the biblical text, where Mary Magdalene is the one who arises early in the morning to go to the tomb.

43. Jacobus de Voragine, *The Golden Legend: Readings on the Saints*, 220; *LA*, 1:361.

44. Jacobus de Voragine, *The Golden Legend: Readings on the Saints*, 220; *LA*, 1:362.

45. Jacobus de Voragine, *The Golden Legend: Readings on the Saints*, 220; *LA*, 1:362.

46. Jacobus de Voragine, *The Golden Legend: Readings on the Saints*, 220; *LA*, 1:362.

47. Jacobus de Voragine, *The Golden Legend: Readings on the Saints*, 375; *LA*, 1:629: "post conuersionem magnifica per gratie superabundantiam, quia ubi abundauit delictum, superbundauit et gratia."

48. Jacobus de Voragine, *The Golden Legend: Readings on the Saints*, 374–75; *LA*, 1:628: "In quantum elegit optimam partem celestis glorie dicitur illuminata."

49. Jacobus de Voragine, *The Golden Legend: Readings on the Saints*, 375; *LA*, 1:628–29.

50. The standard study of the *accessus* is Edwin A. Quain, "The Medieval *Accessus ad auctores*," *Traditio* 3 (1945): 215–64.

51. See Jacobus de Voragine, *The Golden Legend: Readings on the Saints*, 376; *LA*, 1:630, where Jacobus quotes "Ambrose" on this issue. By "Ambrose," here and throughout the *Legenda aurea*, Jacobus refers to prefaces used in the Ambrosian liturgy (alongside passages taken from the Gelasian and Gregorian propers); see André Wilmart, "Saint Ambrose et la *Légende Dorée*," *Ephemerides Liturgicae*, n.s., 50 (1936): 169–206.

52. See Maisch, *Mary Magdalene*, 44–45.

53. Jacobus de Voragine, *The Golden Legend: Readings on the Saints*, 376; *LA*, 1:631.

54. Jacobus de Voragine, *The Golden Legend: Readings on the Saints*, 382; *LA*, 1:641: "Hec autem falsa et friuola reputantur." Maggioni's edition includes the reference to Brother Albert as a textual variant.

55. Jacobus de Voragine, *The Golden Legend: Readings on the Saints*, 220; *LA*, 1:362.

56. In 1376, Catherine herself actively promoted Jacobus's cult in plague-stricken Varazze. On this point, Suzanne Noffke cites Blessed Raymond of Capua, *Opuscula et Litterae*, ed. H. M. Cormier (Rome, 1895), 25–30 (*Dialogue*, 227n32).

57. Jacobus de Voragine, *The Golden Legend: Readings on the Saints*, 380; *LA*, 1:636.

58. Jacobus de Voragine, *The Golden Legend: Readings on the Saints*, 380; *LA*, 1:636.

59. Jacobus de Voragine, *The Golden Legend: Readings on the Saints*, 380; *LA*, 1:636.

60. For this comparison, see Joana Antunes, "The Late-Medieval Mary Magdalene: Sacredness, Otherness, and Wildness," in *Mary Magdalene in Medieval Culture: Conflicted Roles*, ed. Peter V. Loewen and Robin Waugh (New York: Routledge, 2014), 116–39.

61. Antunes, "The Late-Medieval Mary Magdalene," 129, 119. See also Marina Warner, *Alone of All Her Sex: The Myth and Cult of the Virgin Mary* (New York: Random House, 1976), 81–102.

62. See *The Life of Saint Mary Magdalene and of Her Sister Saint Martha: A Medieval Biography*, trans. David Mycoff (Kalamazoo, MI: Cistercian Publications, 1989), 107.

63. Jacobus de Voragine, *The Golden Legend: Readings on the Saints*, 228; *LA*, 1:376–77.

64. Conca also painted a different version of the Magdalene's death that shows her receiving her last Holy Communion from the hands of an angel; see Timothy Clifford, "Sebastian Conca's Communion of Mary Magdalen," *The Burlington Magazine* 114, no. 828 (1972): 142–46. For a study of the reclining posture of Mary Magdalene, see Martha Mel Edmunds, "La Sainte-Baume and the Iconography of Mary Magdalene," *Gazette des beaux-arts* 114 (1989): 11–28. I thank Dianne Philipps for this reference.

65. Jacobus de Voragine, *The Golden Legend: Readings on the Saints*, 381; *LA*, 1:639.

66. J. E. Cross, "Mary Magdalen in the Old English Martyrology: The Earliest Extant 'Narrat Josephus' Variant of Her Legend," *Speculum* 53, no. 1 (1978): 20.

67. Since Mary Magdalene's feast occurs on July 22, it seems likely that "the day of the Lord's resurrection" designates Sunday, rather than Easter per se, but the imagery of a long, preceding sojourn of fasting in the wilderness inevitably recalls Lent, reinforcing the remembrance of the Paschal mystery celebrated at every Mass, and especially at Mass on Sunday, the Lord's day.

68. Jacobus de Voragine, *Golden Legend: Readings on the Saints*, 381; *LA*, 1:638: "corpus et sanguinem domini ab episcopo beata Maria Magdalena cum multa lacrimarum inundatione suscepit. Deinde toto corpusculo ante altaris prostrata crepidinem sanctissima illa anima migrauit ad dominum."

69. *LA*, 1:638.

70. Jacobus de Voragine, *Golden Legend: Readings on the Saints*, 381; *LA*, 1:638.

71. Jacobus de Voragine, *Golden Legend: Readings on the Saints*, 410–11; *LA*, 2:685.

72. Jacobus de Voragine, *Golden Legend: Readings on the Saints*, 411; *LA*, 2:686. According to James Monti, "The use of candles or torches in Christian funeral rites can be traced back to the third century"; see Monti, *A Sense of the Sacred: Roman Catholic Worship in the Middle Ages* (San Francisco: Ignatius, 2012), 597.

73. For Raymond's references to Mary Magdalene, see Raymond of Capua, *The Life of Catherine of Siena*, trans. Conleth Kearns, O.P. (Wilmington, DE: Michael Glazier, 1980), paras. 12, 45, 64, 126, 173, and 185. I use this translation throughout. Kearns's translation conveniently preserves the paragraph numbering in the *Legenda maior*, as found in *AASS*, Vol. 12 (Aprilis III): 853–959.

74. For a discussion of Catherine's relationship to Mary Magdalene that emphasizes preaching, see Astell, *Eating Beauty*, 149–56.

75. *The Letters of Catherine of Siena*, trans. Suzanne Noffke, O.P. (Tempe: Arizona Center for Medieval and Renaissance Studies, 2000), 1:2–5.

76. *Letters of Catherine of Siena*, 1:53.

77. *Letters of Catherine of Siena*, 2:41; for the same image, see 2:48.

78. *Letters of Catherine of Siena*, 2:42.

79. *Letters of Catherine of Siena*, 2:512.

80. *Letters of Catherine of Siena*, 2:512.

81. *Letters of Catherine of Siena*, 2:512–13.

82. Catherine of Siena, *The Dialogue*, trans. Noffke, 136 (para. 74); S. Caterina da Siena, *Il Dialogo*, ed. Giuliana Cavallini (Siena: Cantagalli, 1995), 189.

83. Catherine of Siena, *Dialogue*, 136–37 (paras. 74–75); *Dialogo*, 189–91.

84. William Flete, "The Spiritual Document," trans. Michael Benedict Hackett, in Michael Benedict Hackett, OSA, *William Flete, O.S.A., and Catherine of Siena: Masters of Fourteen Century Spirituality* (Villanova, PA: Augustinian Press, 1992), 84.

85. Hackett, *William Flete, O.S.A., and Catherine of Siena*, 110.

86. *Letters of Catherine of Siena*, 2:513.

87. St. Thomas Aquinas, *Commentary on the Gospel of John*, trans. Fabian Larcher, O.P. (Lander, WY: The Aquinas Institute for the Study of Sacred Doctrine, 2013), 2:469, para. 2517.

88. Aquinas, *Commentary on the Gospel of John*, 2:469, para. 2517.

89. Catherine of Siena, *Dialogue*, 123 (para. 66), 134 (para. 72), 363 (para. 166); *Dialogo*, 167, 186, 583.

90. Catherine of Siena, *Dialogue*, 362–63 (para. 166); *Dialogo*, 581–83.

91. Catherine of Siena, *Dialogue*, 292 (para. 141); *Dialogo*, 456.

92. Catherine of Siena, *Dialogue*, 314 (para. 149); *Dialogo*, 498.

93. Catherine of Siena, *Dialogue*, 315 (para. 149); *Dialogo*, 498.

94. Catherine of Siena, *Dialogue*, 315 (para. 149); *Dialogo*, 499–500.

95. Rudolf M. Bell, *Holy Anorexia* (Chicago: University of Chicago Press, 1985). For a cautionary discussion of the application of this term in relation to Catherine, see Astell, *Eating Beauty*, 156–61.

96. Raymond of Capua, *Life of Catherine of Siena*, para. 174; trans. Kearns, 168.

97. Imitability is a Pauline mark of sanctity: "Imitate me as I imitate Christ" (1 Cor. 11:1).

98. For the listed accusations concerning inedia, see Raymond of Capua, *Life of Catherine of Siena*, para. 172, trans. Kearns, 166.
99. Catherine's canonization by Pope Pius II took place in 1461.
100. Raymond of Capua, *Life of Catherine of Siena*, para. 480; trans. Kearns, 388.
101. Raymond of Capua, *Life of Catherine of Siena*, paras. 173–77; trans. Kearns, 166–72.
102. Raymond of Capua, *Life of Catherine of Siena*, paras. 166–67; trans. Kearns, 159–61. Raymond himself witnessed Catherine's Eucharistic miracles, and William Flete tells of others. For William's descriptions and his Augustinian interpretation of them, see Flete, "Sermon on the Revered Saint Catherine of Siena," trans. Michael Benedict Hackett, in Hackett, *William Flete, O.S.A., and Catherine of Siena*, 185–221, esp. 201–03.
103. Caroline Walker Bynum, *The Resurrection of the Body in Western Christianity, 200–1336* (New York: Columbia University Press, 1995), lays a firm foundation for such a study. Bynum comments on similarities between Jacobus and Aquinas in the final chapter, but she does not discuss Jacobus's legend of Mary Magdalen in particular, nor does she refer here to Catherine of Siena. The Sienese saint figures prominently, however, in Bynum, *Holy Feast and Holy Fast* (Berkeley: University of California Press, 1987).
104. Aquinas, *Commentary on the Gospel of John*, 2:470, para. 2519.
105. Aquinas, *Commentary on the Gospel of John*, 2:457, para. 2473, where Sg 8:6 is quoted; for other citations of the Song of Songs, see 2:453, para. 2466; 2:458, para. 2477.
106. Jean Danielou, *The Bible and the Liturgy* (Notre Dame, IN: University of Notre Dame Press, 1956), 191–207.
107. Raymond of Capua, *Life of Catherine of Siena*, para. 313, trans. Kearns, 290.
108. Raymond of Capua, *Life of Catherine of Siena*, para. 313, trans. Kearns, 290.
109. Raymond of Capua, *Life of Catherine of Siena*, para. 292, trans. Kearns, 270. Kearns cites *ST*, II-II, q. 171, a. 6.
110. Raymond of Capua, *Life of Catherine of Siena*, para. 313, trans. Kearns, 290.
111. Raymond of Capua, *Life of Catherine of Siena*, para. 199, trans. Kearns, 189.
112. Catherine of Siena, *Dialogue*, 339 (para. 158); *Dialogo*, 542: "Tomaso che con l'occhio de l'intelletto suo tutto gentile si specolava nella mia Verità, dove acquistò il lume sopranaturale e scienzia infusa per grazia."
113. Catherine of Siena, *Dialogue*, 339 (para. 158); *Dialogo*, 542. For other references to Aquinas, see *Dialogo*, 155 (para. 85), 181 (para. 96); *Dialogo*, 222–23, 264.
114. Catherine of Siena, *Dialogue*, 210n7.
115. See Noffke's note 25 in Catherine of Siena, *Dialogue*, 339.
116. Catherine of Siena, *Dialogue*, 123 (para. 66); *Dialogo*, 168.
117. Catherine of Siena, *Dialogue*, 123 (para. 66); *Dialogo*, 168.

118. Raymond of Capua, *Life of Catherine of Siena*, para. 165, trans. Kearns, 158–59.
119. Raymond of Capua, *Life of Catherine of Siena*, para.166, trans. Kearns, 160.
120. Raymond of Capua, *Life of Catherine of Siena*, para. 321, trans. Kearns, 297.
121. Raymond of Capua, *Life of Catherine of Siena*, para. 167, trans. Kearns, 160–61.
122. Bynum, *Resurrection of the Body*, 310. She cites *ST* III, q. 15, a. 5, obj. 3 and reply to obj. 3; q. 14, a. 1, obj. 2 and reply to obj. 2.
123. Aquinas, *ST* III, q. 79, a. 1.
124. Aquinas, *ST* III, q. 79, a. 1.
125. Aquinas, *ST* III, q 73, a. 6.
126. Aquinas, *ST* III, q. 54, a. 2, reply to obj. 2.
127. Aquinas, *ST* III, q. 75, a. 8.
128. Aquinas, *ST* III, q. 75, a. 2.
129. Aquinas, *ST* I, q. 1, a. 10.
130. Aquinas, *ST* III, q. 73, a. 4.
131. Aquinas, *ST* III, q. 73, a. 4.
132. Aquinas, *ST* III, q. 73, a. 4.
133. See Raymond of Capua, *Life of Catherine of Siena*, para. 183, trans. Kearns, 177.
134. The phrase is taken from Kearns, note 23, in Raymond of Capua, *Life of Catherine of Siena*, 177–78.
135. See Raymond of Capua, *Life of Catherine of Siena*, paras. 64, 173, 184, 185, and 199, trans. Kearns, 58–60, 166–68, 178, 178–79, 189.
136. Raymond of Capua, *Life of Catherine of Siena*, para. 184, trans. Kearns, 178.
137. See Raymond of Capua, *Life of Catherine of Siena*, para. 118, trans. Kearns, 113–14; para. 206, trans. Kearns, 196.
138. Aquinas, *Commentary on the Gospel of John*, 2:457, para. 2473.
139. Raymond of Capua, *Life of Catherine of Siena*, para. 330, trans. Kearns, 307.
140. Raymond of Capua, *Life of Catherine of Siena*, para. 206, trans. Kearns, 196.
141. See, for example, Bynum, *Holy Feast and Holy Fast*, 166; Karen Scott, "St. Catherine of Siena, *Apostola*," *Church History* 61 (April 1992): 34–46.
142. Bynum, *Holy Feast and Holy Fast*, 81.
143. See Ann W. Astell, "Heroic Virtue in Blessed Raymond of Capua's *Life of Catherine of Siena*," *Journal of Medieval and Early Modern Studies* 42, no. 1 (2012): 35–57, esp. 48–52. This article in a revised and expanded form is republished in chapter 6 in this book.
144. Raymond of Capua, *Life of Catherine of Siena*, para. 91; trans. Kearns, 83–84.

145. Raymond of Capua, *Life of Catherine of Siena*, para. 368; trans. Kearns, 341.
146. Raymond of Capua, *Life of Catherine of Siena*, para. 368; trans. Kearns, 341.
147. Raymond of Capua, *Life of Catherine of Siena*, para. 368; trans. Kearns, 341.
148. Steven Rozenski, *Wisdom's Journey: Continental Mysticism and Popular Devotion in England, 1350–1650* (Notre Dame, IN: University of Notre Dame Press, 2022), 141. See also Jennifer N. Brown, *Fruit of the Orchard: Reading Catherine of Siena in Late Medieval and Early Modern England* (Toronto: University of Toronto Press, 2019).
149. See Rozenski, *Wisdom's Journey*, 131–80; Brown, *Fruit of the Orchard*, 58–81; Dirk Schultze, "Spiritual Teaching by Catherine of Siena in BL Harley 2409: An Edition," *Anglia* 136, no. 2 (2018): 296–325. Hackett notes that Thomas More echoes Flete's *Remedies against Temptations* in his *A Dialogue of Comfort against Tribulation* (1534); see Hackett, *William Flete, O.S.A., and Catherine of Siena*, 119.
150. See Simon Horobin, "Introduction," in Osbern Bokenham, *Lives of Saints*, ed. Simon Horobin (Oxford: Oxford University Press, 2020), 1:xiii–xxxv.
151. See Horobin, "Introduction," xxxiii; Felicity Riddy, "Women Talking about the Things of God: A Late Medieval Sub-culture," in *Women and Literature in Britain 1150–1500*, ed. Carol M. Meale (Cambridge: Cambridge University Press, 1996), 104–27.
152. For the text of these remarkable letters, see Hackett, *William Flete, O.S.A., and Catherine of Siena*, 139–63.
153. Osbern Bokenham, *Legendys of Hooly Wummen*, ed. Mary S. Serjeantson, EETS 206 (1938; repr. London: Oxford University Press, 1997), 139, lines 5065–70. Hereafter I cite this work parenthetically.
154. Sheila Delany, *Impolitic Bodies: Poetry, Saints, and Society in Fifteenth-Century England: The Work of Osbern Bokenham* (New York: Oxford University Press, 1998), 53, 89.
155. Winstead, *Fifteenth-Century Lives*, 135. The *Roman Martyrology* actually includes twenty-eight Old Testament figures, assigned to different days of the calendar.
156. See Eva von Contzen and Anke Bernau, eds., *Sanctity as Literature in Late Medieval Britain* (Manchester: Manchester University Press, 2015); Winstead, *Fifteenth-Century Lives*.
157. Winstead, *Fifteenth-Century Lives*, 126.
158. For a complete prose translation into present-day English, see Osbern Bokenham, *A Legend of Holy Women: A Translation of Osbern Bokenham's "Legends of Holy Women,"* trans. Sheila Delany (Notre Dame, IN: University of Notre Dame Press, 1992). Delany renders the complete passage thus: "Let whoever wishes to

know this not pass hence until they have finished this story, which combines gospel with legend. The reader will find that where sin wretchedly reigned, now grace superabounds" (107).

159. See Michelle Karnes, "Nicholas Love and Medieval Meditations on Christ," *Speculum* 82, no. 2 (2007): 380–408.

160. Delany, *Impolitic Bodies*, 49–64, 91.

161. For an interesting survey of Trinitarian doctrine as presented in English hagiographies, see Winstead, *Fifteenth-Century Lives*, 92–100. Winstead discusses Trinitarian instances in Bokenham's legends of Saints Barbara and Cecilia, but omits treatment of this prayer in the prolocutory.

162. Hackett, *William Flete, O.S.A., and Catherine of Siena*, 181.

163. Hackett, *William Flete, O.S.A., and Catherine of Siena*, 182. The theme of Catherine's creaturely nothingness and God's fullness of being is also emphasized in part 1, para. 92, of Raymond of Capua's *Life*. Borrowing from Raymond's *Life*, the third section of the Middle English text "Cleanness of Soul" (Long Version C) translates God's word to Catherine: "Þu ert she þat ert noght. And I am I þat am"; see Schultze, "Spiritual Teaching," 320.

164. Hackett, *William Flete, O.S.A., and Catherine of Siena*, 182.

165. Delany, *Impolitic Bodies*, 52.

166. See Robin M. Jensen, *Baptismal Imagery in Early Christianity: Ritual, Visual, and Theological Dimensions* (Grand Rapids, MI: Baker Academic, 2012).

167. On the association of milk with blood, see Caroline Walker Bynum, *Jesus as Mother: Studies in the Spirituality of the High Middle Ages* (Berkeley: University of California Press, 1982), 141–42, 150–51, 182. Julian of Norwich (1346–after 1416), Bokenham's near contemporary, compares a breastfeeding mother to Jesus who nourishes us with the Eucharist: "The moder may geve her childe sucke her milke. But oure precious moder Jhesu, he may fede us with himselfe, and doth full curtesly and full tenderly with the blessed sacrament that is precious fode of very life"; see Nicholas Watson and Jacqueline Jenkins, eds., *The Writings of Julian of Norwich* (University Park: Pennsylvania State University Press, 2005), 313.

168. Augustine, *De bono coniugali* 3.3–7.7.

169. On this important dictum, see Michael Tomko, *Beyond the Willing Suspension of Disbelief: Poetic Faith from Coleridge to Tolkein* (London: Bloomsbury, 2016). On literary extensions of the Bible's tropological sense, see Ryan McDermott, *Tropologies: Ethics and Invention in England, c. 1350–1600* (Notre Dame, IN: University of Notre Dame Press, 2016). Dante famously extends the fourfold signification of sacred scripture to the polysemous sense of his *Commedia* in his letter to Cangrande.

170. I thank Dianne Phillips for drawing my attention to this image.

CHAPTER EIGHT. The Ends of Hagiography

1. R. W. Chambers, "The Continuity of English Prose from Alfred to More and His School," in Nicholas Harpsfield, *Harpsfield's Life of More*, EETS o.s. 186 (London: Humphrey Milford, Oxford University Press, 1932), xlv.
2. Chambers, "Continuity of English Prose," xlvii.
3. Chambers, "Continuity of English Prose," xlvii.
4. *The Lyfe of Syr Thomas More . . . by Ro. Ba*, ed. Elsie Vaughan Hitchcock and P. E. Hallett, EETS o.s. 222 (London: Geoffrey Cumberlege, Oxford University Press, 1950), 7.
5. *The Lyfe of Syr Thomas More . . . by Ro. Ba*, 15, 8.
6. *The Lyfe of Syr Thomas More . . . by Ro. Ba*, 11.
7. Helen C. White, *Tudor Books of Saints and Martyrs* (Madison: University of Wisconsin Press, 1963), 129. Robert Bassett (1574–1641) has been tentatively identified as "Ro. Ba."
8. White, *Tudor Books*, 119–20, 116.
9. White, *Tudor Books*, 116.
10. Warren W. Wooden, "Structural Patterning in William Roper's *Life of More*," *Moreana* 16, no. 64 (1980): 100.
11. Hilmar M. Pabel, *Herculean Labours: Erasmus and the Editing of St. Jerome's Letters in the Renaissance*, Library of the Written Word 5 (Leiden and Boston: Brill, 2008), 90–91.
12. In support of Erasmus as a founding figure for modern biblical study, see Marijke H. De Lang, "'Fidelius, apertius, significantius': The New Testament Translated and Edited by Erasmus of Rotterdam, 1516," *The Bible Translator* 67, no. 1 (2016): 5–8; Henk Nellen and Jan Bloemendal, "Erasmus's Biblical Project: Some Thoughts and Observations on Its Scope, Its Import in the Sixteenth Century, and Reception in the Seventeenth and Eighteenth Centuries," *Church History and Religious Culture* 96 (2016): 595–635.
13. On Saint Jerome's hagiographies of Paul, Hilarion, and Malchus, see Susan Weingarten, *The Saint's Saints: Hagiography and Geography in Jerome* (Leiden and Boston: Brill, 2005); Stefan Rebenich, "Inventing an Ascetic Hero: Jerome's *Life of Paul the First Hermit*," in *Jerome of Stridon: His Life, Writings, and Legacy*, ed. Andrew Cain and Josef Lössi (Farnham: Ashgate, 2009), 13–27; Yorick Schulz-Wackerbarth, *Die Vita Pauli des Hieronymus: Darstellung und Etablierung eines Heiligen im hagiographischen Diskurs der Spätantike*, Studien und Texte zu Antike und Christentum 107 (Tübingen: Mohr Siebeck, 2017).
14. Erasmus of Rotterdam, *The Life of the Eminent Doctor Jerome of Stridon Composed Mainly from His Own Writing by Desiderius Erasmus of Rotterdam*, in *Collected Works of Erasmus* [*CWE*], Vol. 61, *Patristic Scholarship: The Edition of St*

Jerome, ed., trans., and annotated by James F. Brady and John C. Olin (Toronto: University of Toronto Press, 1974), 31; Erasmus, *Eximii Doctoris Hieronymi Stridonensis vita*, in *Erasmi Opuscula: A Supplement to the Opera Omnia*, ed. Wallace F. Ferguson (The Hague: Martinus Nijhoff, 1933), 148. For a description of another of Jerome's hermitages, see *CWE* 61:33; *Erasmi Opuscula*, 150–51. On the interpenetration of autobiography and hagiography, see Weingarten, *The Saint's Saints*, 191.

15. See *Life of Paul of Thebes by Jerome*, in *Early Christian Lives*, trans. Carolinne White (London: Penguin, 1998), 77. For another autobiographical reference to eremitical experience, see Jerome's Letter 22.7 to Eustochium, in *The Letters of St. Jerome*, Vol. 1, Ancient Christian Writers 33, trans. Charles Christopher Mierow (Westminster, MD: Newman Press, 1963), 139–40.

16. Pabel, *Herculean Labours*, 11.

17. Lisa Jardine, *Erasmus, Man of Letters: The Construction of Charisma in Print* (Princeton, NJ: Princeton University Press, 1993), 74.

18. Pabel, *Herculean Labours*, 11.

19. For the Latin text, see http//www.thelatinlibrary.com/jerome/vitapauli.html, which credits the research done by Bazyli Degórski, ed., *Edizione critica della "Vita Sancti Pauli Primi Eremitae" di Girolamo* (Rome: Institutum Patristicum "Augustinianum," 1987), which is also the basis for Girolamo, *Vite degli eremita Paolo, Ilarione, e Marco*, ed. Bazyli Degórski (Rome: Città Nuova, 1996), and *Hieronymus, Vita Pauli*, trans. and ed. Vincent Hunink (Leuven: Uitgeverij Press, 2002). Hunink notes that the Latin text established by Degórski differs considerably from the text as found in Migne's edition, *PL* 23:17–28C.

20. Erasmus, "Dedicatory Letter . . . to William Warham, Archbishop of Canterbury," in *CWE*, 61:11. Erasmus also refers in a generic way to Jerome's "exemplary stories" in the revised preface to volume 2 of the second edition; see Pabel, *Herculean Labours*, 144. Pabel notes an unfortunate mistranslation in *CWE*, 61:99.

21. See Letter 10, in *Letters of St. Jerome*, 1:50–52, ed. Mierow.

22. Using Migne's edition of the Latin text, Carolinne White identifies three quotations of Virgil's *Aeneid*, a quotation from a letter of Cyprian, and twelve biblical echoes: Mark 9:23, Ps. 19:4, Rom. 10:18, 1 John 4:18, Matt. 7:7, Luke 11:9, 1 Cor. 13:7, 1 Kings 17:4–6, Phil. 1:23, 2 Tim. 4:7–8, 1 Cor. 13:5, and Eccles. 3:7; see *Life of Paul of Thebes by Jerome*, in White, trans., *Early Christian Lives*, 71–84, 211–12. In his critical edition of the text, Bazyli Degórski identifies six quotations from the *Aeneid* (2.650, 3.56–57, 4.278, 6.672, 7.5–6, 10.211) and thirty-nine biblical references. (See note 27, below.) Weingarten, *The Saint's Saints*, 174–75, 268, gives evidence of Jerome's indebtedness to a Jewish Aggadot about Rabbi Shimon Bar Yohai and discusses biblical typology.

23. Rebenich, "Inventing an Ascetic Hero," 26.

24. White, trans., *Early Christian Lives*, 84.

25. See Augustine, *De doctrina Christiana* 2.40, 60, for the famous analogy to the Israelites' gathering of Egyptian spoils related in Exodus 3:22, 11.2, 12:35.

26. See note 20, above.

27. Girolamo, *Vite degli eremita Paolo, Ilarione, e Marco*, ed. Bazyli Degórski (Rome: Città Nuova, 1996). The footnotes reference Mark 2:23; 1 Sam. 24:8; Judg. 18:26; Eph. 6:16, 14; 1 Thess. 5:8, Rom. 10:2, 18; Luke 6:12; 1 John 4:18; Matt. 7:7–8; Luke 11:10–11; Gen. 3:19; Eccles. 12:7; 1 Cor. 13:7; 1 Kings 17:3–6; Phil. 1:23; 2 Tim. 4:7; 1 Cor. 9:24, 26; Gal. 2:2; Gal. 5:7; Phil. 2:16; Heb. 12:1; Gen. 3:19; Eccles. 12:7; 1 Cor. 10:24; Phil. 2:21; Rev. 14:4; Matt. 17:2; Mark 9:3; Luke 9:29; Luke 2:29; Luke 20:3–8; Rom. 14:8; Matt. 10:29; 2 Sam. 14:11; Matt. 7:11; Luke 11:13; Luke 16:19–31; Rom. 13:14; Gal. 3:27.

28. Jerome's Letter 22 to Eustochium includes twenty quotations from the Song of Songs, which the monk uses to exhort the young woman to an ascetic life of consecrated virginity. In that same letter, Jerome recalls his own life of solitude in the desert; see Jerome, *Letters of St. Jerome*, 1:134–79.

29. Hugh of Saint Victor, *The "Didascalicon" of Hugh of St. Victor: A Medieval Guide to the Arts*, trans. Jerome Taylor, Records of Western Civilization (1961; repr. New York: Columbia University Press, 1991), 4.2, trans. Taylor, 103–4.

30. Ian Christopher Levy, *Introducing Medieval Biblical Interpretation: The Senses of Scripture in Premodern Exegesis* (Grand Rapids, MI: Baker Academic, 2018), 12–13, 209–10, 214–16, 222–23, 247–52.

31. Levy, *Introducing Medieval Biblical Interpretation*, 282.

32. Levy, *Introducing Medieval Biblical Interpretation*, 282.

33. In the oft-quoted words of Augustine, "But Scripture teaches nothing but charity, nor condemns anything except cupidity, and in this way shapes the minds of men"; *On Christian Doctrine*, trans. D. W. Robertson Jr. (Indianapolis: Bobbs-Merrill, 1958), 3.10.15. The recognized intent of the divine author requires the reader's cooperation with that intent: "What is read should be subjected to diligent scrutiny until an interpretation contributing to the reign of charity is produced" (*On Christian Doctrine* 3.15.23).

34. Augustine, *On Christian Doctrine* 2.6.8.

35. Levy, *Introducing Medieval Biblical Interpretation*, 264.

36. I echo Marshall McLuhan's well-known catchphrase, used to sum up his theory of communication, articulated in McLuhan, *Understanding Media: The Extensions of Man* (New York: Mentor, 1964).

37. Augustine, *On Christian Doctrine* 2.16, 24: "An ignorance of things makes figurative expressions obscure when we are ignorant of the nature of animals, or stones, or plants, or other things which are often used in the scriptures for the purposes of constructing similitudes." The Book of Creation thus glosses the scriptures. By its very existence, creatures point to the Creator, but the Bible reveals the natural order to have been created good by the God who is the highest good.

38. See Hebrews 4:12.
39. Gregory the Great, "Preface," in *Morals on the Book of Job*, 3 vols. (Oxford: John Henry Parker, 1844–1850), 1: "Preface," para. 2.
40. Alastair J. Minnis, *Medieval Theory of Authorship: Scholastic Literary Attitudes in the Later Middle Ages*, 2nd ed. (Philadelphia: University of Pennsylvania Press, 2010), 72.
41. Minnis, *Medieval Theory of Authorship*, 58.
42. See Levy, *Introducing Medieval Biblical Interpretation*, 210, 247, 254, 258; Minnis, *Medieval Theory of Authorship*, 76–83.
43. Levy, *Introducing Medieval Biblical Interpretation*, 239–40; Minnis, *Medieval Theory of Authorship*, 21–22, 145–59, 118–45.
44. Levy, *Introducing Medieval Biblical Interpretation*, 238; Minnis, *Medieval Theory of Authorship*, 79–81, 102, 118, 164–65, 170, 173–75.
45. Minnis, *Medieval Theory of Authorship*, 69–70.
46. Minnis, *Medieval Theory of Authorship*, 77, 102.
47. Minnis, *Medieval Theory of Authorship*, 73.
48. The conflicts between the humanists and the Scholastic theologians are more often noted than the continuities; see Erika Rummel, ed., *Biblical Humanism and Scholasticism in the Age of Erasmus* (Leiden and Boston: Brill, 2008).
49. Nellen and Bloemendal, "Erasmus's Biblical Project," 608.
50. Erasmus, Letter 456, in *The Correspondence of Erasmus, Letters 446 to 593: 1516 to 1517*, trans. R. A. B. Mynors and D. F. S. Thomason, *CWS* 4 (Toronto: University of Toronto Press, 1977), 46; *Opus Epistolarum Des. Erasmi Roterodami*, ed. P. S. Allen and H. M. Allen (Oxford: Oxford University Press, 1910–1958/2012), 2:323.
51. *CWE* 4:46; *Opus Epistolarum* 2:324.
52. See Robert Coogan, *Erasmus, Lee, and the Correction of the Vulgate: The Shaking of the Foundations* (Geneva: Droz, 1992); Erika Rummel, *Erasmus and His Catholic Critics*, 2 vols. (Nieuwkoop, Netherlands: De Graaf, 1989).
53. Joseph M. Levine, "Erasmus and the Problem of the Johannine Comma [1 John 5:7–8]," *Journal of the History of Ideas* 58, no. 4 (1997): 573–96.
54. Erasmus translated the Latin word "sacramentum" in Ephesians 5:32 of the *Biblia vulgata* as "mysterium."
55. See Thomas More, *De Tristia Christi*, Vol. 14 of *The Yale Edition of the Complete Works of St. Thomas More* (New Haven, CT: Yale University Press, 1976). For an English translation, see "The Sadness of Christ," in *Saint Thomas More: Selected Writings*, ed. John F. Thornton and Susan B. Varenne (New York: Random House, 2003), 1–116.
56. Nellen and Bloemendal, "Erasmus's Biblical Project," 632.
57. *CWE* 61:19; *Erasmi Opuscula*, 134.
58. *CWE* 61:23; *Erasmi Opuscula*, 137.

59. *CWE* 61:47; *Erasmi Opuscula*, 171.
60. See Pabel, *Herculean Labours*, 185–86; Eugene F. Rice Jr., *Saint Jerome in the Renaissance* (Baltimore: Johns Hopkins University Press, 1985), 37–44.
61. *CWE* 61:24; *Erasmi Opuscula*, 139.
62. *CWE* 61:47; *Erasmi Opuscula*, 171.
63. *CWE* 61:5; Letter 396, *Opus Epistolarum*, 2:212–13.
64. Rice, *Saint Jerome in the Renaissance*, 130.
65. Pabel, *Herculean Labours*, 181.
66. *CWE* 61:22; *Erasmi Opuscula*, 136.
67. *CWE* 61:22; *Erasmi Opuscula*, 136.
68. Peter G. Bietenholz, *History and Biography in the Work of Erasmus of Rotterdam* (Genève: Librairie Droz, 1966), 91.
69. *CWE* 61:24; *Erasmi Opuscula*, 139.
70. *CWE* 61:24; *Erasmi Opuscula*, 138.
71. *CWE* 61:24; *Erasmi Opuscula*, 138.
72. *CWE* 61:25; *Erasmi Opuscula*, 140.
73. *CWE* 61:27; *Erasmi Opuscula*, 143.
74. *CWE* 61:29; *Erasmi Opuscula*, 145–46.
75. *CWE* 61:33; *Erasmi Opuscula*, 151.
76. *CWE* 61:35; *Erasmi Opuscula*, 153–54.
77. Jerome relates the dream to Eustochium in Letter 22.30; see *Letters of St. Jerome*, 1:165–66.
78. *CWE* 61:46; *Erasmi Opuscula*, 169–70.
79. *CWE* 61:36; *Erasmi Opuscula*, 155.
80. *CWE* 61:49; *Erasmi Opuscula*, 174.
81. *CWE* 61:50; *Erasmi Opuscula*, 176.
82. *CWE* 61:51; *Erasmi Opuscula*, 177.
83. *CWE* 61:51; *Erasmi Opuscula*, 177.
84. *CWE* 61:51; *Erasmi Opuscula*, 177.
85. In his famous letter to Eustochium (Letter 22.30), Jerome himself refers to his having taken an oath never again to possess profane books. Against Rufinus's charge (*Apologia* 2.6, 7) that Jerome broke that oath, Erasmus asserts that Jerome could never in fact have made such an oath, but only dreamed in his illness that he had; see *CWE* 61:51–52; *Erasmi Opuscula*, 177–78. Jerome himself refuted Rufinus's charge in *Contra Rufinum* 1.30–31, 3.32.
86. *CWE* 61:51–52; *Erasmi Opuscula*, 178.
87. As a devotee of Cicero, the young Augustine famously disdained the plain style of the scriptures, whose eloquence he later celebrated; see *Conf.* 3.5 (9); *De doctrina Christiana*, bk. 4.
88. *CWE* 61:56; *Erasmi Opuscula*, 184.

89. *CWE* 61:52; *Erasmi Opuscula*, 179.
90. *CWE* 61:54; *Erasmi Opuscula*, 180–81.
91. *CWE* 61:53; *Erasmi Opuscula*, 180. For similar associations of the Fathers of the Church with the senses of scripture, see Henri de Lubac, *Medieval Exegesis: The Four Senses of Scripture*, trans. Mark Sebank and E. M. Macierowski (Grand Rapids, MI: William B. Eerdmans, 1998–2009), 1:3–6.
92. *CWE* 61:53; *Erasmi Opuscula*, 179.
93. *CWE* 61:59; *Erasmi Opuscula*, 187.
94. Pabel, *Herculean Labours*, 87–89.
95. Pabel, *Herculean Labours*, 91.
96. Pabel, *Herculean Labours*, 85–86.
97. Pabel, *Herculean Labours*, 86–87, 224–32, 287–91, 317–34.
98. Martin Luther, *Luther's Works*, Vol. 48, *Letters 1*, ed. Gottfried G. Krodel (Philadelphia: Fortress, 1963), epistle 13. The theological dispute between Luther and Erasmus over free will is of central importance to the Reformation.
99. Levy, *Introducing Medieval Biblical Interpretation*, 264.
100. I echo here the title of Stephen Greenblatt, *Renaissance Self-Fashioning from More to Shakespeare* (Chicago: University of Chicago Press, 1980).
101. Bietenholz, *History and Biography in the Work of Erasmus of Rotterdam*, 91.
102. On this sketch of More, see Clare M. Murphy, "Erasmus as Biographer of Thomas More and His Family," in *Erasmus and the Republic of Letters*, ed. Stephen Ryle (Leiden: Brepols, 2006), 85–103; Germain Marc'hadour, "Erasmus: First and Best Biographer of Thomas More," *Erasmus of Rotterdam Society Yearbook* 7 (1987): 1–30.
103. Bietenholz, *History and Biography in the Work of Erasmus of Rotterdam*, 96. See Erasmus, *Life of Origen: A New Annotated Translation of the Prefaces to Erasmus of Rotterdam's Edition of Origen's Writings*, trans. Thomas P. Scheck (Washington, DC: Catholic University of America Press, 2016).
104. *Harpsfield's Life of More*, 6.
105. See John Maguire, "William Roper's *Life of More*: The Working Methods of a Tudor Biographer," *Moreana* 23 (1969): 59–69; Mark Robson, "Writing Contexts in William Roper's *Life of Thomas More*," in *Writing the Lives of Writers*, ed. Warwick Gould and Thomas F. Staley (New York: St. Martin's Press, 1998), 79–89.
106. Praising More's Christian folly—the wisdom of the cross (cf. 1 Cor. 1:18)—Roper may have had in mind Erasmus's earlier, satiric tribute to More, *Encomium Moriae* (*Praise of Folly*). For this double-sided argument, which deconstructs Roper's praise, see Jonathan V. Crewe, "The 'Encomium Moriae' of William Roper," *English Literary History* (1988): 287–307.
107. Roper, *Lyfe of Sir Thomas Moore, knighte*, 3 (emphasis added).

108. *Harpsfield's Life of More*, 208. See the preface to Erasmus's translation of *Ecclesiastae Libri IV*, in Letter 3036, to Christopher of Stadion, *The Correspondence of Erasmus: Letters 2940–3141*, ed. James M. Estes, trans. Alexander Dalzell (Toronto: University of Toronto Press, 2021), *CWE* 21:324–30; OE 11:189–93.

109. Letter 999, to Ulrich von Hutten, in *The Correspondence of Erasmus, Letters 993 to 1121: 1519 to 1520*, trans. R. A. B. Mynors (Toronto: University of Toronto Press, 1987), *CWE* 7:16; *Opus Epistolarum*, 4:13.

110. *Harpsfield's Life of More*, 4. L. E. Semler notes in the motif of the New Year's gift an echo of More's own New Year's gift in 1505 to Joyce Lee of his translation of the biography of Pico della Mirandola; see Semler, "Virtue, Transformation, and Exemplarity in *The Lyfe of Johan Picus*," in *A Companion to Thomas More*, ed. A. D. Cousins and Damian Grace (Madison, NJ: Fairleigh Dickinson University Press, 2009), 98.

111. *Harpsfield's Life of More*, 56, 74, 92–93, 141–42; Letter 999, *CWE* 7:23, 17–19, 21; *Opus Epistolarum*, 4:16–19.

112. *Harpsfield's Life of More*, 78.

113. *Harpsfield's Life of More*, 80–81.

114. *Harpsfield's Life of More*, 92; Erasmus's Letter 2750, to Johannes Fabri, in *The Correspondence of Erasmus, Letters 2635 to 2802*, trans. Clarence H. Miller, with Charles Fantazzi (Toronto: University of Toronto Press, 1974), *CWE* 19:230; *Opus Epistolarum*, 10:139.

115. *Harpsfield's Life of More*, 101.

116. *Harpsfield's Life of More*, 136.

117. *Harpsfield's Life of More*, 208.

118. *Harpsfield's Life of More*, 109.

119. See Dominic Baker-Smith, "Erasmus and More: A Friendship Revisited," *Recusant History* 30.1 (2010): 7–25; James K. McConica, "The Recusant Reputation of Thomas More," in *Essential Articles for the Study of Thomas More*, ed. Richard S. Sylvester and Germain P. Marc'hadour (Hamden, CT: Archon, 1977), 136–49. For a recent defense and appreciation of Erasmus, see Thomas P. Scheck, "Author's Preface" and "Introduction," in Erasmus, *Life of Origen*, xv–xxviii, xxix–xxxv.

120. *Harpsfield's Life of More*, 107. On this topic, see Jamie H. Ferguson, "Faith in the Language: Biblical Authority and the Meaning of English in More–Tyndale Polemics," *The Sixteenth-Century Journal* 43, no. 4 (2012): 989–1011.

121. *Harpsfield's Life of More*, 114.

122. *Harpsfield's Life of More*, 131.

123. Thomas More, *A Treatice Vpon the Passion*, in *Complete Works of St. Thomas More*, ed. Garry E. Haupt (New Haven, CT: Yale University Press, 1976), 13:158–59.

124. *Harpsfield's Life of More*, 44.

125. *Harpsfield's Life of More*, 48.
126. *Harpsfield's Life of More*, 213.
127. *Harpsfield's Life of More*, 64–65, 177.
128. *Harpsfield's Life of More*, 98–99.
129. *Harpsfield's Life of More*, 153.
130. *Harpsfield's Life of More*, 135. See Isaiah 6:6.
131. *Harpsfield's Life of More*, 217. For the image of Christ as head of his body, the Church, see Col. 1:18; 1 Cor. 11:3; Eph. 5:23.
132. *Harpsfield's Life of More*, 77.
133. *Harpsfield's Life of More*, 179.
134. *Harpsfield's Life of More*, 197. On Saint Stephen as a model for More, see John R. Cavanaugh, "The Saint Stephen Motif in Saint Thomas More's Thought," *Moreana* 8 (1965): 59–66.
135. *Harpsfield's Life of More*, 203.
136. *Harpsfield's Life of More*, 214.
137. Peter Sherlock, *Monuments and Memory in Early Modern England* (Aldershot: Ashgate, 2008), 149.
138. Sherlock, *Monuments and Memory*, 149.
139. Sherlock, *Monuments and Memory*, 1, 3. See Nigel Llewellyn, *Funeral Monuments in Post-Reformation England* (Cambridge: Cambridge University Press, 2000).
140. Sherlock, *Monuments and Memory*, 3.
141. See Letter 2659, from Thomas More, in *CWE* 19:55–59; *Opus Epistolarum*, 10:31–34.
142. See Letter 2831, from Thomas More, in *The Correspondence of Erasmus, Letters 2803 to 2939*, trans. Clarence H. Miller, with Charles Fantazzi, (Toronto: University of Toronto Press, 1974), *CWE* 20:81–86; *Opus Epistolarum*, 10:258–61; for Marcus Haworth's translation of this letter and the epitaph, see Stephen Smith, ed., *For All Seasons: Selected Letters of Thomas More* (New York: Scepter Publishers, 2012), 182–88.
143. Letter 2831, *CWE* 20:82; *Opus Epistolarum*, 10:259.
144. More wrote *The Supplicacion of Soules* in answer to Simon Fish's *A Supplycacion for the Beggars*, which called for the dispossession of the clergy; see Rainier Pineas, "Thomas More's Controversy with Simon Fish," *Studies in English Literature, 1500–1900*, 7, no. 1 (1967): 15–28.
145. Letter 2831, *CWE* 20:82; *Opus Epistolarum*, 10:259.
146. Letter 2750, to Johannes Fabri, *CWE* 19:228; *Opus Epistolarum*, 10:137.
147. The reconstructed epitaph shows a blank space where the word "heretics" would have appeared. Erasmus advised More to expunge it.

148. Letter 2750, to Johannes Fabri, *CWE* 19:228; *Opus Epistolarum*, 10:137. In fact, six heretics were executed; see Richard Rex, "Thomas More and the Heretics: Statesman or Fanatic?," in *The Cambridge Companion to Thomas More*, ed. George M. Logan (Cambridge: Cambridge University Press, 2011), 93–115.

149. Paul Binski, *Medieval Death: Ritual and Representation* (Ithaca, NY: Cornell University Press, 1996), 93.

150. Binski, *Medieval Death*, 93.

151. Binski, *Medieval Death*, 94.

152. See Ann W. Astell, "Retooling the Instruments of Christ's Passion: Memorial Technai, St. Thomas the Twin, and British Library Additional MS 22029," in *The Arma Christi in Medieval and Early Modern Material Culture*, ed. Lisa H. Cooper and Andrea Denny-Brown (Burlington, VT: Ashgate, 2014), 171–202, esp. 173–77.

153. Binski, *Medieval Death*, 114, 115.

154. *Harpsfield's Life of More*, 60.

155. *Harpsfield's Life of More*, 9; the text of the epitaph is included in this volume as appendix IV, 277–81.

156. *Harpsfield's Life of More*, 59.

157. *Harpsfield's Life of More*, 60–61.

158. *Harpsfield's Life of More*, 61.

159. *Harpsfield's Life of More*, 61.

160. *Harpsfield's Life of More*, 18.

161. Roper, *Lyfe of Sir Thomas Moore, knighte*, 6.

162. Letter 999, to Ulrich von Hutten, *CWE* 7:21; *Opus Epistolarum*, 4:17–18.

163. Letter 999, to Ulrich von Hutten, *CWE* 7:21; *Opus Epistolarum*, 4:17–18. I have modified the English translation.

164. *Harpsfield's Life of More*, 18.

165. *Harpsfield's Life of More*, 18.

166. *Harpsfield's Life of More*, 18.

167. *Harpsfield's Life of More*, 18 (emphasis added).

168. *Harpsfield's Life of More*, 17.

169. *Harpsfield's Life of More*, 179.

170. *Harpsfield's Life of More*, 213.

171. *Harpsfield's Life of More*, 209.

172. Letter 2831, from Thomas More, *CWE* 20:85; *Opus Epistolarum*, 10:261.

173. L. E. Semler has argued that Pico della Mirandola, whose biography More translated in 1504 and gave as a New Year's gift to Joyce Lee in January 1505, served as a positive and negative vocational model for More. Pico lived a virtuous life in the world, but his biographer reveals that he suffered in purgatory after

death for having refused God's call to religious life. According to Semler's careful analysis, More's translation of Pico's life influenced More's early biographers, starting with Harpsfield; see Semler, "Virtue, Transformation, and Exemplarity in *The Lyfe of Johan Picus.*"

174. Thomas More, *The Last Things*, in *The Yale Edition of the Complete Works of St. Thomas More*, ed. Anthony S. G. Edwards, Catherine Gardiner Rodgers, and Clarence H. Miller ((New Haven, CT: Yale University Press, 1963), 1:129.

175. *Lyfe of Sir Thomas More . . . by Ro. Ba*, 275.

CHAPTER NINE. Modern Literary Experiments in Biblical Hagiography

1. Emmanuel Levinas, *Beyond the Verse: Talmudic Readings and Lectures*, trans. Gary D. Mole (New York: Continuum, 2007), 109.

2. See Armando Tomo, *Chiara Lubich: A Biography*, trans. Bill Harnett (New York: New City Press, 2012), 28–30, 40, 44–45.

3. William D. Miller, *Dorothy Day: A Biography* (San Francisco: Harper and Row, 1982), 331, 343; John Longery and Blythe Randolph, *Dorothy Day* (New York: Simon and Schuster, 2020), 4, 9.

4. Dorothea M. Schlickmann, *The Hidden Years: Father Joseph Kentenich, Childhood and Youth (1885–1910)*, trans. Mary Jane Hoehne (Waukesha, WI: Schoenstatt Editions U.S.A., 2009), 106–13.

5. Alberto Savorana, *The Life of Luigi Guissani* (Montreal: McGill-Queen's University Press, 2018), 48.

6. On the theme of the need for innovation in the writing of saints' *Lives*, see John A. Coleman, "Conclusion: After Sainthood," in *Saints and Virtues*, ed. John Stratton Hawley (Berkeley: University of California Press, 1987), 205–25. Modernity has seen a range of experiments in hagiographic writing, but few examples exist that show a conscious integration with scripture. For examples of literary experiments, see Fyodor Dostoevsky's *The Idiot* (1868–69), Gustave Flaubert's *La légend de Saint-Julien l'hospitalier* (1877), Mark Twain's *Personal Recollections of Joan of Arc* (1896), Émile Zola's *Lourdes* (1894), Paul Claudel's *L'Annonce faite à Marie* (1910), Charles Péguy's *Le Mystère de la charité de Jeanne d'Arc* (1910), George Bernard Shaw's *Saint Joan* (1924), Sigrid Undset's *Catherine of Siena* (1928), Jean Genet's pornographic *Notre Dame des Fleurs* (1942), Jean Paul Sartre's *Saint Genet, comédien et martyr* (1952), Bertolt Brecht's *Saint Joan of the Stockyards* (1955), and Erik Ehn's *The Saint Plays* (2000). Edith Wyschogrod numbers Henry James's *The Wings of the Dove* (1902) among such literary experiments; see Wyschogrod, *Saints and Postmodernism: Revisioning Moral Philosophy* (Chicago: University of Chicago Press, 1990), 42–48.

7. For a theological engagement with this idea, see Michael Tomko, *Beyond the Willing Suspension of Disbelief: Poetic Faith from Coleridge to Tolkein* (New York: Bloomsbury, 2015).

8. Geir Kjetsaa, *Dostoevsky and His New Testament* (Atlantic Highlands, NJ: Humanities Press, 1984), 5.

9. Kjetsaa, *Dostoevsky and His New Testament*, 8.

10. Kjetsaa, *Dostoevsky and His New Testament*, 13.

11. Kjetsaa, *Dostoevsky and His New Testament*, 13.

12. Henri de Lubac, S.J., *The Drama of Atheist Humanism*, trans. Edith M. Riley (New York: Sheed and Ward, 1950), 165–66.

13. The novel has an earlier, enigmatic reference to the raising of Lazarus, which has awakened Raskolnikov's interest; see Fyodor Dostoevsky, *Crime and Punishment*, trans. Michael R. Katz (New York: Liveright, 2018), 287.

14. For a study of the theological significance of language and speech in the novel, see Rowan Williams, *Dostoevsky: Language, Faith, and Fiction* (Waco, TX: Baylor University Press, 2008).

15. Dostoevsky, *Crime and Punishment*, 360.

16. Fyodor Dostoevsky, *The Brothers Karamazov*, trans. Richard Pevear and Larissa Volokhonsky (1990; repr. New York: Farrar, Straus and Giroux, 2002), dedication page.

17. Dostoevsky, *Brothers Karamazov*, 285.

18. Dostoevsky, *Brothers Karamazov*, 309.

19. Dostoevsky, *Brothers Karamazov*, 309.

20. Dostoevsky, *Brothers Karamazov*, 290.

21. Dostoevsky, *Brothers Karamazov*, 291.

22. Dostoevsky, *Brothers Karamazov*, 293.

23. Dostoevsky, *Brothers Karamazov*, 294.

24. Dostoevsky, *Brothers Karamazov*, 294.

25. Dostoevsky, *Brothers Karamazov*, 294.

26. An allusion to Luke 24:37, "Did not our hearts burn within us while he talked to us on the road, while he opened to us the scriptures?"

27. Dostoevsky, *Brothers Karamazov*, 295.

28. Dostoevsky, *Brothers Karamazov*, 295, 292.

29. See Nadejda Gorodetzky, *Saint Tikhon Zadonsky, Inspirer of Dostoevsky* (London: SPCK, 1951); Thomas Berry, "Dostoevsky and St. Tikhon Zadonski," *New Zealand Slavonic Journal* (1989–90): 67–72.

30. Nel Grillaert, "Dostoevskij's Portrait of a 'Pure, Ideal Christian': Echoes of Nil Sorskij in the Elder Zosima," *Russian Literature* 67 (2010): 185–216.

31. Dostoevsky, *Brothers Karamazov*, 360.

32. Dostoevsky, *Brothers Karamazov*, 361.

33. Dostoevsky, *Brothers Karamazov*, 362.

34. Dostoevsky, *Brothers Karamazov*, 362.

35. Cather's research for the novel involved a close reading of W. J. Howlett, *Life of the Right Reverend Joseph P. Machebeuf, D.D., Pioneer Priest of Ohio, Pioneer Priest of New Mexico, Pioneer Priest of Colorado, Vicar Apostolic of Colorado and Utah* (Pueblo, CO: Franklin, 1908), and of extant letters written by Archbishop Lamy and Father Machebeuf.

36. See Margaret Anne O'Connor, ed., *Willa Cather: The Contemporary Reviews* (Cambridge: Cambridge University Press, 2001), 307–50. In her review for the *Boston Evening Transcript*, Dorothy Foster Gilman writes: "In the first place, this is not a novel" (in O'Connor, ed., *Willa Cather*, 314).

37. Andrew Jewell and Janis Stout, eds., *The Selected Letters of Willa Cather* (New York: Alfred A. Knopf, 2013), 396.

38. Willa Cather, *On Writing* (New York: A. A. Knopf, 1949), 9–10. Cather probably knew Jacobus de Voragine's *Golden Legend* through William Morris's illustrated 1892 edition; see Marilyn Berg Callander, *Willa Cather and the Fairy Tale* (Ann Arbor, MI: U.M.I. Research Press, 1989), 48.

39. Cather, *On Writing*, 9–10. Pierre Cécile Puvis de Chavannes (1824–98) exhibited his *Pastoral Life of Saint Geneviève*, a triptych, in 1879 in Paris. Cather saw it there at the Panthéon in 1902; see Polly P. Duryea, "Paintings and Drawings in Willa Cather's Prose: A Catalogue Raisonné" (PhD diss., University of Nebraska-Lincoln, 1993), 249.

40. Jewell and Stout, eds., *Selected Letters of Willa Cather*, 396.

41. For example, Santiago (Saint James), venerated in New Mexico as the patron saint for caballeros and their horses; Saint Joseph, whose venerated picture of grace at Ácoma secures the fertility of livestock. See Willa Cather, *Death Comes for the Archbishop* (New York: Vintage Classics, 1990), 27, 87.

42. For the apparitions of the Holy Family to Junipero Serra and of Our Lady of Guadalupe to Juan Diego, see Cather, *Death Comes for the Archbishop*, 281–84 and 46–49, respectively.

43. See Pam Fox Kuhiken, "Hallowed Ground: Landscape as Hagiography in Willa Cather's *Death Comes for the Archbishop*," *Christianity and Literature* 52, no. 3 (2003): 367–85.

44. See Cather, *Death Comes for the Archbishop*, 29.

45. Mary-Ann Stouck and David Stouck, "Hagiographical Style in *Death Comes for the Archbishop*," *University of Toronto Quarterly: A Canadian Journal of the Humanities* 41 (1972): 293–307.

46. Cather, *Death Comes for the Archbishop*, 227; cf. Acts 2:44.

47. Cather, *Death Comes for the Archbishop*, 16, 17, 279. Cather's italics call attention to the echoes of 2 Cor. 11:23–29; Heb. 12:35–38.

48. Cather, *Death Comes for the Archbishop*, 260.

49. Cather, *Death Comes for the Archbishop*, 206–7.

50. Cather, *Death Comes for the Archbishop*, 206, 217.
51. Cather, *Death Comes for the Archbishop*, 201, 265.
52. Cather, *Death Comes for the Archbishop*, 209; for Magdalena's previous life of suffering, see 70–73.
53. Cather, *Death Comes for the Archbishop*, 273.
54. Cather, *Death Comes for the Archbishop*, 30.
55. Cather, *Death Comes for the Archbishop*, 31.
56. Cather, *Death Comes for the Archbishop*, 31.
57. Cather, *Death Comes for the Archbishop*, 97–98.
58. Cather, *Death Comes for the Archbishop*, 239–41.
59. Cather, *Death Comes for the Archbishop*, 218, 270.
60. Cather, *Death Comes for the Archbishop*, 105.
61. Strouck and Strouck, "Hagiographical Style," 303.
62. See, for example, Origen, Homily 15, in *Homilies on Joshua*, trans. Barbara J. Bruce, ed. Cynthia White (Washington, DC: Catholic University of America Press, 2002), 147.
63. See Matt. 24:43; Rev. 16:15; 2 Pet. 3:10; 1 Thess. 5:2.
64. In Dante, *Inferno* 5.4–12, Minos the judge wraps his tail around the damned to assign them their proper place in one of the circles of hell. The monster Geryon (*Inferno* 17.1–27) has a tail like a scorpion. Dante depicts Satan in *Inferno* 34.38–57 as eating three sinners in his three mouths: Judas Iscariot, who betrayed Christ, and Brutus and Cassius, who assassinated Julius Caesar.
65. For example, Simplicius and Faustinus, the twins Gervasius and Protasius, Cosmas and Damian, Simon and Jude, Gordianus and Epimachus, Nereus and Achilleus, Primus and Felicianus, Vitus and Modestus, John and Paul, Nazarius and Celsus, Abdon and Sennen, Felix and Adauctus, Gorgonius and Dorotheus, Protus and Hyacinthus, Cornelius and Cyprian, Peter and Paul.
66. Edith Wyschogrod identifies three distinguishing features of the saint's *Life* as a genre: (1) its "temporal character or event structure," (2) its "grammatical mood," and (3) "the social formations it exhibits"; see Wyschogrod, *Saints and Postmodernism*, 6. For Wyschogrod, the "grammatical mood" of a saint's *Life* is the imperative: "Follow me."
67. Franz Werfel, *Between Heaven and Earth*, trans. Maxim Newmark (New York: Philosophical Library, 1944), 250–51.
68. For a longer treatment of Werfel's hagiography with a different focus, see Ann W. Astell, "Artful Dogma: The Immaculate Conception and Franz Werfel's *Song of Bernadette*," *Christianity and Literature* 62, no. 1 (2012): 189–212.
69. Werfel, *Between Heaven and Earth*, 250.
70. At the time of Werfel's writings, the rosary contained fifteen mysteries, so that the total number of Hail Marys numbered 150, to equal the number of bib-

lical psalms—hence the traditional name "Our Lady's Psalter." During the pontification of Pope Saint John Paul II, the number was expanded to twenty, to include five mysteries from the public ministry of Jesus.

71. Franz Werfel, *The Song of Bernadette*, trans. Ludwig Lewisohn (San Francisco: Ignatius, 2006[1942]), 57.

72. The Vulgate translation has "Ipsa" (she), whereas the Septuagint has the masculine pronoun. The linguistic difference in the traditions points to Mary's role as the New Eve at the side of Christ her Son, the "last Adam" (1 Cor. 15:45). Christian art regularly depicts Mary with her bare foot crushing the head of the serpent.

73. Werfel, *Song of Bernadette*, 51.
74. Werfel, *Song of Bernadette*, 51.
75. Werfel, *Song of Bernadette*, xiii.
76. Werfel, *Song of Bernadette*, 147.
77. Werfel, *Song of Bernadette*, 147.
78. Werfel, *Song of Bernadette*, 226.
79. For a historical witness to these phenomena at Lourdes, see Jerry Ryan, "Legacy of a Country Priest, My Friend the Exorcist," *Commonweal Magazine*, October 7, 2011, 18–20.
80. Werfel, *Song of Bernadette*, 305–6.
81. Werfel, *Song of Bernadette*, 511.
82. Werfel, *Song of Bernadette*, 526.
83. Werfel, *Song of Bernadette*, 498.
84. Werfel, *Song of Bernadette*, 577.
85. Quoted in Lionel B. Steiman, *Franz Werfel: The Faith of an Exile: From Prague to Beverly Hills* (Waterloo, ON: Wilfrid Laurier University Press, 1985), 150.
86. See Werfel, *Between Heaven and Earth*, 251.
87. Werfel, *Song of Bernadette*, 249.
88. Werfel, *Song of Bernadette*, 285.
89. Werfel, *Song of Bernadette*, 522.
90. For a detailed treatment of this allegory, see Astell, "Artful Dogma."
91. Werfel, *Song of Bernadette*, 238.
92. Werfel, *Song of Bernadette*, 284.
93. Werfel, *Song of Bernadette*, 517–18.
94. Werfel, *Song of Bernadette*, 121.
95. Werfel, *Song of Bernadette*, 145.
96. Werfel, *Song of Bernadette*, 324.
97. Werfel, *Song of Bernadette*, 549.
98. Dostoevsky, *Crime and Punishment*, 360.
99. Werfel, *Song of Bernadette*, 567.
100. Werfel, *Between Heaven and Earth*, 250–51.

CHAPTER TEN. Historical Truth, Biblical Criticism, and Hagiography

1. See Ann W. Astell, ed., *Lay Sanctity, Medieval and Modern: A Search for Models* (Notre Dame, IN: University of Notre Dame Press, 2000).
2. Hans W. Frei, *The Eclipse of Biblical Narrative: A Study of Eighteenth and Nineteenth Century Hermeneutics* (New Haven, CT: Yale University Press, 1974), 4.
3. Frei, *Eclipse of Biblical Narrative*, 5.
4. Frei, *Eclipse of Biblical Narrative*, 8.
5. Frei, *Eclipse of Biblical Narrative*, 7.
6. Frei has clearly been influenced by Eric Auerbach, "Figura," in *Scenes from the Drama of European Literature*, trans. Ralph Manheim, Theory and History of Literature 9 (Minneapolis: University of Minnesota Press, 1984), 11–78.
7. Frei, *Eclipse of Biblical Narrative*, 7.
8. See Eric Auerbach, *Mimesis: The Representation of Reality in Western Literature*, trans. William R. Trask, 1st Princeton Classics (Princeton, NJ: Princeton University Press, 2013).
9. Thomas J. Heffernan, *Sacred Biography: Saints and Their Biographers in the Middle Ages* (New York: Oxford University Press, 1988), 57.
10. Edward Gibbon, *The Decline and Fall of the Roman Empire* (New York: Modern Library, 1952), 1:467.
11. Heffernan, *Sacred Biography*, 57.
12. See, for example, Thomas Head, *Hagiography and the Cult of Saints: The Diocese of Orléans, 800–1200* (Cambridge: Cambridge University Press, 1990); Sharon Farmer, *Communities of Saint Martin: Legend and Ritual in Medieval Tours* (Ithaca, NY: Cornell University Press, 1991); Raymond Van Dam, *Saints and Their Miracles in Late Antique Gaul* (Princeton, NJ: Princeton University Press, 1993); David Rollason, *Saints and Relics in Anglo-Saxon England* (Oxford: B. Blackwell, 1989); Clare Stancliffe, *Saint Martin and His Hagiographer: History and Miracle in Sulpicius Severus* (Oxford: Clarendon, 1983); Barbara Abou El-Hag, *The Medieval Cult of Saints: Formations and Transformations* (Binghamton, NY: State University of New Your Press, 1994); Karen Jankulac, *The Medieval Cult of St. Petroc* (Woodbridge, Suffolk: Boydell, 2000), among many others.
13. Augustine Thompson, O.P., *Francis of Assisi: A New Biography* (Ithaca, NY: Cornell University Press, 2012), 160.
14. Thompson, *Francis of Assisi*, viii.
15. Influenced by Thompson's method in his biography of Francis, Donald S. Prudlo similarly looks for the historical basis behind the hagiographic accounts in early *Lives* of Thomas Aquinas; see Prudlo, *Thomas Aquinas: A Historical, Theological, and Environmental Portrait* (New York: Paulist, 2020). Prudlo explicitly associates hagiography with a biblical worldview and narrative style (36–39).

16. Thompson, *Francis of Assisi*, 174. This is actually a strangely antihistoric argument, because it fails to acknowledge that Christian parents regularly named their children after saints in the hope that the saints would intercede for them and provide them with a life's model.

17. Thompson, *Francis of Assisi*, 182–83.

18. I think here of the members of the Sant'Egidio Community, which helped to broker the historic 1992 Mozambique Peace Accord, and which, at the request of Pope John Paul II, organizes the annual interreligious day of prayer for peace at Assisi.

19. Heffernan, *Sacred Biography*, 14.

20. Heffernan, *Sacred Biography*, 15.

21. Heffernan, *Sacred Biography*, 31.

22. Heffernan, *Sacred Biography*, 31.

23. Heffernan's case for "sacred biography" bears some resemblance to David Tracy's notion of the "spiritual classic" as imbued with a mystery that "elicits, even empowers the religious self to believe that how we ought to live (for the Jew and Christian, with compassion, in justice, and in love, in righteousness) is grounded in the fundamental nature of reality itself"; see Tracy, *The Analogical Imagination: Christian Theology and the Culture of Pluralism* (New York: Crossroad, 1981), 177. Tracy writes, "To allow for the world of the religious classics is in the end to allow for a world of meaning and truth disclosing the truth of the paradigmatic, the classical, the extraordinary" (177).

24. Heffernan, *Sacred Biography*, 5.

25. Alasdair MacIntyre, *After Virtue: A Study in Moral Theory*, 3rd ed. (Notre Dame, IN: University of Notre Dame Press, 2007), 121.

26. Edith Wyschogrod, *Saints and Postmodernism: Revisioning Moral Philosophy* (Chicago: University of Chicago Press, 1990), 8.

27. Wyschogrod, *Saints and Postmodernism*, 8.

28. Wyschogrod, *Saints and Postmodernism*, 6.

29. Wyschogrod, *Saints and Postmodernism*, 6.

30. See Alexander Lucie-Smith, *Narrative Theology and Moral Theology: The Infinite Horizon* (Burlington, VT: Ashgate, 2007).

31. Frei, *Eclipse of Biblical Narrative*, 13–14.

32. Auerbach, *Mimesis*, 12.

33. Hans W. Frei, "Theology and the Interpretation of Narrative: Some Hermeneutical Considerations," in *Theology and Narrative: Selected Essays*, ed. George Hunsinger and William C. Placher (Oxford: Oxford University Press, 1993), 113.

34. Frei, *Eclipse of Biblical Narrative*, 14–15; Auerbach, *Mimesis*, 12.

35. Robert Alter, *The Art of Biblical Narrative*, rev. ed. (New York: Basic Books, 2011[1981]), 18.

338 Notes to Pages 259–262

36. Auerbach, *Mimesis*, 12.
37. On the importance of the life of the saints in liturgy and devotion, see David Williams, *Saints Alive: Word, Image, and Enactment in the Lives of the Saints* (Quebec: McGill-Queen's University Press, 2010).
38. Wyschogrod, *Saints and Postmodernism*, 28–29.
39. Sherry L. Reames, *The "Legenda aurea": A Reexamination of Its Paradoxical History* (Madison: University of Wisconsin Press, 1985), 45.
40. Reames, *The "Legenda aurea,"* 46.
41. For in-depth studies of Gregory's *Life of Saint Benedict*, see Pearse Cusack, *An Interpretation of the Second Dialogue of Gregory the Great: Hagiography and St. Benedict*, Studies in the Bible and Early Christianity 31 (Lewiston, NY: Edwin Mellen Press, 1993); Gregory the Great, *The Life of Saint Benedict: A Commentary by Adalbert de Vogüé*, trans. Hilary Costello and Eoin de Bhaldraithe (Petersham, MA: St. Bede's Publications, 1993); Sherry L. Reames, "The Richness of Gregory's *Dialogues*," in *The "Legenda aurea": A Reexamination*, 73–84; Michaela Puzicha, *Kommentar zur Vita Benedicti: Gregor der Grosse: des zweite Buch der Dialoge* (St. Ottilien Archabbey, Emming, Germany: Editions of St. Ottilien, 2012).
42. See Michaela Zelzer, "Gregory's *Life of Benedict* and the Bible: The Decoding of an Exegetical Program," *Cistercian Studies Quarterly* 44, no. 1 (2009): 89–102.
43. Matthew Dal Santo, *Debating the Saints' Cults in the Age of Gregory the Great*, Oxford Studies in Byzantium (Oxford: Oxford University Press, 2012).
44. On the dialogue as a late antique genre associated with philosophical *otium*, see Joan M. Petersen, *The Dialogues of Gregory the Great in Their Late Antique Background* (Toronto: Pontifical Institute of Medieval Studies, 1985); Robert A. Markus, *Gregory the Great and His World* (Cambridge: Cambridge University Press, 1997).
45. See Joyce Coleman, *Public Reading and the Reading Public in Late Medieval England and France*, Cambridge Studies in Medieval Literature 26 (Cambridge: Cambridge University Press, 2005); Katharine Breen, *Imagining an English Reading Public, 1150–1400*, Cambridge Studies in Medieval Literature 79 (Cambridge: Cambridge University Press, 2010). Breen argues explicitly for the extension of monastic reading practices to the laity and discusses the reading of saints' *Lives*.
46. Gregory the Great, *Life of Saint Benedict*, chaps. 2 and 3.
47. Gregory the Great, *Life of Saint Benedict*, chap. 16.
48. Gregory the Great, *Life of Saint Benedict*, chap. 23.
49. Gregory the Great, *Life of Saint Benedict*, chap. 8.
50. Gregory the Great, *Life of Saint Benedict*, chap. 8.
51. Gregory the Great, *Life of Saint Benedict*, chap. 8.
52. Gregory the Great, *Life of Saint Benedict*, chap. 8.

53. See Augustine, Homily 7, in *Homilies on the First Epistle of John*, trans. H. Browne, ed. Philip Schaff, Nicene and Post-Nicene Fathers, 1st Series (Peabody, MA: Hendrickson, 1994).

54. Gregory the Great, *Life of St. Benedict*, chap. 33. On the Augustinian associations of this miracle story, see John C. Cavadini, "A Note on Gregory's Use of Miracles in the Life and Miracles of St. Benedict," *American Benedictine Review* 49, no. 1 (1998): 104–20; Jordan Joseph Wales, "The Narrated Theology of *Stabilitas* in Gregory the Great's *Life of Benedict*," *Cistercian Studies Quarterly* 49, no. 2 (2014): 163–98.

55. Gregory the Great, *Life of St. Benedict*, chap. 8.

56. Gregory the Great, *Life of St. Benedict: A Commentary by Adalbert de Vogüé*, 70.

57. See Augustine, *On Christian Doctrine* 3.30.42–3.37.55.

BIBLIOGRAPHY

PRIMARY SOURCES

Aelred of Rievaulx. *De speculo caritatis*. In *Opera ascetica*, Vol. 1 of *Opera Omnia*, edited by A. Hoste, O.S.B., and C. H. Talbot, 3–161. CCCM 1. Turnhout: Brepols, 1971.

———. *The Life of Ninian*. In *The Lives of the Northern Saints*, translated by Jane Patricia Freeland; edited by Marsha L. Dutton, 35–63. CF 71. Kalamazoo, MI: Cistercian Publications, 2006.

———. *The Mirror of Charity*. Translated by Elizabeth Connor, O.C.S.O. Edited by Charles Dumont. CF 17. Kalamazoo, MI: Cistercian Publications, 1990.

———. *Vita Niniani*. In *Pinkerton's Lives of the Scottish Saints*, rev. W. M. Metcalfe, 1:9–39. Paisley, Scotland: Alexander Gardner, 1889.

[Alcuin of York]. *De psalmorum usu*. PL 101: 465–508.

Amalar of Metz. *On the Liturgy*: Vol. 1, *Books 1–2*, and *On the Liturgy*, Vol. 2, *Books 3–4*. Edited by Eric Knibbs. Dumbarton Oaks Medieval Library. Cambridge, MA: Harvard University Press, 2014.

Ambrose of Milan. *Commentary of Saint Ambrose on Twelve Psalms*. Translated by Ide M. NiRiain. Dublin: Halcyon Press, 2000.

The Anglo-Saxon Version of the Life of St. Guthlac. Edited by and translated by Charles Wycliffe Goodwin. London: John Russell Smith, 1848.

Apocalypse of Paul. Edited by Theodore Silverstein and Anthony Hilhorst. Geneva: P. Cramer, 1997.

Aquinas, Thomas. *Catena Aurea: Commentary on the Four Gospels*. 4 vols. Translated by John Henry Newman. Oxford: J. H. Parker, 1842–1845.

———. *Commentary on the Gospel of John*. 2 vols. Translated by Fabian Larcher, O.P. Lander, WY: The Aquinas Institute for the Study of Sacred Doctrine, 2013.

———. *Summa Theologica*. 5 vols. Translated by Fathers of the English Dominican Province. New York: Benziger, 1948. Reprint, Allen, TX: Christian Classics, 1981.

Aristotle. *Nicomachean Ethics*. In *The Basic Works of Aristotle*, edited by Richard McKeon, translated by W. D. Ross, 927–1112. New York: Random House, 1941.

Armstrong, Regis, J. A. Wayne Hellmann, and William Short, eds. *Francis of Assisi: Early Documents*, 3 vols. New York: New City Press, 1999–2001.
Athanasius. *The Life of Antony and the Letter to Marcellinus*. Translated by Robert C. Gregg. Mahwah, NJ: Paulist, 1980.
Augustine. *The City of God*. Translated by Marcus Dods. New York: Modern Library, 1950.
———. *Confessions*. Translated by Henry Chadwick. Oxford: Oxford University Press, 2008.
———. *De utilitate credendi/Über den Nutzen des Glaubens*. Translated by Andreas Hoffman. Freiburg: Herder, 1992.
———. *Enarrationes in psalmos*. Edited by D. Eligivs Dekkers and Johannes Fraipont. CCSL 38–40. Turnhout: Brepols, 1956.
———. *Expositions of the Psalms (Enarrationes in psalmos)*. 6 vols. Edited by Boniface Ramsey. Translated by Maria Boulding. Hyde Park, NY: New City Press, 2004.
———. *Homilies on the First Epistle of John*. Translated by H. Browne. Edited by Philip Schaff. Nicene and Post-Nicene Fathers, 1st Series. Peabody, MA: Hendrickson, 1994.
———. *The Literal Meaning of Genesis*. 2 vols. Translated by John Hammond Taylor. Ancient Christian Writers 41–42. New York: Newman, 1982.
———. *On Christian Doctrine*. Translated by D. W. Robertson Jr. Indianapolis: Bobbs-Merrill, 1958.
———. *Sermons on the Liturgical Seasons*. Translated by Mary Sarah Muldowney, R.S.M. Fathers of the Church. Washington, DC: Catholic University of America Press, 1959.
Bede. *The Ecclesiastical History of the English People*. Edited by Judith McClure and Roger Collins. Translated by Bertram Colgrave. Oxford: Oxford University Press, 1999.
Benedict of Nursia. *The Rule of St. Benedict, Latin and English*. Translated by Luke Dysinger. Santa Ana, CA: Source Books, 1997, repr. 2003.
Bernard of Clairvaux. "Epistola 42. Ad Henricium Senonensem archiepiscopum." In *Sancti Bernardi Opera* Vol. 7, edited by Jean Leclercq and H. M. Rochais, 100–131. Rome: Editiones Cisterciensis, 1974.
———. *De consideratione ad Eugenium papam tertiam libri quinque*. In *Sancti Bernardi Opera* Vol. 3, *Tractatus et Opuscula*, edited by Jean Leclercq and H. M. Rochais, 379–494. Rome: Editiones Cisterciensis, 1957.
———. *De diligendo Deo*. In *Sancti Bernardi Opera*, Vol. 3, edited by Jean Leclercq and H. M. Rochais, 119–54. Rome: Editiones Cisterciensis, 1963.
———. *Five Books on Consideration: Advice to a Pope*. Translated by John D. Anderson and Elizabeth T. Kennan. CF 37. Kalamazoo, MI: Cistercian Publications, 1976.

———. *The Letters of St. Bernard of Clairvaux*. Translated by Bruno Scott James. Kalamazoo, MI: Cistercian Publications, 1998.

———. *The Life and Death of St. Malachy the Irishman*. Translated by Robert T. Meyer. CF 10. Kalamazoo, MI: Cistercian Publications, 1978.

———. *On Loving God*. Translated by Emero Stiegman. CF 13B. Kalamazoo, MI: Cistercian Publications, 1995.

———. "On the Conduct and Office of Bishops." In *On Baptism and the Office of Bishops*, 37–82. CF 67. Kalamazoo, MI: Cistercian Publications, 1974.

———. *On the Song of Songs 1*. Translated by Kilian Walsh. CF 4. Kalamazoo, MI: Cistercians Publications, 1971.

———. *On the Song of Songs 2*. Translated by Kilian Walsh. CF 7. Kalamazoo, MI: Cistercian Publications, 1976, repr. 1983.

———. *On the Song of Songs 3*. Translated by Killian Walsh and Irene M. Edmonds. CF 31. Kalamazoo, MI: Cistercian Publications, 1979.

———. *On the Song of Songs 4*. Translated by Irene Edmonds. CF 40. Kalamazoo, MI: Cistercian Publications, 1980.

———. *Sermones super Cantica Canticorum*, edited by Jean Leclercq, C. H. Talbot, and H. M. Rochais. Volume 2 of *Sancti Bernardi Opera*. Rome: Cistercian Publications, 1958.

———. *Vita Sancti Malachiae*. In *Sancti Bernardi Opera*, Vol. 3, *Tractatus et Opuscula*, edited by J. Leclercq and H. M. Rochais, 307–78. Rome: Cistercian Publications, 1963.

Biblia sacra vulgata. 5th ed. Edited by Robert Weber and Roger Gryson. Stuttgart: Deutsche Bibelgesellschaft, 2007.

Bokenham, Osbern. *A Legend of Holy Women: A Translation of Osbern Bokenham's "Legends of Holy Women."* Translated by Sheila Delany. Notre Dame, IN: University of Notre Dame Press, 1992.

———. *Legendys of Hooly Wummen*. Edited by Mary S. Serjeantson. EETS 206. London: Humphrey Milford, Oxford University Press, 1938, repr. 1997.

———. *Lives of Saints*. 3 vols. Edited by Simon Horobin. Oxford: Oxford University Press, 2020.

Bonaventure. *Breviloquium*. Translated by Dominic Monti. Works of St. Bonaventure 9. St. Bonaventure, NY: The Franciscan Institute, 2005.

———. *Collations on the Six Days*. Edited and Translated by José de Vinck. Volume 5 of *The Works of Bonaventure*. Paterson, NJ: St. Anthony Guild Press, 1970.

———. *Commentary on the Gospel of Luke, Part 1*. Edited and Translated by Robert J. Karris, O.F.M. Works of St. Bonaventure 8. St. Bonaventure, NY: The Franciscan Institute, 2011.

———. *Disputed Questions on Evangelical Perfection*. Edited by Robert J. Karris, O.F.M. Translated by Thomas Reist, O.F.M., and Robert J. Karris, O.F.M.

Works of St. Bonaventure 13. Saint Bonaventure, NY: The Franciscan Institute, 2008.

———. *Doctoris Seraphici S. Bonaventurae opera omnia.* 10 vols. Edita studio et cura Collegii a S. Bonaventura, ad plurimos codices mss. emendate, anecdotis aucta, prolegomenis scholiis notisque illustrate. Quaracchi, Italy: Collegium S. Bonaventurae, 1882–1902.

———. *The Major Legend of Saint Francis.* In Armstrong, Hellmann, and Short, eds., *Francis of Assisi: Early Documents,* 2:525–683.

The Book of Legends, Sefer Ha-Aggadah: Legends from the Talmud and Midrash. Edited by Hayim Nahman Bialik and Yehoshua Hana Ravnitzky. Translated by William G. Braude. New York: Schocken, 1992.

Cather, Willa. *Death Comes for the Archbishop.* New York: Vintage Classics, 1990.

———. *On Writing.* New York: A. A. Knopf, 1949.

———. *The Selected Letters of Willa Cather.* Edited by Andrew Jewell and Janis Stout. New York: Alfred A. Knopf, 2013.

Catherine of Siena. *Il Dialogo della Divina Providenza.* Edited by Giuliana Cavallini. Rome: Edizioni Cateriniane, 1968.

———. *The Dialogue.* Translated by Suzanne Noffke, O.P. New York: Paulist Press, 1980.

———. *The Letters of Catherine of Siena.* 4 vols. Translated by Suzanne Noffke. Tempe: Arizona Center for Medieval and Renaissance Studies, 2000.

Councils and Ecclesiastical Documents relating to Great Britain and Ireland. 3 vols. Edited by A. W. Haddan and W. Stubbs. Oxford: Clarendon, 1869–79.

Daniel, Walter. *The Life of Ælred of Rievaulx.* Translated by F. M. Powicke. CF 57. Kalamazoo, MI: Cistercian Publications, 1994.

Dostoevsky, Fyodor. *The Brothers Karamazov.* Translated by Richard Pevear and Larissa Volokhonsky. New York: Farrar, Straus and Giroux, 2002.

———. *Crime and Punishment.* Translated by Michael R. Katz. New York: Liveright, 2018.

Durandus. *Guillelmi Duranti: Rationale divinorum officiorum I–IV.* Edited by A. Davril and T. M. Thibodeau. CCCM 140. Turnhout: Brepols, 1995.

———. *Le Pontifical romain au moyen-âge.* Vol. 3, *Le pontifical de Guillaume Durand.* Edited by Michel Andrieu. Studi e testi 88. Vatican City: Biblioteca Apostolica Vaticana, 1940.

Eadmer. *Eadmer's "History of Recent Events in England" (Historia novorum in Anglia).* Translated by Geoffrey Bosanquet. Philadelphia: Dufour, 1965.

———. *Historia novorum in Anglia.* Edited by Martin Rule. Rolls Series. Wiesbaden: Kraus, 1965.

———. *The Life of St. Anselm, Archbishop of Canterbury, by Eadmer.* Edited and translated by R. W. Southern. Oxford Medieval Texts. Oxford: Clarendon, 1972.

344 Bibliography

Early Christian Biographies. Translated by Roy Joseph Deferrari. Fathers of the Church 15. Washington, DC: Catholic University of America Press, 1952.
Eleven Old English Rogationtide Homilies. Edited by Joyce Bazire and James E. Cross. Toronto: University of Toronto Press, 1982.
Erasmus, Desiderius. *The Correspondence of Erasmus, Letters 446 to 593: 1516 to 1517*. Translated by R. A. B. Mynors and D. F. S. Thomason. *CWS* 4. Toronto: University of Toronto Press, 1977.
———. *The Correspondence of Erasmus, Letters 993 to 1121: 1519 to 1520*. Translated by R. A. B. Mynors. *CWS* 7. Toronto: University of Toronto Press, 1987.
———. *The Correspondence of Erasmus, Letters 2635 to 2802: April 1532 to April 1533*. Translated by Clarence H. Miller, with Charles Fantazzi. *CWS* 19. Toronto: University of Toronto Press, 1974.
———. *The Correspondence of Erasmus, Letters 2803 to 2939: May 1533 to May 1534*. Translated by Clarence H. Miller, with Charles Fantazzi. *CWS* 20. Toronto: University of Toronto Press, 1974.
———. *The Correspondence of Erasmus: Letters 2940–3141: June 1534 to August 1536*. Edited by James M. Estes. Translated by Alexander Dalzell. *CWS* 21. Toronto: University of Toronto Press, 2021.
———. *Erasmi Opuscula: A Supplement to the Opera Omnia*. Edited by Wallace F. Ferguson. The Hague: Martinus Nijhoff, 1933.
———. *Erasmus's "Life of Origen": A New Annotated Translation of the Prefaces to Erasmus of Rotterdam's Edition of Origen's Writings*. Translated by Thomas P. Scheck. Washington, DC: Catholic University of America Press, 2016.
———. *Eximii Doctoris Hieronymi Stridonensis vita*. In *Erasmi Opuscula: A Supplement to the Opera Omnia*, edited by Wallace F. Ferguson, 134–90. The Hague: Martinus Nijhoff, 1933.
———. *The Life of the Eminent Doctor Jerome of Stridon Composed Mainly from His Own Writing by Desiderius Erasmus of Rotterdam*. In *Collected Works of Erasmus*, Vol. 61, *Patristic Scholarship: The Edition of St Jerome*, edited, translated, and annotated by James F. Brady and John C. Olin, 19–62. Toronto: University of Toronto Press, 1974.
———. *Opus Epistolarum Des. Erasmi Roterodami*. 12 vols. Edited by P. S. Allen and H. M. Allen. Oxford: Oxford University Press, 1910–1958.
Felix's "Life of Saint Guthlac." Edited by and translated by Bertram Colgrave. Cambridge: Cambridge University Press, 1956.
The Five Books of Moses. Translated by Everett Fox. New York: Schocken, 1997.
Flete, William. "Letter to Brother Raymond, Master of Theology," translated by Michael Benedict Hackett. In Michael Benedict Hackett, O.S.A, *William Flete, O.S.A., and Catherine of Siena: Masters of Fourteen Century Spirituality*, 167–77. Villanova, PA: Augustinian Press, 1992.

Bibliography   345

———. "On Remedies against Temptations," translated by Michael Benedict Hackett. In Hackett, *William Flete, O.S.A., and Catherine of Siena*, 127–38.

———. "Sermon on the Revered Saint Catherine of Siena," translated by Michael Benedict Hackett. In Hackett, *William Flete, O.S.A., and Catherine of Siena*, 185–221.

———. "The Spiritual Document," translated by Michael Benedict Hackett. In Hackett, *William Flete, O.S.A., and Catherine of Siena*, 181–84.

Francis of Assisi. "The Later Rule." In Armstrong, Hellmann, and Short, eds., *Francis of Assisi: Early Documents*, 1:99–106.

Gregory the Great. *Dialogi*. 3 vols. Edited by Adalbert de Vogüé. Sources chrétiennes 251, 260, 265. Paris: Éditions du Cerf, 1978.

———. *Homiliae in Hiezechihelem prophetam*. Edited by M. Adriaen. CCSL 142. Turnhout: Brepols, 1971.

———. *The Life of Saint Benedict: A Commentary by Adalbert de Vogüé*. Translated by Hilary Costello and Eoin de Bhaldraithe. Petersham, MA: St. Bede's Publications, 1993.

———. *Morals on the Book of Job*. 3 vols. Oxford: John Henry Parker, 1844–1850.

Gregory IX. *Mira circa nos*. In Armstrong, Hellmann, and Short, eds., *Francis of Assisi: Early Documents*, 1:565–69.

The Guthlac Poems of the Exeter Book. Edited by Jane Roberts. Oxford: Clarendon, 1979.

Harpsfield, Nicholas. *Harpsfield's Life of More*. EETS o.s. 186. London: Humphrey Milford, Oxford University Press, 1932.

Hildegard of Bingen. *Hildegardis Bingensis "Scivias."* Edited by Adelgundis Führkötter, O.S.B., with the help of Angela Carlevaris, O.S.B. CCCM 43 and 43A. Turnhout: Brepols, 1978.

———. *Scivias*. Translated by Mother Columba Hart and Jane Bishop. New York: Paulist, 1990.

Hostiensis. *In Tertium Decretalium Librum Commentaria*, on X.3.45 (*De reliquis* 1; *Audivimus*). Venice edition of 1581, facsimile. Torino: Bottega d'Erasmo, 1965.

Howlett, W. J. *Life of the Right Reverend Joseph P. Machebeuf, D.D., Pioneer Priest of Ohio, Pioneer Priest of New Mexico, Pioneer Priest of Colorado, Vicar Apostolic of Colorado and Utah*. Pueblo, CO: Franklin, 1908.

Hugh of Saint Victor. *The "Didascalicon" of Hugh of Saint Victor: A Medieval Guide to the Arts*. Translated by Jerome Taylor. Records of Western Civilization. New York: Columbia University Press, 1991.

———. *On the Sacraments of the Christian Faith*. Translated by Roy J. Deferrari. Cambridge, MA: Medieval Academy of America, 1951.

Jacobus de Voragine. *The Golden Legend: Readings on the Saints*. Translated by William Granger Ryan. Princeton, NJ: Princeton University Press, 2012.

——— [Iacopo da Varazze]. *Legenda aurea*. 2 vols. Edited by Giovanni Paolo Maggioni. Firenze: SISMEL/Edizioni del Galluzzo, 1998.

Jacques de Vitry. *The Exempla, or, Illustrative Stories from the Sermones Vulgares of Jacques de Vitry*. Edited by Thomas Frederick Crane. New York: Burt Franklin, 1971.

Jardine, Lisa. *Erasmus, Man of Letters: The Construction of Charisma in Print*. Princeton, NJ: Princeton University Press, 1993.

Jerome. *Edizione critica della "Vita Sancti Pauli Primi Eremitae" di Girolamo*. Edited by Bazyli Degórski. Rome: Institutum Patristicum "Augustinianum," 1987.

———. *Hieronymus, Vita Pauli*. Bezorgd, vertaald en toegelicht door Vincent Hunink. Leuven: Uitgeverij Press, 2002.

———. *The Letters of St. Jerome*. Vol. 1. Translated by Charles Christopher Mierow. Ancient Christian Writers 33. Westminster, MD: Newman Press, 1963.

———. *Life of Paul of Thebes by Jerome*. In *Early Christian Lives*, translated by Carolinne White, 71–84, 211–12. London: Penguin, 1998.

———. *Vite degli eremita Paolo, Ilarione, e Marco*. Edited by Bazyli Degórski. Rome: Città Nuova, 1996.

Johannis Beleth: Summa de ecclesiasticis officiis. Edited by Herbert Douteil. CCCM 412. Turnhout: Brepols, 1976.

John of Salisbury. *Anselm and Becket: Two Canterbury Saints' Lives*. Translated by Ronald E. Pepin. Turnhout: Brepols, 2009.

Julian of Norwich. *The Writings of Julian of Norwich*. Edited by Nicholas Watson and Jacqueline Jenkins. University Park: Pennsylvania State University Press, 2005.

Lambertini, Prospero. *De beatificatione Servorum Dei et de Beatorum canonizatione*. Bologna, 1734–38.

Les ordines Romani du Haut Moyen Age. 6 vols. Edited by Michel Andrieu. Louvain: Spicilegium Sacrum Lovaniense, 1961.

The Life of Saint Mary Magdalene and of Her Sister Saint Martha: A Medieval Biography. Translated and Annotated by David Mycoff. Kalamazoo, MI: Cistercian Publications, 1989.

The Lyfe of Syr Thomas More . . . by Ro. Ba. Edited by Elsie Vaughan Hitchcock and P. E. Hallett. EETS o.s. 222. London: Geoffrey Cumberlege, Oxford University Press, 1950.

Luther, Martin. *Works*. 55 vols. Philadelphia: Fortress, 1955–1986.

More, Thomas. *The Correspondence of Sir Thomas More*. Edited by Elizabeth Frances Rogers. Princeton, NJ: Princeton University Press, 1947.

———. *De Tristia Christi*. Volume 14 of *The Yale Edition of the Complete Works of St. Thomas More*. New Haven, CT: Yale University Press, 1976.

———. *For All Seasons: Selected Letters of Thomas More*. Edited by Stephen Smith. New York: Scepter Publishers, 2012.
———. "The Last Things." In *Complete Works of St. Thomas More*, edited by Anthony S. G. Edwards, Catherine Gardiner Rodgers, and Clarence H. Miller, 1:125–82. New Haven, CT: Yale University Press, 1963.
———. *The Sadness of Christ*. In *Saint Thomas More: Selected Writings*, edited by John F. Thornton and Susan B. Varenne, 1–116. New York: Random House, 2003.
———. "A Treatice Vpon the Passion." In *The Yale Edition of the Complete Works of St. Thomas More*, edited by Garry E. Haupt, 13:1–188. New Haven, CT: Yale University Press, 1976.
Origen. *Homilies on Joshua*. Translated by Barbara J. Bruce. Edited by Cynthia White. Washington, DC: Catholic University of America Press, 2002.
———. *Song of Songs, Commentary and Homilies*. Translated by R. P. Lawson. New York: Paulist, 1957.
Pseudo-Dionysius the Areopagite. *The Celestial Hierarchy*. In *The Works of Dionysius the Areopagite*, Part 1, translated by John Parker. London: James Parker, 1897–1899. Reprint, New York: Richmond Publishing Co., 1976.
———. *The Ecclesiastical Hierarchy*. Translated by Thomas L. Campbell. Lanham, MD: University Press of America, 1981.
Raymond of Capua. *De S. Catharina Senensi, virgine de poenitentia S. Dominici*. In *AASS*, Vol. 12 (Aprilis III): 853–959.
———. *The Life of Catherine of Siena*. Translated by Conleth Kearns. Wilmington, DE: Michael Glazier, 1980.
———. *Opuscula et Litterae*. Edited by H. M. Cormier. Rome, 1895.
The Roman Ritual in Latin and English. 3 vols. Edited by and Translated by Philip T. Weller. Milwaukee, WI: Bruce Publishing Co., 1952.
Roper, William. *The Lyfe of Sir Thomas Moore, knighte*. Edited by Elsie Vaughan Hitchcock. EETS o.s. 197. London: Oxford University Press, 1935, repr. 1998.
Thomas of Celano. *The Life of Saint Francis*. In Armstrong, Hellmann, and Short, eds., *Francis of Assisi: Early Documents*, 1:169–318.
———. *The Rediscovered Life of St. Francis of Assisi*. Edited by Jacques Dalarun. Translated by Timothy J. Johnson. St. Bonaventure, NY: The Franciscan Institute, 2016.
———. *Vita prima*. In *Analecta Franciscana sive Chronica aliaque varia documenta ad historiam Fratrum Minorum spectantia*, Vol. 10, edited by College of St. Bonaventure, 1–117. Quaracchi: Collegium S. Bonaventurae, 1926–1941.
The Use of Sarum. 2 vols. Edited by Walter Howard Frere. Cambridge: Cambridge University Press, 1898.

The Vercelli Book Homilies: Translations from the Anglo-Saxon. Edited by Lewis E. Nicholson. Lanham, MD: University of America Press, 1991.
Vercelli Homilies IX–XXIII. Edited by Paul E. Szarmach. Toronto: University of Toronto Press, 1981.
The Vercelli Homilies and Related Texts. EETS o.s. 300. Edited by Donald Scragg. Oxford: Oxford University Press, 1992.
Werfel, Franz. *Between Heaven and Earth*. Translated by Maxim Newmark. New York: Philosophical Library, 1944.
———. *The Song of Bernadette*. Translated by Ludwig Lewisohn. New York: Viking, 1942. Reprint, San Francisco: Ignatius, 2006.
William of St. Thierry. *Exposition on the Song of Songs*. CF 6. Kalamazoo, MI: Cistercian Publications, 1970.

SECONDARY SOURCES

Agnew, Sr. Mary Madeleva. "A Comparison of the Teaching of the Beatific Vision in St. Bonaventure and St. Thomas." Master's thesis, University of Notre Dame, 1960.
Allen, Judson Boyce. *The Ethical Poetic of the Later Middle Ages: A Decorum of Convenient Distinction*. Toronto: University of Toronto Press, 1982.
Alter, Robert. *The Art of Biblical Narrative*. Rev. ed. New York: Basic Books, 2011.
Apczynski, John V. "What Has Paris to Do with Assisi? The Theological Creation of a Saint." In *Finding Saint Francis in Literature and Art*, edited by Cynthia Ho, Beth A. Mulvaney, and John K. Downey, 79–93. New York: Palgrave Macmillan, 2009.
Apel, Willi. *Gregorian Chant*. Bloomington: Indiana University Press, 1990.
Amos, Thomas L. "Early Medieval Sermons and the Holy." In *Models of Holiness in Medieval Sermons: Proceedings of the International Symposium*, edited by Beverly Maayne Kienzle, Edith Wilks Dolnikowski, Rosemary Dragle Hale, Darleen Pryds, and Anne T. Thayer, 23–34. Louvain-La-Neuve: Fédération Internationale des Instituts d'Études Médiévales, 1996.
Antunes, Joana. "The Late-Medieval Mary Magdalene: Sacredness, Otherness, and Wildness." In *Mary Magdalene in Medieval Culture: Conflicted Roles*, edited by Peter V. Loewen and Robin Waugh, 116–39. New York: Routledge, 2014.
Armstrong, Regis J. "*Mira Circa Nos*: Gregory IX's View of Saint Thomas of Assisi." *Laurentianum* 25 (1984): 385–414.
———. "Towards an Unfolding of the Structure of St. Bonaventure's *Legenda maior*." *The Cord* 39 (1989): 3–17.
Astell, Ann W. "Artful Dogma: The Immaculate Conception and Franz Werfel's *Song of Bernadette*." *Christianity and Literature* 62, no. 1 (2012): 189–212.

———. *Chaucer and the Universe of Learning*. Ithaca, NY: Cornell University Press, 1996.

———. "A Discerning Smell: Olfaction among the Senses in St. Bonaventure's *Long Life of St. Francis*." *Franciscan Studies* 67 (2009): 91–131.

———. *Eating Beauty: The Eucharist and the Spiritual Arts of the Middle Ages*. Ithaca, NY: Cornell University Press, 2006.

———. "Heroic Virtue in Blessed Raymond of Capua's *Life of Catherine of Siena*." *Journal of Medieval and Early Modern Studies* 42, no. 1 (2012): 35–57.

———, ed. *Lay Sanctity, Medieval and Modern: A Search for Models*. Notre Dame, IN: University of Notre Dame Press, 2000.

———. "Retooling the Instruments of Christ's Passion: Memorial Technai, St. Thomas the Twin, and British Library Additional MS 22029." In *The Arma Christi in Medieval and Early Modern Material Culture*, edited by Lisa H. Cooper and Andrea Denny-Brown, 171–202. Burlington, VT: Ashgate, 2014.

———. *The Song of Songs in the Middle Ages*. Ithaca, NY: Cornell University Press, 1990.

———. "'To Build the Church: Saint Ælred of Rievaulx's Hexaemeral Miracles in the *Life of Ninian*." *Cistercian Studies Quarterly* 49, no. 4 (2014): 455–81.

Auerbach, Erich. "Figura." In *Scenes from the Drama of European Literature*, translated by Ralph Manheim, 11–78. Theory and History of Literature 9. Minneapolis: University of Minnesota Press, 1984.

———. *Mimesis: The Representation of Reality in Western Literature*. Translated by William R. Trask. 1st Princeton Classics. Princeton, NJ: Princeton University Press, 2013.

———. "Sermo Humilis." In *Literary Language and Its Public in Late Latin Antiquity and in the Middle Ages*, translated by Ralph Manheim, 25–66. New York: Pantheon, 1965.

Bailey, Terence. *The Processions of Sarum and the Western Church*. Toronto: Pontifical Institute of Medieval Studies, 1971.

Baker-Smith, Dominic. "Erasmus and More: A Friendship Revisited." *Recusant History* 30, no. 1 (2010): 7–25.

Balthasar, Hans Urs von. *The Glory of the Lord: A Theological Aesthetics*. Vol. 2, *Studies in Theological Style: Clerical Styles*. Translated by Andrew Louth, Francis McDonagh, and Brian McNeil. Edited by John Riches. San Francisco: Ignatius, 1983.

———. "Theology and Sanctity." In *Explorations in Theology I: The Word Made Flesh*, 181–209. San Francisco: Ignatius, 1989.

Bazire, Joyce, and James E. Cross. "Introduction." In *Eleven Old English Rogationtide Homilies*, edited by Joyce Bazire and James E. Cross, xv–xxxii. Toronto: University of Toronto Press, 1982.

Beaudette, Paul. "'In the World but Not of It': Clerical Celibacy as a Symbol of the Medieval Church." In *Medieval Purity and Piety: Essays on Medieval Clerical Celibacy and Religious Reform*, edited by Michael Frassetto, 23–46. New York: Garland, 1998.

Bell, Rudolf M. *Holy Anorexia*. Chicago: University of Chicago Press, 1985.

Benson, Robert L. *The Bishop-Elect: A Study in Medieval Ecclesiastical Office*. Princeton, NJ: Princeton University Press, 1968.

Bequette, John P. "Reclaiming the Heritage of the Apostles: *Haereditas* in Bernard's *Life of Saint Malachy*." *Cistercian Studies Quarterly* 44, no. 3 (2009): 279–98.

Berry, Thomas. "Dostoevsky and St. Tikhon Zadonski." *New Zealand Slavonic Journal* (1989–90): 67–72.

Berschin, Walter. "*Opus deliberatum ac perfectum*: Why Did the Venerable Bede Write a Second, Prose *Life of St. Cuthbert*?" In *Saint Cuthbert, His Cult, and His Community to AD 1200*, edited by Gerald Bonner, David Rollason, and Clare Stancliffe, 95–102. Woodbridge, Suffolk: Boydell and Brewer, 1989.

Bertini, Stefania Guidetti. *Sermones di Iacopo da Varazze: Il potere della immagini nel Duecento*. Firenze: SISMEL/Edizioni del Galluzo, 1998.

Bettoni, Efrem. *St. Bonaventure*. Translated by Angelus Gambatese. Notre Dame, IN: University of Notre Dame Press, 1964.

Bietenholz, Peter G. *History and Biography in the Work of Erasmus of Rotterdam*. Genève: Librairie Droz, 1966.

Billett, Jesse D. *The Divine Office in Anglo-Saxon England, 597–c. 1000*. London: Henry Bradshaw Society, 2014.

Binski, Paul. *Medieval Death: Ritual and Representation*. Ithaca, NY: Cornell University Press, 1996.

Black, Jonathan. "Psalm Uses in Carolingian Prayer Books: Alcuin and the Preface to *De psalmorum usu*." *Mediaeval Studies* 64 (2002): 1–60.

Blastic, Michael W. "Francis and the Hagiographical Tradition." In *The Cambridge Companion to Francis of Assisi*, edited by Michael Robson, 68–83. Cambridge: Cambridge University Press, 2012.

Blumenthal, Uta-Renate. *The Investiture Controversy: Church and Monarchy from the Ninth to the Twelfth Century*. Philadelphia: University of Pennsylvania Press, 1988.

Borgehammar, Stephan. "A Monastic Conception of the Liturgical Year." In *The Liturgy of the Medieval Church*, 2nd ed., edited by Thomas J. Heffernan and E. Ann Matter, 13–40. Kalamazoo, MI: Medieval Institute Publications, 2005.

Bougerol, Jacques-Guy. "The Moral Reflection of Saint Francis and Saint Bonaventure," translated by Michael Cusato, with Girard Etzkom. In *That Others May Know and Love: Essays in Honor of Zachary Hayes, OFM*," edited by Michael F. Cusato and F. Edward Coughlin, 43–63. St. Bonaventure, NY: The Franciscan Institute, 1997.

Boureau, Alain. *"La Légende dorée": Le systéme narrative de Jacques de Voragine (†1298)*. Paris: Cerf, 1984.
Bradshaw, Paul. *Reconstructing Early Christian Worship*. Collegeville, MN: Liturgical Press, 2010.
Brandt, W. J. *The Shape of Medieval History*. New Haven, CT: Yale University Press, 1966.
Breen, Katharine. *Imagining an English Reading Public, 1150–1400*. Cambridge Studies in Medieval Literature 79. Cambridge: Cambridge University Press, 2010.
Brown, Jennifer N. *Fruit of the Orchard: Reading Catherine of Siena in Late Medieval and Early Modern England*. Toronto: University of Toronto Press, 2019.
Brown, Peter. *The Cult of the Saints: Its Rise and Function in Latin Christianity*. Chicago: University of Chicago Press, 1981.
———. "The Saint as Exemplar in Late Antiquity." In *Saints and Virtues*, edited by John Stratton Hawley, 3–14. Berkeley: University of California Press, 1987.
Brueggemann, Walter. *The Prophetic Imagination*. 2nd ed. Minneapolis, MN: Fortress, 2001.
Brundage, James L. *Law, Sex, and Christian Society in Medieval Europe*. Chicago: University of Chicago Press, 1987.
Burr, David. *Olivi and Franciscan Poverty: The Origins of the "Usus Pauper" Controversy*. Philadelphia: University of Pennsylvania Press, 1989.
———. *The Spiritual Franciscans: From Protest to Persecution in the Century after Saint Francis*. University Park: Pennsylvania State University Press, 2001.
Bynum, Caroline Walker. *Holy Feast and Holy Fast: The Religious Significance of Food to Medieval Women*. Berkeley: University of California Press, 1987.
———. *Jesus as Mother: Studies in the Spirituality of the High Middle Ages*. Berkeley: University of California Press, 1982.
———. *The Resurrection of the Body in Western Christianity, 200–1336*. New York: Columbia University Press, 1995.
Callander, Marilyn Berg. *Willa Cather and the Fairy Tale*. Ann Arbor: U.M.I. Research Press, 1989.
Carragáin, Éamonn Ó. *Ritual and the Rood: Liturgical Images and the Old English Poems of the "Dream of the Rood" Tradition*. Toronto: Toronto University Press, 2005.
Carruthers, Mary. *The Craft of Thought: Meditation, Rhetoric, and the Making of Images*. Cambridge: Cambridge University Press, 2000.
Cavadini, John C. "A Note on Gregory's Use of Miracles in the *Life and Miracles of St. Benedict*." *American Benedictine Review* 49, no. 1 (1998): 104–20.
Cavanaugh, John R. "The Saint Stephen Motif in Saint Thomas More's Thought." *Moreana* 8 (1965): 59–66.

Cervone, Cristina Maria. *Poetics of the Incarnation: Middle English Writing and the Leap of Love*. Philadelphia: Pennsylvania University Press, 2013.
Chambers, R. W. "The Continuity of English Prose from Alfred to More and His School." In *Harpsfield's Life of More*, xlv–clxxiv. EETS o.s. 186. London: Humphrey Milford, Oxford University Press, 1932.
Chenu, M. D. *Nature, Man, and Society in the Twelfth Century: Essays on New Theological Perspectives in the Latin West*. Edited by and translated by Jerome Taylor and Lester K. Little. Chicago: University of Chicago Press, 1968.
Chidester, David. *Word and Light: Seeing, Hearing, and Religious Discourse*. Urbana: University of Illinois Press, 1992.
Ciccarese, M. P. "Le visioni di S. Fursa." *Romanobarbarica* 8 (1984–85): 232–303.
Clairmont, David A. "Bonaventure on Moral Motivation: Trajectories of Exemplification in His Treatments of Voluntary Poverty." *Journal of the Society of Christian Ethics* 25, no. 2 (2005): 109–36.
Classen, Constance, David Howes, and Anthony Synnott. *Aroma: The Cultural History of Smell*. London: Routledge, 1994.
Clifford, Timothy. "Sebastian Conca's Communion of Mary Magdalen." *The Burlington Magazine* 114, no. 828 (1972): 142–46.
Clough, Francis M. "Introduction." In *The Vercelli Book Homilies: Translations from the Anglo-Saxon*, edited by Lewis E. Nicholson, 1–15. Lanham, MD: University of America Press, 1991.
Coakley, John W. "The Conversion of St. Francis and the Writing of Christian Biography, 1228–1263." *Franciscan Studies* 72 (2014): 27–71.
Coleman, John A. "Conclusion: After Sainthood." In *Saints and Virtues*, edited by John Stratton Hawley, 205–25. Berkeley: University of California Press, 1987.
Coleman, Joyce. *Public Reading and the Reading Public in Late Medieval England and France*. Cambridge Studies in Medieval Literature 26. Cambridge: Cambridge University Press, 2005.
Colgrave, Bertram. "Introduction." In *Felix's "Life of Saint Guthlac,"* edited by and translated by Bertram Colgrave, 1–58. Cambridge: Cambridge University Press, 1956.
Collins, David J. "A Life Reconstituted: Jacobus de Voragine, Erasmus of Rotterdam, and Their Lives of St. Jerome." *Medievalia et Humanistica*, n.s., 25 (1998): 31–51.
———. *Reforming Saints: Saints' Lives and Their Authors in Germany, 1470–1530*. Oxford Studies in Historical Theology. Oxford: Oxford University Press, 2008.
Contzen, Eva von, and Anke Bernaud, eds. *Sanctity as Literature in Late Medieval Britain*. Manchester: Manchester University Press, 2015.
Coogan, Robert. *Erasmus, Lee, and the Correction of the Vulgate: The Shaking of the Foundations*. Geneva: Droz, 1992.

Cook, William. "Tradition and Perfection: Monastic Typology in Bonaventure's *Life of St. Francis.*" *American Benedictine Review* 33 (1982): 1–20.

Coolman, Boyd Taylor. *Knowing God by Experience: The Spiritual Senses in the Theology of William of Auxerre.* Washington, DC: Catholic University of America Press, 2004.

Cousins, Ewert H. *Bonaventure and the Coincidence of Opposites.* Chicago: Franciscan Herald Press, 1978.

———. "Introduction." In *Bonaventure: The Soul's Journey into God, The Tree of Life, The Life of St. Francis*, translated by Ewert Cousins, 1–48. Classics of Western Spirituality. Mahwah, NJ: Paulist, 1978.

Crewe, Jonathan V. "The 'Encomium Moriae' of William Roper." *English Literary History* 55, no. 2 (1988): 287–307.

Cross, J. E. "Mary Magdalen in the Old English Martyrology: The Earliest Extant 'Narrat Josephus' Variant of Her Legend." *Speculum* 53, no. 1 (1978): 16–25.

Cross, Richard. "Chapter 10: Thomas Aquinas." In *The Spiritual Senses: Perceiving God in Western Christianity*, edited by Paul Z. Gavrilyuk and Sarah Coakley, 174–89. Cambridge: Cambridge University Press, 2011.

Cubitt, Catherine. *Anglo-Saxon Church Councils, c. 650–c. 850.* London: Leicester University Press, 1995.

Curtius, Ernst R. *European Literature and the Latin Middle Ages.* Translated by William R. Trask. New York: Pantheon, 1953.

Cunningham, Lawrence S. *A Brief History of Saints.* Oxford: Blackwell, 2005.

Cusack, Pearse Aidan. *An Interpretation of the Second Dialogue of Gregory the Great: Hagiography and St. Benedict.* Studies in the Bible and Early Christianity 31. Lewiston, NY: Edwin Mellen Press, 1993.

———. "St. Scholastica: Myth or Real Person?" *The Downside Review* 92 (1974): 145–59.

Dalarun, Jacques. *The Misadventure of Francis of Assisi: Toward a Historical Use of the Franciscan Legends.* Translated by Edward Hagman, O.F.M. Cap. St. Bonaventure, NY: The Franciscan Institute, 2002.

———. "The New Francis in the Rediscovered Life (*Vita brevior*) of Thomas of Celano." In *Ordo et Sanctitas: The Franciscan Spiritual Journey in Theology and Hagiography. Essays in Honor of J. A. Wayne Hellmann, O.F.M. Conv.*, edited by Michael F. Cusato, Timothy J. Johnson, and Steven J. McMichael, 32–46. Leiden: Brill, 2017.

Daley, Brian. "Finding the Right Key: The Aims and Strategies of Early Christian Interpretation of the Psalms." In *Psalms in Community: Jewish and Christian Textual, Liturgical, and Artistic Traditions*, edited by Harold W. Attridge and Margot E. Fassler, 189–206. Atlanta: Society of Biblical Literature, 2004.

Dal Santo, Matthew. *Debating the Saints' Cults in the Age of Gregory the Great.* Oxford Studies in Byzantium. Oxford: Oxford University Press, 2012.
Danielou, Jean. *The Bible and the Liturgy.* Notre Dame, IN: University of Notre Dame Press, 1956.
De Beer, Francis. *La conversion de St. François.* Paris: Éditions franciscaines, 1963.
Dechanet, J. M. "Introduction." In William of St. Thierry, *Exposition on the Song of Songs*, vii–xlviii. CF 6. Kalamazoo, MI: Cistercian Publications, 1970.
Delany, Sheila. *Impolitic Bodies: Poetry, Saints, and Society in Fifteenth-Century England: The Work of Osbern Bokenham.* New York: Oxford University Press, 1998.
De Lang, Marijke H. "'Fidelius, apertius, significantius': The New Testament Translated and Edited by Erasmus of Rotterdam, 1516." *The Bible Translator* 67, no. 1 (2016): 5–8.
Delehaye, Hippolyte. *The Legends of the Saints: An Introduction to Hagiography.* Translated by V. M. Crawford. Notre Dame, IN: The University of Notre Dame, 1961.
Delio, Sr. Ilia. *Simply Bonaventure: An Introduction to His Life, Thought, and Writings.* New York: New City Press, 2001.
de Lubac, Henri. *The Drama of Atheist Humanism.* Translated by Edith M. Riley. New York: Sheed and Ward, 1950.
———. *The Letter and the Spirit: The Understanding of Scripture according to Origen.* Translated by Ann Englund Nash. San Francisco: Ignatius, 2007.
———. *Medieval Exegesis: The Four Senses of Scripture.* 3 vols. Translated by Marc Sebank (Vol. 1), E. M. Macierowski (Vols. 2 and 3). Ressourcement: Retrieval & Renewal in Catholic Thought. Grand Rapids, MI: Wm. B. Eerdmans, 1998–2009.
Desbonnets, Theophile. "The Franciscan Reading of the Scriptures." In *Francis of Assisi Today*, edited by Christian Duquoc and Casiano Floristan, 37–45. Concilium 149. New York: The Seabury Press, 1981.
de Vogüé, Adalbert. *The Life of Saint Benedict: A Commentary.* Translated by Hilary Costello and Eoin de Bhaldraithe. Petersham, MA: St. Bede's Publications, 1993.
———. "One Last Trace of Psalm-Prayers?" In *Praise No Less Than Charity: Studies in Honor of M. Chrysologus Waddell*, edited by E. Rozanne Elder, 17–30. Kalamazoo, MI: Cistercian Publications, 2002.
Ditchfield, Simon. *Liturgy, Sanctity, and History in Tridentine Italy: Pietro Maria Campi and the Preservation of the Particular.* Cambridge Studies in Italian History and Culture. Cambridge: Cambridge University Press, 2002.
Dix, Gregory. *The Shape of the Liturgy.* London: Dacre Press, 1945.
Downey, Sarah. "Too Much of Too Little: Guthlac and the Temptation of Excessive Fasting." *Traditio* 63 (2008): 89–127.

Duby, George. *Medieval Marriage: Two Models from Twelfth-Century France*. Translated by Elborg Forster. Baltimore: Johns Hopkins University Press, 1978.
Duffy, Eamon. "Introduction." In Jacobus de Voragine, *The Golden Legend: Readings on the Saints*, translated by William Granger Ryan, xi–xx. Princeton, NJ: Princeton University Press, 2012.
———. *Stripping of the Altars: Traditional Religion in England, 1400–1580*. New Haven, CT: Yale University Press, 2005.
Dumont, Charles. "Ælred of Rievaulx: His Life and Works." In Ælred of Rievaulx, *The Mirror of Charity*, translated by Elizabeth Connor, O.C.S.O.; edited by Charles Dumont, 11–66. CF 17. Kalamazoo, MI: Cistercian Publications, 1990.
Durand, Alfred. "Inspiration of the Bible." In *The Catholic Encyclopedia*, 8:45–50. New York: Robert Appleton Co., 1910.
Duryea, Polly P. "Paintings and Drawings in Willa Cather's Prose: A Catalogue Raisonné." PhD diss., University of Nebraska–Lincoln, 1993.
Dutton, Marsha L. "Friendship and the Love of God: Augustine's Teaching in *Confessions* and Ælred of Rievaulx's Response in *Spiritual Friendship*." *American Benedictine Review* 56 (2005): 3–40.
———. "Introduction to Walter Daniel's *Vita Ælredi*." In Walter Daniel, *The Life of Ælred of Rievaulx*, translated by F. M. Powicke, 7–88. CF 57. Kalamazoo, MI: Cistercian Publications, 1994.
Eby, John C. "Bringing the *Vita* to Life: Bede's Symbolic Structure of the *Life of St. Cuthbert*." *American Benedictine Review* 48 (1997): 316–38.
Edmunds, Martha Mel. "La Sainte-Baume and the Iconography of Mary Magdalene." *Gazette des beaux-arts* 114 (1989): 11–28.
Emerson Hernández, Marco Carlos. "Augustine and the Seeds of Creation and Recreation." In "The Seeds of Creation and New Creation: St. Thomas Aquinas and His Predecessors on the Generative Principles of Natural and Supernatural Life," chapter 1. PhD diss., University of Notre Dame, 2014.
Emmerson, Richard K., and Ronald B. Herzman. "The *Legenda maior*: Bonaventure's Apocalyptic Francis." In *The Apocalyptical Imagination in Medieval Literature*, 36–75. Philadelphia: University of Pennsylvania Press, 1992.
Ennis, Hyacinth. "The Primacy of the Virtue of Charity in Morality according to Saint Bonaventure." *Antonianum* 50 (1975): 418–56.
Epstein, Steven. *The Talents of Jacopo da Varagine: A Genoese Mind in Medieval Europe*. Ithaca, NY: Cornell University Press, 2016.
Evans, Craig A. "Jesus and Psalm 91 in Light of the Exorcism Scrolls." In *Celebrating the Dead Sea Scrolls: A Canadian Contribution*, edited by Peter W. Flint, Jean Duhaime, and Kyung S. Baek, 541–55. Early Judaism and Its Literature 30. Atlanta: Society of Biblical Literature, 2011.

Evans, Gillian. "St. Anselm and Sacred History." In *The Writing of History in the Middle Ages: Essays Presented to Richard William Southern*, edited by R. H. C. Davis and J. M. Wallace-Hadrill, 187–209. Oxford: Clarendon Press, 1981.

Farris, Giovanni. *Significati spirituali nei "Sermones" di Iacopo da Varazze e nella "Divina Commedia."* Savona: M. Sabatelli, 1998.

Farrow, Douglas. *Ascension and Ecclesia: On the Significance of the Doctrine of the Ascension for Ecclesiology and Christian Cosmology.* Grand Rapids, MI: William B. Eerdmans, 1999.

———. *Ascension Theology.* New York: T&T Clark, 2011.

Fassler, Margot E. *Cosmos, Liturgy, and the Arts in the Twelfth Century: Hildegard's Illuminated "Scivias."* Philadelphia: University of Pennsylvania Press, 2023.

Fawtier, Robert. *Sainte Catharine de Sienne: Essai de critique des sources.* 2 vols. Paris: E. de Boccard, 1921–1930.

Fawtier, Robert, and Louis Canet. *La double expérience de Catherine Benincasa.* Paris: Gallimard, 1948.

Ferguson, Jamie H. "Faith in the Language: Biblical Authority and the Meaning of English in More–Tyndale Polemics." *Sixteenth-Century Journal* 43, no. 4 (2012): 989–1011.

Fiedrowicz, Michael. "Introduction." In *St. Augustine: Expositions of the Psalms (Enarrationes in psalmos)*, edited by Boniface Ramsey; translated by Maria Boulding, 1:13–66. Hyde Park, NY: New City Press, 2004.

———. *Psalmus vox totius Christi: Studien zu Augustins "Enarrationes in Psalmos."* Freiburg im Breisgau: Herder, 1997.

Field, Sean L. "New Light on the 1230s: History, Hagiography, and Thomas of Celano's 'The Life of Our Blessed Father Francis.'" *Franciscan Studies* 74 (2016): 239–47.

Fields, Stephen. "Balthasar and Rahner on the Spiritual Senses." *Theological Studies* 57 (1996): 224–41.

Flanagan, Marie Thérèse. "St. Malachy, St. Bernard of Clairvaux, and the Cistercian Order." *Archivium Hibernicum* 68 (2015): 294–311.

Fleith, Barbara. "The Patristic Sources of the *Legenda aurea*: A Research Report." In *Reception of the Church Fathers in the West*, edited by Irena Backus, 1:237–87. New York: E. J. Brill, 1997.

Fleith, Barbara, and Franco Morenzoni, eds. *De la sainteté à l'hagiographie: Genèse et usage de la "Légende dorée."* Geneva: Droz, 2001.

Fox, Michael. "Vercelli Homilies XIX–XXI, the Ascension Day Homily in Cambridge, Corpus Christi College 162, and the Catechetical Tradition from Augustine to Wulfstan." In *New Readings in the Vercelli Book*, edited by Samantha Zacher and Andy Orchard, 254–79. Toronto: University of Toronto Press, 2009.

Fox Kuhiken, Pam. "Hallowed Ground: Landscape as Hagiography in Willa Cather's *Death Comes for the Archbishop.*" *Christianity and Literature* 52, no. 3 (2003): 367–85.
Frazier, Alison Knowles. *Possible Lives: Authors and Saints in Renaissance Italy.* New York: Columbia University Press, 2005.
Frei, Hans W. *The Eclipse of Biblical Narrative: A Study of Eighteenth- and Nineteenth-Century Hermeneutics.* New Haven, CT: Yale University Press, 1974.
———. "Theology and the Interpretation of Narrative: Some Hermeneutical Considerations." In *Theology and Narrative: Selected Essays*, edited by George Hunsinger and William C. Placher, 94–116. Oxford: Oxford University Press, 1993.
Führkötter, Adelgundis. *The Miniatures from the Book "Scivias"—"Know the Ways"—of St. Hildegard of Bingen from the Illuminated Rupertsberg Codex.* Turnhout: Brepols, 1977.
Fulton, Rachel. *From Judgment to Passion: Devotion to Christ and Mary, 800–1200.* New York: Columbia University Press, 2002.
Gajano, Sofia Boesch, and Odile Redon. "La *Legenda maior* di Raimondo da Capua, costruzione di una santa." In *Atti del simposio internazionale Cateriniano-Bernardiniano, Siena, 17–20 aprile 1980*, edited by Domenico Maffei and Paolo Nardi, 15–36. Siena: Accademia Senese degli Intronati, 1982.
Gaudemet, Jean. "Note sur le symbolisme medieval: Le marriage de l'evêque." *L'année canonique* 22 (1978): 71–80.
Geith, Karl-Ernst. "*Die Abbreviatio in Gestis et Miraculis Sanctorum* von Jean de Mailly als Quelle der *Legenda aurea.*" *Analecta Bollandiana* 105, no. 3–4 (1987): 289–302.
Gerulaitis, Leonardas V. "The Canonization of Saint Thomas Aquinas." *Vivarium* 5, no. 1 (1967): 25–46.
Gibbon, Edward. *The Decline and Fall of the Roman Empire.* 6 vols. New York: Modern Library, 1952.
Gilson, Etienne. *The Philosophy of St. Bonaventure.* Translated by Dom Illtyd Trethowan and F. J. Sheed. New York: Sheed and Ward, 1938.
Glass, Dorothy. "*In Principio:* The Creation in the Middle Ages." In *Approaches to Nature in the Middle Ages*, edited by Lawrence D. Roberts, 67–104. Medieval and Renaissance Texts and Studies 16. Binghamton, NY: Center for Medieval and Renaissance Studies, 1982.
Gorman, Michael. "The Unknown Augustine: A Study of the Literal Interpretation of Genesis (*De Genesi ad litteram*)." PhD diss., University of Toronto, 1974.
Gorodetzky, Nadejda. *Saint Tikhon Zadonsky, Inspirer of Dostoevsky.* London: SPCK, 1951.

Grabmann, Martin. *Die Geschichte der scholastischen Methode*. 2 vols. Freiburg im Breisgau: Herdersche Verlagshandlung, 1909–1911.

Gransden, Antonia. *Historical Writing in England, c. 550 to c. 1307*. Ithaca, NY: Cornell University Press, 1974.

Grant, Robert M. *Miracle and Natural Law in Graeco-Roman and Early Christian Thought*. Eugene, OR: Wipf and Stock, 2011.

Graus, František. *Volk, Herrscher, und Heiliger im Reich der Merowinger: Studien zur Hagiographie der Merowingenzeit*. Praha: Nakladatelství Československé akademie věd, 1965.

Greenblatt, Stephen. *Renaissance Self-Fashioning from More to Shakespeare*. Chicago: University of Chicago Press, 1980.

Gregory, Brad S. *The Unintended Reformation: How a Religious Revolution Secularized Society*. Cambridge, MA: Belknap Press of Harvard University Press, 2012.

Griffiths, Fiona. "Siblings and the Sexes within the Medieval Religious Life." *Church History* 77, no. 1 (2008): 26–53.

Grillaert, Nel. "Dostoevskij's Portrait of a 'Pure, Ideal Christian': Echoes of Nil Sorskij in the Elder Zosima." *Russian Literature* 67 (2010): 185–216.

Gross-Diaz, Theresa. "From *Lectio Divina* to the Lecture Room: The Psalm Commentary of Gilbert of Poitiers." In *The Place of the Psalms in the Intellectual Culture of the Middle Ages*, edited by Nancy Van Deusen, 91–204. Albany: State University of New York Press, 1999.

Hackett, Michael Benedict, O.S.A. *William Flete, O.S.A., and Catherine of Siena: Masters of Fourteen Century Spirituality*. Villanova, PA: Augustinian Press, 1992.

Hall, Thomas N. "Latin Sermons for Saints in Early English Homiliaries and Legendaries." In *The Old English Homily: Precedent, Practice, and Appropriation*, edited by Aaron J. Kleist, 227–63. Brepols: Turnhout, 2007.

Hamilton, Nigel. *Biography: A Brief History*. Cambridge, MA: Harvard University Press, 2007.

Hardon, John. "The Concept of Miracle from St. Augustine to Modern Apologetics." *Theological Studies* 15 (1954): 229–57.

Harper, John. *The Forms and Orders of Western Liturgy from the Tenth to the Eighteenth Century*. Oxford: Clarendon, 1991.

Harris, Stephen J. "The Liturgical Context of Ælfric's Homilies for Rogation." In *The Old English Homily: Precedent, Practice, and Appropriation*, edited by Aaron Kleist, 143–69. Turnhout: Brepols, 2007.

Harrison, Peter. "Miracles, Early Modern Science, and Rational Religion." *Church History* 75, no. 3 (2006): 493–510.

Harvey, Susan Ashbrook. *Scenting Salvation: Ancient Christianity and the Olfactory Imagination*. Berkeley: University of California Press, 2006.

Hayes, Zachary. *The Hidden Center: Spirituality and Speculative Christology in St. Bonaventure*. New York: Paulist, 1981.
Heffernan, Thomas J. "The Liturgy and the Literature of Saints' *Lives*." In *The Liturgy of the Medieval Church*, 2nd ed., edited by Thomas J. Heffernan and E. Ann Matter, 65–94. Kalamazoo, MI: Medieval Institute Publications, 2005.
———. *Sacred Biography: Saints and Their Biographers in the Middle Ages*. New York: Oxford University Press, 1988.
Heffernan, Thomas J., and E. Ann Matter, eds., *The Liturgy of the Medieval Church*. 2nd ed. Kalamazoo, MI: Medieval Institute Publications, 2005.
Hellman, J. A. Wayne. *Divine and Created Order in Bonaventure's Theology*. Translated by Joy H. Hammond. St. Bonaventure, NY: The Franciscan Institute, 2001.
———. "The Seraph in Thomas of Celano's *Vita prima*." In *That Others May Know and Love: Essays in Honor of Zachary Hayes, OFM*," edited by Michael F. Cusato and F. Edward Coughlin, 23–41. St. Bonaventure, NY: The Franciscan Institute, 1997.
———. "A Theology of Preaching–A Theology of Transformation: The *Life of St. Francis* by Thomas of Celano." In *Franciscans and Preaching: Every Miracle from the Beginning of the World Came about through Words*, edited by Timothy J. Johnson, 59–69. Leiden: Brill, 2012.
Heming, Carol Piper. *Protestants and the Cult of Saints in German-Speaking Europe, 1517–1531*. Sixteenth Century Studies 65. Kirksville, MO: Truman State University Press, 2003.
Hiley, David. *Western Plainchant: A Handbook*. Oxford: Clarendon, 1993.
Hill, Joyce. "The *Litania maiores* and *minores* in Rome, Francia, and Anglo-Saxon England: Terminology, Texts, and Traditions." *Early Modern Europe* 9 (2000): 211–46.
Hofmann, Rudolf. *Die heroische Tugend: Geschichte und Inhalt eines theologischen Begriffes*. Munich: Kösel & Rastet, 1933.
Holladay, William L. *The Psalms through Three Thousand Years: Prayerbook of a Cloud of Witnesses*. Minneapolis, MN: Fortress Press, 1996.
Horobin, Simon. "Introduction." In Osbern Bokenham, *Lives of Saints*, edited by Simon Horobin, 1:xiii–xxxv. Oxford: Oxford University Press, 2020.
———. "Politics, Patronage, and Piety in the Work of Osbern Bokenham." *Speculum* 82, no. 4 (2007): 932–49.
Hughes, Kevin L. "Chapter Five: Living the Word." In *The Oxford Handbook of Mystical Theology*, edited by Edward Howells and Mark MacIntosh, 109–28. Oxford: Oxford University Press, 2020.
Illich, Ivan. *In the Vineyard of the Text: A Commentary to Hugh's "Didascalicon."* Chicago: University of Chicago Press, 1993.

Jankofsky, Klaus. "*Legenda aurea* Materials in the *South English Legendary*: Translation, Transformation, Acculturation." In *"Legenda aurea": Sept siècles de diffusion: Actes du colloque international sur le "Legenda aurea," text Latin et branches vernaculaires*, 317–29. Paris: Vrin, 1986.

Jensen, Robin M. *Baptismal Imagery in Early Christianity: Ritual, Visual, and Theological Dimensions.* Grand Rapids, MI: Baker Academic, 2012.

Jeremy, Sister Mary. "Caxton's Golden Legend and Varagine's *Legenda aurea.*" *Speculum* 21, no. 2 (1946): 212–21.

Jiroušková, Lenka. *De Visio Pauli: Wege und Wandlungen einer orientalischen Apokryphe in lateinischen Mittelalter unter Einschluss der alttsechischen und deutschsprachigen Textzeugen.* Leiden: Brill, 2006.

Kantorowicz, Ernst H. *The King's Two Bodies: A Study in Medieval Political Theology.* Princeton, NJ: Princeton University Press, 1957.

Karnes, Michelle. "Nicholas Love and Medieval Meditations on Christ." *Speculum* 82, no. 2 (2007): 380–408.

Karris, Robert J., O.F.M. "Introduction." In Bonaventure, *Disputed Questions on Evangelical Perfection*, edited by Robert J. Karris, O.F.M; translated by Thomas Reist, O.F.M., and Robert J. Karris, O.F.M., 7–24. Works of St. Bonaventure 13. Saint Bonaventure, NY: The Franciscan Institute, 2008.

Kaufman, Peter Iver. "Augustine, Martyrs, and Misery." *Church History* 63, no. 1 (1984): 1–14.

Kemp, Eric Waldram. *Canonization and Authority in the Western Church.* London: Oxford University Press/Geoffrey Cumberlege, 1948.

———. "Pope Alexander III and the Canonization of Saints." *Transactions of the Royal Historical Society* 27 (1945): 13–28.

Kearns, Conleth. "Introduction." In Raymond of Capua, *The Life of Catherine of Siena*, translated by Conleth Kearns, O.P., xiii–lxxxiv. Wilmington, DE: Michael Glazier, 1980.

Kienzle, Beverly Maayne, Edith Wilks Dolnikowski, Rosemary Dragle Hale, Darleen Pryds, and Anne T. Thayer, eds. *Models of Holiness in Medieval Sermons: Proceedings of the International Symposium.* Louvain-La-Neuve: Fédération Internationale des Instituts d'Études Médiévales, 1996.

Kincella, Sean. "Athanasius' *Life of Anthony* as Monastic Paradigm for the *First Life of St. Francis* by Thomas of Celano: A Preliminary Outline." *Antonianum* 72 (2002): 541–56.

Kjetsaa, Geir. *Dostoevsky and His New Testament.* Atlantic Highlands, NJ: Humanities Press, 1984.

Klingshirn, William E. "Defining the *Sortes Sanctorum*: Gibbon, Du Cange, and Early Christian Lot Divination." *Journal of Early Christian Studies* 10, no. 1 (2002): 77–130.

Kolb, Robert. *For All the Saints: Changing Perceptions of Martyrdom and Sainthood in the Lutheran Reformation.* Macon, GA: Mercer University Press, 1987.

Kozlowski, Matthew William. "The Man of Perfect Virtue: Bonaventure's *Legenda maior* in the Tradition of Hagiography." PhD diss., Catholic University of America, 2020.

Krahmer, Shawn M. "The Virile Bride of Bernard of Clairvaux." *Church History* 69, no. 2 (2000): 304–27.

Kraus, Wolfgang. "Ps 40 (39): 7–9 in the Hebrew Bible and the Septuagint, with Its Reception in the New Testament (Heb 10:5–10)." In *XVI Congress of the International Organization for Septuagint and Cognate Studies: Stellenbosch, 2016*, edited by Gideon R. Kotzé, Wolfgang Kraus, and Michael N. van der Meer, 119–32. Atlanta: Society of Biblical Studies, 2019.

Kurtz, B. P. "From St. Anthony to St. Guthlac: A Study in Biography." *Modern Philology* 12 (1926): 103–46.

Kwatera, Michael. "A Critique of Vatican II's Directives Regarding the Hagiographical Readings in the Liturgy of the Hours." MA thesis, University of Notre Dame, 1980.

Lakoff, George, and Mark Johnson. *Philosophy in the Flesh: The Embodied Mind and Its Challenge to Western Thought.* New York: HarperCollins, 1999.

———. *Metaphors We Live By.* Chicago: University of Chicago Press, 1980.

Lambert, Malcolm. *Franciscan Poverty: The Doctrine of the Absolute Poverty of Christ and the Apostles in the Franciscan Order, 1210–1323.* London: SPCK, 1961.

LaNave, Gregory F. "Chapter 9. Bonaventure." In *The Spiritual Senses: Perceiving God in Western Christianity*, edited by Paul Z. Gavrilyuk and Sarah Coakley, 159–73. Cambridge: Cambridge University Press, 2011.

Lapidge, Michael. "Introduction." In *Anglo-Saxon Litanies of the Saints*, edited by Michael Lapidge, 1–61. London: Henry Bradshaw Society, 1991.

Lawler, Michael G. "Grace and Free Will in Justification: A Textual Study in Aquinas." *The Thomist* 35, no. 4 (1971): 601–30.

Leclercq, Jean. *The Love of Learning and the Desire for God: A Study of Monastic Culture.* Translated by Catherine Misrahi. New York: Fordham University Press, 1974.

Le Goff, Jacques. *In Search of Sacred Time: Jacobus de Voragine and "The Golden Legend."* Translated by Lydia G. Cochrane. Princeton, NJ: Princeton University Press, 2014.

Lerner, R. E. "A Collection of Sermons Given in Paris c. 1267, including a New Text by Saint Bonaventure on the Life of Saint Francis." *Speculum* 49 (1974): 466–98.

Levinas, Emmanuel. *Beyond the Verse: Talmudic Readings and Lectures.* Translated by Gary D. Mole. New York: Continuum, 2007.

Levine, Joseph M. "Erasmus and the Problem of the Johannine Comma [1 John 5:7–8]." *Journal of the History of Ideas* 58, no. 4 (1997): 573–96.
Levy, Ian Christopher. *Holy Scripture and the Quest for Authority in the Later Middle Ages.* Notre Dame, IN: University of Notre Dame Press, 2012.

———. *Introducing Medieval Biblical Interpretation: The Senses of Scripture in Premodern Exegesis.* Grand Rapids, MI: Baker Academic, 2018.

Llewellyn, Nigel. *Funeral Monuments in Post-Reformation England.* Cambridge: Cambridge University Press, 2000.

Lucas, Peter. "Easter, the Death of St. Guthlac, and the Liturgy for Holy Saturday in Felix's *Vita* and the Old English *Guthlac B.*" *Medium Aevum* 61 (1992): 1–16.

Lucie-Smith, Alexander. *Narrative Theology and Moral Theology: The Infinite Horizon.* Burlington, VT: Ashgate, 2007.

Luongo, F. Thomas. *The Saintly Politics of Catherine of Siena.* Ithaca, NY: Cornell University Press, 2006.

MacIntyre, Alasdair. *After Virtue: A Study in Moral Theory.* 3rd ed. Notre Dame, IN: University of Notre Dame Press, 2007.

MacQueen, John. "The Literary Sources for the Life of St. Ninian." In *Galloway: Land and Lordship*, edited by Richard D. Oram and Geoffrey P. Stell, 17–25. Edinburgh: Scottish Society for Northern Studies, 1991.

———. *Numerology: Theory and Outline History of a Literary Mode.* Edinburgh: Edinburgh University Press, 1985.

———. *St. Nynia: A Study of Literary and Linguistic Evidence.* Edinburgh: Oliver and Boyd, 1961.

MacQueen, Winifred W. "Miracula Nynie Episcopi." In *Transactions of the Dumfriesshire and Galloway Natural History and Antiquarian Society, 1959–1960*, 21–57. Dumfries: Council of the . . . Society, 1961.

Madigan, Kevin. "Aquinas and Olivi on Evangelical Poverty: A Medieval Debate and Its Modern Significance." *The Thomist* 61 (1997): 567–86.

Maguire, John. "William Roper's *Life of More*: The Working Methods of a Tudor Biographer." *Moreana* 23 (1969): 59–69.

Maisch, Ingrid. *Mary Magdalene: The Image of a Woman through the Centuries.* Translated by Linda M. Maloney. Collegeville, MN: Liturgical Press, 1998.

Mâle, Emile. *The Gothic Image: Religious Art in France of the Thirteenth Century.* Translated by Dora Nussey. New York: Harper and Row, 1958.

Marc'hadour, Germaine. "Erasmus: First and Best Biographer of Thomas More." *Erasmus of Rotterdam Society Yearbook* 7 (1987): 1–30.

Markus, Robert A. *Gregory the Great and His World.* Cambridge: Cambridge University Press, 1997.

Matter, E. Ann. *The Voice of My Beloved: The Song of Songs in Western Medieval Christianity.* Philadelphia: University of Pennsylvania Press, 1990.

Mattison, William III. *The Sermon on the Mount and Moral Theology: A Virtue Perspective.* Cambridge: Cambridge University Press, 2017.

Mayeski, Marie Anne. "New Voices in the Tradition: Medieval Hagiography Revisited." *Theological Studies* 63, no. 4 (2002): 690–710.

McConica, James K. "The Recusant Reputation of Thomas More." In *Essential Articles for the Study of Thomas More*, edited by Richard S. Sylvester and Germain P. Marc'hadour, 136–49. Hamden, CT: Archon, 1977.

McCready, William D. *Signs of Sanctity: Miracles in the Thought of Gregory the Great.* Toronto: Pontifical Institute of Medieval Studies, 1989.

McDermott, Ryan. *Tropologies: Ethics and Invention in England, c. 1350–1600.* Notre Dame, IN: University of Notre Dame Press, 2016.

McGinn, Bernard. "Apocalypticism and Church Reform, 1100–1500." In *The Continuum History of Apocalypticism*, edited by Bernard J. McGinn, John J. Collins, and Stephen J. Stein, 273–98. New York: Continuum, 2003.

———. *The Flowering of Mysticism: Men and Women in the New Mysticism, 1200–1350.* Vol. 3 of *The Presence of God: A History of Western Christian Mysticism.* New York: Crossroad, 1998.

———. *The Growth of Mysticism: Gregory the Great through the 12th Century.* Vol. 2 of *The Presence of God: A History of Western Christian Mysticism.* New York: Crossroad, 1994.

———. *Visions of the End: Apocalyptic Traditions in the Middle Ages.* 2nd ed. New York: Columbia University Press, 1998.

McGuire, Brian Patrick. *Brother and Lover: Ælred of Rievaulx.* New York: Crossroad, 1994.

McLaughlin, Megan. "The Bishop as Bridegroom: Marital Imagery and Clerical Celibacy in the Eleventh and Early Twelfth Centuries." In *Medieval Purity and Piety: Essays on Medieval Clerical Celibacy and Religious Reform*, edited by Michael Frassetto, 209–327. New York: Garland, 1998.

McLuhan, Marshall. *Understanding Media: The Extensions of Man.* New York: Mentor, 1964.

Miller, William D. *Dorothy Day: A Biography.* San Francisco: Harper and Row, 1982.

Minnis, Alastair J. *Medieval Theory of Authorship: Scholastic Literary Attitudes in the Later Middle Ages.* 2nd ed. Philadelphia: University of Pennsylvania Press, 2010.

Moberly, R. W. L. "To Hear the Master's Voice: Revelation and Spiritual Discernment in the Call of Samuel." *Scottish Journal of Theology* 48, no. 4 (1995): 443–68.

Monti, Dominic. "Do the Scriptures Make a Difference in Our Lives?" In *Franciscans and the Scriptures: Living the Word of God*, edited by Elise Saggan, O.S.F., 1–17. St. Bonaventure, NY: The Franciscan Institute, 2005.

Monti, James. *A Sense of the Sacred: Roman Catholic Worship in the Middle Ages.* San Francisco: Ignatius, 2012.

Mowinckel, Sigmund. *The Psalms in Israel's Worship.* 2 vols. Translated by D. R. Ap-Thomas. Oxford: Blackwell, 1962.

Murphy, Clare M. "Erasmus as Biographer of Thomas More and His Family." In *Erasmus and the Republic of Letters*, edited by Stephen Ryle, 85–103. Leiden: Brepols, 2006.

Muscat, Noel. *The Life of Saint Francis in the Light of Saint Bonaventure's Theology on the "Verbum Crucifixum."* Studia Antoniana Cura Pontificii Anthenaei Antoniani Edita 33. Roma: Editrice Antonianum, 1989.

Musseter, Sally. "Type as Prophet in the Old English *Genesis B.*" *Viator* 14 (1983): 41–58.

Nellen, Henk, and Jan Bloemendal. "Erasmus's Biblical Project: Some Thoughts and Observations on Its Scope, Its Import in the Sixteenth Century, and Reception in the Seventeenth and Eighteenth Centuries." *Church History and Religious Culture* 96 (2016): 595–635.

Newman, Barbara. "*Innova dies nostros, sicut a principio:* Novelty and Nostalgia in Thomas of Celano's First and Second Lives of St. Francis." *Franciscan Studies* 81 (2023): 169–93.

Newman, Martha G. *Boundaries of Charity: Cistercian Culture and Ecclesiastical Reform, 1098–1180.* Figurae Reading Medieval Culture. Stanford, CA: Stanford University Press, 1996.

———. "Contemplative Virtues and the Active Life of Prelates." In Bernard of Clairvaux, *On Baptism and the Office of Bishops*, 11–36. CF 67. Kalamazoo, MI: Cistercian Publications, 1974.

Nocentini, Silvia. "The *Legenda maior* of Catherine of Siena." In *A Companion to Catherine of Siena*, edited by Carolyn Muessig, George Ferzoco, and Beverly Mayne Kienzle, 339–57. Leiden: Brill, 2012.

Novikoff, Alex J. "Anselm, Dialogue, and the Rise of Scholastic Disputation." *Speculum* 86 (2011): 387–418.

Nussberger, Danielle K. "Saint as Theological Wellspring: Hans Urs von Balthasar's Hermeneutic of the Saint in a Christological and Trinitarian Key." PhD diss., University of Notre Dame, 2007.

O'Connor, Margaret Anne, ed. *Willa Cather: The Contemporary Reviews.* Cambridge: Cambridge University Press, 2001.

O'Dwyer, B. W. "St. Bernard as Historian: *The Life of St. Malachy of Armagh.*" *Journal of Religious History* 10 (1978): 128–41.

Ohly, Friedrich. *Hoheleid-Studien: Grundzüge einer Geschichte der Hoheliedauslegung des Abendlandes bis um 1200.* Frankfurt am Main: F. Steiner, 1958.

O'Leary, John. "The Substantial Composition of Man according to Saint Bonaventure." PhD diss., Catholic University of America, 1931.

Olesiejko, Jacek. "Heaven, Hell and Middangeard: The Presentation of the Universe in the Old English *Genesis A*." *Studia Anglica Posnaniensia: International Review of English Studies* 45 no. 1 (2009): 153–62.

Pabel, Hilmar M. *Herculean Labours: Erasmus and the Editing of St. Jerome's Letters in the Renaissance.* Library of the Written Word 5. Leiden–Boston: Brill, 2008.

Pansters, Krijin. *Franciscan Virtue: Spiritual Growth and the Virtues in Franciscan Literature and Instruction of the Thirteenth Century.* Leiden: Brill, 2012.

Pelle, Stephen. "Sources and Analogues for Blickling Homily V and Vercelli Homily XI." *Notes and Queries* 59, no. 1 (2012): 8–13.

Pellegrini, Luigi. "A Century Reading the Sources for the Life of Francis of Assisi." *Greyfriars Review* 7 (1993): 323–46.

Petersen, Joan M. *The "Dialogues" of Gregory the Great in Their Late Antique Background.* Toronto: Pontifical Institute of Medieval Studies, 1985.

Pineas, Rainier. "Thomas More's Controversy with Simon Fish." *Studies in English Literature, 1500–1900* 7, no. 1 (1967): 15–28.

Poirel, Dominique. "L'écriture de Thomas de Celano: Une rhétorique de la rupture." *Franciscan Studies* 70 (2012): 73–99.

Poppi, Antonino, O.F.M. "The Gifts of the Holy Spirit according to Bonaventure." Translated by Solanus M. Benfatti, C.F.R. *The Dunwoodie Review* 35 (2012): 154–72.

Poulain, Augustin. "Revelations, Private." In *The Catholic Encyclopedia*, 13:5–7. New York: Robert Appleton Co., 1912.

Prentice, Robert P. *The Psychology of Love according to St. Bonaventure.* St. Bonaventure, NY: The Franciscan Institute, 1951.

Prinzivalli, Emanuela. "A Saint to be Read: Francis of Assisi in the Hagiographic Sources." *Greyfriars Review* 15 (2001): 253–98.

Prudlo, Donald S. *Certain Sainthood: Canonization and the Origins of Papal Infallibility in the Medieval Church.* Ithaca, NY: Cornell University Press, 2015.

———. *Thomas Aquinas: A Historical, Theological, and Environmental Portrait.* New York: Paulist, 2020.

Puzicha, Michaela. *Kommentar zur Vita Benedicti: Gregor der Grosse: Des zweite Buch der Dialoge.* St. Ottilien Archabbey, Emming, Germany: Editions of St. Ottilien, 2012.

Quain, Edwin A. "The Medieval *Accessus ad auctores*." *Traditio* 3 (1945): 215–64.

Radle, Gabriel. "Embodied Eschatology: The Council of Nicaea's Regulation of Kneeling and Its Reception across Liturgical Traditions" (Part 1 and Part 2). *Worship* 90 (July and September 2016): 345–71, 433–61.

Rahner, Karl. "The Doctrine of the 'Spiritual Senses' in the Middle Ages." Translated by David Morland, O.S.B. In *Theological Investigations* 16:109–208. New York: Crossroad, 1979.

Randle, Jonathan T. "The Homiletic Context of the Vercelli Book Poems." PhD diss., Cambridge University, 1999.
Ratzinger, Joseph. *The Theology of History in St. Bonaventure*. Translated by Zachary Hayes, O.F.M. Chicago: Franciscan Herald Press, 1971.
Rava, Elenora and Filippo Sedda. "Sulla trace dell'autore della *Legenda ad usum chori* beati Francisci: Analisi lessicografica e ipotesi di attribuzione." *Archivum Latinitas Medii Aevi* 69 (2011): 109–68.
Reames, Sherry L. *The "Legenda aurea": A Reexamination of Its Paradoxical History*. Madison: University of Wisconsin Press, 1985.
———. "The Cecilia Legend as Chaucer Inherited It and Retold It: The Disappearance of an Augustinian Ideal." *Speculum* 55, no. 1 (1980): 38–57.
Rebenich, Stefan. "Inventing an Ascetic Hero: Jerome's *Life of Paul the First Hermit*." In *Jerome of Stridon: His Life, Writings, and Legacy*, edited by Andrew Cain and Josef Lössi, 13–27. Farnham: Ashgate, 2009.
Reeves, M. *The Influence of Prophecy in the Later Middle Ages: A Study in Joachism*. Notre Dame, IN: University of Notre Dame Press, 1994.
Renan, Ernst. *The Life of Jesus*. Translated by Charles E. Wilbour. New York: Carleton, 1864.
Rex, Richard. "Thomas More and the Heretics: Statesman or Fanatic?" In *The Cambridge Companion to Thomas More*, edited by George M. Logan, 93–115. Cambridge: Cambridge University Press, 2011.
Rice, Eugene F., Jr. *Saint Jerome in the Renaissance*. Baltimore: Johns Hopkins University Press, 1985.
Riddy, Felicity. "Women Talking about the Things of God: A Late Medieval Sub-culture." In *Women and Literature in Britain 1150–1500*, edited by Carol M. Meale, 104–27. Cambridge: Cambridge University Press, 1996.
Roberts, Jane. "An Inventory of Early Guthlac Materials." *Mediaeval Studies* 32 (1970): 193–233.
Robertson, Duncan. *Lectio Divina: The Medieval Experience of Reading*. Collegeville, MN: Cistercian Studies, 2011.
Robson, Mark. "Writing Contexts in William Roper's *Life of Thomas More*." In *Writing the Lives of Writers*, edited by Warwick Gould and Thomas F. Staley, 79–89. New York: St. Martin's Press, 1998.
Rozenski, Steven. *Wisdom's Journey: Continental Mysticism and Popular Devotion in England, 1350–1650*. Notre Dame, IN: University of Notre Dame Press, 2022.
Rozier, Charles C. "Between History and Hagiography: Eadmer of Canterbury's Vision of the *Historia novorum in Anglia*." *Journal of Medieval History* 45, no. 1 (2019): 1–19.
Rubenstein, Jay. "Liturgy against History: The Competing Visions of Lanfranc and Eadmer of Canterbury." *Speculum* 74, no. 2 (1999): 279–309.

Rummel, Erika, ed. *Biblical Humanism and Scholasticism in the Age of Erasmus.* Leiden and Boston: Brill, 2008.

———. *Erasmus and His Catholic Critics.* 2 vols. Nieuwkoop, Netherlands: De Graaf, 1989.

Ryan, Jerry. "Legacy of a Country Priest, My Friend the Exorcist." *Commonweal Magazine*, October 7, 2011, 18–20.

Ryan, William Granger. "Introduction." In Jacobus de Voragine, *The Golden Legend: Readings on the Saints*, translated by William Granger Ryan, 1:xiii–xviii. Princeton, NJ: Princeton University Press, 1993.

Ryba, Thomas. "Reality, Imagination, and the Sensuous in Theology: Newman, Milbank, and Pickstock on the Perception of God." Paper Given at the International Newman Conference Oxford University, UK, August 2004.

Saggan, Elise, O.S.F., ed. *Franciscans and the Scriptures: Living the Word of God.* St. Bonaventure, NY: The Franciscan Institute, 2005.

Savorana, Alberto. *The Life of Luigi Guissani.* Quebec: McGill-Queen's University Press, 2018.

Saward, John. "The Fresh Flowers Again: St. Bonaventure and the Aesthetics of the Resurrection." *The Downside Review* 110 (1992): 1–29.

Schlauri, Ignace. "Saint François et la Bible: Essai Bibliographique de sa Spiritualité Évangélique." *Collectanea Franciscana* 40 (1970): 365–437.

Schlickmann, Dorothea M. *The Hidden Years: Father Joseph Kentenich, Childhood and Youth (1885–1910).* Translated by Mary Jane Hoehne. Waukesha, WI: Schoenstatt Editions U.S.A., 2009.

Schmucki, Octavian. *The Stigmata of St. Francis of Assisi: A Critical Examination in Light of Thirteenth-Century Sources.* St. Bonaventure, NY: The Franciscan Institute, 1991.

Schultze, Dirk. "Spiritual Teaching by Catherine of Siena in BL Harley 2409: An Edition." *Anglia* 136, no. 2 (2018): 296–325.

Schulz-Wackerbarth, Yorick. *Die Vita Pauli des Hieronymus: Darstellung und Etablierung eines Heiligen im hagiographischen Diskurs der Spätantike.* Studien und Texte zu Antike und Christentum 107. Tübingen: Mohr Siebeck, 2017.

Scott, Karen. "Catherine of Siena and Lay Sanctity in Fourteenth-Century Italy." In *Lay Sanctity, Medieval and Modern: A Search for Models*, edited by Ann W. Astell, 77–90. Notre Dame, IN: University of Notre Dame Press, 2000.

———. "'Io Catarina': Ecclesiastical Politics and Oral Culture in the Letters of Catherine of Siena." In *Dear Sisters: Medieval Women and the Epistolary Genre*, edited by Karen Cherewatuk and Ulrike Wiethaus, 87–121. Philadelphia: University of Pennsylvania Press, 1993.

———. "Mystical Death, Bodily Death: Catherine of Siena and Raymond of Capua on the Mystic's Encounter with God." In *Gendered Voices: Medieval*

Saints and Their Interpreters, edited by Catherine M. Mooney, 136–67. Philadelphia: University of Pennsylvania Press, 1999.

———. "St. Catherine of Siena, 'Apostola.'" *Church History* 61 (April 1992): 34–46.

Scragg, Donald C. "The Compilation of the Vercelli Book." *Anglo-Saxon England* 2 (1973): 189–207.

Scullion, James P., O.F.M. "A Love Supreme: The Writings of Francis of Assisi and the Gospel of John." In *Franciscans and the Scriptures: Living the Word of God*, edited by Elise Saggan, O.S.F., 19–32. St. Bonaventure, NY: The Franciscan Institute, 2005.

Seybolt, Robert Francis. "Fifteenth Century Editions of the *Legenda aurea*." *Speculum* 21, no. 3 (1946): 327–38.

———. "The *Legenda aurea*, Bible, and *Historia scholastica*." *Speculum* 21, no. 3 (1946): 339–42.

Sellers, Gordon B. "The Old English Rogationtide Corpus: A Literary History." PhD diss., Loyola University Chicago, 1996.

Semler, L. E. "Virtue, Transformation, and Exemplarity in *The Lyfe of Johan Picus*." In *A Companion to Thomas More*, edited by A. D. Cousins and Damian Grace, 95–113. Madison, NJ: Fairleigh Dickinson University Press, 2009.

Sherlock, Peter. *Monuments and Memory in Early Modern England*. Aldershot: Ashgate, 2008.

Silverstein, Theodore. *Visio Sancti Pauli*. Studies and Documents 4. London: Christophers, 1935.

Simon, David L. "Comment." In *Approaches to Nature in the Middle Ages*, edited by Lawrence D. Roberts, 105–6. Medieval and Renaissance Texts and Studies 16. Binghamton, NY: Center for Medieval and Renaissance Studies, 1982.

Simpson, James. *Sciences and the Self in Medieval Poetry: Alan of Lille's "Anticlaudianus" and John Gower's "Confessio Amantis."* Cambridge Studies in Medieval Literature 25. Cambridge: Cambridge University Press, 1995.

Sinding, M. "Assembling Spaces: The Conceptual Structure of Allegory." *Style* 36, no. 3 (2002): 503–23.

Smalley, Beryl. *The Study of the Bible in the Middle Ages*. Notre Dame, IN: University of Notre Dame Press, 1964, repr. 1978.

Smyth, Marina. "The Body, Death, and Resurrection: Perspectives of an Early Irish Theologian." *Speculum* 83, no. 3 (2008): 531–71.

———. "The Origins of Purgatory through the Lens of Seventh-Century Irish Eschatology." *Traditio* 58 (2003): 91–132.

Smith, Lesley Janette. *The Glossa Ordinaria: The Making of a Medieval Bible Commentary*. Leiden and Boston: Brill, 2009.

Southern, Richard W. "Introduction." In *The Life of St. Anselm, Archbishop of Canterbury, by Eadmer*, edited by and translated by R. W. Southern, ix–xxxvi. Oxford Medieval Texts. Oxford: Clarendon Press, 1972.

———. *Saint Anselm and His Biographer: A Study of Monastic Life and Thought, 1059–c. 1130*. Cambridge: Cambridge University Press, 1963.

———. "Sally Vaughn's Anselm: An Examination of the Foundations." *Albion* 20, no. 2 (1988): 181–204.

Staunton, Michael. "Eadmer's *Vita Anselmi*: A Reinterpretation." *Journal of Medieval History* 23, no. 1 (1997): 1–14.

Steadman, John M. "Heroic Virtue and the Divine Image in *Paradise Lost*." *Journal of the Warburg and Courtauld Institute* 22, no. 1/2 (1959): 88–105.

Steiman, Lionel B. *Franz Werfel: The Faith of an Exile: From Prague to Beverly Hills*. Waterloo, ON: Wilfrid Laurier University Press, 1985.

Stouck, Mary-Ann, and David Stouck. "Hagiographical Style in *Death Comes for the Archbishop*." *University of Toronto Quarterly: A Canadian Journal of the Humanities* 41 (1972): 293–307.

Szittya, Penn R. *The Antifraternal Tradition in Medieval Literature*. Princeton, NJ: Princeton University Press, 1986.

Taylor, Jerome. "Introduction." In *The "Didascalicon" of Hugh of Saint Victor: A Medieval Guide to the Arts*, translated by Jerome Taylor, 3–39. Records of Western Civilization. New York: Columbia University Press, 1991.

Tichelkamp, Craig. *The Mystified Letter: How Medieval Theology Can Reenchant the Practice of Reading*. Minneapolis, MN: Fortress, 2023.

Tierney, Brian. *Origins of Papal Infallibility, 1150–1350: A Study in the Concepts of Infallibility, Sovereignty, and Tradition in the Middle Ages*. Leiden: Brill, 1988.

Thompson, Augustine. *Francis of Assisi: A New Biography*. Ithaca, NY: Cornell University Press, 2012.

Tracy, David. *The Analogical Imagination: Christian Theology and the Culture of Pluralism*. New York: Crossroad, 1981.

Tedoldi, Fabio Massimo. *La dottrina del cinque sensi spirituali in san Bonaventura*. Rome: Pontificium Athenaeum Antonianum, 1999.

Thibodeau, Timothy M. "*Enigmata Figurarum*: Biblical Exegesis and Liturgical Exposition in Durand's 'Rationale.'" *Harvard Theological Review* 86, no. 1 (1993): 65–79.

Thompson, Billy Brussell. "'Plumbei cordis, oris ferrei': La reception de la teologia de Jacobus de Voragine y su *Legenda Aurea* en la Península." In *Saints and Their Authors: Studies in Medieval Hispanic Hagiography in Honor of John K. Walsh*, 97–106. Madison, WI: Hispanic Seminary of Medieval Studies, 1990.

Tomko, Michael. *Beyond the Willing Suspension of Disbelief: Poetic Faith from Coleridge to Tolkein*. London: Bloomsbury, 2015.

370 Bibliography

Tomo, Armando. *Chiara Lubich: A Biography*. Translated by Bill Harnett. New York: New City Press, 2012.

Truhlar, K. V. "Virtue, Heroic." In *New Catholic Encyclopedia*, 2nd ed., 14:554–55. Washington, DC: Catholic University of America Press, 2002.

Turner, Mark. *The Literary Mind: The Origins of Thought and Language*. New York: Oxford University Press, 1996.

———. *The Way We Think: Conceptual Blending and the Mind's Hidden Complexities*. New York: Basic Books, 2002.

Tylus, Jane. *Reclaiming Catherine of Siena: Literacy, Literature, and the Signs of Others*. Chicago: University of Chicago Press, 2009.

Vauchez, André. "Jacques de Voragine et les saintes du XIII siècle dans la *Légende dorée*." In *Legenda aurea: Sept siècles de diffusion: Actes du colloque international sur le Legenda aurea, text Latin et branches vernaculaires*, 27–56. Paris: Vrin, 1986.

———. *The Laity in the Middle Ages: Religious Beliefs and Devotional Practices*. Edited by Daniel E. Bornstein. Translated by Margery J. Schneider. Notre Dame, IN: University of Notre Dame Press, 1993.

———. *Sainthood in the Later Middle Ages*. Translated by Jean Birrill. Cambridge: Cambridge University Press, 1993.

———. "The Stigmata of St. Francis and Its Medieval Detractors." *Greyfriars Review* 13 (1999): 66–89.

Vaughn, Sally N. "Anselm: Saint and Statesman." *Albion* 20, no. 2 (1988): 205–20.

———. "Eadmer's *Historia novorum*: A Reinterpretation." In *Anglo-Norman Studies 10: Proceedings of the Battle Conference 1987*, edited by R. Allen Brown, 259–89. London: Boydell Press, 1988.

Wack, Mary F., and Charles D. Wright. "A New Source for the 'Three Utterances' Exemplum." *Anglo-Saxon England* 20 (1991): 187–202.

Waddell, Chrysogonus. "The Two Saint Malachy Offices from Clairvaux." In *Bernard of Clairvaux: Studies Presented to Dom Jean Leclercq*, edited by M. Basil Pennington, 123–50. Cistercian Studies 23. Washington, DC: Cistercian Publications, 1973.

Wales, Jordan Joseph. "The Narrated Theology of *Stabilitas* in Gregory the Great's *Life of Benedict*." *Cistercian Studies Quarterly* 49, no. 2 (2014): 163–98.

———. "'Sacrifice' in the Theology of Gregory the Great." PhD diss., University of Notre Dame, 2014.

Wandel, Lee Palmer. *Voracious Idols and Violent Hands: Iconoclasm in Reformation Zurich, Strasbourg, and Basel*. Cambridge: Cambridge University Press, 1995.

Warner, Marina. *Alone of All Her Sex: The Myth and Cult of the Virgin Mary*. New York: Random House, 1976.

Webb, Catherine. "St. Catherine of Siena's Heart." *Speculum* 80, no. 3 (2005): 802–17.

Weinert, Franz-Rudolf. *Christi Himmelfahrt. Neutestamentliches Fest im Spiegel alttestamentlicher Psalmen: Zur Entstehung des römischen Himmelfahrtsoffiziums.* St. Ottilien Archabbey, Emming, Germany: Editions of St. Ottilien, 1987.

Weingarten, Susan. *The Saint's Saints: Hagiography and Geography in Jerome.* Leiden and Boston: Brill, 2005.

Wendland, Ernst R. "'Blessed is the man who will eat at the feast in the Kingdom of God' (Lk 14:15): Internal and External Intertextual Influence on the Interpretation of Christ's Parable of the Great Banquet." *Neotestamentica* 31, no. 1 (1997): 159–94.

White, Helen C. *Tudor Books of Saints and Martyrs.* Madison: University of Wisconsin Press, 1963.

Willard, Rudolph. "The Latin Texts of the Three Utterances of the Soul." *Speculum* 12, no. 2 (1937): 147–66.

Williams, David. *Saints Alive: Word, Image, and Enactment in the Lives of the Saints.* Montreal and Kingston: McGill-Queen's University Press, 2010.

Williams, Rowan. *Dostoevsky: Language, Faith, and Fiction.* Waco, TX: Baylor University Press, 2008.

Wilmart, André. "Le manuel de prières de saint Gaulbert." *Revue bénédictine* 48 (1936): 236–65.

———. "Saint Ambrose et la *Légende dorée*." *Ephemerides Liturgicae*, n.s., 50 (1936): 169–206.

Winstead, Karen A. *Fifteenth-Century Lives: Writing Sainthood in England.* Notre Dame, IN: University of Notre Dame Press, 2020.

Wooden, Warren W. "Structural Patterning in William Roper's *Life of More*." *Moreana* 16, no. 64 (1980): 100–106.

Woodward, Kenneth L. *Making Saints.* New York: Simon and Schuster, 1996.

Wright, Charles D. "The Pledge of the Soul: A Judgment Theme in Old English Homiletic Literature and Cynewulf's *Elene*." *Neuphilologische Mitteilungen* 91 (1990): 23–30.

Wrisley Shelby, Katherine. "*A Christo sub specie Seraph*: Revisiting St. Bonaventure's Theology of the Stigmata." *Cithara* 61, no. 1 (2021): 10–38.

Wyschogrod, Edith. *Saints and Postmodernism: Revisioning Moral Philosophy.* Chicago: University of Chicago Press, 1990.

Zacher, Samantha. *Preaching the Converted: The Style and Rhetoric of the Vercelli Book Homilies.* Toronto: University of Toronto Press, 2009.

Zahlten, Johannes. *Creatio mundi: Darstellungen der sechs Schöpfungstage und naturwissenschaftliches Weltbild im Mittelalter.* Stuttgarter Beiträge zur Geschichte und Politik 13. Stuttgart: Klett-Cotta, 1979.

Zelzer, Michaela. "Gregory's *Life of Benedict* and the Bible: The Decoding of an Exegetical Program." *Cistercian Studies Quarterly* 44, no. 1 (2009): 89–102.

INDEX

A
Accessus ad auctores, 182
Aelred of Rievaulx, St.: and Augustine's *Confessions*, 42–43; *Life of Ninian*, 38–60; *Mirror of Charity*, 40, 42, 51, 53–57, 276n.9
agency, divine and human, 131–34, 215, 223, 234
Agnes of Montepulciano, St., 189
allegory, 69; in Bernard of Clairvaux, 69; in Francis of Assisi, 127; in Hugh of St. Victor, 88, 92–93; as sense appropriated to Ambrose, 222. *See also* biblical senses; numerology
Alcuin of York, 18, 21–23, 37
Alter, Robert, 259
Ambrose, St., 59, 215, 222, 308n.18, 315n.51
anagogy: definitions of, 177–78; and eschatology, 176–77, 241; literalized in *Legenda aurea*, 176; and liturgy, 178; and mystical exegesis, 177; and sacraments, 203; as sense assigned to Augustine, 222
angels: at Annunciation, 247; at Ascension, 34; Catherine of Siena as angel, 149, 156, 171; creation of, 47; Francis of Assisi as angel, 147, 159; on Jacob's ladder, 157; in *Life of Guthlac*, 23, 31– 32, 35; with Mary Magdalene, 183–84, 189, 195, 202–3; nine choirs of, 305n.158; as readers, 57; at the Resurrection, 187; as watchmen, 79
Anselm, St.: boyhood dream-vision, 101; canonization of, 114–15; in dispute over ecclesiastical jurisdiction, 105–6; in the furnace of Babylon, 109–11; in investiture controversy, 94–95, 98; and Matilda of Scotland, 99; miracles of, 102–3, 108–9; Muslim reception of, 103; ordination as archbishop, 95–96; reception of pallium, 97–98; resistance to election, 107; use of similitudes, 102, 106
Anthony of Egypt, St., 2, 17, 212–14
Anthony of Padua, St., 126–27, 138
Antunes, Joana, 184
apocalypticism, 92, 130, 263, 292n.52. *See also* Bonaventure, St.; Catherine of Siena, St.; Raymond of Capua, Blessed; Werfel, Franz
Ascension, 18, 22, 28, 33–37. *See also* Eucharist; rogation days
Athanasius, St.: "Letter to Marcellinus," 19, 23; *Life of Antony*, 2, 17, 23, 30–31; in Jerome's *Vita Pauli*, 213

372

Auerbach, Erich, 258–59
Augustine, St.: Christmas sermons, 53; *City of God*, 41, 44, 53, 151, 167; *Confessions*, 38, 40–43, 51–59, 121–22; *De doctrina Christiana*, 89, 146, 201, 215, 262, 324n.33, 324n.37; *De Genesi ad litteram*, 40; *De Trinitate*, 201; *Enarrationes in psalmos*, 17–18; model for conversion of Francis of Assisi, 121–22, 133; and the *Totus Christus*, 17–18
authorship: of human writers, 216; of the saint, 132–34, 215, 223; of the scriptures, 214–15

B
baptism, 59, 76, 191, 203, 249
Bartholomew, St., 25, 27, 30, 34, 37
beatitudes, 121, 124, 135; in Bonaventure's *Commentary on Luke*, 135–38; in *Breviloquium*, 139–41; in *Legenda maior*, 141–45
Bede the Venerable: *De Templo*, 44; *Ecclesiastical History*, 31, 39, 86; *Glossa* on Luke, 137; *Life of Saint Cuthbert*, 23, 33; model for "heroic" hagiography, 86
Beleth, John, 178–79
Bell, Rudolf, 189
Benedict, St. *See* Gregory the Great, St.; Rule of St. Benedict
Bernard of Clairvaux, St.: *De consideratione*, 64; *Life of Malachy*, 62–82; *On Loving God*, 79; *On the Conduct and Office of Bishops*, 64; *Sermons on the Song of Songs*, 61, 62–63, 68

biblical senses: in Bonaventure, 139, 146–47; disassociation of, 6, 10, 92, 177; four, 2, 6, 176, 178, 214, 222; and Ephesians 3:14–19, 137–38; and "letter" and "spirit," 92. *See also* allegory; anagogy; *sensus litteralis*; tropology
Bietenholz, Peter, 219, 224
Billett, Jesse, 32, 33
Binski, Paul, 232
bishop's insignia: Gospel book, 96; pallium, 97–98, 99; ring, 67; staff, 67
Black, Jonathan, 21, 22
Bloemendal, Jan, 217–18
Bokenham, Osbern, 172, 198–205
Bollandists, 253–54
Bonaventure, St., 8; *Breviloquium*, 136, 139–41, 143; *Collations on the Six Days*, 146, 147; *Commentary on Luke*, 136; *De donis*, 142; *Disputed Questions on Evangelical Perfection*, 123; *Legenda maior*, 121–31, 133–35, 141–46; on senses of scripture, 139, 146–47
Bougerol, Jacques-Guy, 135
Boureau, Alain, 175
Bradshaw, Paul, 19
Brendan, St., 4
Bridget of Sweden, St., 166, 198
Brown, Peter, 254
Brueggemann, Walter, 31
Bynum, Caroline Walker, 194, 196, 254, 318n.103

C
candles, symbolism of, 1, 186, 239, 250, 263

canonization: of Anselm, 114–15; of Bernadette Soubirous, 249; of Bonaventure, 151–52; of Catherine of Siena, 151, 190, 196; changes in process of, 8, 12, 112–15, 120, 135–36, 151–52, 170, 308n.13; of Empress Adelaide, 112; of Francis of Assisi, 119, 122; of Gerard of Toul, 112; of Malachy, 63; of Nicholas Peregrinus, 112; of Peter of Anagni, 112; of Thomas Becket, 115; of Thomas More, 233
Carruthers, Mary, 68–69
Cather, Willa: biblical imagery, 243–44; *Death Comes for the Archbishop*, 12, 242–46; and *Golden Legend*, 242
Catherine of Siena, St.: apocalyptic mission of, 154–56, 167, 171; *Dialogue*, 151, 157, 167–68, 169; *Letters*, 157; and Revelations 20:1, 156; and the Song of Songs, 196, 307n.2; as Thomistic teacher, 191–94. *See also* Flete, William; Mary Magdalene, Raymond of Capua, Blessed
causality, 8, 132, 216
Caxton, William, 174, 200
celibacy, 65, 67–68, 112
Chambers, R.W., 209
charity: as bond of unity, 74–75, 143, 167, 195, 287n.67; and bridal union, 64; as chief virtue, 44, 143; and death, 79, 127, 142–43, 145, 166; as Franciscan charism, 135; and gift of piety, 139, 142; and gift of wisdom, 139; God as, 262; and humility, 157–59; and patience, 166–69; as rule of exegesis, 89, 214, 291n.34, 324n.33; and Sabbath, 44, 282n.110; as theological virtue, 151, 158, 166, 304n.137
Chenu, M. D., 11, 84, 92
Clairmont, David, 131
Coakley, John, 121, 125, 132–33
coal, symbolism of, 228, 236
Coleridge, Samuel Taylor, 203
Colgrave, Bertram, 23, 29, 33
compunction, 21, 74, 76, 99, 157, 161, 287n.63, 287n.65, 304n.140. *See also* tears
Conca, Sebastian, 184–85, 316n.64
Cousins, Ewert, 144
Cross, James, 184

D
Dal Santo, Matthew, 260
Danielou, Jean, 17, 19–20, 34, 191
Dante Alighieri, 175, 245, 321n.169
Day, Dorothy, 237
Degórski, Bazyli, 213, 323n.19
Delany, Sheila, 199, 201–2
Delehaye, Hippolyte, 5–7, 253–56, 260
de Lubac, Henri, 5, 92, 177–78, 238
de Vives, Luis, 175
de Vogüé, Adalbert, 262
Divine Office, 2, 4, 32–34, 183, 186
Dominic, St., 123, 176, 189, 191
Dostoevsky, Fyodor, 12; *The Brothers Karamazov*, 239–42; *Crime and Punishment*, 238–39
Downey, Sarah, 275n.107
dragon, 2, 247
Duffy, Eamon, 174, 175, 179–80
Dunstan, St., 86, 113
Durandus, William, 178–79
Dutton, Marsha, 38, 42

E
Eadmer of Canterbury: and biographical dualism, 84–87; cult of saints, 112–15; *Historia novorum*, 84, 93–100; *Vita Anselmi*, 100–111
ekphrasis, 69
Emerson Hernández, Marco Carlos, 40, 277n.10
energeia, 69
Erasmus, Desiderius: as another St. Jerome, 212, 218; as biblical editor, 217–18; as biographer of Jerome, 218–23; as correspondent with More, 231; as friend of More, 225–26
etymology: of Catherine, 154, 156, 158–59; of cattle, 55; of Jerome, 219–20; of Mary Magdalene, 182
Eucharist: and Ascension, 33, 35, 188; as bodily food, 192–94; and breastfeeding, 203, 321n.167; and Catherine of Siena, 189–93, 195–97; and fasting, 153, 163; as food of martyrs, 165, 178; and Mary Magdalene, 183, 184–86; as memorial, 227; and miracles of bread and fish, 103; as offering for souls in Purgatory, 70–71; and pelican, 59; in Thomas Aquinas, 191–95; and Tree of Life, 72; as viaticum, 26

F
Felix of Croyland. *See* Guthlac, St.
Flete, William, 158–59, 174, 198–99, 201
Francis of Assisi, St.: as angel of the sixth seal, 147, 159, 305n.158; canonization of, 199, 122; death, 129; first follower of, 126; at Greccio, 127–28; hearing Gospel at Portiuncula, 124–25, 133; pre-conversion, 133; military service, 299n.36; reverence for scripture, 127, 299n.53; trip to Apulia, 124–25, 133. *See also* Bonaventure, St.; stigmata; Thomas of Celano
Frei, Hans, 10–11, 252–53, 258–59
Fursey, St., 31

G
Geoffrey of Auxerre, 63
gifts of the Spirit, 137, 141, 145
Girona tapestry, 47, 49, 279–80n.56
Glass, Dorothy, 45–46, 47
Grandsen, Antonia, 86, 87, 294n.70
Graus, František, 254
Gregori, Luigi, 250–51
Gregory the Great, St.: *Homilies on Ezekiel*, 1, 21; *Life of St. Benedict*, 13, 260–62, 338n.41, 339n.54; and Lives of saints, 89, 265n.10; *Moralia in Job*, 74, 132, 177. *See also* tropology
Grillaert, Nel, 240
Grosseteste, Robert, 151
Guissani, Luigi, 237
Guthlac, St.: and animals, 24; and Bartholomew, 25, 27; conversion of, 23; death, 33–35; dragged by demons, 26–27; dream of Britons, 28; and foreknowledge, 29; and King Aethelbald, 24, 29–30; novitiate at Repton, 23; and psalm 15, 27, 33, 37; and psalm 17, 25, 30, 33, 37; and psalm 30, 30; and psalm 55, 26, 33, 36–37; and psalm 67, 28, 31,

Guthlac, St. (*cont.*)
  34, 36–37; and psalm 77, 36; and psalm 80, 29; and psalm 83, 27, 31, 35; and psalm 117, 25, 30, 33; rule of, 25–26; temptation to despair, 25; temptation to presumption, 25–26

H
hagiography: and autobiography, 9; bi-partite, 87–88; and biography, antique, 5; and biography, modern, 9, 12, 209, 211, 224, 236; commemorative, 86; dualist, 8–9, 12, 87, 114; features of, 334n.66; as intimate biography, 87; in modern literature, 236–50, 331n.6; patterns for, 86–87; as sacred biography, 93, 112, 255–56; as studied by historians, 254–55, 336n.12, 336n.15; as studied by moral philosophers, 256–57; as studied by theologians, 267n.27, 337n.23; as Wisdom literature, 3, 90
Harpsfield, Nicholas, 224–35
Heffernan, Thomas, 87, 93, 253–54, 255–56
Hellman, Wayne, 124
Hildegard of Bingen, St., 47–48
historical sense. See *sensus litteralis*
Hostensius, 4, 115
Hughes, Kevin, 12, 92
Hugh of St. Victor, 2–3, 147; *De sacramentis*, 46; *Didascalicon*, 86–93
humility: of Anselm, 103; and charity, 153, 157, 158; of exegetes, 89; and fear of the Lord, 141; as foundational virtue, 140, 153, 158, 169; of Jesus, 127, 156, 165; ladder of, 153, 157; and piety, 145; and obedience, 147, 155; and sorrow for sin, 160; of Thomas More, 226, 231–32; as virtue opposed to pride, 140, 153

I
investiture controversy, 94–95, 98

J
Jacobus de Voragine, 174–75, 312n.6. See also *Legenda aurea*
Jerome, St.: Erasmus's biography of, 218–23; *Life of Saint Paul the Hermit*, 211–14; literal sense ascribed to, 222; miracles of, 218–19; as model for Erasmus, 212, 218; as received by reformers, 222
John of St. Paul, 126
John the Baptist, St., 82; 112–13
Julian of Norwich, 321n.167

K
Karris, Robert, 123
Kaufman, Peter Iver, 165
Kearns, Conleth, 150, 162
Kentenich, Joseph, 237
Kjetsaa, Geir, 238
Kozlowski, Matthew, 119, 132
Krahmer, Shawn, 63, 68

L
Lawler, Michael G., 134, 302n.99, 302n.102
Leclercq, Jean, 178
lectio divina, 11, 179
Legenda aurea: and anagogy, 175–78; contents of, 174–75; dissemination of, 174–75, 312n.4; liturgy and, 9, 178–79;

reception of, 4, 9, 174–75;
    as Scholastic work, 9, 179–83
LeGoff, Jacques, 175, 178
Levinas, Emmanuel, 236, 257
Levy, Ian Christopher, 5, 214–15, 223
literal sense. See *sensus litteralis*
liturgy: seasonal, 179, 314n.36; as
    time-ending, 31, 43, 173, 176;
    in typological interpretation,
    273n.83. *See also* Divine Office;
    Eucharist; sacraments
Love, Nicholas, 200
Lubich, Chiara, 237
Lucie-Smith, Alexander, 257
Luongo, F. Thomas, 309n.23
Luther, Martin, 217, 222–23

M
MacQueen, John, 39, 43–44, 57
MacQueen, Winifred, 39, 52
Madigan, Kevin, 131
Malachy, St.: as archbishop of Armagh,
    66–68; and Bernard of Clairvaux,
    63–64, 75, 81–82; as bishop of
    Connor, 65–66; as bridegroom,
    74; in Cistercian liturgy, 63;
    and *cross-figil*, 79; death of, 63,
    81; and dove, 75–76; and hands,
    80–81; as pastor, 77–78; sister of,
    69–73
marriage: of bishop to diocese, 66–67,
    285n.23; at Cana, 241; of Christ
    and church, 71, 74; of mystic
    union, 78, 150, 229; of priest in
    celibacy, 65; as sacrament, 65, 67,
    203, 217, 227, 231
Martha, St., 186
Martin of Tours, St., 38, 59
martyrdom: accounts of, 5; anticipated
    by saints, 66, 110, 132, 142,
    164–65, 166, 212; ascetical, 212;

of Carthusians, 234–35; and
    heroic patience, 165–71; of
    insults, 220; roses of, 61; spiritual,
    197; of St. Elphege, 104; of
    Thomas More, 229, 235
martyrs: as Christian heroes, 151, 165;
    cult of, 165, 178, 244; food of,
    178, 194; John the Baptist as,
    112–13; Thomas Becket as, 229;
    Thomas of Dover as, 229; virtues
    of, 166–67; witness of, 3, 89,
    151, 157, 177, 210, 229
Mary Magdalene: as biblical composite,
    182–83; in *Bokenham's Legends of
    Holy Women*, 199–205; as
    illumined disciple, 182; in the
    Legenda aurea, 179–86; as model
    for Catherine of Siena, 186–89,
    195–98; in Thomas Aquinas, 191;
    as type of repentant sinner, 181,
    182; as witness to the
    Resurrection, 182, 188
Mary of Egypt, St. 183–84
McLaughlin, Megan, 65
Meyer, Robert T., 79
Minnis, Alastair, 132, 216
miracles: at Cana, 241; as criteria for
    canonization, 112, 120, 122, 135,
    152; as documenting belief, 258;
    in legend of St. Jerome, 218–19;
    in legend of Mary Magdalene,
    183; in *Life of Anselm*, 83, 91,
    102–3, 108–111, 290n.2; in *Life
    of Benedict*, 261; in *Life of
    Catherine of Siena*, 150, 161, 162,
    169; in *Life* of Francis, 122, 128,
    144, 255; in *Life of Malachy*,
    71–74, 81; in *Life of Ninian*,
    38–60, 279n.45; as mythic, 10,
    259; purpose of, 40–42, 261–62;
    in *Song of Bernadette*, 248

Monti, Dominic, 128, 296n.5
Monti, James, 316n.72
morality plays, 245
More, Thomas: *A Dialogue of Comfort against Tribulation*, 228; epitaph, 229–35; martyrdom of, 235; on Henry VIII's marriages, 227–28; *On the Sadness of Christ*, 225; polemic against Tyndale, 227; as remembered by Erasmus, 225; *The Soul's Supplication*, 231, 329n.144; vocation of, 233–35
Mowinckel, Sigmund, 20
Musseter, Sally, 17, 18

N
Nellen, Henk, 217–18
Newman, Martha, 63, 287n.67
Nil of Sora, St., 240
Nocentini, Silvia, 150, 151
Noffke, Suzanne, 311n.1
numerology, 7, 44, 135, 137

O
ordination: of Anselm, 96–97; of Malachy, 69; of Ninian, 43
Origen of Alexandria, 177

P
Pabel, Hilmar, 212, 219
parables: and *Aggadot*, 1, 243, 245; of the foolish rich man, 245; of the Good Shepherd, 66–67, 77, 79, 94; of the great banquet, 11, 84, 96–105; of the hidden treasure, 124, 243; of the sower and the seed, 243; of the wheat and tares, 111. *See also* Anselm: use of similitudes

patience, 161–70
Paul the Hermit, St., 5, 211–14
Pico della Mirandola, 235, 330n.173
popes: Adrian VI, 222; Alexander III, 114; Alexander IV, 130; Clement XI, 115; Eugenius III, 64, 75; Gregory IX, 119, 122; Gregory XI, 164; Gregory XIII, 307n.3; Honorius III, 120, 134; Innocent III, 120, 126; as judge for canonization, 4, 115; Leo IX, 112; Pascal, 94–95; Paschasius II, 112; Pelagius, 175; Pius II, 151; Pius XI, 249; Sixtus IV, 151; Urban II, 94, 97, 99, 103, 111–12; Urban VI, 164
Poppi, Antonino, 142
Poirel, Dominique, 119
Poulain, A., 307n.3
poverty: disputed by anti-mendicants, 123–24, 130; and fear of the Lord, 145; as foundational for evangelical perfection, 142; of John the Baptist, 159; of Malachy, 73; and Matthew 5:3, 136, 140, 142; practiced by Christ, 131; as religious vow, 140, 141; and Spiritual Joachites, 130, 301n.75; and temperance, 137–38; as a virtue, 131, 135–36, 142, 169
Praxedes, St., 176–77, 313n.22
Prudlo, Donald, 115
psalms: in Alcuin of York, 21–22; as exorcisms, 19, 29, 30, 273n.73; in *Life of Guthlac*, 23–35; as prophecy and prayer, 17–21. *See also* Divine Office; Guthlac, St.
Pseudo-Dionysius, 177

R

Ratzinger, Joseph, 146–48, 305n.160
Raymond of Capua, Blessed: as apocalyptic writer, 149, 153, 156–61; as Catherine's confessor, 150, 157, 159, 169; as defender of Catherine against detractors, 190–95; as doubting Thomas, 152; sources for his *Legenda maior*, 151
Reames, Sherry, 175, 260
Rebenich, Stefan, 212
Renan, Ernst, 10
Rice, Eugene, 219
"Ro. Ba.," 209–10, 235
Roberts, Jane, 31
rogation days, 18, 36
Roper, William, 224–25
Rozier, Charles, 85–86
Rubenstein, Jay, 112–13
Rule of St. Benedict, 90, 153, 157
Rules of Tychonius, 146, 262
Ryan, William Granger, 176

S

sacraments. *See* baptism; Eucharist; marriage; ordination
sensus litteralis: as ascribed to Jerome, 222; as duplex, 216; and Eucharist, 195; as foundational, 91, 93, 146, 227; as *historia*, 6, 10–11, 88, 91–92, 146, 255; and "historical-critical" method, 13, 20, 252, 254; and historical writing, 84, 86, 98, 100, 106–07, 114; as "history-like," 253, 258; as "letter" vis-à-vis "spirit," 8, 12, 92–93, 110, 214; in Reformation controversies, 211, 217, 227; of saints' *Lives*, 2, 9–10, 68, 176, 223, 229, 253; as seedlike, 92–93
Sherlock, Peter, 230, 232

Simon, David L., 46
Smalley, Beryl, 5, 92
sortes bibliae, 96, 126, 128–29, 293n.63
Southern, R. W., 83, 85, 86–87, 105
Staunton, Michael, 87, 102, 104, 106, 108
stigmata: and approval of Franciscan Rule, 120, 126, 134; of Catherine and Francis of Assisi, 159–60; of Catherine of Siena, 150, 196; denied, 130, 135, 144; of Francis of Assisi, 8, 119, 127, 128, 132; and virtues, 138, 143; and wisdom, 144–45
Strauss, David F., 10
Suetonius, 86–87, 226
Sulpicius Severus, 23, 90, 101

T

tears: and anointing, 72, 181–82; gift of, 74, 161, 240; of joy, 186; kinds of, 188–89, 287n.63
Thomas Aquinas, St.: compared to Jacobus de Voragine, 180–81, 190–94; on Eucharist and biblical senses, 194–95; on heroic virtue, 135–36; on martyrdom, 166
Thomas of Celano: compared to Bonaventure as hagiographer, 131–35; education of, 296n.10; other writings, 122, 297n.20; sources for the *Vita prima*, 121; *Vita prima*, 124–29; witness to Francis's canonization, 122
Thompson, Augustine, 254–55
Tracy, David, 337n.23
tropology: and allegory, 2, 8, 88, 92; and history, 88; and morals, 88, 89, 256–58, 260; sense assigned to Gregory the Great, 222. *See also* virtues

V

Vauchez, André, 254
Vaugh, Sally, 84–85, 86
Vercelli "Homily 23," 18, 36–37
Virgin Mary, 3, 52, 181, 184, 195, 197, 246–49; and Song of Songs, 61, 196
virtues: cardinal, 136–37, 151, 156, 167; chain of, 154–56; exemplary, 136, 308n.12; habits of, 136; heroic, 8, 12, 120, 132, 135–36, 149–52, 307n.11, 308n.13; hierarchy of, 134; of the perfected, 136, 308n.12; perfecting, 136, 308n.12; social, 156, 308n.12; theological, 139, 151, 155, 167

W

Waddell, Chrysologus, 63
Werfel, Franz, 12–13, 246–50
White, Carolinne, 213
White, Helen C., 210–11
William of Saint-Amour, 123, 126, 130, 300n.73
Winstead, Karen, 200
Wooden, Warren, 211
Woodward, Kenneth, 151, 170, 307n.7, 308n.13
Wrisley Shelby, Katherine, 138
Wyschogrod, Edith, 257, 260, 334n.66

Z

Zacher, Samantha, 36
Zadonsky, St. Tikhon, 240
Zore, Mary J., 49, 280–81n.64

ANN W. ASTELL

is professor of theology at the University of Notre Dame.
She is the author of many books, including *Eating Beauty:
The Eucharist and the Spiritual Arts of the Middle Ages*,
and the editor of *Saving Fear in Christian Spirituality*.